# Columbans on Mission

The Missionary Society of St. Columban

# Columbans on Mission

Stories by Columban priests, Sisters, lay missionaries and the lay men and women
with whom they work

## Compiled by
# Peter Woodruff
## and edited by Kate Kenny
## and Connie Wacha

| Library of Congress Control Number: | | 2013921618 |
|---|---|---|
| ISBN: | Hardcover | 978-1-4931-4751-9 |
| | Softcover | 978-1-4931-4750-2 |
| | eBook | 978-1-4931-4752-6 |

Rev. date: 12/06/2013

**To order additional copies of this book, contact:**
Xlibris LLC
1-888-795-4274
www.Xlibris.com
Orders@Xlibris.com
142987

# TABLE OF CONTENTS

Preface ........................................................................................................9
Introduction—Prophetic Dialogue ........................................................11

Chapter 1—Deeds and words.................................................................17
    On the Mission Trail with a Horse Named "Horse" .......................18
    Why Stay Home..............................................................................21
    A Place of Joy before Dying............................................................22
    The Grain of Sand that We Offer ...................................................26
    A Courageous Woman.....................................................................28
    Ministry to the Deaf in Holy Rosary Parish,
        Archdiocese of Cagayan de Oro ..........................................29
    Community Based Rehabilitation.....................................................30
    Seek and You Shall Find..................................................................34
    Two Prisoners Freed .......................................................................36
    Bearers of Joy and Good News........................................................37
    In Honor of the God of Life ...........................................................39
    The Aetas (Negritos) and the Columbans .......................................43
    Anita ..............................................................................................45
    A Valiant Woman ...........................................................................47
    Dreams of a Missionary and Their Outcome....................................48
    Adapting Well-honed Pedagogical Skills.........................................50
    Solidarity with Shanghai's Migrant Workers ...................................53
    Compassionate Solidarity................................................................56
    Just Being There ............................................................................59
    Cycles of Renewal...........................................................................61
    Reaching Out..................................................................................63
    St. Bernadette's Children's Centers.................................................67
    Cattle Have the Right of Way .........................................................70
    Challenging and Changing Times....................................................73
    Fire in My Heart.............................................................................75
    Things We Do.................................................................................78

Chapter 2—Liturgy and prayer .................................................................. 81
    Sacramentals—A Form of Mission ................................................. 82
    An Unfinished Spiritual Journey .................................................... 84
    No, Is an Answer .......................................................................... 87
    A Pilgrimage Towards Dialogue .................................................... 89
    Trusting in God ............................................................................ 91
    Jesus Loves Me and You Too ......................................................... 93
    As We Forgive: Redemption and Reconciliation ............................ 95
    Renewed in Spirit ........................................................................ 97
    Welcomed by Children ............................................................... 100
    WHY IRELAND? ........................................................................ 102
    Drawing All to Himself ............................................................... 104
    Dancing .................................................................................... 107

Chapter 3—Commitment to justice, peace and integrity of creation ......... 111
    Street Children Locked Up .......................................................... 114
    The Path to My Missionary Vocation ............................................ 116
    The Power of a Few Good Christians ............................................ 119
    Connecting to Country ................................................................ 121
    A David and Goliath Case ........................................................... 123
    Getting at the Root of the Problem .............................................. 125
    Passion for Justice and Peace ...................................................... 127
    Organic and Sustainable Agriculture .......................................... 129
    Rooted in the Earth ................................................................... 133
    A Man Who Has Lived for His Family .......................................... 136
    Doing Christianity ..................................................................... 138
    Awards All Round ...................................................................... 140
    Questioning Voices in South Korea .............................................. 142
    Beacons of Hope ........................................................................ 145
    Climate Change Campaign .......................................................... 148
    Solidarity with the Poor on His Own Turf .................................... 150
    La Monja ................................................................................... 152
    Human Trafficking in the Philippines ........................................... 154
    Witnesses of a Long and Continuing Struggle ............................... 157
    Fr. Jim the Editor/Fr. Jim the Pastor .......................................... 163
    Migrant Ministry ....................................................................... 166
    Standing with Our People in a Foreign Land ................................ 169
    Recovering What We Have Lost ................................................... 173
    Solidarity in the Ongoing Struggle for Justice for the Poor ........... 176
    Planting the Seed ....................................................................... 180
    Caring for what Has Been Entrusted to Us ................................... 182
    Sowing Seeds of Hope ................................................................ 185

Comments on the Experience of Being a
    Prison Chaplain in Lima, Peru ........................................ 188
Bus Ride ............................................................................... 190

Chapter 4—The practice of interreligious dialogue ................. 194
Christian/Muslim Dialogue in Mindanao,
    Republic of the Philippines ........................................... 196
High Mountain, Flowing Water ........................................... 202
Chinese Friends Welcoming Me to Mission .......................... 203
Comments from Fr. Warren Kinne's Students in Shanghai, China ........... 205
Interreligious Dialogue with Candomblé ............................. 209
More Than Ecumenism ........................................................ 212
Asia on Mission to Asia ...................................................... 215
Dialogue of Deeds .............................................................. 217
Friendship, God and Hope .................................................. 219
Her Own Woman ................................................................ 221
Waqt ki Awaz—Call of Today ........................................... 223
A Church with Room for All ............................................... 227
Soon to Go on Mission ....................................................... 230
Adapting and Learning ....................................................... 232
Finding Ways to Be Who I Am ........................................... 234
Traipsing from House to House .......................................... 236

Chapter 5—Efforts of Inculturation ....................................... 238
Recreating Andean Identity ................................................ 239
Poetry Has Shaped My Life ................................................ 241
Shudh Hindi and Fiji Hindi ................................................ 244
Post-parish Mission Era ...................................................... 246
Helping the Korean Church Grow ...................................... 248
In the Church in the World ................................................. 250
Mission, a Constant Opportunity ....................................... 253
Post Vatican II Renewal in Labasa Parish ........................... 255
Yes, I Can Be a Missionary ................................................. 257
Last Man In and Last Man Out ........................................... 261
Getting into the Nuts and Bolts of Life .............................. 264
Managing a Cooperative for the Poor ................................ 266
Undaunted and Determined ............................................... 267
Interview with Roweena Cuanico, Coordinator of the
    Columban Lay Missionary Program in the Philippines ...... 267
Anita, a Peruvian Lay Missionary in the Philippines ........... 269
Subanen Ministry ............................................................... 271
Valiant and Respectful Women ........................................... 273

A Leader's Vision ...................................................................................... 275

Health Care and Education ...................................................................... 276

The Seeds of Our Own Education System ............................................ 277

One church, two communities ................................................................ 280

My Passion as a Missionary ..................................................................... 281

Becoming More Missionary ...................................................................... 283

Women of Faith ......................................................................................... 287

Let Your Light Shine ................................................................................. 288

Shapes of Solidarity .................................................................................. 292

A Spirit Filled People ................................................................................ 295

A Pastoral Reading of the Bible .............................................................. 298

Two Steps Forward and One Step Back .................................................. 301

An Evangelizing Faith Community .......................................................... 304

Peruvian Laity on Mission within Peru ................................................. 306

Rural Missionary Catechist ...................................................................... 309

Christian Communities Growing towards Maturity .............................. 311

Christmas Gift ............................................................................................ 314

On Being Good News ................................................................................ 316

Living My Faith Quietly ............................................................................ 319

Rebirth ........................................................................................................ 321

Steady Comeback ...................................................................................... 323

The Journey of Our Local Church in Myanmar .................................... 325

Wedded to the Church of the Pacific ..................................................... 330

Chapter 6—The ministry of reconciliation ............................................ 333

Beginning of a New Life—March 16, 1992 .......................................... 335

A Scout Troop Drawn from Sons and Daughters of
    Malate Street Families ........................................................................ 337

Finding Hope through Scouting .............................................................. 340

'We are the miracle girls!' ........................................................................ 342

Breakfast in Nancheng .............................................................................. 345

Reclaiming Space ....................................................................................... 347

A Valiant Community ................................................................................ 348

A Program that Works .............................................................................. 351

Against the Odds ....................................................................................... 355

Drug Addiction, Family and God ............................................................. 358

Growing ...................................................................................................... 360

A Space for Children ................................................................................ 363

Conclusion .................................................................................................. 367

# PREFACE

Since leaving Peru in 2009 I have traveled to places where Columbans work to seek and ghost-write their stories. Some I wrote under my own name, and in some cases all I needed to do was ask the story teller to write. I both took and borrowed photos taken by others. I was welcomed and guided along the way as I did not speak the local language in most places that I visited. In some cases locals, with the help of a Columban translator, gave me a story. Before I sent the stories to the editors of each of the three English language editions of the Columban Mission magazine the main source for what I had written gave his or her approval.

Recently, it was suggested (I don't remember by whom and maybe a few people mentioned the possibility independently of each other) that I make a book of "mission stories." Kate Kenny, the director of the Columban Communications Office in the U.S., supported the idea when I put it to her. I then began the search for a suitable framework for the stories. The book, *Constants in Context: A Theology of Mission for Today*, by Divine Word Missionaries, Stephen B. Bevans and Roger P. Schroeder, outlines the missiological framework that I have used.

I am most grateful for those who have helped me with this project. Three friends from varied backgrounds made positive critical comments on the description of the framework used for the book: Mary Beth Moore, a short story writing nun with a long-term commitment to solidarity with the poor in Peru and more recently with Latinos in New York, read the text with an eye to clarity and economy of words; Ana Lanyon, already an author of three books on Mexican history, offered suggestions that broadened the presentation of this Catholic story; Elisabeth McDonald, the unchurched but searching young university graduate, homed in on the in-house language that makes little sense to her generation. Columban Fr. Trevor Trotter, a companion of seminary days, did a critical read of an early draft of the whole text and made suggestions that helped me improve the draft I handed to the editor.

# PREFACE

# INTRODUCTION

## Prophetic Dialogue[1]

Within the Catholic Church and non-fundamentalist Christian churches mission has changed significantly during the past 50 years, and I believe it will continue to evolve as missionaries strive to be who we are in an ever changing world. The following framework seeks to provide a context for stories of mission as it is lived in today's world by a relatively small group of missionaries. All the protagonists belong to or in some way work with the Missionary Society of St. Columban, a missionary organization of the Catholic Church. This framework and the accompanying stories will be like most products of our age—constantly in need of updating.

This book considers Christian mission as a participation in the life and mission of God. In Baptism every Christian is invited to participate in "God's mission" of loving care for all that is. The mission of the Christian is to share in the mission that the Father entrusted to his Son and the Holy Spirit: to do God's work of all-embracing love, proclaiming the Good News of salvation, namely that love has the power to overcome death and actually did so in the person of Jesus of Nazareth. He loved in truth, which He placed at the heart of the life of our world[2].

Invited into the infinitely loving relationships between the Father, the Son and the Holy Spirit, the three persons of the one God, Christians are called and moved to love each other as we take on the shared challenge to be messengers of the Good News of Jesus Christ. God invites us to share this task "in Christ"[3] precisely

---

[1]   To some this phrase may seem to be an oxymoron but I hope that as you read the following text it will become clear that it can be otherwise understood.

[2]   See Jn 18, 37-38: So Pilate said to him, "Then you are a king?" Jesus answered, "You say I am a king. For this I was born and for this I came into the world, to testify to the **truth**. Everyone who belongs to the **truth** listens to my voice." Pilate said to him, "What is **truth**?"

[3]   In him we have redemption by his blood, the forgiveness of transgressions, in accord with the riches of his grace that he lavished upon us. In all wisdom and insight, he has

because we are God's adopted sons and daughters and so we are incorporated into Christ; we are literally the "mystical body of Christ."[4] We are drawn into the life of God and so we become, at the root of our being, enlivened by God, not simply inspired by God as if we were apart from or at a distance from God. That is why we complete the Eucharistic prayer with the following: "through him [Christ], with him, in him, in the unity of the Holy Spirit, all glory and honor is yours, almighty Father, for ever and ever."

Consequently, we appreciate that our role as missionaries is to accomplish what God would want. It is not about our mission, meeting our needs, nor is it about the Church's mission but rather God's mission. In so far as we [the Church] listen to God and take on God's mission God renews and strengthens us. In this sense, followers of Jesus have assumed God's mission from the very beginnings of Christianity, as shown by the first preaching of the apostle, Peter: "God raised this Jesus; of this we are all witnesses. Exalted at the right hand of God, he received the promise of the Holy Spirit from the Father and poured it forth, as you (both) see and hear." (Acts 2, 32-33)

God, who is love, which is the passion for and the will to life, raised Jesus, who, having completed his mission, departed and sent the Holy Spirit to accompany his friends as they took on the task of continuing his (God's) mission. In fact, Jesus' friends were invited to be even more—his brothers and sisters, as adopted sons and daughters of the Father. As the apostle, Paul, wrote: "The Spirit itself bears witness with our spirit that we are children of God, and if children, then heirs, heirs of God and joint heirs with Christ, if only we suffer with him so that we may also be glorified with him." (Romans 8, 16-17)

God does not enforce belief. God invites belief. God's invitation may come to us in the context of a major and traumatic experience; it may come to us in a time of quiet and inner peace. To receive God's invitation we need to listen, to be attentive and therefore we pray, which of course includes listening to God. God may call us through church leaders or the members of our church community. God may call us through the events of our lives. There is so much that can move us towards God in the daily events of our lives.

We can also help God communicate with others when we, as God's messengers, assume towards them the attitude of patient respect God has for each of us. To be a missionary in the spirit of the Father, Son and Holy Spirit, requires

---

made known to us the mystery of his will in accord with his favor that he set forth in him as a plan for the fullness of times, to sum up all things in Christ, in heaven and on earth. (Eph 1, 7-10)

4    If we would define and describe this true Church of Jesus Christ . . . we shall find nothing more noble, more sublime, or more divine than the expression "the Mystical Body of Christ." (Pope Pius XII, Mystici Corporis Christi, No. 13)

that we befriend those to whom we have been sent and who have welcomed us, to develop open and respectful relationships, to hear what they have to say to us and to be ready to share with them. As the mission stories illustrate, these relationships often arise in the context of a shared project, rather than in extensive discussions.

Today the Catholic Church demands that her missionaries do not set out on mission with a sense of cultural superiority over those to whom they are being sent. Missionary activity under the protection of European colonizing projects has ceased and, in fact, many of those peoples who were once under colonial governments are the seed bed of vibrant local churches, which are sending missionaries around the world. Present circumstances call us to a respectful dialogue among cultures, where all participants might hope to be enriched. Appreciation of customs and values in another culture often leads us to deepen our appreciation for aspects of our own culture.

The dialogue in which today's missionary engages is prophetic in so far as all parties involved, both the missionary and those to whom the missionary has been sent, become aware of God speaking to them precisely in the context of their friendship, dialogue, collaboration and shared joy. The missionary is frequently sent to the poor, for whom God has a preference and through whom God speaks to the missionary. The CELAM (Conference of Bishops of Latin America and the Caribbean) meeting in Puebla, Mexico in 1979 referred to the many and varied faces of the poor in which "we should recognize the suffering features of Christ, the Lord, that question us and ask us for explanations." (Cf. Puebla, 31-40) The missionary sometimes engages with men and women who profess another religious faith. While the missionary proclaims that Jesus of Nazareth is the way, the truth and the life, he or she is also open to discovering something of the beauty and wisdom of God in the encounter with people of a different faith. Dialogue and mutual enrichment, not the intention of conversion, characterize this approach to Christian mission. A moving and well publicized example of this was the life-long commitment of a group of Trappist monks to share life with their Muslim neighbors in a rural Algerian village. In 1996 an armed group hostile to the Algerian government of the day abducted and killed seven monks.

There was a time when the Christian missionary focused primarily on establishing and promoting the development of the Church; in all probability, the priority uppermost in the missionary's mind would not have been the reign of God. However, his or her hope would have been that the Church might make a contribution to the growth of God's reign on earth, even though this would not have been described in such terms. Only in recent years has the idea of the reign of God begun to have prominence in the thinking of Catholic missionaries. Given that the reign of God was the primary focus of the mission of Jesus of Nazareth, this may seem rather strange. However, unfortunately for Christianity and more specifically Christian mission the building up of the Church tended to be the primary focus of her own activity and the understanding of the reign of God was limited to what happened beyond our life on earth.

When Jesus began his preaching, the first thing that he said was, "The reign of God is at hand." (Matthew 4, 17) The reign of God, sometimes called the Kingdom of Heaven, is God's way of love embracing all the people of the earth; it is everyone living in a fully human way. Obviously this is a project that never even approaches completion. The followers of Jesus of Nazareth (Christians) strive to let the reign of God enter into the life of our world. Many men and women of goodwill, with or without a religious faith, also embrace and promote values that Jesus preached and lived and so they too, without necessarily being Christians, also promote the reign of God. How many millions of men and women around the world would espouse the values set forth in the following summary of Jesus' preaching?

When he saw the crowds, he went up the mountain, and after he had sat down, his disciples came to him. He began to teach them, saying:

Blessed are the poor in spirit, for theirs is the kingdom of heaven.
Blessed are they who mourn, for they will be comforted.
Blessed are the meek, for they will inherit the land.
Blessed are they who hunger and thirst for righteousness, for they will be satisfied.
Blessed are the merciful, for they will be shown mercy.
Blessed are the clean of heart, for they will see God.
Blessed are the peacemakers, for they will be called children of God.
Blessed are they who are persecuted for the sake of righteousness, for theirs is the kingdom of heaven.
Blessed are you when they insult you and persecute you and utter every kind of evil against you [falsely] because of me. (Matthew 5, 1-11)

So, while Christian Churches may point to and partially embody the reign of God, as preached by Jesus of Nazareth, God and God's ways are welcomed into our world in a variety of beautiful and mysterious ways beyond the initiatives and structures of the Christian Churches.

So, it is clear that in our times Christian mission goes beyond the task of setting up and running parishes or church communities; nor is its outreach limited to setting up educational and health services. To help us reflect upon and talk about Christian mission in all its complexity the following presentation will refer to Christian mission under six headings that have been proposed by Divine Word missionaries and missiologists Stephen Bevan and Roger Schroeder. The following list[5] is by no means definitive and will surely evolve as the circumstances of our world change:

1.  Deeds and words
2.  Liturgy and prayer
3.  Commitment to justice, peace and integrity of creation
4.  The practice of interreligious dialogue
5.  Efforts of inculturation
6.  The ministry of reconciliation

---

[5]     List taken from Bevans, S. & Schroeder, R., Constants in Context, Orbis, New York, 2004, P. 351.

# CHAPTER 1

## Deeds and words

Jesus, a Jewish man of deep faith and commitment, lived His mission both doing and speaking; His deeds and words complemented each other. He healed the sick, fed the hungry, forgave those who hurt Him, threw the money changers out of the temple and so on. He also taught in a variety of ways, especially through parables. He spoke out against the hypocrisy of the religious leaders of His people—In the course of His teaching he said, "Beware of the scribes, who like to go around in long robes and accept greetings in the marketplaces, seats of honor in synagogues, and places of honor at banquets. They devour the houses of widows and, as a pretext, recite lengthy prayers. They will receive a very severe condemnation." (Mark 12, 38-40) He put the command to love at the heart of His teaching: "I give you a new commandment: Love one another. As I have loved you, so you also should love one another. This is how all will know that you are my disciples, if you have love for one another." (John 13, 34-35)

To a large extent, the deeds that Jesus requires of us are the big and little things of living our ordinary lives with integrity. Some may take on great and impressive ventures but most Christians will speak of our faith in Christ through the ordinary stuff of our ordinary lives. However, we also speak to others communally: through our local Christian community, our church institutions and the Church as institution at local, national and international levels. We Christians form a complex web; when we network in a creative, life-giving way, that web can generate hope in ourselves and others.

When we have opportunities to speak to others about our faith, we share with them the teaching of Jesus and its relevance to our times. We want them to know the man, Jesus of Nazareth, and to appreciate His approach to life, human existence and destiny—What is our purpose on this earth? Where are we going? How might we hope to get there? We act and speak in the hope that our approach to life might encourage others to discover some of the spiritual riches that we have discovered in Jesus and in His teaching.

"Always be ready to give an explanation to anyone who asks you for a reason for your hope, but do it with gentleness and reverence . . ." (1 Peter 3, 15) Jesus was certainly not afraid to proclaim God's message but He never did so from a position of strength. He was well aware that He was on the "losing side," but He kept at it until the end. His way of being with others challenges us to be confident and clear in the proclamation of our faith and yet unassuming and respectful. Our attitude of respect is the fruit of the conviction that it is precisely in the dialogue, with its moments of listening and speaking that the Good News of Jesus can be proffered, appreciated and, in some cases, accepted.

The rest of this chapter is made up of mission stories illustrating the above paragraphs. After each story or, in some cases, groups of stories there is a link to our religious tradition, which, for the most part, is taken from the Bible but, also from teachings of the Popes, General Councils and Episcopal Conferences.

## On the Mission Trail with a Horse Named "Horse"

Seminarians and a priest travel to the rain-swept edges of the Peruvian Amazon
By Columban Fr. John Boles

"There is rain, heavy rain and Mendoza rain." That was the warning we received from Fr. Antonio, the pastor of Rodriguez de Mendoza, before we left the Peruvian capital of Lima for our visit to his parish. Every year during the summer holidays, I accompany our Columban seminarians from Peru and Chile on a month-long mission experience to a different part of the Peruvian hinterland. This particular year, Fr. Antonio had invited us to his area, a region of great beauty but with one undeniable and unstoppable problem—the rain.

Mendoza nestles in the Northern Andes of Peru, close to the border with Ecuador. It is on the eastern side of the great mountain chain, overlooking the Amazon jungle. It is covered in lush forest and ideal for the cultivation of coffee, one of the country's main cash crops. But its location also makes it susceptible to huge amounts of annual rainfall. Westerly winds sweep across the Atlantic and grow heavy with moisture. They pick up yet more humidity as they journey over the vast Amazon Basin. As they smash into the natural wall of the Andes, they let drop all this stored water vapor in the form of torrential summer downpours. The worst month is February. And yes, we were going to Mendoza in February, the rainiest month of the year.

We had a dozen students going on the mission experience. Fr. Antonio split them into pairs and sent them to live in six remote villages. These villages are communities which rarely benefit from visits by the priest or parish workers, particularly during the wet season. Many of the residents of these villages are subsistence farmers (*campesinos*) barely eking out enough food to survive. The seminarians soon busied themselves by visiting the *campesinos* in their homes, organizing liturgies and preparing people for Baptism and First Holy

Communion. My role was to circulate by visiting each village on a rotating basis and celebrating the sacraments.

It was easier said than done. No sooner had the seminarians established themselves in their respective settlements than the heavens opened. The jeep we had borrowed was no match for the road which had been transformed into a muddy stream. We had driven only a few miles before getting bogged.

So, we turned to "Plan B." Antonio managed to get me a horse. It was named, imaginatively, "Horse" (*Caballo* in Spanish). Horse was strong but apparently bad-tempered. Consequently, instead of mounting my less-than trusty steed I stowed my rucksack and Mass kit on his back, donned my Wellington boots, and away we went, guided by a couple of local catechists.

Taking our time, we successfully slopped our way from village to village. We slept in the houses of *campesinos* and gathered in their humble chapels for the sacramental celebrations.

The visit to *Nueva Luz* (New Light) was particularly memorable. We arrived a little late since Horse balked at a series of swollen river crossings. It was twilight by the time we were able to join the congregation in the chapel where we huddled beneath the single light-bulb. "New Light" turned out to be a rather optimistic name, given the general lack of electric illumination in the community.

Mass had barely started when the deluge began. We had to suspend operations almost immediately. The rain was beating on the tin roof with such intensity that you could barely hear yourself think. Moreover, the waters of a flash flood began to seep into the building, and we were soon up to our ankles. Everyone had to rush out and help unclog the storm-drains of accumulated leaves. Then all hands turned to swishing the water off the sodden floor.

The storm passed as quickly as it had come. With calm restored we resumed the ceremony, only to face a new challenge. Encouraged by the dank night air, clouds of mosquitoes and moths began to assail us or, more precisely, began to assail ME, who as the priest had been given the favored position directly under the lone bulb. I continued with the Eucharist, maintaining as much dignity as possible while every few seconds slapping at little blood-suckers feasting on any and all exposed skin.

However, the biggest threat to decorum was posed by the moths. Some of them seemed to be as big as Vulcan bombers. One particular flying fortress, with wings the size of soup-spoons, decided to plunge into the chalice. We were at the Consecration, and so the cup was uncovered. Flapping desperately in its attempts to escape, our winged friend momentarily had the sacred vessel wobbling on the altar. For a time I think some of the faithful believed a miracle was taking place, until I unceremoniously scooped the bedraggled but, presumably by now, very holy insect out of the wine.

All of these adventures made me aware of the enormity of the task that faces the Church as it seeks to reach out to communities it had formerly underserved, especially at a time when the Latin American bishops are launching what they term a "Continental Mission" promoting evangelization throughout the Americas. I felt proud to have participated in this movement, albeit only briefly. It was humbling to witness the extraordinary hospitality the *campesinos* extended to the seminarians and me.

Most of all, I was heartened by the effect all this had on the seminarians themselves. It had been a major step in their formation as future Columban missionary priests, capable of taking the Word to all parts of the world, through rain, sleet or snow, and with or without the help of a horse called "Horse."

Link to our tradition:

After this the Lord appointed seventy two others whom he sent ahead of him in pairs to every town and place he intended to visit. He said to them, "The harvest is abundant but the laborers are few; so ask the master of the harvest to send out laborers for his harvest. Go on your way; behold, I am sending you like lambs among wolves. Carry no money bag, no sack, no sandals; and greet no one along the way. Into whatever house you enter, first say, 'Peace to this household.'" (Luke 10, 1-5)

## Why Stay Home

Rachel & David Winton

When David and Rachel Winton retired from teaching, they were looking for a new challenge. Now they are teaching English to university students in China, a far cry from their careers as school teachers in England.

David and Rachel found this new life through *AITECE* (Association for International Teaching, Educational and Curriculum Exchange), an organization based in Hong Kong and linked with the Columban Fathers.

We were accepted to teach English in Wuhan in central China and live in a serviced apartment on the campus of Hubei University. The facilities we need are on our doorstep: supermarket, post office, bank, and restaurant . . . even a hairdresser. One further pleasant aspect for us is that the generations live here together in harmony: students, teachers with their young children, and former teachers now in their old age.

Most of the 16,000 students are from Hubei province and live on campus. They are enrolled in graduate and post-graduate programs in the arts and sciences. The campus is leafy and despite the number of students, is not overwhelming in size. The university has contracted us to teach English to students at various stages of proficiency. Each of us has eight contact sessions of two hours a week with eight different groups of students, the number of students in each class ranging from 16 to 50.

Both of us taught high school students in state schools in England until our retirement, so one would reasonably conclude that we have learnt most of the skills needed to teach effectively. However, we are finding that teaching Chinese tertiary students with just one contact session each week, challenges us in new ways.

Some classrooms are well-equipped, having air-conditioning that makes it much easier to work in the extremes of hot and cold weather. Older rooms are not so well equipped with long rows of desks screwed to the floor, so there is no chance of re-arranging the furniture for small group work or whole class activities in a circle. Some of the classrooms are on the fifth and sixth floor, and there is no elevator, but the students would not think of complaining.

When we arrive for class at 8:00 a.m. we find the students seated at their desks with their textbooks open. We were provided with a basic textbook and whilst we found it helpful, we needed to move beyond it. We needed to get our students discussing topics in which they had some genuine interest and spark discussion. Such discussions often demand that the students use vocabulary that they may not have already learnt, so we teach them some of the words and phrases they might need in the discussion of the day.

We have introduced topics such as "better city/better life" (the slogan of the 2010 Shanghai Expo), "China's one child policy" and the difficulties of life on a live-in campus. We have also taught them to sing some English songs, such as "You are my sunshine" and organized role-plays.

This has helped the students to be less stiff and formal, and to move the lesson away from one way traffic to an interaction between us and them or between the students themselves. We feel we are making progress, but we keep in mind that our cultural backgrounds are so different.

They are respectful and always well-dressed; being scruffy is not part of their style. The students are used to the teacher doing all the talking and so are inclined to be passive.

Unlike our experience back home, there is no need to expend energy keeping order in the classroom; the students are co-operative and work with the teacher. A major difference between our cultures is that while ours is individualistic, their culture puts emphasis on a sense of belonging to a group. This may explain in part their unwillingness to volunteer their individual views to the class, but will agree to do so if directly asked.

It is a great joy to be trying something new at this stage of our lives. Retirement has meant an opportunity to branch out in our chosen profession. We will also take advantage of the opportunity to travel in China and have already had six days in Beijing.

Over the winter break we plan to travel to the south-west and over the summer to the north-west, from where some of our students come, and finally to Shanghai . . . before we fly home to London.

Link to our tradition:

As each one has received a gift, use it to serve one another as good stewards of God's varied grace. (1 Peter 4, 10)

## A Place of Joy before Dying

Setting up St. Columban's Nursing Home, Chuncheon, South Korea
By Columban Sister Nora Wiseman, SSC

I was working in our clinic in the city (Chuncheon) and was totally dedicated to the home care of terminally ill patients. We had to travel a lot as the more seriously ill patients lived well out in the country; often they were also poorer than our city patients. Also, those living near the city could more easily get to the hospital.

We worked with a group of volunteers who trained and visited with us. One of our volunteers, together with her husband, owned land just outside the city. They offered us this land to build a hospice so that a greater number of terminally ill patients might benefit from our care. We were given three years to start something before the property reverted to the donor. On finding out that the government gave no subsidy for a hospice but would give about 50% of the cost of a nursing home, we chose to build a nursing home.

From small donations and one major fund-raising activity we created a fund that allowed us to begin to draw up building plans. We obtained the necessary building permits from the municipal and provincial governments, but we had not adequately negotiated the backing of our neighbors, who were, for the most part, fruit farmers. When the builders we had contracted attempted to begin work on the site they found the entrance barricaded and placards protesting the project.

At a community meeting organized by both parties a city government representative attempted to begin the discussion outlining the history of our service to the community in the Chuncheon area, but he was immediately interrupted by a local farmer who harangued the meeting about not wanting or needing such a building near their homes. He claimed that it would bring down the price of land in the area. His fiery speech brought all present to their feet; the meeting broke up, and we realized that we would have to find another way around the obstacle of local resistance.

A local politician who is a Catholic then offered to help us with the negotiation. Things gradually began to move, and soon the builders were able to enter the construction site unimpeded. I have discovered over the course of the 40 years I have lived in this country that Koreans have a talent for negotiating their way through almost any kind of difficult situation. With the support of the Church, the community and local government we opened St. Columban's Home on March 25, 2004.

Prior to opening our nursing home I visited the neighborhood representative with a bundle of invitations to our formal opening. He took advantage of my visit to ask me to visit a terminally ill neighbor. When I went to the patient's home I recognized him as someone I had met and soon realized that he was the man who had sabotaged our community meeting two years previously. We continued to visit him with medicine twice a day for a few weeks until he died of cancer.

Neither he nor his family ever discussed with us our initial encounter at the meeting in the communal hall. In fact, as we have lived and journeyed with the people of this neighborhood, many who once opposed our coming have expressed regret for not welcoming us in the beginning.

We now have room for 75 nursing home patients and five hospice patients, all of whom remain in our home until they die. We have 44 staff members working three shifts. Among them are nurses, social workers, cooks, office workers and others. Doctors come to our home regularly, and we have easy access to the local hospital. We have our own ambulance that can get a patient to the hospital in 20 minutes.

We try to run our home in a hospice style, looking at the person and all their needs and then doing all we can to help meet them. Our staff are great at finding out the needs of the patients and when it comes to gift giving on the occasion of Easter, Christmas and birthdays, they choose gifts according to the needs and wants of each patient.

Most of our patients can only leave their beds in a wheelchair. We help as many as possible to come to the front foyer to begin the day with prayers, followed by exercises and a snack. After that the daily routine of programs begins. In the same way we help the patients come to the dining room for meals, rather than serve meals in bed. They get great joy from communal activities.

On entering our home patients give us access to their bank account into which the government deposits a stipend each month. We ensure that each patient has the cash in hand that they need to cover personal expenses. It is a small thing but does ensure a degree of autonomy that helps maintain personal dignity.

When accepting residents for our Home, we do not differentiate between religions, so we have residents who are Buddhist, Christian, and those of no religion as well as Catholics. Here in the Home we have weekly Sunday Mass, morning prayers together, May Procession and other religious ceremonies. Often through their attendance at these events, residents get interested in religion and ask to be baptized. In the eight years that our Home has been in existence, 264 have been baptized and 27 confirmed. The Lord continues to share the "Good News" with those who are open to hearing it.

When I was based in the city clinic doing home visits to terminally ill patients I had no thought or plan for such a home as we have now. We had no money for such a venture. Nor did we know how we might find the thousands of dollars it would cost to build and run a home such as this. Local people came to us with the offer of land, effective support in negotiating both local resistance and government bureaucracy, and donations. The project has unfolded in such a way that I am convinced that it is God's work.

Link to our tradition:

Care and respect for the aged has been part of the Judeo-Christian tradition from early times as indicated by the following quotes. The Book of Leviticus states clearly that this is a command from God. Matthew reports Jesus challenging the legalistic and specious attempt of his contemporaries to nullify this command:

"Stand up in the presence of the aged, show respect for the old, and fear your God. I am the LORD." (Leviticus 19, 32)

"For God said, 'Honor your father and your mother,' and 'Whoever curses father or mother shall die.' But you say, 'Whoever says to father or mother, 'Any support you might have had from me is dedicated to God,' need not honor his father.' You have nullified the word of God for the sake of your tradition." (Matthew 15, 4-6)

The following four stories focus on empowering people with physical or mental disabilities.

## The Grain of Sand that We Offer

Helping the intellectually disabled discover their own dignity as they find a place
in modern society
By Gemma Kim Myeong Seon

I had recently completed a degree in sociology at Gwangju University. I was looking not just for a job but for my way in life. I had participated in the student protests in 1980, as had many of my companions in the faculty of sociology. I had witnessed the slaughter of hundreds of fellow students by government forces. Seeing my companions mowed down by guns held by other young Koreans, my own people, left me feeling shattered and struggling to make sense of life.

I got a job with a welfare agency run by a religious organization but did not like it as I felt pressured to embrace their religion. After a month or so I left that job, and my sister, who had gone to Ecuador as a lay missionary in 1978, introduced me to Columban Fr. Noel O'Neill. Fr. Noel had just begun work with the intellectually disabled. At that stage he had no funds to pay staff, so we worked as volunteers.

At that time, Korean society did not recognize nor address the issue of the wellbeing of the intellectually disabled. Fr. Noel first began work with those who had been institutionalized by the state and lived caged like wild animals. We knew others lived with their families, who were ashamed to admit they had disabled members and hid them. With a very simple survey form we went about the locality looking for these hidden people. I had already been quite disturbed by seeing our military and police shoot my fellow students as if their lives had no worth. It did not take me long to grow into the conviction that it would be worthwhile spending my life at the service of people whose lives were accorded little or no value by society. Stark experience challenged me and led me to the conviction that life is both precious and sacred.

In about 1985 I joined a lay association called, "Apostolic Auxiliaries," which works in coordination with the local bishop. We commit to a celibate life, but each member finds his or her own way in life. We do not live in community, but we meet regularly for a day of prayer and study, and we do an annual eight day retreat. At some stage of our life, we spend two years at our international formation center in Lourdes, France, to focus on deepening our relationship with Christ.

This lay association continues to sustain me in my work with the mentally disabled. It has helped me discover and live by the values that matter to me. I feel that I have grown as a human being by focusing my energies on the wellbeing and growth of some of the weakest and insignificant members of society.

If asked now what advice I might offer a young person embarking on life's journey I would say something like, "Do not simply take on board what society may be pushing. Be wary of building your life around the quest for money, fame or power. Do not allow personal, physical beauty to become an obsession. Rather, discover your true values and through them find your own way to be fully human."

In the course of the past 30 years I have held many jobs with the mentally disabled. I also did further studies and completed a Master's degree in social welfare in a university in Seoul. I have also lectured part time in a number of universities on work with the mentally disabled.

At present I am director of the Emmaus Workplace, which provides a variety of jobs for the intellectually disabled. Our basic goal is to do what we can to enable them to feel that they are part of society. We help the disabled integrate in society as best they can. Most, if not all, have been treated as rejects, and we want to welcome them as members of society.

In the area of work, we have jobs for three categories and do all possible to help them move into the first category, which means they are able to do full time work and receive the legal minimum wage. In this center there are eleven men and women in this category at present; there are fifteen in the second category, which means they can work for six hours a day and receive one third to one sixth of the legal minimum wage; in the third category there are ten people in programs for about six hours each day, which are designed to help them cope with the basics of life and work a little. They receive pocket money.

What we do may be like the grain of sand on the seashore, but it's the grain of sand that we offer.

A few words from three young mentally disabled people who work in a factory set up by Emmaus Industries

My name is Matthias Lee Tae Soo, and I have been working in the candle factory for six years. Now I am the leader of a group of nine workers in the factory. Even though I only earn the basic wage I dream of making money and being famous. I participate in the Legion of Mary with the youth of our parish. I have friends in the youth group, and we keep in touch with each other by texting with our mobile phones. Before I got this job I was not involved in the parish; I had no friends, no social life. I became a Catholic and then persuaded my mother and father to go out to the church and be baptized. Becoming more active socially has been good for my family.

I am Lee Jong Won, and it is so much fun working in this factory. We supply toilet paper to the local army base. The teamwork is great. I like to practice speaking English. I have been working here for seven years. At first I wanted to buy a house on Jeju Island and marry my girlfriend who works in another sheltered workshop, but now I want to get a job in Pusan and live there. I earn about $900 a month and if I were to leave this job tomorrow I would receive a severance pay of about $20,000. This is a not for profit factory so what we earn goes to the workers and the development of the factory.

My name is Cho Gratia, and I have been working in the toilet paper factory for ten years. We work as a team to produce the toilet rolls, and I feel good about that. Before coming to work in the factory I attended a center for learning skills to see what I might do in the future. One of the things I like about this place is that every Friday evening members from a theater group come to help us prepare a play, which we present in the city cultural center in October. I like acting and have had major parts in a few of our plays, and I always play the role of Our Blessed Mother in our Passion play during Holy Week. Also, with four other workers I participate in a weekly scripture study session which lasts one hour. We learn as we fill in the drawings that the team from the diocesan center brings along with them. We also go to the Emmaus Center for cooking lessons, and there is a yoga program here in which eleven of us from the factory participate.

## A Courageous Woman

By Monika Lewatikana (Columban lay missionary from Fiji)

Twice a week the mothers bring their disabled children to the clinic for therapy; some also come on Saturdays. If their children cannot walk they must carry them. Even if they did have a wheelchair it would be extremely difficult to push it along the sandy roads of Rancho Anapra, located in the desert sands on the north-west edge of Ciudad Juárez, Mexico.

I grew up in Fiji and spent nine years as a lay missionary in Chile, but I had never had the opportunity to work with disabled kids. I worked with youth in Chile and that continues to be my main commitment in the Columban mission in Rancho Anapra.

When I saw the struggle of mothers with their disabled children I wanted to support them in some way. I have no special medical skills, so I decided to simply be with them, to accompany them. I went to the clinic regularly for some months, but in recent months I have not been going. Maybe I became busy with other things; maybe I was not so sure that I was making any contribution to the lives of these poor women and their kids.

At the clinic I got to know Martin and his mother, Martha. Martin was about nine years of age; he cannot walk, swallow or talk. He is fed through a tube inserted through the wall of his stomach. However, he can understand, and he laughs and smiles when we are together at the clinic.

It really hit me that these are the forgotten people, especially the mothers. Martha has five kids to look after so what can she expect to do for Martin? One day she asked me, "Where is God in all this?" I just looked at her; I had no experience of such a situation. I did not know what to say. I thought for a while and then began to speak in the hope that what I said might mean something to Martha.

I believe that in and through the struggles of our lives God speaks to us. I said to Martha, "People have come into your life through your disabled son—the Sisters who run the clinic, me and others." Martha thought for a moment and responded, "Yes, it is true that if I just stayed at home I would not know so many people. Also, even among the mothers who bring their children for therapy we share and I feel encouraged watching and listening to them. I find strength in knowing that I am not the only one who struggles to bring up a disabled child."

## Ministry to the Deaf in Holy Rosary Parish, Archdiocese of Cagayan de Oro

By Marisol Rojas (Peruvian lay missionary)

The Ministry to the Deaf began in this parish in 1999 when Columban Fr. Shaun O'Donnell was parish priest. In 2009 Archbishop Antonio Javellana Ledesma formally gave his support to this ministry at archdiocesan level, and five parishes have joined the program. Vilma Arante is the archdiocesan coordinator, and I work with her with deaf students from the Holy Rosary Parish.

There is a privately run school for the deaf in the city, but all the costs must be covered by the families of the students. There is also a State-run school, but the students still have to pay for food, transport to and from school and other miscellaneous expenses. The archdiocesan program is totally free, so we are able to open our doors to the very poor.

My work in the Ministry to the Deaf means so much to me. I have learned sign language and have made friends with the students. They are so perceptive with their eyes, which seem especially sharp as they compensate for their lack of hearing. They quickly read a person by their facial expression and are most welcoming to anyone they sense to be a friend. I suspect it would be extremely difficult to fool them. I would like to introduce you to two students with whom I work.

Jeaneva Veligaño is a sixteen year old orphan who has been brought up by her grandparents. She was a pioneering student who began at the school in 1999 when our school opened. She helps her grandmother sell fish, but still her family often goes without. If they don't sell they have no food. Four families share the house where Jeaneva lives. In her family there is her sister and grandparents, and all of them share the same room. There are a total of 30 residents in the house. They have no toilet between all four families, so they either use the seashore or at times a neighbor's toilet. Jeaneva also buys lottery tickets on commission for people, who believe they might have more luck if a deaf person buys the ticket for them. She is also a great card player and swims like a fish. She has beautiful handwriting. On finishing her schooling she hopes to get work in domestic service and be able to help her family economically.

Pelros Yangwas is thirteen years old and his grandfather took him in when he was three months of age because his father was sent to jail for drug related offences. He is still in jail, and Pelros has visited him there. He is the second of five children as the jail allows matrimonial visits. Pelros' father was a Jeepney driver before he was sent to prison. His grandfather is now 73 years old and ailing, and his 60 year old grandmother does not enjoy the best of health either. When Pelros first came to school at the age of nine, he was very shy but after meeting others who are also deaf he began to grow in confidence. School became like a family for him where he could share so much more. He now expresses himself with enthusiasm and flair. He is a ball of confidence and helps new students learn. Like Jeaneva, he also lives in a very crowded house.

## Community Based Rehabilitation

By Columban Fr. Fintan Murtagh

I arrived in the Philippines in 1964 and was assigned to work in parishes to the north of Manila in Zambales province. In 1972 I became aware that I was suffering from multiple sclerosis. I was able to deal with the illness and continue with in the parish mission, but it was not until 1985 that I began to develop a systematic approach to the disabled where I was working. I suppose I saw the need earlier but did not consider the possibility that I might do something about it. I had always helped the needy in a piecemeal way but had not tried to work out a more effective response.

Melody got me moving. She was thirteen years old and paralyzed from the waist down from polio. Meeting her was like a new beginning for me. Her father made a side-car attached to his bicycle to take her to school. I then helped make a tricycle that Melody could propel. One of her neighbors made parallel bars from bamboo poles so that she could do daily therapeutic exercises. She helped me see a world of struggle, pain and endurance that had been hidden from me. Maybe my interest was also stimulated in part by own experience of sickness but, in my case, I feel I was lucky to be able to call on medical attention, but these people had nothing.

I began the project in Candelaria Parish where I was parish priest at that time. Once people heard about the priest who was showing interest in the disabled, many began to come out of the woodwork. They were hidden in family homes because their families did not know what to do with them. I had heard about a program for helping the disabled that was running in Malate Parish in Manila. I contacted the organizer, Barney McGlade, an Irish psychologist sponsored by GOAL, an Irish sports group that helps people in third world countries. Barney helped me as a consultant to set up a program in Candelaria Parish, and then he set up another in Santa Cruz Parish, and the ball began to roll.

Facts and figures may not be the most imaginative way of describing a project but, I think, in this case, such an approach will help you appreciate how that initial insight has grown in to a continually growing service that is now bringing help and joy to lives of over 1,000 disabled people. The following is a brief description of what we did in favor of the disabled recently.

Community Based Rehabilitation (CBR) for People with Disabilities and Families (PWD) is presently serving in thirteen parishes of the diocese of Iba. It has grown steadily since its foundation in Candelaria Parish in 1985. Now there are 1,037 members in a broad variety of programs for people with disabilities, 315 in the 13-21 years of age group, 234 in the 7-12 years of age group, 169 in the 0-6 years of age group, and 159 in the 36-70 years of age group.

Topping the list of disabilities is cerebral palsy with 181, mostly children. There are 348 who suffer from strokes, Parkinson's disease, spinal cord injury, epilepsy, and other brain or spinal infections or injuries. There are 206 who are deaf, hearing impaired, mute, blind or partially blind. There are 198 with a congenital anomaly, such as club foot, harelip and cleft palate, heart disease, missing one or more limbs, etc. There are 170 with slow learning disabilities, and there are others with a variety of disabling conditions.

Our programs aim to help members achieve as much personal development and independence as possible. We have 161 members enrolled in the public schools and most of them are on a scholarship which provides for school fees, books and other utensils. We have four members in a vocational school where they learn a basic skill that will help them earn a living. Then we have eleven in kindergarten, 90 in primary school and 39 in high school.

We have 120 children in our home and center based program, where parents learn to work with their disabled child. For those who need it we also offer massage therapy and this year 166 availed of this service. Medical assistance of some kind has been given to 876 members, 34 of whom have been hospitalized. The Philippine Band of Mercy, with whom we network, regularly performs operations for us on children with harelip and cleft palate.

We are not alone in this work with people with disabilities. Willing helpers, professionals, local government units, private and public agencies, NGOs and a variety of institutions lend a hand where needed. We are never short of support for social and religious activities. We have been duly accredited by the relevant government agencies and recently received a Certificate of Accreditation recognizing the CBR Foundation as a NGO at the service of people with disabilities.

Our members are not simply beneficiaries of free services. They too are required to do their bit in so far as they are able. They help out by paying some of the cost of services, giving materials, collecting empty bottles for recycling, cleaning the center or office, paying membership fees, volunteering in activities, attending meetings and training seminars, and generally helping out in any way they can.

Our members and networks generate much of our funding. However, we do rely to a certain extent on outside help. Price increases, which we know will always be a part of life, have put us under pressure, especially regarding much needed medicines. There was a flood last year in part of the province that destroyed our files and other materials.

However, seeing ever more members gradually learning to deal and live with their disabilities gives all of us on the team the heart and the will to push ahead.

Link to our tradition:

Jesus empowered many men and women who were in some way disabled, as seen in a well-known incident related in Luke 15, 18-25: "And some men brought on a stretcher a man who was paralyzed; they were trying to bring him in and set [him] in his presence. But not finding a way to bring him in because of the crowd, they went up on the roof and lowered him on the stretcher through the tiles into the middle in front of Jesus. When he saw their faith, he said, 'As for you, your sins are forgiven.' Then the scribes and Pharisees began to ask themselves, 'Who is this who speaks blasphemies? Who but God alone can forgive sins?' Jesus knew their thoughts and said to them in reply, 'What are you thinking in your hearts? Which is easier, to say, Your sins are forgiven, or to say, Rise and walk? But that you may know that the Son of Man has authority on earth to forgive sins'—he said to the man who was paralyzed, 'I say to you, rise, pick up your stretcher, and go home.' He stood up immediately before them, picked up what he had been lying on, and went home, glorifying God."

# Seek and You Shall Find

By Columban Fr. P. J. McGlinchey

It was 1966 and our program to develop greater land use in the central part of Jeju Island, South Korea, was well underway. We were developing pig farming, which requires a plentiful supply of water. Normally we had that from the many wells on the island. However a severe drought was threatening the water supply of all on Jeju Island. Such was the crisis that the most common human activity during the drought period was fetching water. Men, women, children and animals were to be seen constantly carrying water. There never had been piped water on the island as the wells had been adequate.

Being an island that was formed from one volcano and its lava flow, which subsequently fractured, the rain quickly seeps through the surface, in through the many crevices and cracks and then gradually filters down towards the sea. The seepage forms creeks or rivulets above and below ground and parts these are naturally blocked and so springs appear and wells can be dug. It was also common knowledge that some rain water was being trapped high up in the mountain in the center of the island. However, residents, most of whom lived on the narrow coastal strip and made a living from farming and fishing, had never needed to tap that source in the hills above.

At that time in Korea, there was no modern pig industry. People were extremely poor, so I concentrated on modernizing the pig industry, and St. Isidore Farm was born. Since our pig farming enterprise needed a lot of water, I looked into the possibility of tapping into the water stored higher up the central mountain. It quickly became clear that we could tap it but would need a 20 kilometer pipeline to bring the water down to our locality. At the time, Korean manufacturing industry had not developed so we had to import the PVC pipe from Japan.

I put together a project outline and costing details and set off to the U.S. to look for funding. I stopped first in San Francisco, but it was coming up to St. Patrick's Day and the Columbans were organizing a big fund raiser. They advised me to travel east, but in Chicago I was told the same story and continued on my way to New York, where there was also a St. Patrick's Day Columban fund raiser. However, the Columban in charge did suggest I approach Catholic Relief Services (CRS).

This marked the beginning of a new approach to my fundraising for development projects on Jeju Island. At that time CRS did a lot of emergency food distribution, but we were not focusing on that kind of aid. Rather we wanted to help people to help themselves—give them a fishing line, not the fish. However, I did attempt to put our project to CRS, which had offices occupying a whole floor of the Empire State Building. There I was greeted by the Monsignor in charge who told me that they did not have any cash for projects but that I should try a funding organization in Europe, maybe OXFAM. So, with the help of some friends in Chicago who paid for my airline ticket, to OXFAM I went, was well received and left my water pipe project with them, and soon after returned to Korea to await their response to my request.

Weeks passed, maybe a couple of months, and then one day I saw a cloud of dust in the distance. It was summer, all was dry and the roads were as yet unpaved. The jeep eventually arrived and out stepped the British ambassador to South Korea. With his wife, a native of County Antrim, he was touring the provinces of the country to which he had been assigned—a standard practice among British ambassadors in those days. They had taken two days to reach my place, starting in Jeju Town (as it was then), traveling around the coast on a poor road, staying the night at a house along the way, and then completing the 120 mile journey on the second day. His wife had had enough.

I invited them in for a cup of tea and my cook's version of my mother's buns. My mother's version rose but my Korean cook's version remained flat. Tea and buns put new life into the ambassador's wife. So, we chatted about this and that and I had occasion to tell them about my funding request to OXFAM for our water pipe project. The ambassador told me with enthusiasm that he knew the head of OXFAM as they had studied in Oxford together, and he would bring the matter to his attention as soon as he returned to Seoul. Within a few days I received a positive response from OXFAM.

We piped the water down from the mountain, and the farm turned out to be a great success. We now have a pig cooperative which is exporting pig meat to the Korean mainland and even to Japan. When the time was ripe I turned the whole enterprise over to the cooperative and turned my attention to modernizing the beef cattle and dairy industries on our St. Isidore Training Farm. In recent years we have been breeding racehorses for the local racing industry. The profits from these enterprises finance the running of an 85 bed nursing home, a 29 bed hospice, a retreat center and a youth education center.

Link to our tradition:
Moses had some trouble finding water for his people. He had to trust in God and so too did Columban Fr. P. J. McGlinchey. "So Moses cried out to the LORD, 'What shall I do with this people? A little more and they will stone me!' The LORD answered Moses: 'Go on ahead of the people, and take along with you some of the elders of Israel, holding in your hand, as you go, the staff with which you struck the Nile. I will be standing there in front of you on the rock in Horeb. Strike the rock, and the water will flow from it for the people to drink.' Moses did this, in the sight of the elders of Israel. The place was named Massah and Meribah, because the Israelites quarreled there and tested the LORD, saying, 'Is the LORD in our midst or not?'" (Exodus 17, 4-7)

The following two stories tell of missionaries in solidarity with prisoners.

## Two Prisoners Freed

### By Columban Fr. Liam O'Keeffe

Around Easter 1994 I received a request from a Dominican priest who was visiting from Pakistan. He asked me to visit two Pakistani prisoners who had been sentenced to death for murder and were in a Korean jail.

My first task was to locate them, so I went to the Pakistani embassy where I was informed that they were in Kwangju prison, which was a five hour trip from where I was living in Seoul. I went to see them every three months for the first two years. The only other visitors they had were personnel from their embassy who visited about once a year. Initially all they asked of me was news, some books and a little friendship.

In 1993 they had been sentenced to death for the 1992 murder of another Pakistani. Not until 1996 did the prisoners plead with me to help appeal their death sentence. I did what I could to look into their case but, not having expertise in jurisprudence; I had to rely on the judgment of others. Even though the prisoners insisted on their innocence I was never personally convinced either way. However, if they were guilty it may have been closer to a manslaughter verdict than that of murder.

I did wonder whether the prosecution's case had been proven beyond reasonable doubt. Also, I was and am personally opposed to the death penalty. I was aware that it was not unknown for cases to be rushed through the system just to get a result on record. The men who had been sentenced did claim a mistranslation of evidence from English to Korean, and I knew this to be a reasonable claim.

Being foreigners there was not much likelihood of the death sentence being carried out, but without a pardon they would remain in prison indefinitely. Being on death row the prisoners enjoyed a degree of protection from other prisoners. On the other hand, they were not able to work in the prison's factories so had no way of earning money. Their initial request to me was for books. Then, after about two years they asked me to help them mount their appeal against the death sentence.

Fortunately, in 1996 I was transferred to Kwangju to do mission promotion work so had easy access to their prison. While in Kwangju I was able to avail of the services of the diocesan office. Through them I found help to approach the appropriate groups and individuals in order to further the appeal of my prisoner friends. The Columban secretary in Kwangju typed the case description and the argument for appealing the death sentence written by the sentenced men in long hand.

The Kwangju diocesan office helped us approach the Catholic Human Rights Committee of Korea, who then did most of the leg work that eventually led to the release of the prisoners. They lobbied the then President of Korea, Kim Dae Jung, and Cardinal Stephen Kim Su-Hwan, Archbishop of Seoul. We also contacted and got support from Amnesty International and the United Nations Commission for Human Rights, based in Geneva, Switzerland.

On August 15, 1998, President Kim Dae Jung commuted the death sentence to one of life imprisonment. The story goes that he consulted his legal advisers about whether such a severe sentence had ever been reduced at one stroke to complete freedom and, on hearing that it had never been done, he decided to commute the sentence to life in prison as the first step.

Soon after that the prisoners were moved to Daejeon prison, about half way between Kwangju and Seoul. The two prisoners were very disappointed with the President's decision largely because they had been assured by prison officers that they would be set free on August 15. Due to distance, visiting became more difficult for me but, between September 1998 and February 1999, I visited them four or five times. I was hopeful that their complete pardon was not too far distant and was overjoyed when they were given the presidential pardon leading to their release on February 25, 1999. The Secretary General of the Catholic Human Rights Committee of Korea accompanied them from Daejeon prison to the airport and their deportation.

Soon after, I met the Cardinal at a baptism ceremony and, much to my surprise, he mentioned the matter to me. He was relieved that the long saga had at last ended successfully. The Cardinal had quite a reputation for being in touch with the poor and marginalized wherever he met them.

## Bearers of Joy and Good News

### By Columban Sister Rebecca Conlon

Abeeda, a 28 year old mother with one small child, had been sentenced to 15 years jail for trafficking marihuana. She was caught in possession of one kilogram of the drug. Her husband, a laborer, was out of work at the time, and she needed money to feed her family, as do so many others in a similar situation. She took her child to prison with her.

The women in jail here at present are Muslims and Hindus. The Christians who were also here previously have been moved to a jail in Karachi. They are for the most part Nigerians who have been caught peddling drugs. My friends in the local jail do not seem to be worried about their fate. I often hear them say: "Koe bat nehi. (It doesn't matter)." They also respond to my query about how they are coping with, "Allah's heart is good." It may sound fatalistic to some, but it is also faith.

I visit the prison regularly and do what I can to support and share with the women and their children. My main contribution to their material welfare is an income generating scheme. We have a bag making project using traditional Sindhi cloth (Ajorak). We provide the cloth and sewing materials; the women make the bags, the long-term spin-off for them being a skill that they might use after release from prison. We then sell the bags locally and overseas (25% of our market). Income from the sale covers the cost of material and wages.

Abeeda and her companions are able to buy extra food for their children with this income, and some who work assiduously at the bag making have been able earn enough to cover the cost of paying their lawyer without whom they would have no hope of being released.

To an outsider this ministry may seem so disheartening, but I find it anything but that. We have a great laugh together, and we celebrate our religious faiths together. We do things the way we want to do them. In a way we are very free to do things our own way in the prison.

We also try to support the prisoners' children. Abeeda's child was one of twelve in the jail for whom we bring educational toys to stimulate their learning process. Also, this year a great moment for the children was our celebration to mark Universal Children's Day. A group of children from the Christian community visited the jail (with special permission) to play games with the children of the inmates.

They began their celebration by ceremonially cutting and sharing a cake. They ate the cake even before they got into the soup. They then shared poems and songs, with the prisoners' children also participating. They played games together. Then, the coup de grace was a performance by a magician for whom we also had to obtain special permission from the authorities.

Finally, the children from our Christian community also presented a gift pack of clothes, toys and sweets to each of the children accompanying their mothers in the jail. They were truly bearers of Good News as they prompted a moment of laughter and joy for all in the jail.

Link to our tradition:

In the passage about the last judgment in Matthew 25 Jesus highlights the importance of doing what we can for those in need, in particular, prisoners: "For I was hungry and you gave me food, I was thirsty and you gave me drink, a stranger and you welcomed me, naked and you clothed me, ill and you cared for me, in prison and you visited me.' When did we see you ill or in prison, and visit you?' And the king will say to them in reply, 'Amen, I say to you, whatever you did for one of these least brothers of mine, you did for me.'"

## In Honor of the God of Life

Interview with Columban Fr. Kevin Mullins by Columban Fr. Peter Woodruff

Kevin, you have now been in this parish for eleven years. What is the story behind your coming to this part of the world?

I had been in Britain for eighteen months doing mission appeals and was on my way back to Chile where I had been working for the previous seventeen years. Columban Frs. Arturo Aguilar and Bill Morton from the U.S. invited me to stop off in El Paso, Texas, where they were stationed.

While they lived and worked in El Paso, Fr. Bill was also looking for an opportunity to work with poor families across the border in Ciudad Juárez.

Through a Mexican priest he had entered into a working relationship with residents of Rancho Anapra, a poor suburb on the northwest edge of Ciudad Juárez. Bill had devised a project to help home owners with roofing and sanitary facilities. Part of my visit to El Paso was a trip across the border to Rancho Anapra.

Bill and Arturo invited me to stay, but I returned to Chile for two more years. However I could not get Rancho Anapra out of my mind.

So, how did you resolve that?

I emailed the Columban general council requesting an appointment to the U.S. so that I might work in Rancho Anapra. My initial request was turned down, but I was asked to present the reasons why I had discerned that this might be my future as a Columban missionary. I did this and soon after was appointed to the U.S. and then to El Paso.

Following negotiation with the bishop of Ciudad Juárez, Rancho Anapra was made a parish, and I was appointed parish priest. Two other Columbans, Bill and John, were also appointed to the parish. And so we began our ministry here with about 35 Catholics coming to Sunday Mass. There were nearly 20,000 residents within the jurisdiction of our new parish and most were Catholics, so clearly we had much to do to help them feel that they belonged to the Church.

Could you say something about your dreams for what was then a new parish?

We realized that we were working with a stable, poor and marginalized population. Even now the main ring road of the city excludes our small suburb from the urban sprawl of the city, and this road was only completed a few years ago. We did not see ourselves as saviors or problem solvers. Rather we set out to help Catholics feel that this Church is theirs; we aimed to help them feel that they belonged; we wanted their belonging to the Church to be a life giving experience for them—joyous and empowering.

I have seen that you now have hundreds participating in the life of this parish. Have you found support from local Church leadership for your ministry?

I always go to the weekly priests' meetings, and I feel that we understand and appreciate each other. Our bishop seemed a little aloof when I first came but, in recent years, he has become more hands on and sensitive pastorally.

We also feel significant support from the national Church leadership, especially since the Latin American Bishops' meeting in Aparecida, Brazil in 2007. A couple of years ago the Mexican Bishops issued a statement titled, "May Mexico Achieve Life with Dignity in Christ Our Peace." It is a long pastoral statement, based largely on the conclusions of the Aparecida meeting, and aims to encourage and inspire the local Church at grassroots level. I found a brief section on parish life most affirming.

Would you like to highlight some of the points the bishops make in their statement?

Yes, I will touch on just a few that are taken from section 197 of the Bishops' statement. The following points (not a full translation of the text) have inspired and continue to inspire me in my commitment in this parish.

Community life is where people shape and strengthen the social fabric—the sense of belonging.

We [the Catholic Bishops of Mexico] are committed to renewing our parishes, making them a network of groups and communities whose members share their lives as disciples and missionaries of Jesus Christ. The bread of the Word and of the Eucharist and the service of charity urges parish community members to achieve reconciliation and justice for the life of the world.

We are committed to making the communal aspect of parish life more dynamic so that, in the midst of a fragmented society, the parish might provide opportunities for strengthening community life, and so help the community rediscover the security necessary for living together in peace.

We are committed to making all parishes a place and sign of reconciliation, which is the best antidote for the poison of hate and the desire for revenge.

We urge the small communities and groups that constitute our parishes to contribute to the recovery of communal spaces and to develop projects that strengthen the social fabric.

What have you found in this parish that nourishes your own life?

I have seen so much drug related violence and killing, and yet families seem to be so resilient. It's as if they grieve "on the run." They quickly get back into life with a dogged determination. They do not let violence perpetrated by others destroy their lives. It seems that everyone knows about the violence in Juárez, but I see and hear the untold story of creativity, commitment to family, to work and to parish.

The rhythm of parish life seems to support families in their daily lives. It is as if the relentless progress of the liturgical calendar, with its seasons and cycles, reflects, supports and steadies people as they take on the stuff of their lives.

I have found that men, women and youth want to participate; they want to do things together; they are also ready to try new things. We get on well. I feel easy with them and them with me. Some said to me recently, "You are not a bossy priest; you enjoy us."

They can also laugh in the midst of tragedy and at times show a rather black humor, which I enjoy. Even though we do experience fear and see our hands trembling after being close to dangerous violence we then find a way to joke and laugh about it. It's inexpensive therapy, I guess.

To sum up—I feel so accepted here, by the eight Columbans with whom I have shared this mission over the past eleven years, by my neighbors, by the parish community, by fellow diocesan priests, by the bishop. I could not want for a better place to be a missionary priest.

Link to our tradition:

John records Jesus' prayer for his followers in John 17, 20-26: "I pray not only for them, but also for those who will believe in me through their word, so that they may all be one, as you, Father, are in me and I in you, that they also may be in us, that the world may believe that you sent me. And I have given them the glory you gave me, so that they may be one, as we are one, I in them and you in me, that they may be brought to perfection as one, that the world may know that you sent me, and that you loved them even as you loved me. Father, they are your gift to me. I wish that where I am they also may be with me, that they may see my glory that you gave me, because you loved me before the foundation of the world. Righteous Father, the world also does not know you, but I know you, and they know that you sent me. I made known to them your name and I will make it known, that the love with which you loved me may be in them and I in them." Kevin Mullins, with his parish team, has helped a parish community in a poor suburb of Ciudad Juárez, Mexico, respond in the spirit of this prayer of Jesus.

# The Aetas (Negritos) and the Columbans

By Columban Fr. Donal O'Dea

In April 1999 an Aeta Catholic community came of age when the Franciscan Missionaries of Mary formally handed over responsibility to the community leaders. The Lakas is an alliance of 150 Aeta families living in Bihawo, Botolean. Since Paddy Duggan invited the Sisters to the area Columbans have worked with them in their mission and Columban Fr. Peter Steen, who was the Columban Director in the Philippines when the Sisters first took on the mission among the Aeta in 1982, was there to celebrate with them.

The Columban contribution to the tribal apostolate in Zambales began when we arrived in the area in 1951. The largest concentration of Aetas was in the Botolan Parish. Fr. Joe Conneely took over the parish in the late 1950s and initiated a movement in the eastern barrios in the mountains through parish catechists.

After a few years, Fr. Jude McGeough joined Joe as assistant and went to live in the mountains at Poonbato in 1967. He organized the building of the church and school, learned the local language and traveled through the whole area.

As the population of the whole province grew, ever more lowlanders moved into Aeta territory, prompting the Aetas to withdraw further into the mountains. The Church reached out to them with a new initiative, with the parish priest, Fr. Paddy Duggan, inviting the Franciscan Missionaries of Mary to help develop the apostolate. These Sisters put their mark on the Church's pastoral work with the Aeta People from the beginning and continue to do so today.

The Church personnel and the Aeta leaders agreed that the basic thrust of our apostolate should be to work to secure justice for the Aeta people, protect their ancestral land, and preserve their cultural heritage. We decided to foster among the Christian majority a greater awareness and appreciation of the Aeta people in order to lessen the deep-seated prejudice against them.

The Sisters lived in the communities and returned to their home base in Poonbato on weekends. They did not go where other NGOs were working, nor where they were not accepted. Their work was made particularly difficult during the martial law years (1972 to 1986) as they were suspected of being subversives. The lack of roads, bridges, transport and other conveniences made life stressful for them.

However, they did truly walk with the people, identifying their needs and hopes and working with them to find adequate solutions. They also had to combat the prejudice of the majority who generally referred to the Aetas with derogatory terms, such as, Minority Tribes, non-Christian Tribes, Kulots (kinky haired); all these terms denote inferiority.

It was slow work. Basic literacy programs suited to their culture and life style were developed. Leadership training, health and nutrition, new agricultural methods, care for the environment, and protection for their ancestral lands were some of the topics they developed together.

Many came to learn and imitate. Aeta leaders went to learn from and share with others, even beyond the shores of the Philippines. The ferment among the Aetas and other indigenous groups marked the beginning of the process which led to the State recognizing their rightful place in the nation through an Act of Congress.

The Aeta lived around Mt. Pinatubo, which is for them a sacred mountain. The mountain's eruption in June 1991 changed everything for them. The volcano dumped four cubic kilometers of volcanic sand (lahar) on the surrounding hills and valleys. The Aeta had to move. The Lakas, a group working with the Sisters, managed to stay together and continue in a new location. Others were scattered and found it very difficult to cope with the new life.

They had lost their land; their culture and customs were threatened; their future as a people with its own identity was in jeopardy; many were seen begging on the roads; they received a mere trickle of relief aid. A new journey began, a search for a new home.

In 1993, at the request of the local bishop to the Columban superior, I was asked to work fulltime with the Aetas. I began by finding out who was working with them and what were their short and long-term needs. I established that there were 14,000 Aetas in twenty two areas. The large resettlement areas (those with 500 to 1,500 families) have schools, a clinic, doctors and centers for meetings and water distribution. However, even soon after the volcano's destruction of their land many Aetas were returning to their barrios to start again and the Sisters went with them.

The Aeta People know from their own harrowing experience that life and growth have their pains and trials, hopes and disappointments, joys and sorrows. Three years ago I resigned as diocesan coordinator of the apostolate to the Aeta people, and the bishop appointed a Filipino priest. I am now over 80 years old so am happy to continue in the role of advisor. The journey goes on, the challenges remain. There is much to be done here in the diocese of Iba and elsewhere.

Link to our tradition:

Battered by a long-term and steady invasion of their traditional lands and, in more recent times, the massive eruption of the Mt. Pinatubo volcano, the Aeta people may well identify with sentiments expressed in the prayer of Mary when she visited her cousin, Elizabeth: "My soul proclaims the greatness of the Lord; my spirit rejoices in God my savior. For he has looked upon his handmaid's lowliness; behold, from now on will all ages call me blessed. The Mighty One has done great things for me, and holy is his name. His mercy is from age to age to those who fear him." (Luke 1, 46-50)

## Anita

### By Columban Fr. Peter Woodruff

Anita grew up in what used to be a Columban-run parish in the northern suburbs of Lima. Her barrio was first settled by migrants from the provinces in the 1960s. From her family and her personal life experience she learned about poverty, solidarity and struggle. Anita joined the Columban lay missionary program and in 2008, with three companions, arrived in the Philippines.

In Cagayan de Oro Anita was introduced to the local St. Vincent de Paul conference, Alliance of Two Hearts, whose president, Fe Jaquilmac, knew the Columbans from the days when Columban Archbishop Paddy Cronin was her boss in the social action program in the early 1980s. The St. Vincent de Paul Society had arrived in the Cagayan de Oro in the early 1980s, thanks to the concern and initiative of a Filipino diocesan priest. However, some of those in charge of the conference misappropriated funds, and when Fe was asked to take on the presidency she first had to put the house in order. Fe has been president of the archdiocesan conference since 1988, but finds she has to push to get local support for the work. People may have goodwill, but then they also seem to be so busy about whatever may be the business of their lives.

Fe was so pleased to be able to help Anita find a way of being with and supporting the poor with whom the local conference worked. As Fe explained to me, the focus of their work is to enable the poor and, in the context of this task, help them discover the person of Jesus Christ. Their projects do require funding, but it all happens in a context of supporting the efforts of the poor to stand on their own feet. Progress is slow and some do not make it. The poverty of the poorest is grinding and can leave its victims devoid of hope and so lacking in the determination to take hold of the reins of their lives. The gentle accompaniment of the St. Vincent de Paul workers, such as Anita, encourages families, often headed by women, to push ahead.

The St. Vincent de Paul Society also has other projects such as a consumer cooperative that offers loans for house repair, small businesses and tuition. The size of the loan given to a member depends on the size of their capital build-up. Those who do not build up their capital are asked to leave the co-op. There are also three small grocery stores and a massage clinic under the umbrella of the conference's works.

The place I visited was a day-care center run by the women of the group who took turns looking after the many small children I met running about at will. Rotating the job of caring for the children allows the women to work and so earn.

The group I met have a small workshop where they make candles, for which there is a constant demand due to regular brown-outs as the local electricity supply cannot always keep up with the demand, even more so when there is drought since the generators are water driven.

Anita had taken me to meet her friends in one of the poorest places I have ever seen. They welcomed me with joy and a courtesy that I had noticed seemed to be typical of Filipinos. After taking a few photos, which the children absolutely reveled in, we settled down to chat and watch the children playing their games.

I left the day-care center and the candle making workshop knowing that most of those I had met will spend the rest of their lives in poverty but, at the same time, they gave me heart.

Link to our tradition:

A Peruvian lay missionary in the Philippines accompanies the poor with the support of the local St. Vincent de Paul Society. She does not go to them with money or grand projects, just herself. In Matthew 19, 24 Jesus says to his disciples, "Again I say to you, it is easier for a camel to pass through the eye of a needle than for one who is rich to enter the kingdom of God."

# A Valiant Woman

By Beth Sabado, Columban lay missionary

A-Hang (this is not her real name), a 29 year old Vietnamese care-giver, arrived in our shelter as a victim of rape. She was looking after an elderly man, and his son, who was her employer, raped her repeatedly. She arrived in the shelter in August 2005. I had worked as a nurse for nine years in a hospital in the Philippines and was head nurse when I resigned to join the Columban Lay Mission program. However, I had no experience of trauma counseling so did not know how to deal with A-Hang's case.

I would see her looking out the window with a vacant look on her face. I knew she was so lonely and probably depressed, but I felt that I could do little more than be silently present to her. My Chinese language was quite limited at that time even though I had done one year of fulltime language study. I soon realized that by being present to her I was comforting her. One day she said to me, "You are very good."

After about four months A-Hang started talking to me about how she had been raped. She cried and let me see her feelings. I knew that was good, that she was beginning the road back to recovery. She also started participating in activities and talking with others in the shelter.

When the time came for her court hearings I helped her prepare herself for the ordeal. We looked at a movie about a court case dealing with rape and that made her hesitate. She told me she was afraid to relive the feeling of being raped. I told her that if she showed such feeling it would help her case. I advised her to be focused, not to worry whether or not she cried or felt bad, and to consult the translator if necessary.

I admired her sense of confidence, her strength and courage. She would say, "I am doing this because I am fighting for my rights. This is my time to speak the truth."

A-Hang won her case. Her criminal employer was sentenced to time in jail and was obliged by the court to pay her compensation. She was also the first migrant worker to win the right to a cross-sector (care giver to factory worker) transfer.

Like so many others A-Hang had arrived at our shelter weary of life, depressed and seemingly broken. She found the inner strength to gradually come back to life. We at the shelter were privileged to accompany her along the road of that difficult year long journey. Her facial expression told me that she was moving on. In fact, she was the first of many I have seen make a similar comeback after being abused or exploited in some devastating way.

She confirmed for me in a striking way that I had made the correct decision when I applied to join the Columban Lay Mission program. When I was a young nurse I had the timeline of my life worked out—profession, good job, better job, migrate to U.S., marry, have a family and a nice home. A Chilean couple, both of whom were lay missionaries with the Columbans, began to help me see radically different, undreamt of possibilities.

I had the idea that only Sisters and priests could be missionaries. They showed me that was not so. They had a baby and lived in the small town of Midsalip. Life was not easy there. I noticed that they also spoke our language (Cebuano) among themselves. I knew Columban priests who came to the hospital at times, Lar Ryan and Mick Sinnott, so I asked them about the Columban Lay Mission program.

I applied to join the program, was accepted, did the initial orientation course and was assigned to Taiwan. Following Chinese language study I expressed my preference for work in the mountains with the indigenous with whom I thought I'd have a good chance of improving my Chinese. I ended up with the migrant workers who generally speak Chinese poorly. The story of A-Hang and so many others has ensured that I never regretted the path I have walked.

I visited my sister in the U.S. to see what life was like there. I still wondered whether I might like to work and live in the U.S. I soon realized that it was not for me. Here I am empowering women who have been abused and exploited. This makes so much more sense to me. I also learn a lot from the different cultures of the women who come to our shelter.

At times, it may be tiring, frustrating and disappointing here because many women feel hopeless and give up only partway through their court cases. Still, the A-Hangs of this world assure me that this work is very worthwhile. In August 2010, A-Hang came to say, "Goodbye." She told me, "I've earned enough money for my daughter's education. I'm going home now." I asked her how she was, whether the troubles of the past still affected her. She laughed and said, "The past is over; I just want to move on with my life." A-Hang is a practicing Buddhist, and I know that she finds a steady strength in her religious faith.

Link to our tradition:

Mary was there for her son as are missionaries, on occasion, simply there for others. See John 2, 1-5: "On the third day there was a wedding in Cana in Galilee, and the mother of Jesus was there. Jesus and his disciples were also invited to the wedding. When the wine ran short, the mother of Jesus said to him, 'They have no wine.' [And] Jesus said to her, 'Woman, how does your concern affect me? My hour has not yet come.' His mother said to the servers, 'Do whatever he tells you.'"

## Dreams of a Missionary and Their Outcome

### By Columban Fr. Joe Houston

I returned to Ireland from Chile in 1987 to accompany my sick mother who died in early 1988. At that time I intended to return to Chile. While in Ireland I heard from Columban Fr. John O'Connell, the director of the Irish Region at the time, that there was material available about going to China as an English teacher.

There was a report by Matt Carpenter, an Irish Mill Hill missionary, on his work in China. In fact, he is still in China, in a remote, poor area where he helps locals with community development projects, such as installing a clean water supply system. His report in particular influenced me and also a report by a lawyer who had visited China.

At that stage, I saw teaching English as a contribution to the Chinese people, a way of furthering their educational opportunities. This seemed to me to be a missionary response along the lines suggested by Vatican II's document, *Gaudium et Spes*, on our outreach to the modern world. I also hoped that, in some way, I'd find openings for preaching the Gospel.

Both worked out for me, but the second not to the extent that I had hoped. I felt bound by the orientation of AITECE (the organization that recruited and placed teachers in China), which was to teach English. However, on some special days, especially Easter, Christmas and St. Patrick's Day I discussed the Christian meaning of these religious celebrations, but I used to frame my explanation in terms of culture.

While teaching English I was hesitant to look for contact with the underground Church for fear of what I might give away if interrogated. However, I did have some discreet contact with people in both the underground and over-ground Church.

At the time I first decided to go to China, Deng Xiaoping, a top Chinese leader, had been moving the country towards a hybrid economic model involving private ownership of industry and a greater openness to foreign investment and international trade. This new trend prompted me to hope for ever greater democratic freedoms and the opportunity to work openly as a Catholic missionary in collaboration with the Chinese Church. I did not realize then that Deng's vision did not go beyond economic reform.

Zhao Ziyang, Chairman of the Communist Party of China (CPC) in 1989, supported the student movement's demands for greater democracy, but he lost the internal political struggle and was put under house arrest, during which he recorded and smuggled out his memoirs, which were published in Hong Kong in both Chinese and English after he died (Prisoner of the State—the secret journal of Chinese Premier, Zhao Ziyang, Simon and Schuster, Hong Kong, 2009). In his memoir Zhao pointed out that Deng was not open to greater democracy or cultural freedom, but rather to aspects of the capitalist economic system.

I am now beyond the mandatory retirement age of 65 years and no longer teach English but I do see scope for further engagement in our China mission. The Church continues to be persecuted, but the trend is towards greater freedom, so I think it is important that we take advantage of the openings presently available to us.

There is a strong trend towards reconciliation between the underground and over-ground Church. We no longer refer to two churches in China; rather there is one Catholic Church. Information available on the state of the Catholic Church in China from The Holy Spirit Study Centre in Hong Kong indicates strong growth and ever-growing collaboration among Catholics.

The modern day Church in China dates to the time of Matteo Ricci, the Italian Jesuit missionary who died in Beijing in 1610, so clearly our missionaries have not been sent to China to establish the Church. Rather we have been invited to support the Chinese Church, which constantly invites us to do precisely that in a variety of ways. We have to find effective ways to serve and what we do depends so much on opportunities that present themselves, our own personal gifts and maybe a certain amount of luck, also frequently described as the providence of God.

Some of our priests are helping out in a local seminary; some help facilitate advanced studies in China and abroad for young Chinese Church leaders; some teach English under the aegis of AITECE; some are helping build bridges between conflicting parties in the Church; one edits an English edition of the Hong Kong Catholic weekly, which has a strong outreach to the approximately 130,000 domestic workers from the Philippines; one works with migrant workers and their families who have come from rural China to the big city in search of work and education.

Link to our tradition:

To dream of and search for a more humane world find support in the final chapters of the Bible: "Then I saw a new heaven and a new earth. The former heaven and the former earth had passed away, . . . I also saw the holy city, a new Jerusalem, . . . I heard a loud voice from the throne saying, 'Behold, God's dwelling is with the human race. He will dwell with them and they will be his people and God himself will always be with them [as their God]. He will wipe every tear from their eyes, and there shall be no more death or mourning, wailing or pain, [for] the old order has passed away.'" (Revelation 21, 1-4)

## Adapting Well-honed Pedagogical Skills

By Rachel and David Winton, AITECE volunteers

### David

I was born and brought up in north London. After studying Classics at university I taught English and History at Canisius College, an Irish Jesuit Mission School, in southern Zambia from 1971 to 1974. After a year back home studying for a teaching certificate, I taught English and history at a boys' Catholic comprehensive secondary school in north London for over thirty years. I got married in 1977 to Rachel, also a teacher, and we have three children, now all adults. I retired in July 2009, but still enjoyed teaching and wanted a new challenge. Through AITECE, an organization based in Hong Kong and linked with the Columbans, we were accepted to teach English here in Wuhan in central China.

## Rachel

I was born and brought up in Hertfordshire and Norfolk, England. My father was a minister in the United Reformed Church, and my mother was born in Taiyuan, NW China, the daughter of Baptist missionaries who were active there in the early twentieth century. I studied French and German at university, spent a year teaching English in Paris, and subsequently taught languages in comprehensive secondary schools in London. After marrying David in 1977, I took time out of teaching to raise our three children, and became a Catholic in 1986, just before our third child was born. I returned to teaching in 1991, working as a learning support teacher, to enable children with special needs to remain in mainstream education. I retired in 2005, and helped teach English as a Second Language on a voluntary basis to immigrant mothers in north London. I was very pleased to come to China, once David had retired, to teach English to university students in Wuhan, and to follow up our family interest in the development of Christianity in China.

## Rachel and David

We live in a very serviceable apartment on the campus of Hubei University in the city of Wuhan in the province of Hubei in central China. The 16,000 students, most of which are from Hubei province, also live on campus. They are enrolled in graduate and post-graduate programs in the arts and sciences. The southern side of this city is home to 20 universities where nearly 500,000 students pursue the numerous study programs available. Two of the city's universities are among the top ten in China. The campus is very leafy and, despite the number of students, is not overwhelming in size. All the facilities you might need are here on your doorstep: supermarket, post office, bank, restaurant and even a hairdresser's shop. One further pleasant aspect is that all the generations live here together in harmony—students, teachers with their young children and former teachers now in their old age.

The university has contracted us to teach English to students at various stages of proficiency. They provide us with a basic textbook, a copy of which the students buy. We each have eight contact sessions of two hours a week with eight different groups of students, the number of students in each class ranging from 16 to 50. Both of us taught high school students in state schools in England until our retirement, so one would reasonably conclude that we have learnt most of the skills needed to teach effectively. However, we are finding that teaching Chinese tertiary students with just one contact session each week challenges us in new ways.

Some classrooms are equipped for using multimedia but, at the same time, they might still have a blackboard rather than a whiteboard. Some classrooms have air conditioning which makes it so much easier to work in the extremes of hot and cold weather, but some older rooms are not so equipped. Some of the classrooms we teach in are on the fifth or sixth floor and there is no elevator, but the students would not even think of complaining. When we arrive for class at 8.00 a.m. we find them seated at their desks with their textbooks open. They are respectful and always well dressed; being scruffy is not part of their style.

Most classrooms have long rows of desks screwed to the floor, so there is no chance of rearranging the furniture for small group work or whole-class activities, say in a circle. The students seem to be used to the teacher doing all the talking and are inclined to be passive. We usually begin by going through some of the oral exercises in the textbook, and they seem happy to continue the lesson doing things more or less mechanically by rote.

So, while we have found the textbook helpful, we also saw that we needed to move beyond it. We needed to get our students discussing topics in which they had some genuine interest, topics that would spark discussion and a variety of opinions. Of course, such discussion demands that the students use vocabulary that they may not have already learnt, so we teach them some of the words and phrases they might need in the discussion of the day. So far we have introduced topics such as children and television, better city/better life (the slogan of the 2010 Shanghai Expo), China's one child policy, the difficulties of life on a live-in campus and the happiest day of my life. We have also taught them to sing some English songs, such as "You are my sunshine," and organizing role playing exercises. All of this has helped the students to be less stiff and formal, and to move the lesson away from being a one way traffic process to an interaction between us and our students and between the students themselves. We feel we are making progress, but we always need to keep in mind that our cultural backgrounds are so different.

Unlike our experience back home, there is no need to expend energy keeping order in the classroom; the students are always co-operative and work with the teacher. Perhaps a major difference between our cultures is that while ours tends to be rather individualistic, theirs seems to emphasize more a sense of belonging to a group. This may in part explain their unwillingness to volunteer their individual views to the class but will agree to do so if directly asked. Apart from being taught good manners from childhood, conformity rather than a selfish individualism is reinforced in the students during the first two weeks of their first university term, when, dressed in military fatigues, they do military-type drills from 6:30 a.m. to 5:00 p.m. Even though there is no obligatory military service in China, the military ethos of conformity has a significant influence on reinforcing social behavior and attitudes.

We are finding that this job constantly challenges our creativity as teachers but, despite all the difficulties, it is a great joy to be trying something new at this stage of our lives. Retirement has meant an opportunity to branch out and do so in our chosen profession. We will also take advantage of the opportunity to travel in China, which is such a vast and varied country. We have already had six days in Beijing; over the winter break we plan to travel to the south-west and over the summer to the north-west, from where some of our students come, and finally to Shanghai before we fly home to London.

Link to our tradition:

Rachel and David, retired teachers from England, teach English to university students in Wuhan, China. "Do not neglect to do good and to share what you have; God is pleased by sacrifices of that kind." (Hebrew 13, 16) According to The Catechism of the Catholic Church, No. 1911, "Human interdependence is increasing and gradually spreading throughout the world. The unity of the human family, embracing people who enjoy equal natural dignity, implies a universal common good. This good calls for an organization of the community of nations able to provide for the different needs of men [and women] . . ." (cf. Gaudium et Spes, No. 29)

## Solidarity with Shanghai's Migrant Workers

### By Puisana Chaw

I was born in Hong Kong and was brought up speaking Cantonese. I then went to the U.S. to the University of Wisconsin in Madison where I completed a degree in Developmental Psychology, with a personal emphasis on the development of children. I then worked as a preschool teacher for two years and saw the need to work with parents as well as to coordinate what they and I were trying to achieve with their children. That motivated me to complete a second degree in child and family studies in Syracuse University, New York. I also married Etienne, but my husband's job with a multinational company meant moving home often. When we arrived in Pasadena, California, it seemed like a good place to bring up a family. We had our first child, Kelly. After a few years there, the company made him an offer he could not refuse in their Shanghai office. This also gave us the opportunity to help Kelly learn Mandarin as we spoke Cantonese at home. Even though she is only five years old she moves so easily between English, Cantonese and Mandarin.

I began my work with the You Dao Foundation[6] as a volunteer and was recently asked to take on the job of Executive Director, which I also do voluntarily. Our foundation works to raise awareness of the plight of migrants; we build alliances and partnerships to support migrants; we look for practical ways to support migrants. Working in a formal association with the local Church in the social apostolate is very complex, so we have decided to pursue our objectives in other ways. Also, due to government rules we cannot establish and run educational institutions. Some of our projects have prospered for a time but then, for reasons beyond our control, they might finish overnight. We take on what we do knowing that we are working in a grey, insecure area.

The local Church is reasonably good in its response to emergency situations created, for example, by an earthquake or a flood. However, it seems that it is difficult for the Church to take on longer term social outreach projects; first, because generally the government does not want the Church systematically reaching out as it opposes the development of civil society independent of its control; second, the Church has been pushed in on itself and, in a sense, is finding its way to get going again with its primary focus for now being the development of the Church itself as an institution.

We have projects in two places, Fengxian District (on the southern outskirts of Shanghai city) and Baoshan District (on the north western outskirts of the city).

In the former we offer a number of scholarships to migrant children attending two kindergartens. It is a five day a week program from 7:30 a.m. to 4:30 p.m. The scholarship covers the cost of tuition fees, three meals per day and other miscellaneous costs. With the support of our sponsors we are also setting up a community center to support the ongoing formation of migrant children.

For various social purposes, including healthcare and education to the end of high school, the 33 provinces of China are run to a certain extent as if they were independent countries. Healthcare and education are available in each province for all who are born there, but such basic services are much harder to come by once provincial borders are crossed. This has become a significant social problem in the major urban centers along the eastern seaboard. The government

---

6    *You Dao was initiated in Shanghai when Columban priest, Fr. Warren Kinne invited a group of friends to discuss the issue of migrant workers over dinner in June 2005. A lawyer at the dinner, Audrey Leung, later initiated a research project about the plight of the migrant workers. She did extensive research on all aspects of the phenomenon and started to give seminars to various groups including professional and women's leadership groups about the fruit of her research and her own growing commitment to do something helpful. The story unfolds as the members of the You Dao Foundation better understand the situation of migrant workers and try to respond in appropriate ways to help them contribute to the development of their country. For more details see: http://www. youdao.org.hk/*

is in the process of partially addressing the educational needs of migrant children in Shanghai by collaborating with some of the better privately run schools, and offering the children free education from grades one to nine. However, such schools continue to offer a second rate education to the migrant children, who still cannot attend the State-run, fee-based kindergartens, a circumstance that our Foundation sees as a window of opportunity.

When we first began to offer scholarships the migrants were quite suspicious. Is it at all possible that an organization might offer something for nothing? What do these people really want? Do they want to win our trust so that later they might kidnap our children and sell them? By visiting and talking to them we persuaded some of our honorable intentions and then what we did for their children won their trust.

We began with home visits to obtain basic information about the families applying for scholarships. Once we determined the list of children to receive scholarships we arranged to visit each family monthly in order to update ourselves with regard to their work and health situations, and how the children were doing. Our goal is to promote an integral formation of the child, which of course requires parental participation in the education of their children. In many parts of China parents are forced to leave their children with their grandparents while they go to work in distant urban centers. As a consequence, thousands of children have grown up without knowing their parents, and the rate of delinquency among such children has risen. While the families with whom we work are poor, they are also together and we want to help them remain that way.

In Baoshan District volunteers from two universities come to the small center that the local Catholic parish lets us use on weekends. The center was built, maybe 100 years ago, in the town of Beiyaowan, which at that time was a rural town surrounded by farms. It is now hemmed in by small factories and workshops and is a temporary home to thousands of migrants from neighboring provinces, whose lives are a constant struggle to make ends meet.

On Saturday and Sunday afternoon the children from the neighborhood are queued up outside the gate anxious to enter and get on with the afternoon's fun. The university students, who for the most part are not Catholics, play games with them and do activities around tables with those who prefer that. One student commented to me: "We may not be doing much, but we are doing something, and I know that if I don't do this I will not try to change anything."

I support the volunteers with training sessions each quarter on child development, and I go to the center every two weeks to talk to the students about their experience with the children. We would like to have a student do an internship with You Dao and then take on a job of home visiting. This would be a step towards a partnership with a university. As in all our projects, we are always on the lookout for openings and coordinate as best we can to take advantage of them.

Link to our tradition:

Shanghai is the biggest and richest city in China. How might some of the city's 20 million residents discover the face of a compassionate God? From its most ancient tradition the Bible associates compassion with God: "If one of your kindred is in need in any community in the land which the LORD, your God, is giving you, . . . you shall freely open your hand and generously lend what suffices to meet that need . . . . When you give, give generously and not with a stingy heart; . . . The land will never lack for needy persons; that is why I command you: 'Open your hand freely to your poor and to your needy kin in your land.'" (Deuteronomy 15, 7-11)

## Compassionate Solidarity

By Jhoanna Resari (Philippines) and Kim Jung Woong (Korea), Columban lay missionaries

### Jhoanna Resari

I was 26 years old when I first arrived in Taiwan, a little apprehensive about how I might cope with all that is so different from what I had grown up with in the Philippines, my home country.

Even while I was in college I was interested in reaching out to others and doing something worthwhile with my life, but I did not know quite what that might mean in practical terms. One Sunday on my way to Mass, I saw a big banner outside a church announcing, "Columban Lay Mission." I realized immediately that as a lay person I could also be a missionary, but when I phoned the Columban contact person and answered her questions about my age, studies and work experience, I was advised to get a job and come back in three years.

I found a job and continued discerning. I worked as a graphic artist and in my free time did volunteer work in emergency relief and community outreach, all of which seemed close to my idea of mission work. I thought that if I liked this then I'd probably like mission work.

At the same time, I was exploring other options and over the course of a year I attended monthly discernment retreats for vocational discernment with a community of the Carmelite Missionary Sisters. That experience led me to reflect: "If, for me, it's not about taking vows as a nun maybe God is calling me to lay mission."

When I was 23, I contacted the Columban lay missionaries and was welcomed to their preparation program, but my parents cried when I told them. They were afraid for my safety and wondered whether I might end up in Africa. However, they ended up telling me that, "Wherever you are happy we will support you." They soon got to know the Columbans and my companions in the lay mission preparation program. Much to their relief, I was also able to inform them that the Columbans had no mission in Africa, and they were quite pleased when I told them that I was being sent to Taiwan, not so far away from home.

On arrival in Taiwan I began a one year full-time Chinese language course and also made time for discerning which apostolate I might take on. The Columbans asked me to consider their mission priorities, but they were also open to other suggestions. I ended up opting for work with people living with and affected by HIV/AIDS and Columban Fr. Peter O'Neill, the Columban lay mission contact person at that time, put me in touch with Nicole Yang, the Taiwanese founder of Harmony Home Association Taiwan.

Nicole began her work with people living with HIV/AIDS in 1986 when a friend who was sick with AIDS asked her for help. She took the young man into her house where she was bringing up two young children and, as the saying goes, "The rest is history!" That initiative of kindness and compassion has steadily expanded in Taiwan and beyond to mainland China.

While previously those we sheltered were mostly homosexuals, today drug users are the biggest group (although not by much), followed by homosexuals and children. We have more men than women coming to our shelters, and the shelter for the women and children is now separate from that of the men (an inadequate budget prevented us from doing this until recently).

Nicole asked me to help with whatever might involve English. I also help out with hands-on work with patients, especially the children, so I have had to educate myself about HIV/AIDS. The women's shelter takes up quite a bit of my time, along with accompanying migrant women involved in legal cases (sheltering migrant women and their children is another service rendered by Harmony Home). At first, I was a little afraid and nervous being in the shelter for adult patients because of my lack of knowledge about HIV/AIDS, but I soon came to understand more about the disease, its cause, consequences and treatment.

Nicole has always given priority to publicity and fundraising so I took charge of communication via English outside Taiwan. While the Taiwanese Government does contribute around fifteen percent of our annual budget, we rely on private donations for the rest.

The administration of Harmony Home is centralized in Taipei from where we send funds to our various works in other places. I represent Harmony Home at fundraising events where we ask for direct donations and also grants and scholarships, especially for the education of the children. I also help with the design of printed material and do some Chinese to English translation.

I was not the only Columban lay missionary to choose Harmony Home as my place of mission in Taiwan. One Korean, Kim Jung Woong (Bosco) joined me after two years, but I will leave it to Woong to say more about that.

### Kim Jung Woong (Bosco)

Before joining the Columban Lay Mission program I had a varied experience of life. Among other things, I worked in a hotel chain in Seoul, South Korea, as a room sales manager for eight years. For three years I wandered around Australia and New Zealand working and learning English.

During the Columban lay mission orientation period in Seoul, I visited Columban Sisters who were running a shelter for HIV/AIDS patients. I was afraid when I shook hands with patients, but I was moved and wanted to overcome this fear. Later, in Taiwan, I chose to work at Harmony Home with people living with and affected by HIV/AIDS.

I was told that the Columbans in Taiwan had a number of priorities and that I might choose an apostolate in the area of one of those priorities. However, none of us were native English speakers, and I think I mistranslated the word "priority" as something akin to "suggestion," which of course left me free to choose an apostolate outside the boundaries of the priorities—one of the hazards of belonging to a multi-cultural, cross-cultural mission group.

At Harmony Home Nicole asked me to supervise the nannies and mothers at the shelter for women and children. I became Nicole's eyes and ears, but the nannies saw me as a spy for Nicole, who wants to create more of a home than an institutional atmosphere in the shelters. However, given all the circumstances she has to insist on some rules. The nannies were generally infected by HIV because of drug use and were in the shelter to help them kick their addictions. Also many of the children's mothers are still in prison so we take the children to prison to visit. Harmony Home is also a halfway home for these women.

I am also the photographer who provides pictures so that Harmony Home can make an album for each child to take with them when they leave. The photos are also used in Harmony Home publicity and decorate many walls of the children's shelter.

I am now beginning my second three year term as a Columban lay missionary and have recently returned from Korea with my new bride, Lee Ji Young (Tina). Tina was also a member of our Korean lay mission group so clearly mission work was not my only focus during my first term in Taiwan. Tina and I were married in Korea; Nicole traveled north to be at our wedding. Tina continues to work at Harmony Home but now as an employee, not a lay missionary. The Columban lay missionaries are funded by the Columbans. But Harmony Home gives monthly allowances to help with both Jao's and my expenses as Nicole's way of thanking the Columbans for allowing us to work in Harmony Home as full-time volunteers.

Now Tina and I know and understand what we might do with and for people living with HIV/AIDS who come to Harmony Home. We look forward to sharing this mission and supporting each other as husband and wife lay missionaries. I am 44 and Tina is 39 years old and life continues to be an adventure for both of us.

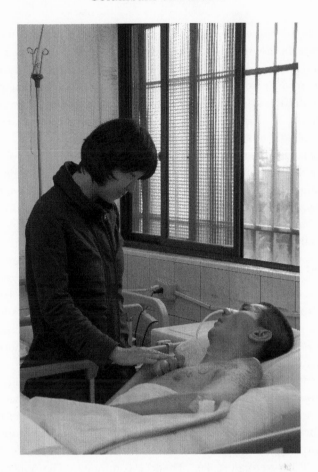

Link to our tradition:

The following verse, Psalm 119, 77, might serve as a mantra for those working with people living with and affected by HIV/AIDS: "Show me compassion that I may live, for your law is my delight."

## Just Being There

### By Columban Fr. Peter Woodruff

Francisco and Cecilia are pillars of a small parish community in a new and dusty suburb on the outskirts of Lima, Peru. They live in a small house located on an unpaved street where the government authorities, after about 20 years since families first came to live in the area, have recently begun to put in water and sewerage pipes. They are welcoming, diligent and loving with their three children and hard workers. They help their neighbors in need in so far as they can and coordinate in the activities of the local church community.

Francisco has worked as a diesel-engine mechanic in the navy for many years and just two years ago, soon before he turned 50, he retired. He and his wife had done all they could to bring up their children in a healthy and loving way but, all of a sudden, their world fell apart. Their eldest son had become a marihuana addict. They did not know to whom they could turn. They felt that other family members would be judgmental. Cecilia's parents were dead as was Francisco's father. Francisco did not want to worry his elderly mother.

Distraught and confused he went in search of Padre Leo (who had been parish priest in that area for a few years when they were beginning to get the community up and running). He found Columban Fr. Leo Donnelly in the Columban headquarters house and when Fr. Leo hugged him Francisco just sobbed aloud for ten minutes. He could not understand why all this had happened to them. Cecilia came along too and poured her heart out to Fr. Leo.

Fr. Leo was like a father to them, firm, gentle and compassionate. With an understanding word and strong hug they were confident that they would always find in him acceptance and compassion. "Who on earth will judge you?" he said. "Don't be getting upset. Just let the Father act in freedom. Things will work out." They felt that they could have drowned in despair, and Fr. Leo was like a life-saver. He stopped them from despairing, and they knew they had found someone in whom they could trust.

They gradually began to get on with tackling the issue as a family but did not involve the two younger children. Things have moved on, but they know that such matters are never definitively solved and that they are not safe from further family trauma. Francisco remarked to me, "I now know that no one is immune from anything. Anything can happen to anyone. One can do everything correctly, so to speak, and still disaster can strike." Then he continued, "The only response that will work in the face of this kind of thing is love."

A huge part of their concern was the wherewithal to cover needed medical assistance. Recovery meant weekly meetings with psychologists and social welfare people, and if they went ahead it also meant they had to accompany their son at each session, a requirement the hospital authorities demanded. They already knew that this could go on for months. Fares, and medicines had to be included, and their relief was palpable when Fr. Leo assured them he had Columban benefactors who would help and that he was merely a channel for such aid.

Both told me that they already knew all this from their experience of standing by others in their need, but the experience of having to deal with it in their own lives radically changed their way of knowing. Their experience of standing by their own son, still fragile and still struggling to find his way, lets them feel the depth of pain that others might be enduring as they face their own family problems. Francisco also said in the course of our conversation, "It's so important not to judge anyone. I was down and Padre Leo lifted me up. If he had judged me in some way he could have pushed me further into despair and confusion."

Cecilia commented, "There were times when we used to wonder with our friends in the parish community, 'what is God preparing us for?' We never expected this." They told me that Fr. Leo told the men manning the gate of the headquarter's house, where he lives as retired, that they should wake him if he were asleep when either of them came to see him.

Francisco mentioned a most pleasant surprise that Fr. Leo gave him when he turned up at their home for Francisco's 50th birthday and enjoyed two special dishes that people from Chiclayo (Francisco's home city in on the north coast of Peru) delight in. *

*Espesado: mix and grind maize, coriander and kaiwa (Chenopodium pallidicaule—native Andean vegetable), cook in a pot and serve as a puré, and place a piece of boiled beef on top; then, the second dish, Ceviche de caballa (dark fleshed fish from the waters of the Pacific Ocean near Chiclayo): dice the fish and marinate in lime; add peppers and spices according to taste.

Link to our tradition:

Francisco and Cecilia found in Columban Fr. Leo Donnelly the support they needed. Like the Samaritan Fr. Leo was in the right place at the right time with the right disposition, compassion. "But a Samaritan traveler who came upon him was moved with compassion at the sight. He approached the victim, poured oil and wine over his wounds and bandaged them. Then he lifted him up on his own animal, took him to an inn and cared for him. The next day he took out two silver coins and gave them to the innkeeper with the instruction, 'Take care of him. If you spend more than what I have given you, I shall repay you on my way back.'" (Luke 10, 33-35)

## Cycles of Renewal

### By Mausio Tifanue

A Raiwaqa parishioner in Fiji describes his role in a parish renewal initiated 25 years ago and suggests the need for another period of renewal.

Ours has always been a dynamic parish, with lots of lay participation, but the style of lay involvement has changed radically over the years, due basically to Vatican II's vision of the role of the laity in the Church's mission.

Our Archbishop of over 30 years, Petero Mataca, now in his 80th year, was the first parish priest of Raiwaqa. He put in place the original parish structure that endured until 1989. Later, when he was Archbishop, we renewed our parish life according to the insights of Vatican II.

Initially the heart of our parish organization was "The Men's Club," which drew in men from all sectors of the parish. The sectors existed but did not function as such but rather the basic lay structure of our parish was this centralized organization of men. The men took their cue from the parish priest, and so the parish was structured along the lines of traditional Fijian society. The chief made the decisions in consultation with the men and then instructed people what to do. It was a top-down affair.

The Columbans took over the parish when Fr. Petero became archbishop. I arrived in Fiji in 1975 but lived in another area until 1982, when I married Vamarasi Mausio, a Rotuman[7] and born Catholic like myself. Columban Fr. Dermot Hurley was parish priest at that time. I was used to the traditional ways of being a Catholic, and I fit into the local Catholic community easily. I got to know my neighbors, and they got to know me and so I gradually became involved in parish life.

I was elected parish chairman in 1988 under our new parish priest, Columban Fr. Tom Rouse. With Fr. Tom's backing, our parish committee and I oversaw the process of parish reorganization on the basis of sectors. We decentralized the parish and so the Men's Club soon became irrelevant. However, we had to deal with considerable resistance as we put in place the changes. Some argued that we should leave things as the Archbishop had left them when he was parish priest.

However, what we were proposing was very much in tune with the archdiocesan momentum. In 1987 the archdiocesan vision was developed and published. This vision urged us to develop our local parish church as a "Family of God." It gave us support in our project of more inclusive participation in parish life. We had also been doing workshops on reforming our parish structure, and our parish constitution was approved in 1987. And so, with this backing, during the years 1988-89, we put in place the reforms and broadened the participation base generating a spirit of revival in parish life.

We developed lay participation in our Sunday celebrations. We prepared unleavened bread (something like roti) and used it in the Eucharist. Parishioners had to chew it, and we were not used to doing that with the wafer that simply dissolved in one's mouth. Jesus told us to take and eat so we felt we were eating when we used this unleavened bread.

We introduced Good Friday Stations of the Cross that invited participants to reflect on the passion and death of Jesus in the context of our own lives. Our Stations of the Cross carried a message for present day Fiji. This generated opposition from within and outside our parish. In April 1989 our parish priest, Fr. Tom Rouse, was refused an extension of his visa due to his participation in a public protest against the recent military coup.

Around that time our parish delegation to the National Lay Assembly had to deal with an accusation by other participants of doing things not approved by the Archbishop, and this in the presence of the Archbishop. As leader of our parish

---

[7]    There are more Rotumans in Fiji than in Rotuma.

delegation, I had to defend our actions to the Archbishop and he agreed that we were on the right track, encouraging us to do well what we were doing.

After Fr. Tom left, our parish committee more or less ran the parish. Columban Fr. Arthur Tierney soon arrived to take over and wanted to make some changes, but we insisted that he must work through the parish committee. For a while we clashed on the method of decision making but eventually ended up being close friends. Fr. Arthur realized that by working with us there was so much that he would not need to concern himself with.

I completed my term as parish chairman and a new chairman was elected, and our decentralized parish structure survived to shape our way until today. As we said goodbye for a second time to Fr. Tom as our parish priest I wonder whether it is time for another renewal. The first was about lay participation and education in the Catholic faith. What might be the heart of an archdiocesan renewal program for our times? I think the moment is propitious as our bishop elect, Fr. Peter Joy Chong, will be assuming the reins of the local church in June 2013.

Link to our tradition:

"The Christian faithful are those who, inasmuch as they have been incorporated in Christ through Baptism, have been constituted as the people of God; for this reason, since they have become sharers in Christ's priestly, prophetic, and royal office in their own manner, they are called to exercise the mission which God has entrusted to the Church to fulfill in the world, in accord with the condition proper to each one."

"In virtue of their rebirth in Christ there exists among all the Christian faithful a true equality with regard to dignity and the activity whereby all cooperate in the building up of the Body of Christ in accord with each one's own condition and function."

The very differences which the Lord has willed to put between the members of his body serve its unity and mission. For "in the Church there is diversity of ministry but unity of mission. To the apostles and their successors Christ has entrusted the office of teaching, sanctifying and governing in his name and by his power. But the laity are made to share in the priestly, prophetical, and kingly office of Christ; they have therefore, in the Church and in the world, their own assignment in the mission of the whole People of God." (The Catechism of the Catholic Church, 1993, # 871-873)

## Reaching Out

By Columban Fr. Ed O'Connell, Milka Rosas, Rosario Salinas and Vanesa Cardosa

In 1999 I was appointed to the parish, Our Lady of the Missions, where I have since led the parish team in the development of parish communities and social outreach. From a socio-economic perspective our parishioners are predominantly working and lower middle class. They are not the poorest of the poor, but many families do struggle to make ends meet. A major priority in our parish work at all levels is to empower those with whom we work. With this in mind, I helped establish a small organization called Warmi Huasi, (Quechua for Women's House), which develops programs of social outreach, especially in response to needs of women and children.

In recent years Warmi Huasi has developed a second center in the township of San Benito[8], where 5,000 people live in extreme poverty on the foothills of the Andes, some 25 kilometers to the north east of our parish. In the following paragraphs staff members of the San Benito Warmi Huasi describe their work and dreams.

We have two outreach programs running in San Benito, Peru, each staffed by three young women, all of whom are university graduates in areas such as, midwifery, nutrition, education, psychology and social welfare. One program focuses on the nutrition of children under five years of age (Rosario Salinas, Vanesa Cardosa y Luz) and the other on the prevention of family violence (Amelia Palacios, Shirley Almeida and Milka Rosas). Both programs insist on community involvement in the strategies they develop and also coordinate with state institutions to help make things happen and to ensure continuity of service. Also, we do not attempt to duplicate the services provided by the State.

### Nutrition

Our nutrition program is now in its third year. We began with a study of 500 children below the age of five years. We did this in coordination with parents, kindergarten teachers and staff at the local state medical center. We identify the children with problems and visit their homes on a weekly basis until the children are well. We recognize the structural factors of our society that ensure the poverty of millions, a situation that challenges the political culture of all citizens of Peru. Following the recent presidential elections we are hopeful that much more will be done at a political level to address some of the structural causes of large scale poverty in all parts of our country. We have also shown in our work that, even in the present situation, much can be done through family and community initiative to overcome some of the consequences of malnutrition in small children.

---

[8]    Located in Las Lomas de Carabayllo: *http://maps.google.com.au/maps?hl=en&q=map+loma s+de+carabayllo+lima+peru&bav=on.2,or.r_gc.r_pw.&biw=1293&bih=639&wrapid=tlif13077 1848974810&um=1&ie=UTF-8&hq=&hnear=0x9105d64220e89703:0x7755431d170e3f89, Lomas+de+Carabayllo&gl=au&ei=bDPyTcHXPOix0AGVmZzUCw&sa=X&oi=geocode_result& ct=title&resnum=1&ved=0CBwQ8gEwAA*

We run workshops to show mothers how to use the food available in the local market in more interesting and nutritious ways. What is commonly on sale is produce that is in season and inexpensive. In the supermarkets in other parts of the city customers have access to better quality and greater variety provided of course they can pay.

Some children are born underweight or have bouts of sickness when they are quite small. They then might not get the right kind of food so end up undernourished.

The lack of piped water and sewerage leads to a lot of sickness, especially in infants. The water is trucked in and sold by the barrel to residents who store it in a tank in front of their house so, even with the best will of family members, beating parasites and stomach infections is a constant battle. Boiling the water and washing hands before handling food are musts but both are either an expense and/or a hassle, so parents need to be educated to appreciate the dangers, in particular to their children, of unwashed hands and unboiled water.

Martha took seriously what she learned in our workshops, and her once undernourished child is now quite healthy. She and others have demonstrated that parents can find ways of caring adequately for their small children even in the midst of multiple adverse circumstances. Some mothers don't go beyond fried food and pasta and even when there is more variety, often there is little attempt to balance the children's diet. Parents at times seem to give in to the dictates of whatever is easy and what status demands.

### Family Violence

State institutions that deal with family violence are not present in this area. To reach the municipal center of our district, where State-run services are located, we have to follow a circuitous route over a range of hills and cross a river, all of which would take residents over one hour and a couple of buses to get there. However, we do have a small police station that is staffed by two policemen. When a resident reports an incident of family violence, the police register the complaint but do not act on it unless serious injury is involved.

We hope to provide an adequate and suitable service in response to family violence. The women of this barrio are often quite lonely. They have come from other parts of Lima and are cut off from friends and family. From San Benito to the center of Lima is a 90 minute bus trip. As yet, neighbors in general have not forged bonds of friendship. The barrio has been populated slowly over the past fifteen years with each family looking out for itself. There has been some local community organization but not to the same extent as in the squatter settlements where many of Lima's poor have found a block of land, built their housing bit by bit and joined in with neighbors to organize the installation of a variety of communal services.

However there are a few community spaces where parents might meet each other, such as, the parents' associations at the local schools, the glass of milk groups (milk for small children program run by the municipality of Lima for over 25 years), and the barrio organization charged with seeing to the installation of the water and sewerage systems.

We have looked for and found local residents who want to collaborate in our programs, and with them we run workshops that prepare them to be able to detect and notify us of others who are having difficulties. Some teachers also help us detect problem cases and often advise women who are affected by family violence. Also, children are more likely to talk to their companions about family violence than to adults, so in our program we orient them towards doing something positive with such information.

Most victims of family violence that come to our attention are women. Some men, due mainly to their own personal security issues, have fits of jealousy and beat their wives or partners. Because of work the men may be away from the home for lengthy periods of time and, with or without evidence, presume their wives or partners have been with another man. Others may be absent for long periods as they have their second family in San Benito, which they see as a suitable location for this, as the barrio is relatively isolated from the rest of the city. Then there are arguments over money, mainly because there is not enough; such a dispute can become heated and end with physical violence.

Then there is a rather common form of violence against children, namely that their fathers are slow or unwilling to sign their birth certificate, so the box for the father's name is left empty. The municipality has a system for rectifying this, based first on persuasion and, if that does not achieve the desired result, on DNA evidence. However, without easy access to the municipal office that deals with this matter we can do little about the problem.

Children may also be victims of physical violence. However we need the competent state institutions to make their presence felt in this department. We have signed an agreement for a working arrangement with the Ministry for Women that might help in this regard. Next year we also hope to have the Ministry of Justice involved. Without such government presence in the locality there is little chance of long term solutions. We believe that it is important that citizens have confidence in the institutions of the state, beginning with the police. Such institutions are necessary to help develop and maintain a basic support network for those needing help, which of course includes helping residents understand how to ask for the help they may need.

Link to our tradition:

A church-backed NGO seeks to respond to basic needs of the poor, empowering both them and the Peruvian professional staff dedicated to implementing the NGO programs. "Peripheral-urban culture is the result of the huge migrations of generally poor people who settled around cities in peripheries of extreme poverty. In these cultures, the problems of identity and belonging, relationship, living space and home are increasingly complex." (Aparecida[9], No. 58) The perennial challenge to respond is echoed in Proverbs 21, 13: "Those who shut their ears to the cry of the poor will themselves call out and not be answered."

## St. Bernadette's Children's Centers

### By Columban Fathers Tony Coney and Peter Woodruff

There is an unbreakable link between Christianity and human nature which can be seen in action whenever the good in every child is allowed to emerge and be valued in an environment of respect, freedom and tolerance. As people develop and mature, so also will they give witness to ever deepening human values, which are also Christian values. So it is for us as we try to promote justice, equality

---

[9]    Conclusions of the meeting of the Bishops' Conference of Latin America and the Caribbean, held in Aparecida, Brazil, 2007.

and the human rights of children, leaving no doubt in anyone's mind that the inspiration behind all that we do is Christian.

Christianity is by implication hope filled, other centered with the optimism that all will be well. If you expect to see the good which is inherent in another, good will eventually shine through irrespective of the brokenness that assails all of us. But this goodness has to be nurtured and valued so that the person might live in the way he sees him mirrored in another's eyes.

In the Children's Centers we provide an environment that celebrates all that is good in childhood through making sure that the children feel valued and cared for. Through listening to them, individually and in group meetings, we try to discern their needs and respond accordingly, therefore adapting our outreach to better facilitate their growth. We also believe that if the children are treated as valuable human beings they in turn will learn to appreciate their own value. We accept them in whatever condition they arrive without asking them to change, and when we receive very troubled children, who require special help, they usually responded to positive treatment.

In choosing our staff we do not discriminate on the basis of religious belief. Our project's purpose does not include inculcating religious belief of any kind in the children who come to us. We believe that is the responsibility of their parents, who are free to share whatever may be their beliefs with their children. We basically attempt to give witness to our faith in Jesus Christ, whom we profess as Lord, through what we do with the children.

The principal idea behind the Children's Centers is to provide a safe environment for children to play and enjoy their childhood which will give them the space and the opportunities to discover and develop their talents. The basis of our approach is "freedom with responsibility," the child being free to do what he or she wants, while valuing and respecting the freedom of others. To this end the children are free to participate in any activity, so that through trial and error, they may realize where their strengths and interests lie.

In many situations involving children, whether in school or in the home, the adults generally decide what is best for them and what they should be doing, with little reference to the desires of the children themselves. So, we organize meetings of the children in different age groups, where they can set their own norms and rules for acceptable behavior, etc., and also to express how they feel the project should be progressing. We, as the adults and staff, are there to guide, encourage and help, but ultimately we want the children to decide and make decisions through listening and dialoguing with us and each other.

The official education system is quite militaristic, especially around the time of Independence Day when the children parade in the streets, singing the national anthem and saluting the national flag. We decided to celebrate this day with a different mindset, highlighting the cultures and customs of Peru through dance, drama and song, and only with those who wanted to participate, therefore giving these celebrations a very different focus.

We don't want the children to feel that we are attempting to impose specific values, as we prefer them to experience a freedom that may not be available to them in other spaces of their lives. We want them to know and remember that we respect their individuality. We do what we can to help them grow into who they want to be. We don't want them to remember their time with us as one more experience of being shaped or formed by their elders. Rather we hope that they will have happy memories of freely playing, mutual respect and genuine fun with their friends as they go about being children and beginning to put their own shape on their lives.

I do not think that our approach is the only way of working with children, but I do maintain that it is a valid way. The children may or may not grow up as Catholics, but they will surely remember their time with us with gratitude. They will remember that we treated them with respect, offered them freedom in ways that they may not have experienced elsewhere but, at the same time, that we demanded a certain discipline based on mutual respect and responsibility. Whether or not, at a later date, they choose to delve into the nature of our Christian faith will be their free choice.

I believe that, given the circumstances of this traditionally Catholic society, this is a valid approach to Christian mission. In Peru, Catholicism is no longer imposed on people but some may still feel family or social pressure to conform. I quote some paragraphs from the Vatican II Constitution on the Church in the Modern World that I feel supports our integral approach to the educational and formative challenges we are at least partially addressing:

35 . . . . A person is more precious for what s/he is than for what s/he has . . . . the norm of human activity is this: that in accord with the divine plan and will, it harmonizes with the genuine good of the human race, and that it allow men and women as individuals and as members of society to pursue their total vocation and fulfill it.

In brief, we can say that, according to these key paragraphs from the Council conclusions, by making our world more human, that is, more just and respectful of the dignity of every person, we are doing God's work. Also, by acting in love among ourselves and in favor of others we please God and give witness to our Christian faith.

. . . Not everyone who cries, "Lord, Lord," will enter into the kingdom of heaven, but those who do the Father's will by taking a strong grip on the work at hand. Now, the Father wills that in all men and women we recognize Christ our brother and love Him effectively, in word and in deed.

Link to our tradition:

Columban Fr. Tony Coney, with a team of Sisters, lay men and lay women has developed a service for children to help them be themselves. Fr. Tony describes the project as an integral approach to Christian mission. "Amen, I say to you, whatever you did for one of these least brothers [or sisters] of mine, you did for me." (Matthew 25, 40)

## Cattle Have the Right of Way

### By Columban Fr. Tomás King

Since my appointment to the remote parish of Nagar Parkar, Pakistan, in November 2008 I have crossed the Thar Parkar several times a month. It is a four hour drive from the Columban parish of Badin, and it is located on the bottom right hand corner of the Pakistani map, right on the border with India. Though small it is the main town near the border between Pakistan and India in this area. It is the homeland of the Parkari Kohli tribal people, one of the ethnic groups among whom the Columbans work. There is a small but vibrant Catholic community of nearly one hundred families living in fifteen villages scattered over an area half the size of Ireland. For the past 35 years an important Christian presence has been a high school hostel. It was badly damaged in the 2001 earthquake the epicenter of which was just across the border in India. It is only now that a new hostel has been built. It was blessed and opened by Bishop Max Rodrigues on December 17, 2011.

Without such subsidized hostel facilities rural families would not be able to afford the cost of education. Experience has proven that with access to higher education youth will have the chance to grow in confidence and be better equipped to face the challenges of their lives. The hope and dream is that this will make possible the formation and education of young people who will be motivated to live among and serve their own community.

But I am far from the only one crossing the desert! Twice a year there is also the migration of thousands of cattle. It is an amazing sight watching the cattle and their drovers trek slowly across the desert. It highlights the reality of people being away from home for weeks and months on end. They are people on a journey seeking to make a living for their families. It brings to mind my own years as a farmer and also the words of a poem by Padraic Colum which I studied in high school which evokes the images of pilgrimage, journey, longing and the relationship between humans and animals.

During and after the monsoon rains which occur during July, August and September, cattle migrate from interior Sindh across the Thar to the Nagar Parkar area to take advantage of the new grass growth and sometimes even squash and watermelon which are in abundance after the monsoon rains. Then a few months

**The Drover, Padraic Colum**

O! farmer, strong farmer!
You can spend at the fair
But your face you must turn
To your crops and your care.
And soldiers—red soldiers!
You've seen many lands;
But you walk two by two,
And by captain's commands.
O! The smell of the beasts,
The wet wind in the morn;
And the proud and hard earth.
Never broken for corn
To Meath of the pastures,
From wet hills by the sea,
Through Leitrim and Longford
Go my cattle and me.
I hear in the darkness
The slipping and breathing.
I name them the by-ways
They're to pass without heeding.
Then the wet, winding roads,
Brown bogs with black water;
And my thoughts on white ships
And the King o' Spain's daughter . . .

later when the grasses have dried up, there is the return trip back to the interior of Sindh to forage along the sides of roads, in uncultivated fields and where the leftovers from crops are still there for the taking.

Salinization is ruining the land in some parts of interior Sindh, but the big landowners, who often have more land than they know what to do with, are not doing anything about it. It is an expensive and slow process to reclaim the land for crop production. In Pakistan, about 6.30 million hectares of land are salt-affected, of which 1.89 million hectares are saline and the area of productive land being damaged by salinity is about 40,000 hectares annually. The landlords do not want to face the expense of curing the land so it is just left fallow and is a source of fodder for migrating cattle.

I have been the pastor in Nagar Parkar for a few years now and have made the four hour road trip to and from Nagar Parkar many times. When I first made the journey in 1991, as a student, it took eighteen hours on the back of a truck to cross the sand track. Since a metaled road was laid in 2005 that journey takes four hours. My trips in and out seldom coincide with the cattle drive, but in August 2011, I spent four hours on the first half of the journey mostly in second gear, which should have only taken two hours, because of the sheer volume of cattle migrating. Thousands of cattle divided in numerous herds were seeking to escape the devastating floods that inundated Sindh in August and September 2011. Their food supply had been ruined, so they sought refuge across the desert, to the Nagar Parkar region, now freshly covered with grass.

Their drovers walk and sleep with their cattle, gazing up at myriad stars as they go to sleep. Like the good shepherd in the parable of Jesus, the drovers know their cattle, and their cattle know them. Drovers often have some goats of their own and can be seen carrying a young kid wrapped around their shoulders like a scarf. What milk the cows have is sold to villagers along the seven day trek across the desert. When the grass is plentiful, as it is when they feed well in interior Sindh, milk is sold to milk suppliers who come in their pickup wagons and take the milk back to nearby towns to process and sell.

The herders belong to a Sindhi Muslim ethnic people who pass on their way of life from generation to generation. Some herders own their own flocks but many work as employees of the herd owner. Wealthy cattle owners who employ herders believe that their savings are more safely invested in cattle than in the bank.

As well as flocks of cattle, there are other obstacles to the journey across the desert. Local security forces, as is their right, are extremely vigilant of ex-patriots coming and going in this border region with India. At this stage those manning the check posts come to know me and let me pass without much fuss.

Obstacles? Maybe not! But rather moments of opportunity to enter more deeply the freedom, the spontaneity and the mystery that is life's journey!

Link to our tradition:

The biannual cattle drive across the Thar desert in south east Pakistan is suggested as a metaphor for the life of a missionary in that land, so evocative of the Bible text: "So Jesus said again, 'Amen, amen, I say to you, I am the gate for the sheep. All who came [before me] are thieves and robbers, but the sheep did not listen to them. I am the gate. Whoever enters through me will be saved, and will come in and go out and find pasture. A thief comes only to steal and slaughter and destroy; I came so that they might have life and have it more abundantly. I am the good shepherd. A good shepherd lays down his life for the sheep.'" (John 10, 7-11)

# Challenging and Changing Times

Columban Fr. Peter Woodruff reports on a conversation with Bishop Max Rodrigues of Hyderabad, Pakistan

In a conversation with Bishop Max Rodrigues of Hyderabad, Pakistan, we touched on a number of topics, in particular, the impact of missionaries on the development of the local church and the challenges ahead for Pakistani society.

The diocese of Hyderabad extends over southeast Pakistan, roughly from the Indus River to the border with India; this is all the Sindh Province with the exception of Karachi. It is basically a rural diocese with hundreds of towns, villages and hamlets. The country people are predominantly of the Kholi people— Parkaris and Kutchis. The Bheels are another tribal group scattered throughout the south east. They usually do not own the land they work and are, for the most part, illiterate.

Most of these people, known as tribals, are Hindus and are open to a variety of religious faiths, provided of course they encounter a tolerant attitude on the part of the other religion. Some, especially among the Parkaris, have become Christians. The bishop related an experience of visiting a Parkari Kachi village where the whole village was present at Mass and just three Christians received communion, but the majority who are Hindus also like to come along. They join in the singing and listen to the Word.

Bishop Max explained to me that various groups of missionaries have worked among these rural people for over 60 years, and their approach to their mission has varied greatly. Some have focused on human development projects and have funded and supervised a great variety of projects that benefit the local people, especially in the field of water storage, sanitation, medical care and education.

In recent times missionaries have also done quite a lot to overcome inter-tribal barriers among the rural folk. In Badin there has been a good gelling of Parkari and Punjabis, so now we don't need to run separate services for them. Missionary accompaniment and dialogue with the various ethnic groups has been crucial to achieving this breakthrough.

However there is a pitfall for any priest, foreign or local, who is running a rural parish. If, in his commitment to helping the people escape the bondage under the landlord, the priest, in the eyes of the people, ends up replacing the landlord even though in a benign way, I think he is making a serious mistake. It is merely replacing one feudal relationship with another. On the other hand, projects that empower people are most welcome, especially education, which I believe does much to help lift up our people.

The bishop told me that the local priests, who are mostly Punjabis, are ready to work with the tribal peoples. They may not necessarily have the financial backing that most missionaries seem to have. It can be difficult for them to work alongside missionaries as they cannot offer people the material benefits that missionaries often bring with them. They will need to feel free to develop their particular way of working with the rural tribal peoples.

This can lead to a certain amount of misunderstanding, which, in the long run will be worked through. The model of priest for so many people has been the foreign missionary with a large vehicle and funding for this and that. In time, I would hope that our local priests will develop their ways of being with our poor rural people. For me, it's not a matter of saying that one way is right and another wrong. Rather it is all part of a process, which hopefully will help our people rise up. For this to be a process with direction we need to review our approaches constantly to ensure that we are on target.

Bishop Max expressed his appreciation of all the missionaries who have worked in the Province of Sindh, both in the past and in the present. He gave the example of the work done by Columban Fr. Robert McCulloch. Fr. Robert would see a need and address it in such a way that our local Christians would be committed in the task of responding and assuming responsibility. He helped train seminarians, helped put in place the academic link between the NCIT with the Yarra Theological Union, has collaborated significantly in the development of St. Elizabeth's Hospital, established an after school coaching center for Christian boys (who due to their families' lack of resources were not able to keep up with their Muslim fellow students) in years (academic classes) 8 through to 12. He also recognized the economic assistance given for these projects by the St. Vincent de Paul Society in Australia.

The bishop also commented that the way Pakistan is moving it might be difficult for missionaries in the near future. He assured me that the majority of Muslims in Pakistan are moderate, but in recent times, radical Muslim groups have become more influential and are prepared to use violence to achieve their goals. They even blow up the shrines in honor of Muslim saints as they see such devotional centers as a deviation from true Muslim religious practice.

If Pakistan is to survive as a country, it will have to change course. We are a diverse people, ethnically and religiously. We cannot afford to be building walls, physical, religious and ethnic, around each ethnic and religious group. I believe that respectful dialogue and mutual acceptance must be the cultural basis underpinning the long-term development of a viable and healthy Pakistani nation.

Link to our tradition:

The observations of an experienced bishop on pitfalls and possibilities for the missionary priest working among tribal peoples of the Sindh recall the words of Pope Paul VI in his Encyclical *Ecclesiam Suam*: "Speaking generally of the dialogue which the Church of today must take up with a great renewal of fervor, we would say that it must be readily conducted with all men and women of good will both inside and outside the Church." (No. 93)

## Fire in My Heart

### By Columban lay missionary Gloria Canama

"The fire which is in the sun, the fire which is in the earth, that fire is in my own heart." Upanishad

My childhood dream was always to be a religious Sister. The seed of this dream must have been sown by the Columban missionaries, Sisters and priests, who were my educators and friends from my early years.

I tried to follow my childhood dream and joined a religious community in Davao City, the Philippines, but it ultimately was not for me. After two years, I made the difficult decision to leave. I spent the long hours of the bus journey back home crying. I was fighting with God who I felt had abandoned me. Amazingly when the tears subsided, there was peace within me. There was this inner knowing that Jesus was very present and hurting with me as I left the community I had come to love. In my life's journey, I always go back to that faith experience of God's abiding presence and assuring love in my moment of desolation and confusion.

There were more years of searching for God's will for me, of how to respond to the persistent call within, of how to live a meaningful way of life. The Spirit who kept the fire burning in my whole being eventually led me to the Philippine Catholic Lay Missionaries (PCLM). Years with PCLM affirmed and strengthened my lay missionary vocation. By baptism we are called to follow and participate in the mission of Jesus. It was also my baptism of fire. I literally crossed rivers, seas and mountains, had the same simple meals for days and had nothing extra. My cup was overflowing. I received more than I had given. I had found my pearl of great price. I had found a meaningful way of life, and the fire within kept on burning.

In 1990 I joined the Columban lay missionary program and together with Pilar Tilos and Emma Pabera formed the first lay missionary team from the Philippines. Why did I choose the Columbans? Partly, it was because of a special affinity with them. Not only had they been significant in my life formation, the Columbans I knew inspired me deeply by their commitment and way of mission, especially their option for the poor, their passion for justice and the care of the earth. There's a deep resonance with my own passion and commitment in life.

Pilar, Emma and I arrived in Lahore, Pakistan, on a Mission Sunday. It was one of those synchronistic moments confirming my yes. When we experienced difficulties and doubted our decisions, the three of us found it helpful to remember why we came. Being on mission is a gift from God, our *magnificat in praxis.* All three of us had long connections with Columban missionaries as friends and mentors. Now as Columban lay missionaries we joined them as partners, sharing Columban life and mission and witnessing to a new way of being Church. It has been over twenty years now since I first set foot in the "land of the pure." My first years in mission had been purifying years. I came with excitement and confidence. "I am a woman of experience. I've brought with me my faith, my lived experiences of working to earn a living and my voluntary Christian community involvement. Moreover, I know the Columbans!"

Learning the language alone was like being back in first grade, struggling and getting excited when I was able to read the word Lahore in Urdu script. My first big difficulty was the many don'ts that apply to women, myself included, in Pakistani culture. What I considered as a simple piece of cloth to cover my head was a cultural symbol indicating whether or not I am a good woman. The late Archbishop Armando Trindade of Lahore, on our first courtesy call to him asked us, "What are you three women doing here in Pakistan? How can you travel on your own in a very male-dominated society? How do you hope to empower Pakistani women?" We didn't have the answers and honestly told the Archbishop with the assurance that we'd share with him our mission experiences. We did and in the process gained his trust and support.

While on mission in my own home country, I was working closely with community leaders, men and women alike. In Pakistan, I found myself in the midst of women sharing their deep aspirations to be treated with dignity and justice. My years in the Columban parish of Sheikhupura were very meaningful and fulfilling, a lived experience of Jesus' words "I have come that you may have life, life to the full." I left the parish over ten years ago now, yet I continue to be enriched with the continued friendship with some families there and the countless life-giving mission moments. It is a lasting gift of mission, a living well where I continue to draw water of joy, nurturance, strength and hope.

On the other hand, I continue to share the pain of my women friends still carrying the twin burdens of being women and of being poor. Joining the Columbans is a gift and a privilege but not without cost. Partnership in mission, especially 20 years ago, was more an ideal or a dream. It took a lot to change attitudes, to be seriously valued as laity on mission and to be integrated in Columban life as partners in mission. Earlier on, lay missionaries were often asked, "What do you do on mission?" There was no easy answer as many of us, if not all, joined with no blueprints except the faith and commitment of a disciple to actively participate in the mission of Jesus.

Sometimes, the light within seemed to be flickering, dimming as I struggled to find seeds of hope and meaning in chaotic, worsening situations, locally and globally. A quote from Clarissa Pinkola Estes resonates with my own experience, "Struggling souls catch light from other souls who are fully lit and willing to show it." I can partly identify with St. Paul who went through many trying moments in his missionary journey. I experienced sickness; the deaths of Pilar and Columban Fathers Pat McCaffrey and Tanvir Tommy O'Hanlon; armed robbery in the Columban house, deportation from Karachi airport and the "given" challenges just by being here as a woman, a lay missionary and part of the minority Christian community in an Islamic country which has been fighting against terrorism, violence, intolerance and the many forms of poverty and injustice.

When I almost gave up this Columban lay missionary journey of mine, I realized that the cost to continue is nothing compared to the gifts with which I have been lavishly blessed. I highly value this partnership, this sharing of Columban life and mission. It is indeed a pearl of great price to be part of peoples' lives—with Pakistanis, with Filipino migrants in Lahore and the whole community of life.

It's a privilege to be involved in ministries that I love, to be part of creative relevant responses to changing missionary challenges. There is this inner knowing that there is always enough cosmic grace not only to continue but to thrive and glow in my missionary journey. "Only in burning itself that a candle gives light."

Link to our tradition:

The life of the disciple who follows Jesus has always been a mix of joy and hardship; the Apostle Paul wrote of his experience on more than one occasion:

Blessed be the God and Father of our Lord Jesus Christ, the Father of compassion and God of all encouragement, who encourages us in our every affliction, so that we may be able to encourage those who are in any affliction with the encouragement with which we ourselves are encouraged by God. For as Christ's sufferings overflow to us, so through Christ does our encouragement also overflow. If we are afflicted, it is for your encouragement and salvation; if we are encouraged, it is for your encouragement, which enables you to endure the same sufferings that we suffer. Our hope for you is firm, for we know that as you share in the sufferings, you also share in the encouragement. (2 Corinthians 1, 3-7)

# Things We Do

By Columban Sister Perlita Ponge

Every couple of months or so Sr. Marie and I along with Fr. James Kajo or Master Lawrence our catechist visit the Vimo family in a small village in our parish (Kunri). They are Parkari Kholi people and very poor, but each time we visit they insist on killing a chicken and preparing a pot of chicken *karai* (stew) and inviting us to a meal. They continually remind me that poor people are often more generous than those who have plenty.

We visited them to give them tokens for food rations soon after the recent floods washed away most of their village. Their house, like the houses of their fellow villagers, had been constructed of dried mud so was washed away by the floods. The only building left standing was the parish school, which is built of brick and concrete.

We planned to do what we had gone to do and move on to the next needy family, but they insisted that we stay; the mother of the house said that she had already sent someone out to kill the chicken. They lost so much in the flood and don't even have a roof over their head, and yet they want to offer us hospitality.

I see the poor I meet in the course of my daily work as the soft and gentle side of Pakistan. Whatever their religious faith may be, they are so hospitable, and sharing food seems to break down barriers. Even with so little they are grateful to God for what they have; they see our visit as a blessing and a moment to celebrate.

Since the floods in the parish we have traveled the roads, especially the back roads far from the main highways, in the parish four wheel drive as along the sides of these roads refugees in the thousands from the floods have camped (the roads are raised between one and two meters above the level of the adjacent fields). Those on the back roads generally receive little or no aid. We have been able to give them food ration tokens, blankets and sometimes two kilogram food parcels with rice, sugar, lentils, flour, oil and tea, the basics of the local diet. We were able to give freely without discrimination and without demanding an identity card.

Most of those we meet are strangers to us and us to them. We don't introduce ourselves but rather just leave them something to alleviate their difficult situation and move on. One woman told us with a smile of gratitude that we were the first to give them a hand. We would return on another occasion and some remained, but some were no longer there. Hopefully the flood waters had subsided enough for them to return to their villages to make a new start.

Floods come and go and the meteorological experts tell us to expect more frequent flooding in the coming years. However, life goes on and some of our parishioners asked us to take on a new project. Some women told me that they would like to be able to read the Bible. Consequently, we organized a pilot project to teach women to read and write and presently have a group of 21 women aged from 15 to 45 years. They are Parkari Kholi and Punjabi women. We began in September but had to close for the floods. We called the group to class again in October and, much to my surprise, all 21 turned up.

One member of the class told her brother in another village about our class, and he requested adult literacy classes for his village. We want to respond, but first we will complete the course we have started and evaluate it. We don't want to fail by attempting to bite off more than we can chew. Also, we feel that it's a matter of hastening slowly.

Our teacher is Berna. She receives a salary, and we charge the participants 30 rupees a month (around 20 cents). The classes run from Monday to Friday from 1:30 to 3:00 p.m.

A key element to the success of this program is the teacher who has to be someone who treats those in the class with courtesy and respect. Also, we would need to find a person in or near the other village who might take on the task.

We feel the project is off to a good start as the initiative to begin came from the women of the village, and the invitation to extend also came from residents of another village.

Link to our tradition:

Missionaries are sent but they are also invited as in the case described above. In the spread of the early Church, Acts 10, 30-34 reports: "Cornelius replied, 'Four days ago at this hour, three o'clock in the afternoon, I was at prayer in my house when suddenly a man in dazzling robes stood before me and said, 'Cornelius, your prayer has been heard and your almsgiving remembered before God. Send therefore to Joppa and summon Simon, who is called Peter. He is a guest in the house of Simon, a tanner, by the sea.' So I sent for you immediately, and you were kind enough to come. Now therefore we are all here in the presence of God to listen to all that you have been commanded by the Lord.' Then Peter proceeded to speak and said, 'In truth, I see that God shows no partiality . . .'"

# CHAPTER 2

## Liturgy and prayer

"The liturgy is the summit toward which the activity of the Church is directed; at the same time it is the font from which all her power flows." (Constitution on the Sacred Liturgy, No. 10, Vatican II, December 4, 1963) In the liturgy we experience God in and among us, bonding us, moving us, giving us life and sending us out on mission. The mix of public and silent prayer, reading the word from the books of the Bible and listening to the same word, hearing the homily and applying it to our lives, sharing the song and music, recognizing each other as fellow pilgrims at the sign of peace, and identifying totally with Christ and God's mission at communion, all come together to give us new life, encouraging us to continue to find ways of identifying with God's mission.

Being engaged in God's mission presumes being engaged with God in prayer. This is exemplified in a variety of situations in the Acts of the Apostles, which describes moments in the life of the early Christian Church. In all that the apostles and the community do they call on God for guidance and support. Their prayer is constant and in service of God's mission. The following are but some of the passages from the Acts of the Apostles that refer to the prayer of the early Church.

"When they [the apostles] entered the city they went to the upper room where they were staying, Peter and John and James and Andrew, Philip and Thomas, Bartholomew and Matthew, James son of Alpheus, Simon the Zealot, and Judas son of James. All these devoted themselves with one accord to prayer, together with some women, and Mary the mother of Jesus, and his brothers." (Acts 1, 13-14)

When the first Christians were about to choose another apostle to replace Judas Iscariot they prayed: "You, Lord, who know the hearts of all, show which one of these two you have chosen to take the place in this apostolic ministry from which Judas turned away to go to his own place. Then they gave lots to them, and the lot fell upon Matthias, and he was counted with the eleven apostles." (Acts 1, 24-26)

Prayer was clearly an integral part of the life of the first community: "They devoted themselves to the teaching of the apostles and to the communal life, to the breaking of the bread and to the prayers." (Acts 2, 42)

Even as he was being stoned to death Stephen continued to pray and forgive: "As they were stoning Stephen, he called out, "Lord Jesus, receive my spirit." Then he fell to his knees and cried out in a loud voice, "Lord, do not hold this sin against them; and when he said this, he fell asleep." (Acts 7, 59-60)

The rest of this chapter is made up of mission stories illustrating the above paragraphs. After each story or, in some cases, groups of stories, there is a link to our religious tradition, which, for the most part, is taken from the Bible but, also from teachings of the Popes, General Councils and Episcopal Conferences.

## Sacramentals—A Form of Mission

### A Sacred Time
### By Columban Fr. Barry Cairns

I am a blessings priest! I use the ritual with its numerous liturgical blessings and find it a powerful form of mission.

As I write this, I have just come from blessing an expectant mother. After receiving the blessing she said, using a special Japanese simile, "My fears have evaporated like the morning dew. My tension and aloneness have gone. I feel confidant." And this first-time expectant mother really meant it. Her eyes just lit up. It is a beautiful blessing. It starts with a prayer expressing how this mother is sharing in God's own creation. The short Gospel reading is from Mark 10:13-16. Jesus blesses each child and mother. The prayers emphasize joy and trust.

In Japan on November 15, there is a traditional blessing of children aged 7, 5 and 3. In the country, parents take their children to their local Shinto shrine. But urbanized and Christian Japanese have no such shrine. We give the children and their parents a blessing at the Church. I would usually have about 250 children, plus their parents (95% non-Christians) from the local kindergartens. I urge the parents to seek God's help in raising their children in our present unsettled society. To the children, my message is this: "Say thank you from your heart—to God—and to your mom and Dad. They do so much for you. Thank you is the most beautiful word in the language."

I have noticed the great influence that blessings have on people's hearts. God enters into their daily lives. In talks, in the catechumenate, and in sermons we can tell people that our God is close and cares for each one of us, but often it is not until a blessing is received at a time of crisis for a particular purpose that realization comes. Yes, I can rely on my God. Yes, the Church is relevant in my daily life.

Blessings have been part of Church life for a long, long time. They are mentioned in the third century Apostolic Tradition by Hippolytus. One, called in Latin *Itinerarium* (Going on a Journey), became popular in the sixth century when monks, such as St. Columban, were setting out on dangerous missionary journeys. I recently blessed a young student who was going overseas to attend a meeting on behalf of her university. Kaori-san had never been on a plane before nor had she ever left the country. She had never traveled alone even within Japan. The blessing had an amazing effect. Fear was replaced by trust in God. She looked forward to the experience. The Scripture reading used is from Genesis 28:21. Jacob sets out on a journey and promises, "If God will be with me and watch over me on this journey of mine till I return home, the Lord shall be my God."

When I was pastor in the southern village of Sakitsu, the Catholic communities were all connected with fishing. Near my home town in Island Bay, New Zealand, our bishop used to bless the Italian fishing fleet every year. So in Sakitsu I held the annual blessing of boats. What a festival they made of it! All the boats were festooned with a mass of colorful flags. I remember as I went across from boat to boat each man lifted the hatch cover to allow the holy water to fall directly onto the small but vital diesel engine. The Gospel was the storm on the Sea of Galilee where Jesus calls from the fog, "Fear not, it is I," and then creates a calm sea. The final prayer is beautiful: May Jesus lead you always to a safe harbor and to the final harbor which is Heaven.

I bless the ground before work starts at a building site. Here there is much scattering of blessed salt. There is another blessing when the roof beam is raised, and finally another when the family moves into their new home. During this blessing, a medal is put over the front entrance. I emphasize the blessing of the family altar which is very much a part of Japanese households following the Buddhist tradition. I pray with the family before the altar and urge them to keep praying before it as a family.

I also bless cars and motor bikes. Here the blessing emphasizes safe driving and road courtesy as a practical way to love one's neighbor. Driving with thoughtfulness for others is part of living a Christian life.

And there is a blessing for the saddest of occasions when a mother loses a baby through a miscarriage, a stillbirth or SIDS (sudden infant death syndrome). This blessing embraces the distraught mother with gentleness, using words like, "Comfort this woman in the emptiness which gnaws within her. God's love seems to be contradicted. Give her hope O Lord." The document from Rome, The Hope of Salvation for Infants Who Die Without Baptism (January 19, 2007), is a great help here. Prior to the release of the document from Rome, I just gave the sorrowing mother my own opinion on the limitless expanse of Abba's tender loving kindness. I never was a "limbo man!" Now Heaven for unbaptized babies is official!

I have found it is important to give time and care to these blessings. A perfunctory set of words is disastrous. This time is sacred for the person receiving the blessing. God is showing His personal love for this person in this particular circumstance.

I have found that blessings touch people. They feel that the gentle Jesus comes directly into their ordinary everyday lives. He really does walk the road of life with them. Through blessings Jesus says in a living voice that reaches the ears of the heart, "Fear not! I am with you." That surely is the Good News. That is mission!

Link to our tradition:

And people were bringing children to him that he might touch them, but the disciples rebuked them. When Jesus saw this he became indignant and said to them, "Let the children come to me; do not prevent them, for the kingdom of God belongs to such as these. Amen, I say to you, whoever does not accept the kingdom of God like a child will not enter it." Then he embraced them and blessed them, placing his hands on them.

## An Unfinished Spiritual Journey

By Ariel Presbitero, former Columban lay missionary from the Philippines

My grandfather was a motor mechanic who repaired the motors of small boats; in fact, he could repair any kind of motor. My father was also a motor mechanic, so I grew up in our family repair shop in the town of Binangonan, Rizal, 35 kilometers south of Manila, the Philippines. We lived near a huge lake, Laguna de Bay, where many fishermen plied their trade. For them, paying my grandfather and my father to repair their boat engines was more economical than buying a new engine, so we always had work.

Columbans ran our parish, probably since before World War II. I was baptized by Columban Fr. Kieran White who was from Ireland. I remember seeing the photo of Columban Fr. Martin Strong (d. 1981) on the wall of the lobby of our local high school. Fr. Martin was the New Zealand Columban who oversaw the building of our town's first high school. When I was growing up I knew many Columbans but in fact did not realize they were Columbans. For me, they were simply the priests who came to work with us in our parish, named after Santa Ursula.

I was raised in our motor repair workshop, but after completing high school I went to a university in Manila to study social work. Afterwards I worked with fishing communities living on the shores of Laguna de Bay. I belonged to a non-government organization (NGO) that was founded from within our university. We focused on supporting community organization, advocacy, networking and, in the case of the fisherman working on our lake, organizing to help them defend their way of life.

The central government was considering tapping the lake to supply drinking water to Manila. If that had gone ahead it would have seriously disrupted the fishing industry and the lives of thousands of families. Our organization (OTRADEV—ORGANIZATION FOR TRAINING, RESEARCH AND DEVELOPMENT), which was founded by seven students from our social work faculty, promoted a dialogue between the Government, the People's Organization (PO) made up of fishermen and their families, and NGOs with a view to coming to an agreement on the use of the lake's water. Eventually, the Government decided to look for another solution to the problem of Manila's water supply. In fact, relying on the lake's water would have required an expensive filtration plant as its water quality was rated 'D' and for drinking it had to be 'A.'

I worked on that project for just over three years and then participated in a community development project with an indigenous group (pre-dating the Malay people who form the majority of the population of modern day Philippines) living on the island of Mindoro, south of Manila. I liked the work and the people with whom I worked. Our NGO was made up of professors, students and graduates sharing a similar vision of development. For us social work was not simply about solving the immediate problem of the poor, but rather fostering attitudes and systems that would allow the poor to take hold of the reins of their own lives. We were not a static organization but rather our research and our service arms worked in tandem mutually enriching and supporting each other.

However, I felt that the spiritual dimension was missing in our way of life. There was no faith discussion, no reflection on a sacred text, no shared prayer. Maybe we did not know how to address the need as our group included people professing a variety of religions and also atheists. When I told my companions that I was leaving the job to join the Columban lay missionaries they were surprised but most supportive. They organized a party for my send-off and gave me a beautiful painting of a fish. That was nearly 20 years ago, and I am still in touch with some of them.

My way into the Columban lay missionary program was gradual. Our local school principal gave my mother a copy of a mission magazine published by the Columbans, and it lay there on a table in our house for some weeks before I opened it. I read an article about lay missionaries and wanted to know more. I contacted Columban Fr. Mickey Martin who listened patiently and gave me some books to read. Later, another Columban, Fr. Peter Leonard, gave me a booklet outlining an Ignatian discernment process. I joined the Columban lay missionary program and following the preparation program, was appointed to Brazil along with three others.

Around the end of the first three year term in Brazil I was profoundly moved by the death of two lay missionaries whom I had never met. Pilar Tilos, from the

Philippines, died in Pakistan and Elizabeth Kim, from Korea, died in Fiji. Their dying on mission has had so much to do with my maintaining my missionary commitment. Their life commitments became a powerful spiritual force in my life. No other person, group or event has touched me as have Pilar and Elizabeth in death. The following are excerpts from what I wrote about Elizabeth soon after her death of hepatitis in 1996:

. . . there was a deep sense of connection when I heard the news [of her death] . . . . I was confronted by my own vulnerability that it could possibly happen to me too while in the mission. What if I got malaria? What if I got bitten by an unvaccinated dog? What if I met an accident? What if somebody shot me? A lot of "ifs" but one thing that stood out when I was reflecting on Yean Sin was her faith in God. Yean Sin was born in a non-Catholic faith tradition. She was baptized only for a few years when she joined the Columban Lay Mission Program. She was the only Catholic in her family at the time. She let go of everything to follow Christ in a place unknown to her.

At that time I was finishing my first term in Brazil and felt I was at a crossroad. I had promised my family that I would serve for only three years. When I heard of the death of Yean Sin in Fiji, a different awareness came into me and asked my heart whether it might be worth continuing no matter what. Yean Sin probably didn't think that she would stay in Fiji forever. She did not know until it happened to her. At that time, death didn't mean so much for me. All I remember was I had gone on a mission to be available to the call of God and to the people whom I was called to serve. I did not imagine that death might be part of missionary experience, even though during my CPE course (part of the preparation for overseas mission) I was asked to write my own obituary.

Because of Yean Sin I decided to renew for a second term as a Columban lay missionary in Brazil. Yet I never thought that I would continue for twelve years— six in Brazil and six in Peru. Yean Sin demonstrated love of God by offering her life and inspired other people like me to continue God's mission on earth. I am very thankful to her family for allowing her to follow her heart and so offer new hope for the world. Her death means new life for us who are in the crossroad discerning the will of God. Thank you Yean Sin and may your legacy live on.

After completing six years in our Brazil mission and a further six years in Lima, Peru, I came to Los Angeles, California. I was not sure where I was heading in life. I worked as a caregiver and then in a machine workshop where we ground metal parts for machines; I liked the work. It reminded me of my time in my grandfather's workshop in Binangonan. Then, one day I received the news that my grandfather had died. I told the workshop boss that I needed to go away for a few days as my grandfather had died. I never returned; I could no longer return to work in a machine workshop after my grandfather's death. As he had left this world so did I feel that I must leave the world in which I had known him.

After that I accepted the offer to work with the Columbans in U.S. First, I formed an affiliate support group among Filipinos in California, which continues to run fundraising activities twice a year. I moved on to coordinating with the Columban Center for Advocacy and Outreach (CCAO) office in Washington, as West Coast Associate promoting the programs of our CCAO Office and helping with exposure trips to South America.

For me, the clear recognition of God present in my life is so important. I thank the Columban lay missionary program for offering me this opportunity to consciously walk with God.

Link to our tradition:

Jesus quoted the prophet Isaiah when He spoke of His mission in the synagogue of Nazareth: "The Spirit of the Lord is upon me, because he has anointed me to bring glad tidings to the poor. He has sent me to proclaim liberty to captives and recovery of sight to the blind, to let the oppressed go free, and to proclaim a year acceptable to the Lord." In the preceding article Ariel sheds some light on his statement: "I do not pretend to be Jesus or any kind of Messiah but I do feel the Spirit of God within, guiding me along my way."

## No, Is an Answer

### By Columban lay missionary Angelica Escarsa

"God answers our prayers all the time. Believe me—all the time!"

This is what I share with the children when I visit parish schools to do mission promotion. But I am sure you would want to know why I say this. Let me explain by giving you an example.

When I was eight years old, I suffered from a urinary tract infection. It was not a very serious illness, but at that tender age, taking big tablets the size of kidney beans three times a day was like life coming to an end. It was an awful experience, and I felt scared. However, even at that young age, I knew about God. I knew that I could pray to God, who could make me well. That was what my godmother assured me. So I did. I prayed to God; actually I bargained with God. I said, "God, if you make me better I will go to Mass every Sunday." Then I got well. No doubt the big tablets did the job, but I did not see it that way!

I never prayed as hard as I did in 1995. It was the year I took my board exam to become a teacher. Then, it was the most important thing in my life as it was where my future lay. If I passed the board exam I could get a teaching job and help my family. I do trust in God's mercy, but without prayer I know I won't get it. I did my best during the exam, but on my own I couldn't be sure. I need God's help, so I prayed every day until the results came out. It was the most exciting and life-giving experience of my life when I saw my name on the list of those who had passed. God answered my prayer once again.

In January 27, 2002, I was standing in front of Our Lady in the Columban Church in Olongapo City, the Philippines. That night I surrendered my sister to God as she struggled for her life with the help of a life-support machine. She had been in a coma for almost a week. Entrusting her to God was the only way I could comfort myself. At four o'clock the following morning my sister passed away due to complications from her rare illness of systemic lupus E.

During my first year on mission there were moments when I was homesick, lonely and upset. I took refuge in a chapel in the Ilac Center in Dublin, Ireland. There I knelt in front of the Blessed Sacrament and started to cry. Then a woman came to me and asked me, "Are you okay?" I told her that I was upset and missed my family and that I wished I was at home. She was so sympathetic and was trying to console me. Pointing to the Blessed Sacrament, she told me, "Pour out everything to Jesus. Tell Him everything. He will listen to you, and you will be okay."

I thanked her for her kindness, and my heart was lifted. I was longing for my mother and there she was, a woman who talked to me the way my mother would speak to me. After few minutes, she came back and handed me 20 pounds. She said she returned the trousers she bought and had her money back. She was giving it to me so I could go to the cinema and treat myself. It was such an overwhelming experience. You see, I was only asking God for comfort when feeling sad and alone. But I got more than comfort. God sent me to the cinema.

Maybe for that woman what she did was just a simple act of kindness, but the impact for me was tremendous. It was like experiencing God face to face. It was an affirmation that God is so close to me and walks with me always. In that simple act I was assured that every person I meet reveals something of God, allowing me to know that God loves me no matter what, especially in the lowest times of my life.

Not long after my sister died, I was lying on my bed in tears, praying so hard after getting the text message from home that my father was in hospital after suffering cardiac arrest and had a 50/50 chance of survival. He was in coma.

I asked God to help my father, but he died twelve hours after having a cardiac arrest. Did God answer my prayer? Yes, I know God heard me and helped my father die.

God answers our prayer according to what is best for us. God knows exactly what is planned for us. Remember the words spoken to the prophet Jeremiah (Jeremiah 1, 5): "even before you were born, I knew you." When we pray to God and don't get a "yes," it doesn't mean God did not answer our prayer. No, is also an answer.

Link to our tradition:

LORD, you have probed me, you know me: you know when I sit and stand; you understand my thoughts from afar. You sift through my travels and my rest; with all my ways you are familiar. (Psalm 139, 1-3)

In the same way, the Spirit too comes to the aid of our weakness; for we do not know how to pray as we ought, but the Spirit itself intercedes with inexpressible groaning. And the one who searches hearts knows what is the intention of the Spirit, because it intercedes for the holy ones according to God's will. (Romans 8, 26-27)

## A Pilgrimage Towards Dialogue

### By Columban Fr. Frank Hoare

Pilgrimage is common to all religions. People undertake a pilgrimage to experience a more intense connection with the divine. They believe that journeying to a holy place which has associations with a divine or saintly person will change them for the better. They expect to have particular petitions granted. Pilgrims leave aside for a while the ordinary routine of daily life. Inspired by the pilgrimage experience they return to ordinary life with renewed faith.

In Fiji, Catholics like to carry the cross on pilgrimage during Lent and especially in Holy Week. But this kind of pilgrimage remains within the boundaries of our own religious tradition. In pluralist Fiji where Catholics are only 10% of the population we need a way to dialogue with Hindus, Muslims, and Sikhs, all who are fellow travelers, whose journey may be along a different path but who are aspiring to reach the same destination.

For this reason on the day before Diwali, the Hindu festival of Lights, a group of thirty young Fijian Catholics came together to make a pilgrimage of dialogue.

A bus dropped us at a Sikh temple about twelve miles from Ba town. Bearded turbaned men greeted us hesitantly at the gate. This was a new experience for them too. Before entering the temple we left our shoes outside and covered our heads with the scarves they supplied. We all sat on the floor of the temple in front of a baldachin with a large lectern on which was placed the Guru Granth Sahib, the Sikh scriptures. A Sikh priest, swishing a fly whisk in front of the holy book, chanted some verses. The president of the community, a high school teacher, explained the prayer in English and went on to explain the main teachings, rituals and symbols of the Sikh religion.

Sikhism which was founded in sixteenth century India puts emphasis on the equality of people, on prayer, hard work and on hospitality to strangers. Our group experienced this when our Sikh hosts served us a tasty lunch before we departed.

We walked for two hours towards Ba, arriving at a Muslim mosque in Varavu around 4 p.m. The president and some committee members of the mosque invited us to sit together in the porch of the mosque. We asked to hear about the main beliefs of Islam and how worship was conducted at the mosque. Our Muslim hosts were very happy with this. They seemed to have feared a debate about whether Islam or Christianity is the true religion. Afterwards they presented me with a copy of the Holy Koran, invited us to return again and to visit their high school at Ba. Again we were offered refreshments before we continued our journey.

About an hour later we arrived at a Hindu temple at the edge of Ba town. The temple priest was speaking with a Muslim couple when we arrived. We heard later that the wife's arm was shaking uncontrollably, and they had come to the temple for a healing. Due to some misunderstanding we were not expected that evening so we agreed to return the next day. Our group slept in the parish hall that night.

The next day the temple priest and an Indian lady devotee explained to us the layout of the temple and the identity of the different statues. It was remarkable that the images of the high gods, Shiva and Vishnu were outside the main temple at the back porch whereas five female goddesses were enthroned inside with various pictures and items of worship on the ground in front of them. The central goddess was believed to have power to cure female infertility. Some grateful devotees had placed small dolls in the temple in thanksgiving for the children they had conceived.

As we were leaving, a young female bank official arrived in a taxi. She consulted the temple priest about her facial skin problems, and he told her what materials to bring for the rituals. We were surprised when we heard that she too was Muslim. The temple catered for the everyday problems of life which are believed to be the special preserve of the female Hindu deities (whereas salvation is the preserve of the male deities). This explained why the female deities held center stage. It also seemed that the mosque did not cater for some of the needs of Muslim women and so they came to the temple. This, of course, did not mean that they were changing their religion.

That evening we went to the Sai Baba temple in Ba town. His devotees believe that Sai Baba, who lives in South India, is an avatar (incarnation) of God. Here we participated in celebrating Diwali, the feast of lights, which commemorates the return to his kingdom of Lord Rama, believed to be an incarnation of Vishnu, from fourteen years of exile. We joined in lighting candles around the periphery of the temple symbolizing joyfully the victory of good over evil and then sat inside for an hour as the devotees chanted hymns in Hindi and English. We respectfully refused the offer of prasad, fruits and sweets which have been offered to the god and bear his blessing. Our group sang a hymn when requested and I, on behalf of the group, explained our mission pilgrimage. Here too we were given a very warm welcome and invited to return again.

Some weeks later I heard a Fijian elder ask one of the youths who had participated in the mission pilgrimage what he had learned. The youth replied that he was impressed by the sincerity with which the people we met practiced their faith and prayed. It made him realize that he was a lukewarm Christian, and it motivated him to deepen his commitment in the future.

Different as it seemed to a traditional Catholic pilgrimage our Fiji pilgrimage of dialogue also brought us to a deeper sense of God in the world and in our lives. It helped us to develop friendly and respectful links with fellow believers in God in a multi-cultural and multi-religious country where reconciliation, respect and cooperation are so important to peace and progress.

Link with our tradition:

We never know who we will meet along the way, just as the two disciples did not even dream of meeting Jesus as they walked along the road to Emmaus (Luke 24, 28-32): As they approached the village to which they were going, he gave the impression that he was going on farther. But they urged him, "Stay with us, for it is nearly evening and the day is almost over." So he went in to stay with them. And it happened that, while he was with them at table, he took bread, said the blessing, broke it, and gave it to them. With that their eyes were opened and they recognized him, but he vanished from their sight. Then they said to each other, "Were not our hearts burning [within us] while he spoke to us on the way and opened the scriptures to us?"

## Trusting in God

My first year on mission in Rancho Anapra, Ciudad Juárez, Mexico, next to the
U.S. border
By Columban lay missionary Sainiana Tamatawale

While working as a lay missionary in Manila, the Philippines, I read stories about the "Border Mission" in the Society's magazine and the lay missionary newsletter. I wanted to come here to work as a missionary so requested an appointment to this mission. I knew it would be tough but was happy to do God's will; I was confident that God would show me the way and walk with me.

I felt afraid when I heard of all the violence and killing in Ciudad Juárez. Last year there were nearly 200 murders a month in the city, most of them related to drug cartel wars. Still, there was something in me that urged me to come and trust in God.

A short piece of advice from St. Columban has helped a lot: "A life unlike your own can be your own teacher." I have found this to be true as the faith of the people of Rancho Anapra, in the midst of violence and hardship, has moved and strengthened me.

Many of my neighbors asked me, "Are you not afraid to be here?" I said, "No, God sent me here and is with me every day." I also feel that God is with me in the faith and courage of those who live here. One woman whose husband wanted to leave because of all the violence insisted on staying; she said to me, "What keeps me here is the faith of my neighbors; we have got to know each other in our troubles and many of us meet in the chapel."

I can see that many have come to know and support each other. It is true that there is much suffering, but there is also much care for others and solidarity with those who are suffering. All this has strengthened my faith in God accompanying us in this mission.

Everything here is different from Fiji—the food, the way people relate to each other, religious practice, family customs and so on. My Mexican friends realize that I have come from a different way of life, and they welcome me into their lives, especially when they see that I make an effort to adapt to their ways.

Learning a new language and adapting to the customs of another people are demanding and tiring, but I understand this as simply part of my way in life, what God has called me to. While this first year in Rancho Anapra has challenged me, it has also been a very happy time for me.

The Columban border team is also quite diverse. We have priests, lay men and women and religious Sisters from a variety of countries—the U.S., Fiji, Australia, Ireland, the Philippines and Mexico. We also come from a wide variety of life and mission experience. Some have been on mission in other countries for many years, but I feel that each one contributes to the team's work according to their abilities.

Having been on this mission for only one year the challenges that I have had to face are not what others with longer experience here might mention. I still feel that I have a way to go before I can say that I am fluent in Spanish; it's a slow business learning a new language. Then there is the violence, which, even though it is less this year than last, continues to strike fear into the residents of our suburb.

In March two men were killed in our barrio. I had been with the confirmation group in our chapel a few blocks away and I returned to see two men lying dead on the sandy road a few meters from the front of my house. Both had been shot by police; for a while I was afraid to go out.

Also, crossing the bridge from Juárez to El Paso is at times a major problem. One time I had to wait in line for five hours to be processed by U.S. immigration officials. Passing from the U.S. to Mexico is no problem.

Now, whenever I go out I pray that God will guide and protect me, and that when I need to cross to El Paso that the line through immigration will be short.

Link to our tradition:

The invisible inner life of the Trinity is reflected in the visible work of salvation-history—incarnation, cross/resurrection and sending of the Spirit—that we call God's mission. God's mission is at the heart of our Christian faith; it's what we strive to live; it is a way of being into which we are drawn by our faith: "Father, they are your gift to me. I wish that where I am they also may be with me, that they may see my glory that you gave me, because you loved me before the foundation of the world." (John 17, 24)

## Jesus Loves Me and You Too

### By Columban Sister Mihua Kim (from Korea)

I used to see him every day in the street as I passed him on my way to our center (Community of Hope). At first I did not realize who he was, but after he came to an activity in our center I realized that he was one of our oldest members with a disability. We introduced ourselves, but he knew me from my work as a staff member in the center. After that he would greet me every morning.

He is mentally retarded and much older than me, probably in his forties. What most struck me was that he had his rosary with him every day. Whenever I saw him he had his rosary in his hand. That's how I remember him even before I got to know him. He is big and walks slowly; he is always praying.

I recall one morning seeing him coming towards me and then entering the chapel behind our center. He made the sign of the cross a few times and then stood in front of the statue of our mother, Mary. As a Korean I was so moved by this man freely expressing his faith in God in public, as we don't do that in Korea. However, here I see people everywhere saying in some way or other that God loves us.

My praying friend inspired me because I was having a bad morning, and he was praying in front of the Virgin Mary. So often I had passed by that chapel but I never entered to pray to Mary or make the sign of the cross, so seeing him praying made me say to myself, "I am saying to the people that I am a Sister and a missionary but this man puts me to shame." He made me ask myself, "What am I doing here?" He was really a great teacher for me.

This is my first mission and this being a Catholic country, I wonder what am I here for. As a missionary, what should I do? Every morning when I saw him, this question came to me. It was not just shame that he prompted in me, but he left me with this question that continued to come back to me.

I like to see him. One time I saw him near the center of the city; I was on my way to the center. I asked him where he had been and he replied, "In Cota," which is a shrine in honor of the Virgin Mary. He had been there to pray, part of his daily routine. It is quite a long walk and his fidelity to his religious practice amazed me. Comparing myself with him I feel that he is a much more religious person.

By being who he is this Filipino man has helped me work out why I am here on mission. There are many ways of life, many ways of responding to God's call. This is my way of responding to God's call. As a Sister I came to know myself better than before. Some might say that I'm selfish being here because I feel that this is in part a response to my needs too. However, since I realized how much Jesus loves me I feel happy to be with other people, here or anywhere else. I can sense Jesus's compassionate love in others. I just enjoy seeing how Jesus loves me and others. I don't get tired of this.

Before I joined the Sisters, I never experienced being loved by other people. Of course I would always say that my mother and father love me, but it seemed like something coming out of my head, not my heart. During my novitiate I realized that Jesus loves me really. Though I may be very weak, though I am not perfect, Jesus still loves me. Even with my faults and mistakes He accepts me as I am. He understands me because He knows me. He has known me totally since I was born. In the Gospels it is easy to see His love.

So, since then I want to help people come to understand that Jesus loves them. That's why I am here—so that others may know that Jesus loves them. I am not here to give to them but to simply be with them, to give myself to them, to empathize with them, to help them feel that I am truly with them.

Link to our tradition:

"As the Father loves me, so I also love you. Remain in my love. If you keep my commandments, you will remain in my love, just as I have kept my Father's commandments and remain in his love. I have told you this so that my joy may be in you and your joy may be complete. This is my commandment: love one another as I love you." (John 15, 9-12)

## As We Forgive: Redemption and Reconciliation

### By Columban Fr. Frank Hoare

New Year celebrations were in full swing in Namoto village in western Fiji. It was after midnight, but loud music was blaring from the radios and groups of people were noisily drinking alcohol. Samu, a powerfully built man in his thirties, staggered to his feet and followed Manoa, an unmarried youth from a neighboring village, out of the communal shed. Samu was obsessed by rumors that Manoa was carrying on a liaison with his wife. His suspicions and resentment, fueled by the alcohol, gnawed at him. His anger quickly boiled over.

Outside on a path between two houses, Samu challenged Manoa and cursed him roundly. He struck Manoa with a savage blow from his fist. Manoa fell to the ground, hit his head against a rock and lay motionless. A young man died as suddenly as an unexpected flash of lightning.

The following Sunday I faced a full church in Namoto. It was a difficult homily to preach. People were stunned. A Catholic family in a nearby village was mourning a son. A Catholic family in Namoto was weighed down with guilt and shame. I could not ignore or avoid the situation. It was important to put words on the shock and acknowledge the rupture of an ordered existence. But it was not my place to point the finger of blame. The tragedy was wider than lust and revenge.

It was a teachable moment in which to examine the contributing factors of alcohol abuse, rumor mongering and the failure of leadership. Manoa's tragic death pointed to a breakdown in the communal ethos as well as the religious values of the village. We all shared some responsibility. It was a moment for communal conversion. Forgiveness and reconciliation might come later, but it would take time.

In the wake of the tragedy, Samu received a three-year sentence for manslaughter. During that time, I visited him in prison. Samu was glad to see me. He requested a rosary and asked how he could learn more about the Bible after he completed his sentence. Wary of a sudden but shallow conversion, I recommended that Samu attend the weekly village liturgy preparation meeting.

During those meetings, the Bible was brought in procession to the family responsible for reading in church on the following Sunday. The family, together with the catechist and liturgy committee, read, reflect and share on the Scripture readings.

This, I suggested, would bring him in regular contact with God's word with the support of a faith community. The catechist and his wife could be Samu's mentors and the midwives of a new life for him.

Meanwhile, Samu's clan felt alienated and defensive. Manoa's family was in shock and rejected early overtures of reconciliation. The village catechist and liturgy leaders discussed the situation during Lent. As Holy Week approached, the liturgy leader approached me to request a different Good Friday Stations of the Cross. Instead of holding them in the church, he suggested incorporating them into a procession that would embrace both villages, both of the extended families, the living and the dead.

But would the two key families agree to participate? The liturgy leader approached them and persuaded them to take part in faith. Good Friday morning was hot and humid. A large crowd of villagers gathered outside the house of the deceased Manoa.

His family gathered around the seven-foot cross as we began with a prayer linking their sorrow with the sorrow of Mary and sufferings of Jesus. I was asked to carry the cross from the first station to the second followed by the people singing a hymn. At the third station commemorating the first fall of Jesus, Manoa's father took the cross and led the procession from his village to the outskirts of Namoto a few hundred yards away.

The fourth station commemorates Mary's sorrowful meeting with her son Jesus. After the Biblical reflection, Samu's widowed mother offered, as a profound sign of apology, a whale's tooth, the most sacred symbol in Fijian culture, to Manoa's father. Tears were shed as Manoa's father accepted this traditional and much revered symbol from Samu's uncle. With that acceptance, Manoa's family accepted Samu's clan's apology and reconciled with them.

Another emotional station was the twelfth where Jesus dies on the cross for the salvation of the world. At the spot where the fatal accident happened, we meditated on how Jesus' acceptance in love and forgiveness of His death overcame the evil let loose in the world by Adam's original sin and the sin of Cain's killing of his brother Abel.

Afterwards I requested that the large wooden cross we had carried that day be planted and erected on that spot as a reminder to the community of a needless tragedy but also of a memorable process of reconciliation of not only two families but also two communities.

Link to our tradition:

Put on then, as God's chosen ones, holy and beloved, heartfelt compassion, kindness, humility, gentleness, and patience, bearing with one another and forgiving one another, if one has a grievance against another; as the Lord has forgiven you, so must you also do. And over all these put on love, that is, the bond of perfection. And let the peace of Christ control your hearts, the peace into which you were also called in one body. And be thankful. (Colossians 3, 12-15)

## Renewed in Spirit

### By Columban Fr. Dominic Nolan

For many years, in fact for most of time since I was ordained in 1969, I was at sea as regards the Bible. We had good Bible teachers in the seminary. Columban Fr. Chris Baker offered us a solid basis for further study, but in general our program of studies in the seminary did not attempt to challenge us. Then Leo McMorrow arrived, fresh from post-graduate studies in Rome. Leo did push us but was too much for some of us. I did not understand what he was trying to teach us about the Bible, but my classmates thought he was fantastic. I just could not get on his wavelength.

Then in 2003, thanks to a pastoral biblical course in Nemi at an SVD institute just south of Rome, a new world began to open up for me. I could not believe my luck; I was sitting there and hearing this stuff, and it was so clear. The lecturers crammed a semester of classes into a week, which meant five hour lectures a day. That was not easy for me as I'd been so long away from the books. They had experts on a variety of subjects. However, that experience gave me a confidence in myself and in my knowledge.

I had always been concerned about the enormous chasm between academic scripture studies and what was available to the average person. So much seemed inaccessible to most Catholics. I wanted to do something to change that, but I returned to our mission in the Philippines without knowing how. Still I was full of hope and enthusiasm.

On arriving in the Philippines after the course, a Philippine priest with whom I'd made friends with in Nemi, connected me with the Episcopal Commission on Biblical Apostolate (ECBA), which runs the biblical outreach for the whole country. I met great men and women on that team, many of whom are much more highly qualified than I am, but all of us share the same passion—to make the message of the Bible more accessible to the members of our church communities all over the country. Being in touch with this group of people helped me feel part of something bigger than myself; it gave me zest and affirmation to get on with doing something about the chasm between the scholars and the average church member, that had troubled me for so long.

Fr. Mick Mohally, the Director of the Spiritual Year, gave me an opening. He said, "Dom, will you come over and give these new lads in the Spiritual Year a course on introduction to the Bible?" In the Philippines, the Spiritual Year is the first year of the Columban initial formation program. Our first year students are relatively mature young men. They have made the decision to leave their jobs and join us. It's a huge step for them. Just having a job is no little achievement for most young men in this country. However, despite all this, as far as knowledge of the Bible is concerned, they generally arrive with vague memories of Bible stories from primary school. They're scraping to know what a chapter and verse is.

I had no skill in teaching. I did not know how much I needed to fill an hour; I didn't know how to present material and work the dynamic of the class. For me it was a whole new venture. At the beginning, for one hour of class I would put in twenty four hours of preparation. I had to learn to leave time for questions and reflection, for note taking and review. I've taught our students the introduction to the Bible course for six years now. It's easier these days but continues to fascinate and open me to new insights and joys. I've also branched out to teach similar courses to other groups, and I use my new found understanding of the Bible in retreat work with a variety of groups. I'm not a scripture expert, but I do know where to find information; I know what commentaries are available and useful; I can point students in the direction they might want to go.

Basically, I want to help students get a feel of the Bible, to know how to find the various books, to know what it is about as a whole, to know the historical context. Even though the Bible is not history as such, every one of the 72 books of the Bible was written in an historical context, for a specific group of people, in response to their religious needs. The student will understand the Bible much better if he or she has an appreciation of the historical background of the people and events whose story of search for God is related in a variety of ways in the Bible. Doing the timeline of people and events over and over may have frustrated the students, but they learned its value soon enough. I know for a fact that it definitely helps them get the broad picture, which is what an introduction to the Bible is about.

What I really look for in my students is their passion in life. I'm constantly on the lookout for what are their interests. If they don't have a passion in life I don't think they have a future with the Columbans, but I don't tell them that. Rather I push them to identify what might be their core interest, what engages them. They share their answers in an informal way, and I then keep the answers in the back of my mind. There was a Fijian in the class who had a fascination with the prophets, so I gave him a book on the prophets.

The course is called Scripture, Life and Prayer, but I don't teach it in those three parts. Everything gets mixed, because life is also a jumble of so many things. In my teaching, I try to identify their passion, but just for myself, and then I do what I can to feed and foster it. I don't attempt to process anything with them. Others might do that; it's not my strength. Some like history, some ecology and so on. There is always some part of the Bible story that will, in some way, speak to the passion of each person. I try to direct my students to the parts of scripture that might help them.

One of the exercises they do regularly is reflect in four stages on the Gospel of the coming Sunday. They work on the Gospel text using footnotes and cross references. They then share in groups in the class.

These few years of bringing a better understanding of the Bible to Columban students, lay groups and religious Sisters has meant so much to me. I am much more conscientious about preparing my homily; I pray in a way that makes more sense to me. This teaching experience has made me even more aware of the chasm between what would be the ideal as regards knowledge of the Bible and what in fact most people do know. However I realize that in order to get to know one has to want to know, but once the spark has been lit my students really push me because they do want to know. Their thirst for knowledge and understanding makes me say to myself: "Dominic, don't let them down." It motivates me to do what I can to make the scriptures relevant to their lives.

All this has driven me to become a better announcer of the Word, a better priest, to be more conscientious. We can never take the mystery out of all we find in the Bible, but I am sure we can remove some of the ignorance; we can help people start on a path of discovery, rather than simply drifting along. It gives me such joy to see others fired up about something.

I may challenge students if I see they are not putting in, but if they don't respond I don't push. However, I do let them know that they could make a lot more of themselves. I'm sure the courses we offer our Columban students in this first year give them a fantastic basis for the course of studies they will be taking on. I've got good feedback from the Director of the Spiritual year, as he can see that this course is helping the students get a handle on the Bible and so equipping them to use it in other courses in the program.

Link to our tradition:

Indeed, the word of God is living and effective, sharper than any two-edged sword, penetrating even between soul and spirit, joints and marrow, and able to discern reflections and thoughts of the heart. No creature is concealed from him, but everything is naked and exposed to the eyes of him to whom we must render an account. (Hebrews 4, 12-13)

## Welcomed by Children

By Columban Fr. Pat Baker

"If you want to learn Cebuano well, make sure that you spend as much time as you can with kids," was the advice I was given by Fr. John Wanaurny, Director of the Columban Language School in Ozamiz City, the Philippines, in 1972.

I tried to follow that advice when I was assigned to the parish of Plaridel in June 1973. Almost every afternoon a group of about six kids used to sit on a bench under a tree just outside the door of the *convento* (presbytery). Some were in Grade 2, others in Grade 3. They were a lively, talkative group. They welcomed me to sit with them. They asked me all sorts of questions, some quite personal. They laughed at some of my answers and they made some side remarks amongst themselves that I could not understand. More laughs. They were patient in trying to understand and answer my questions. They encouraged me when I tried to tell them a bit of a story. In contrast to some other kids whom I approached, this group would persevere with me. Others would give up and walk away after three or four minutes, but this group would hang in. There were times when they just chatted amongst themselves, but I did not feel excluded. They were not ignoring me. It was still good practice for me to try to follow and understand what they were saying. Occasionally one of them would explain for me what they were talking about. We became friends. We looked forward to these gatherings most afternoons.

A benefit from this was that the group could assure other friends that I was more approachable than they thought. The circle began to widen. Also when I met kids as I was going around the parish, they were not so shy. They were more courageous in stopping to talk with me. There were some nice beaches within walking distance of the *convento*. I liked swimming. Two or three days a week I would go to one of the beaches, and a crowd of kids often gathered to swim and chat with me. They certainly proved the validity of the advice that Fr. Wanaurny gave us.

I was two years in Plaridel before being transferred to Pagadian City. I kept in touch with five members of that "core group" of six. I would send them a card for their birthdays and meet them when I went back for the annual Fiesta. They remembered my birthday. Down through the years, as some of them got married and had children I was able to be with them for various celebrations. Joy Ronulo married a Belgian—Stefaan Gouwy—and went to live near Ypres. I visited them there in 2004. Nenette Lobino became a Nun. She sometimes called in to see me in Ozamiz on her way to Plaridel for her home vacation. We also met in Manila occasionally. AnnAnn Ratilla moved to Zamboanga City and married Samuel Sereno. They have three daughters. Fe Rebadajo moved to Manila where she married Jojo Tungala. They have seven children. Angie Dumalagan also moved to Manila and married, but we lost touch with her.

Their link with me helped them keep in touch with each other as well. But it was only in January 2010, that four of them managed to meet up with each other, to have a reunion. Joy was back in the Philippines from Belgium to celebrate her mother's 80th birthday in Plaridel. It was she who suggested some months previously that we organize a reunion. Sr. Nenette was going to come from Cebu City to Manila for a meeting in January, so we set that as the target date. AnnAnn came from Zamboanga City. It was easier for Fe to join us, once her husband and older kids agreed to look after the younger ones for three days.

My task was to find a place where they could stay. Any kind of a religious place was ruled out, because they wanted to be able to make as much noise as they liked. They wanted to be together in the one room. The one and only purpose of the reunion was to talk and laugh together for the whole three days. This is exactly what they did with so much news to catch up on, so many juicy bits of gossip to share. I joined them for some meals. They had many stories to share about me. Most of them I had not heard before—mistakes I made with the language, little tricks that they played on me without my knowing it, the intrigues that were going on in the group to get more of my attention. The diners at the neighboring tables were somewhat distracted by all our laughter. They must have been wondering too what was a Sister in full habit doing in a group like that. It was evident how excited they were to be with each other again after more than 30 years. They were profuse in their thanks for the attention that I gave them when they were kids and ever since. I also thanked them again for the help that they gave me with the language.

But there was more to these friendships than just getting help with the language. They helped me to realize how important it was to give attention to "little people"—not just kids, but the poor, marginalized, those with little formal education. Just to take time to sit with these people and listen to them with respect was a very important ministry. I became more and more convinced of this as I moved into working with basic Christian communities. I was continually being impressed by the gifts and talents that poor farmers and fishermen displayed, once I listened to them and encouraged them to express their opinions and to make decisions together.

Link to our tradition:
"Then children were brought to him that he might lay his hands on them and pray. The disciples rebuked them, but Jesus said, 'Let the children come to me, and do not prevent them; for the kingdom of heaven belongs to such as these.'" (Matthew 19, 13-14) Listening to children helped Fr. Pat discover the value of listening to the poor: "But in the city lived a man who, though poor, was wise, and he delivered it through his wisdom. Yet no one remembered this poor man. Though I had said, 'Wisdom is better than force,' yet the wisdom of the poor man is despised and his words go unheeded. The quiet words of the wise are better heeded than the shout of a ruler of fools." (Ecclesiastes 9, 15-17) "Listen, my beloved brothers. Did not God choose those who are poor in the world to be rich in faith and heirs of the kingdom that he promised to those who love him?" (James 2, 5)

## WHY IRELAND?

By Columban lay missionary Gracia Kibad

Why Ireland? Is there mission here? Do you think there is a future for the Church in Ireland? These are some of the questions people asked me. I received comments such as, "You're great to leave your family and come this far to do what you're doing." I'm convinced that there is mission in Ireland as anywhere else, for mission goes beyond geographical and cultural boundaries.

What does it mean for me to work in the Church in a so-called "post-Christian" society? The Irish church has a long tradition of sending missionaries overseas including the Philippines where I am from originally. Now Ireland is receiving missionaries! Over time, the concept of mission has changed and so too is the manner in which it is done, with a greater emphasis on friendship and dialogue. Missionaries now engage and immerse themselves in people's lives and the reality in which they find themselves.

The call to respond to God's call to mission was compelling. I've never dreamt of doing great things. Sometimes being on mission is difficult. It seemed daunting to face the risks that went with answering the call, but I felt that no one could stop me from responding to it. It was something that had been there, and it was time to let that desire burst forth to bear fruit. Leaving my family and friends was not easy, but leaving to face the unknown has been very challenging. I came to Ireland with very little expectation, but I was conscious of coming in response to a call.

My initial sense of being in Ireland was revulsion. The consumerist way of life of the people made me angry. To me it was deplorable. Coming from a country where so many people are poor and a country burdened by world debt, I initially disliked living and working in Ireland. I felt that they didn't care about us in developing countries like the Philippines, so why did I have to live here among them and be generous to them. This may sound silly. Of course, individual citizens are not the culprits. It's the global economic system which prevails that I was angry about.

I had to convince myself that while "Third World" citizens are victims of the global economic system, the citizens in developed countries are victims too— victims of a consumerist, materialistic lifestyle. This is a challenge that people in the West need to face.

I realized that I needed to grow out of my own preconceptions to be true to God's call. I needed to work on my anger in order to look positively at the situation I found myself in. If I was to witness to my Christian values, I needed to understand the underlying issues in order to focus on my vision and mission in Ireland.

In the two parishes where I was assigned, I worked with young people, the travelers (people living a nomadic life), the elderly, prayer groups, liturgy groups and migrant workers. Working with a variety of people young and old, Irish and foreign, has been very enriching. Indeed it was life-giving. It also gave me a good grounding in the reality of Irish society and the Irish Church.

My experience of cross-cultural mission has taught me to let go of my notions of how things should be. I had to enter into a new way of doing things, of relating with people. I had to allow myself to be surprised by the newness of my life in Ireland and to be open to those who were different from me.

I have gone beyond my prejudices towards the so-called "First World" to a better understanding of its people and where they're at. I now realize that there's a need for God's compassion everywhere.

Living in a culture other than my own and belonging to a Church that is quite different from what I was used to have deepened my faith. I am very grateful to God for this. I've grown out of my childish notion of God, who would be there and wipe my tears away, making everything okay. Now in my adult life, I have experienced God in a different way. While God is still there to wipe my tears away, God is present in my weeping, in my loneliness. God is always there in my joys and to see me through my trials, not necessarily to take them away.

Living my life on mission has been strengthened by the Columban missionaries in their work for justice and peace, dialogue with other faiths and their work in caring for the earth. I believe in the work they do. Being a part of this enterprise is giving meaning to my life as a person.

On mission, I discovered that I don't have all the answers, and it feels good to know that I don't. This has allowed me the opportunity to struggle with others and share their lives, their joys and successes, their questions and answers, as we struggle with issues of our lives and our Christian faith. If it were not for this mission experience I wonder whether I would have had the chance to feel vulnerable and helpless, to experience just being with people in their daily life.

All this became an occasion for affirming my own uniqueness, and with that a recognition of my own limitations and gifts. I learned to receive and, in receiving, to give. Perhaps the little that I gave made a difference in another's life. As the adage goes, "We are not so poor as to give nothing nor so rich as to receive nothing." I found joy in both giving and receiving.

Reflecting on mission, I also learned that listening is essential to understanding others; otherwise dialogue would be futile. To listen is to have an open heart and an open mind. There can be no authentic listening when we are so full of ourselves that there is no room for others in our hearts.

As I look back at my experience in Ireland, I thank the God of many surprises, who asked me to leave the familiar and embrace the unknown. God has shown me compassion and blessed me with the opportunity to be compassionate towards the people I came across during my missionary journey. I have felt God constantly affirming His love for me through the people I've met.

Link with our tradition:

In John 10, 7-11 Jesus assures us of the wisdom of seeking life in Him:

So Jesus said again, "Amen, amen, I say to you, I am the gate for the sheep. All who came [before me] are thieves and robbers, but the sheep did not listen to them. I am the gate. Whoever enters through me will be saved, and will come in and go out and find pasture. A thief comes only to steal and slaughter and destroy; I came so that they might have life and have it more abundantly. I am the good shepherd. A good shepherd lays down his life for the sheep."

## Drawing All to Himself

By Fr. Francis Ko Latt (Associate priest from Myanmar working with the Columbans in Naleba, Fiji)

"And when I am lifted up from the earth, I shall draw all men and women to myself." (John 12, 32)

I met with the church community leaders to plan the Stations of the Cross, which, if simply walking from the beginning to the end, would take about one hour. There had been much heavy rain, which did not look like letting up, but we decided to depart at 1:00 p.m., rain or shine.

Our first station was in a small Indo-Fijian village on the coast. The rain had stopped. There are only three Catholic families in the village, the majority being Hindus. Most Catholics in our community live in Naleba where we have our church. The three Catholic families were so pleased to welcome the rest of our parish community to their village. The village is rarely visited by the rest of the community as it is a bit out of the way. Very few parishioners have a car.

The three families prepared sweets and drinks for all at the first station. I told them that Good Friday was a day of prayer and fasting and that I had already eaten one full meal. However, I explained that they were welcome to do as they saw fit. Then I blessed the snacks and those who wished to do so shared the food. It was a lively social moment, and the families of the village felt blessed by so many coming from afar to be with them, in particular a widow of three years who had opened her home to us.

We set out from the first station with the three women, all widows, from the three families carrying the rather heavy cross. We prayed and sang hymns in Hindi along the way. Sometime later, I think around the fifth station, we noticed a truck was following us. It stopped with us at the following station and those in the truck, all of whom were Hindus from another village, offered us sweets and drinks. They explained to us that it was also their festival day (the festival of Holi).

Soon after we reached the top of the hill and began to go down towards Naleba. Around the eighth station we came to a family who had put out pancakes and juice for us. They were not Catholic, nor Muslim, nor Hindu, but rather Fijian Methodists. They shared food and drink with us, and then three of them took up the cross with us. At the ninth station another Methodist family was waiting for us. We prayed and they sang a hymn to Jesus Christ in Hindi, even though they were Fijian.

I was so moved by adults, youth and children singing together without song sheets or books. All present joined in with a quiet reverence. As they were singing the second hymn the rain began to come down. Our leader invited the group of Methodists to continue with us and many did.

The rain continued as we approached the eleventh and twelfth stations, and we were about to go up another hill. Here I asked a group of four strong men to take turns carrying the cross, so it was no longer being carried by three persons but one. Not long after this a physically disabled older man approached and insisted that he carry the cross alone.

His obvious struggle to carry the cross prompted a change in the atmosphere in the group; people seemed to pray more intensely as they identified more closely with the sufferings of Jesus Christ. Then a young girl, short and small, wanted to carry the cross, saying: "I also want to be like Jesus; let me carry the cross." She did, and all were moved. A school teacher and then another young girl later took up the cross.

It was slippery and muddy coming into the dip before the final uphill stage. As I was the only one with gumboots I said that I'd carry the cross, a gesture the rest did not expect. So, we reached the top of the hill, and an old lady took over and cried as she went. The road was rough, and she had to let some men help her. Near the end an Indian woman who was sick also carried for a short way, and three youth from the Methodist Church carried the final stage to the foot of the cross inside our church.

So much of this Good Friday Stations of the Cross was not planned, in particular the participation of Hindus and Methodists, and one instead of three people carrying the cross. Our holy walk began as a social occasion with a religious backdrop and gradually became ever more prayerful and deeply moving. Many of the Hindus and Methodists stayed with us in our church for the Good Friday liturgy and also returned for our Resurrection Mass on Easter Sunday.

It struck me that our crucified and risen Lord does indeed draw all to Himself.

Link to our tradition:

From Mount Hor they set out by way of the Red Sea, to bypass the land of Edom, but the people's patience was worn out by the journey; so the people complained against God and Moses, "Why have you brought us up from Egypt to die in the wilderness, where there is no food or water? We are disgusted with this wretched food!" So the LORD sent among the people seraph serpents, which bit the people so that many of the Israelites died. Then the people came to Moses and said, "We have sinned in complaining against the LORD and you. Pray to the LORD to take the serpents from us." So Moses prayed for the people, and the LORD said to Moses: Make a seraph and mount it on a pole, and everyone who has been bitten will look at it and recover. Accordingly Moses made a bronze serpent and mounted it on a pole, and whenever the serpent bit someone, the person looked at the bronze serpent and recovered. (Numbers 21, 4-9)

". . . And just as Moses lifted up the serpent in the desert, so must the Son of Man be lifted up so that everyone who believes in him may have eternal life." (John 3, 14-15)

## Dancing

### By Columban lay missionary Vida Hequilan

I've always loved to dance. As a teenager and even later I'd often return from a night out partying with my friends when others in my house were getting up. I think that may have worried my Dad a little, but he let me be. He is a quiet man who has no interest in social life. He would say, "Why would you want to go out to eat when there is plenty of food here at home?" I'm more like my mother who was outgoing and vivacious, but she died when I was 17 years old. I was just devastated since we were such close friends.

I am from the Philippines, and when I finished high school I went to college and qualified as a high school teacher. I liked teaching and did my job well, but I had no particular commitment to anything. I went to church on Sunday but was not involved in church activities. On weekends I would go out with my friends to parties and to the disco.

Then a friend began to talk to me about being a lay missionary, which was the furthest thing from my mind. I think she wanted someone she knew to go with her. I never thought I had a calling to anything like this. I had become accustomed to and content with a routine of work, family and fun with my friends. I am an only child, and my family is not wealthy but I have always had what I needed.

My friend's urging probably got me wondering whether there might be more to life than what I was living. I decided to look into the lay missionary idea and began to go through the hoops to get into the Columban program. I was pessimistic about my chances of making the grade, but I kept advancing through interviews and discernment exercises until I ended up in the overseas mission orientation program.

My Dad and my relatives tried (not very hard) to dissuade me, but since I'd progressed so far I decided to dig my heels in and go for it. In fact, now I know that leaving home and taking on this new life-challenge have deepened my relationship with my father, who is not a naturally affectionate man, nor does he share his feelings readily. He is a quiet, introverted, stay-at-home man. However, now we can say to each other, "I love you, and I miss you!"

I was assigned to the Columban mission in Taiwan and dreamt of doing all kinds of good things with the people, but even after a year of fulltime Chinese language study I felt so helpless. The accent of the people in the hills where I went to work is different from that of my language teacher. Also, my teacher spoke slowly and distinctly. All I could do was clean the church and visit people but I, the party going extrovert, could not converse.

My teacher encouraged me to just talk and keep talking until I got through the barrier. She urged me to go back to being like a small child. Luckily for me the people here are patient and understanding but also correct me when I make a mistake. The going back to being a little child lasted for about six months. It was a humbling experience.

I had never done any farm work and knew nothing whatsoever about it. Still, I offered to help in the fields, and the job we were doing was covering the fruit (persimmon) with bags to protect it from bugs and so on. When I covered 500 on my first day of work they told me that was pretty good for a first day on the job. Later I also helped with the harvest. I accepted no payment for my work, but they gave me lots of fruit. I learnt so much from that experience and also felt that it allowed me to draw closer to the people of the village.

I experienced the way my new neighbors worked. We began the day with an energy drink, laced with a wee drop of alcohol, something like Red Bull. As we worked we chatted, joked and sang. We lunched together in the field, rested in the shade of a tree and then work again until dusk. All this gave me a new appreciation of nature; I'd grown up with it in the Philippines but had never really seen or felt it. I had a feeling of peace as I sat and, for the first time, really looked.

This is still a strongly patriarchal society. I have also noticed that many women are quite strong and influential so, despite the patriarchal tradition that endures, maybe such women are the glue that holds things together in the relatively poor rural communities of Taiwan's mountain area. I worked in the fields with five women and two men, and I noticed that the women in particular worked hard. They now feel free to call on me when they need my help.

An essential part of my mission in this area is to collaborate with the parish priest in parish ministry. Columban Fr. Larry Barnett, our parish priest, attends to eight communities, so he asked me to help with a number of things, the most challenging of which is leading the Sunday worship in a number of communities each weekend. We have a rotation system.

I like to lead the communion service even though I never did anything like this in the Philippines. For me it is a humbling experience to share about God and even more so when I have to do so in my very simple Chinese. I prepare well and write everything in Chinese characters. I try to relate the Word of God to our experience of life and if I can make them laugh that helps too. I want my homily to be personal and funny as I don't want them to go to sleep. It feels great to get positive feedback about my homily as I do feel quite inadequate. One time I was able to talk about my mother's death, and I know it was very moving.

When I left the Philippines, I could not have imagined that I would be dancing in church halls and on basketball courts with the wives and children of Taiwanese farmers, and then with the farmers themselves. The women love the way I teach them to move their hips, and I have the impression that their men love it even more. I began teaching some dances for a Christmas gathering of the whole parish. Women of the neighboring Presbyterian community then asked me to teach them. Then one of the men asked me to teach the men. This year I am teaching Christmas dances to people from three villages. If being a Christian is taking on life with joy, then dancing has to be the way to go.

Link to our tradition:

Prayer takes many forms. See the account of David dancing around the Ark of the Covenant: "Thus David, the elders of Israel, and the commanders of thousands went to bring up the ark of the covenant of the LORD with joy from the house of Obed-edom. While God helped the Levites to carry the ark of the covenant of the LORD, they sacrificed seven bulls and seven rams. David was vested in a robe of fine linen, as were all the Levites who carried the ark, the singers, and Chenaniah, the leader of song; David was also wearing a linen ephod. Thus all Israel brought up the ark of the covenant of the LORD with joyful shouting, to the sound of horns, trumpets, and cymbals, and the music of harps and lyres. But as the ark of the covenant of the LORD was entering the City of David, Michal, daughter of Saul, looked down from her window, and when she saw King David leaping and dancing, she despised him in her heart." (1 Chronicles 15, 25-29)

# CHAPTER 3

## Commitment to justice, peace and integrity of creation

Throughout the ages many Christians have dedicated themselves to addressing the needs of the poor, working for peace and attending to the wellbeing of the earth. Unfortunately many so-called Christians have done just the opposite, enriching themselves at the expense of the poor, bringing death and destruction to the poor through wars they have instigated, and using the resources of our planet irresponsibly to enrich themselves. In our time, it is ever clearer that one cannot engage in such activities and hope to ease one's conscience by giving alms.

Only in recent times has systemic analysis and criticism been possible. The gradual move towards democracy in many parts of the world has allowed ever more freedom to analyze and criticize social structures and then form or join movements seeking to change what is wrong. In the west, especially since the days of the industrial revolution, social movements of various kinds have worked for major changes in society.

The ongoing movements championing the cause of millions of poor in Latin America are gradually achieving the changes necessary to achieve a reasonable basic standard of living. Women around the world continue to organize and campaign for equality with men in all areas of life. Millions who have been subjected to systemic exclusion because of their race have organized and worked to change such situations of discrimination. When the status quo happens to permit massive injustice men and women are finding ways to challenge and change this. Following World War II many nations living under the domination of colonial rule sought their independence by both peaceful and violent means.

Christians have been involved in all such movements, but not always on the side of the poor. That lack of solidarity with the poor has been questioned and challenged in recent times by Christians reflecting upon their experience of working against abuse and injustice and for a more just society. Various forms of "Liberation Theology," beginning with what began to emerge in Latin America in the late 1960s and 1970s, have developed our understanding of what it might mean to stand in solidarity with the poor. This understanding has been taken on board by the leadership of many Christian Churches. In the case of the Catholic Church, formal statements on social justice from Pope Leo XXIII to the present day are ample and constant witness to this radical shift in the Church's understanding of her role in God's mission. In his encyclical letter, *Centesimus Annus* (1991), commemorating the 100th anniversary of Pope Leo XXIII's encyclical letter, *Rerum Novarum*, Pope John Paul II wrote:

Re-reading the Encyclical [*Rerum Novarum*] in the light of contemporary realities enables us to appreciate the Church's constant concern for and dedication to categories of people who are especially beloved to the Lord Jesus. The content of the text is an excellent testimony to the continuity within the Church of the so-called "preferential option for the poor," an option which I defined as a "special form of primacy in the exercise of Christian charity." Pope Leo's Encyclical on the "condition of the workers" is thus an Encyclical on the poor and on the terrible conditions to which the new and often violent process of industrialization had reduced great multitudes of people. Today, in many parts of the world, similar processes of economic, social and political transformation are creating the same evils. (No. 11)

In recent times national and continental Church leadership has similarly applied universal Church teaching to local situations, in particular the Bishops of Latin America and the Caribbean, in a series of meetings held since Vatican II: Medellin, Colombia, (1968), Puebla, Mexico, (1979), Santo Domingo (1992), and Aparecida, Brazil, (2007). The U.S. Catholic Bishops have also brought to bear the riches of the Church's social teaching on challenges facing the U.S., perhaps the better known statement being their pastoral letters of 1986 and 1983, "Economic Justice for All: Pastoral Letter on Catholic Social Teaching and the U.S. Economy", and on the issue of global peace, "The Challenge of Peace: God's Promise and Our Response." Since the second Vatican Council individual bishops and national or regional bishops' conferences have sought to apply the social teaching of the Church to local situations.

Such statements by Church leadership outline general principles but challenges such as economic justice for all and peace among nations are permanently on the agenda of humanity. There is usually a close link between the challenges of economic justice and that of peace. In so far as people feel that justice is not being done there is little chance of achieving peace through negotiation and mutual agreement; rather peace in such circumstances will necessarily be imposed by force and fear, and a fear-based peace was never part of Jesus' proposal for the reign of God.

Jesus said in His sermon on the mount: "Blessed are the peacemakers, for they will be called children of God."(Matthew 5, 9) A son or daughter of God does not instill fear into others. We are called to trust in God as in a loving father. Jesus commanded His disciples to love each other and such love engenders trust and peace. Violence and force impose a kind of peace that bears no relationship to what Jesus proposes to His followers. At all levels of human activity we can be peacemakers, sharing an endeavor that is intrinsic to the mission of God. (Matthew 5, 21-26; 38-48)

The dream of the prophet Isaiah (Isaiah 2, 2-4) evokes a basic yearning of humanity to move beyond warfare as the way to resolve our differences. Isaiah foresees a time when peoples will choose to resolve disputes in the presence of and with the help of God, which means that we will seek to have our disputes resolved by negotiation and mutual agreement, not by superior strength and military might:

In days to come, the mountain of the Lord's house shall be established as the highest mountain and raised above the hills. All nations shall stream toward it. Many peoples shall come and say:

"Come, let us go up to the Lord's mountain, to the house of the God of Jacob that he may instruct us in his ways, and we may walk in his paths."

. . . He shall judge between the nations, and set terms for many peoples. They shall beat their swords into plough shares and their spears into pruning hooks; one nation shall not raise the sword against another, nor shall they train for war again.

Respect for the earth and all the forms of life that it sustains emerges from an abiding commitment to justice and peace, because at the root of that commitment is respect for life in all its forms, a concern for harmony with all that is, for we have been entrusted with care of the earth as stewards:

Genesis 1, 26: Then God said: Let us make human beings in our image, after our likeness. Let them have dominion over the fish of the sea, the birds of the air, the tame animals, all the wild animals, and all the creatures that crawl on the earth.

Psalm 8, 7-9: You have given him rule over the works of your hands, put all things at his feet: all sheep and oxen, even the beasts of the field, the birds of the air, the fish of the sea, and whatever swims the paths of the seas.

Romans 8, 19-23: For creation awaits with eager expectation the revelation of the children of God . . . We know that all creation is groaning in labor pains even until now; and not only that, but we ourselves, who have the first fruits of the Spirit, we also groan within ourselves as we wait for adoption, the redemption of our bodies.

These Bible texts point to the responsibility that God has given us to care for the earth and the life that it sustains.

The rest of this chapter is made up of mission stories illustrating the preceding paragraphs. After each story or, in some cases, groups of stories, there is a link to our religious tradition, which, for the most part, is taken from the Bible but, also from teachings of the Popes, General Councils and Episcopal Conferences.

## Street Children Locked Up

Poverty, Abuse and Neglect
By John A. Keenan

Maria, 15, and Lourdes, 16, were abducted one night near their homes and taken to a detention center near Manila City Hall because of *bagansa*, or vagrancy, for being out after curfew. Instead of being taken home to their parents, they were dumped into an already overcrowded, poorly ventilated detention center called Reception and Action Center (RAC). Most children do not know what or when curfew is nor do most of them have watches or know how to observe the curfew hours. The plight of such children abducted from the streets was highlighted a couple of years ago in the local and international media. It is estimated that there are up to 20,000 children behind bars in the Philippines.

In RAC some 70 children aged between one and sixteen years are packed into three rooms barely big enough for 30 people. They have to sleep on the bare wooden floors side by side like sardines in stifling heat and poor ventilation. This center is run by the City of Manila and the Department of Social Welfare and Development. The main problems are over-crowding, lack of sufficient food, clothing, adequate facilities, privacy and staff.

In another building in the same compound, some 170 children are in trouble with the law for petty crimes such as stealing cell-phones, ear-rings and cash, although some are charged with serious bodily crimes. Those children are held in six dormitories in a building called the Manila Youth Reception Center. It is run by the same authorities as the RAC and has the same problems with over-crowding, lack of furniture, bedding, privacy, ventilation, adequate recreation, reading materials and so on. For many children it is a place without hope as their cases may go on for months or years due to lack legal representation and due process. As minors, according to law they are supposed to be released from behind bars after eight hours and turned over to the Department of Social Welfare and Development (DSWD) for re-education, counseling, although this doesn't always occur.

A third section called "Lingap" houses in a large tent of displaced families, the destitute, the sick and dying, mentally ill, the old and abandoned. It reminds me very much of the homes run by Blessed Mother Teresa's Missionaries of Charity. Again, they lack trained staff, privacy, medical supplies is rampant.

The children are abducted by local officials in the local barangay and by the police. The children come mainly from poor and deprived families have been abducted for simply begging, selling goods, being alone even in broad daylight or just sleeping. Instead of taking them home they are impounded, irrespective of their rights to know why they are being abducted, the right of their parents to know about it and their right to know where they are being taken by complete strangers. For them it is a terrifying and traumatic experience. According to RA 9344, Section 21 regarding the procedure for taking a child into custody the arresting officer must, among other things, explain to the child: a) the offense committed, b) identify himself to the child, c) refrain from slapping . . . or using vulgar words, d) avoid displaying weapons or handcuffs. Their parents or guardians must also be informed.

To compound the trauma, the children are herded into sub-human conditions, small children along with big teenagers in an atmosphere of fear and trepidation. Such crammed conditions can spawn all kinds of abuse, introduction to vice and fights among themselves. They are only allowed out for half an hour of recreation and for their meals three times a day. The rest of the time they are cooped up inside in the stifling heat. They have no opportunity for study or improving themselves. Sometimes they may be there for over a month or longer before being released by being sent to a children's home or to their parents or guardians if they can be found. The resident staff does their best to help them and succeed admirably in many cases, but they are hampered by numbers.

The fact is that most of them should not be there in the first place since they are innocents, the victims of poverty, broken families and neglect both in the city and in the provinces. Instead of being rescued they are being condemned to sub-human conditions. It has been suggested that the barangay officials and police are being rewarded for filling their quota of arrests. The Center is understaffed, and there are not enough social workers to pursue their cases and set them free. They have an impossible job because of the lack of financial and personnel support. RAC is probably one of the better detention centers as compared with similar institutions in other cities in metro Manila and in the provinces. If the community became more aware and helped poor families, paid just wages and made genuinely free education a reality, many of these children would not end up in RAC.

I celebrate Mass in RAC every Sunday morning, which is much appreciated by the children and staff. Before Mass the volunteers give the children religious instruction, and I usually meet them individually. This gives me a chance to get to know them and their background. They are lovely children. They are simply victims of poverty with broken families, abusive parents, the lack of a decent home with water, electricity and food and no access to education. I feel pity for them and angry at society, the government and the Church, that they are not doing more to respond to these basic human needs. Most have dropped out of school by 10 or so due to lack of food and *pamasahe* (fares for public transport). Education is supposed to be free, but it isn't without fees. What hope is there for them?

Without education or a livelihood will they end up as prostitutes and criminals? It is very sad indeed.

The RAC staff, who are social workers, are very committed to the welfare of the children and do their best to feed and take care of them on a slim budget, until they find their parents or guardians. I feel that my presence there gives them spiritual and moral support in what could easily be a very depressing job. They are very welcoming and accommodating. Our work there complements what they are trying to do in convincing the children to avoid *barkadas* (groups of peers, in this context with a negative connotation), vices and to go back to school.

Editor's Note: The names of all children mentioned in this article have been changed for their protection and privacy.

Link to our tradition:

Religion that is pure and undefiled before God and the Father is this: to care for orphans and widows in their affliction and to keep oneself unstained by the world. (James 1, 27)

## The Path to My Missionary Vocation

By Columban Associate Fr. Enrique Escobar

In my youth I never thought of being a priest. In fact, even though I was from a Catholic family, I did not want to have anything to do with the Church. My brothers and sisters went to a Catholic school, but I went to the local state school, where I heard lots of criticism of the Church, which I could verify by what I saw in our local parish.

I grew up in a fishing village, which has now been transformed into a seaside resort, just eleven kilometers from Chiclayo on the north coast of Peru. Ours is a middle class family, so I never knew poverty. My Dad ran a transport business, and after he died in 1982, my elder brother took over the business.

Even though my family was reasonably well off I saw the results of poverty among my companions at school. I completed high school in 1980 so grew up during the time of the military government of General Juan Velasco Alvarado (who was also from the north of Peru, Sullana, to be precise). His government put in place some major social reforms, in particular the agrarian reform. I was in high school during the second phase of the military government that was headed by another general who did much to undo social reforms favoring the poor of Peru. It was a time of social ferment into which so many of my generation were drawn.

I thought that a military career would allow me to do something about social justice in Peru so, on completing secondary school and turning 18 years of age, I signed up for two years military service. I notified my parents after signing on. It took me just a few weeks to realize that I was not going to be able to do much good as a soldier. I experienced so much inhuman treatment within the military and was stationed on the border between Peru and Ecuador during that absurd conflict between the two countries. However, I made the best of the situation, learned the mechanics of diesel engines, completing the two years of voluntary service with the rank of sergeant.

I left the army while stationed in Lima where I remained and continued my search for meaning in my life. I signed up for a course as an accountant's assistant at the night school run by the Salesians in Breña. That put me in touch with a youth group with whom I shared my concerns. We began to go to summer courses on Theology of Liberation that were run by the Catholic University, which of course introduced me to another way of understanding the Catholic faith, so different from what I had seen in my home parish.

Then in 1988 Pope John Paul II visited Peru and spoke to over a million people gathered on the sand hills to the south of Lima. He spoke of "hunger for God and hunger for bread," two basic essentials of life. In the summer courses, Gustavo Gutierrez spoke about God's preference for the poor and our corresponding call to live out the same preference. This finally undid my negative image of God and undid my resistance; I surrendered and began to walk with God.

I was not sure where all this was leading me but, on the recommendation of one of the priests in Our Lady Help of Christians Parish, I journeyed to Huaraz to see Bishop Gurruchaga, who was a Salesian from the Basque area of Spain. I lived in the bishop's house for a short time and what I witnessed helped me change my negative idea of the hierarchical church. The bishop was always up and about between 4:00 and 5:00 a.m. to attend the (subsistence) farmers of the area who came to see him to talk about a variety of matters. He also served them breakfast. This was so different from what I'd seen in my home parish where the priests seemed so aloof from the ordinary people.

After a few days the bishop offered to send me to a small town further into the mountains. I went there for a year and shared the parish house with the parish priest. It was a time to discern my vocation in life. I think that if I had not discovered the God who is concerned for the suffering of the poor I probably would have joined some armed revolutionary movement. The bishop told me that I would be a good priest but not in Huaraz. He offered to help find a suitable place for me. He introduced me to Maryknoll missionary Fr. Tom Garrity who was trying to develop a group of Peruvian missionaries comprised of lay persons, priests and religious.

I began to work as a lay missionary in the Amazon jungle and then in Canto Grande, a newly settled poor area to the north east of the old city center of Lima. The priests in the parish were Columban associates from Australia, Frs. Rom Hayes and Tom Martin. We got on well. Then, in 1989 Fr. Tom Garrity invited me to be a priest. I was 25 years of age when I began the formal studies. Another Basque bishop, Fr. Jose Luis Astigarraga who is a Passionist and heads a mission prelature in the Peruvian jungle, gave me formal support to study for the priesthood. Fr. Tom could not give me such support as he had not been able to obtain official recognition for the missionary organization that he was developing.

I found the three men who were so helpful to me, Tom and the two bishops, to be understanding and compassionate. They did not judge or condemn but rather lifted up the person who was down. They had a job to do and did it well, but they also focused primarily on the person with whom they were dealing, be it me or the person who came to the door. Their way of living their Christian faith made them so thoroughly human and welcoming of the other.

Fr. Tom had the idea that if other youth had to work to help finance their tertiary studies so too should the student for the priesthood. I found a job at a service station in the afternoons and continued to live with a team of lay missionaries in Canto Grande. I never lived in a seminary. For Fr. Tom it was all about having an experience similar to that of other youth. I was ordained a priest on December 12, 1994, by Bishop José Luis Astigarraga. From 1995 to 2000 I accompanied lay missionaries in the jungle during the year and helped them with courses in Lima during the summer months.

Around the year 2000 one of the lay missionaries asked me about my missionary commitment and, coincidentally, I had received a leaflet from the Columbans advertising their priest associate program. I talked to the bishop about the Columban option, and he told me to keep at what I was doing. I went back to him six months later and he suggested I contact the Columbans. In 2001 the Columbans asked me to work with Columban Fr. John Boles (originally from England) in a parish where I remained for seven months and from there was appointed to the Philippines.

Working with the poor in Manila had a major impact on me. My time there was akin to being born again as I had to learn two new languages at the same time, English and Tagalog. I wondered whether or not to stay with the Columbans but realized that there was something drawing me to their style of being missionaries. I also feel that we of Latin America have a lot to offer the Church in the Philippines. I had an interesting and challenging experience in Manila living in close proximity and sharing with Muslims. In Peru, because of the make-up of our society, we have a long tradition of dialogue and tolerance. Some look down on others but most of us are open to respecting and living with difference. Our experience of small church communities also challenges us to treat each other as equals, so I feel that much of our life in Peru might speak to our fellow Christians in the Philippines. I would like to continue as a missionary in that inter-cultural dialogue.

Link to our tradition:

In his inaugural address to the fifth meeting of CELAM in Aparecida, Brazil, on May 13, 2007, Pope Benedict XVI stated: "We can ask ourselves a further question: what does faith in this God give us? The first response is: it gives us a family, the universal family of God in the Catholic Church. Faith releases us from the isolation of the 'I', because it leads us to communion: the encounter with God is, in itself and as such, an encounter with our brothers and sisters, an act of convocation, of unification, of responsibility towards the other and towards others. In this sense, the preferential option for the poor is implicit in the Christological faith in the God who became poor for us, so as to enrich us with his poverty (cf. 2 Corinthians 8, 9: "For you know the gracious act of our Lord Jesus Christ, that for your sake he became poor although he was rich, so that by his poverty you might become rich").

## The Power of a Few Good Christians

By Columban lay missionary John Din

Working as a Columban lay missionary in Brazil for six years and in Peru for eleven years gave me the opportunity to do things that I think helped make a difference but, perhaps even more importantly, to meet a few very impressive people who have inspired me in some way to deepen my commitment to mission.

However, it all began for me in my own part of the Philippines, namely in Mindanao near Midsalip. It was 1987, and I was in my last year in high school when activists protesting the illegal logging in the hills where the Subanen people live were picketing the road along which the trucks with loads of logs had to pass. They helped stop the logging, and I realized then that social change is possible. The fact that things are as they are does not mean that they must remain that way.

I worked on a variety of projects in Brazil and Peru, and it was while working with Columban Fr. Colin McLean on a project promoting black identity, specifically how to use the body to express oneself in dance, that a chance encounter prompted me to rethink some of my basic assumptions. I had joined in a street march protesting racism in Salvador, in north east Brazil. Much of the march was also dance, but I was happy to just march. Along the way an elderly woman from our group of friends asked me why I was in Brazil. She then said, "If you are here to save us you might as well just go home; we can save ourselves." Not that I was feeling messianic at the time but maybe one of my hidden reasons for being on mission was to help others.

That was a very important moment to me because it opened me to life on mission with uncertainties and questions about my presence and work as a missionary. I quite wrongly presumed that the image of Church that I had from the Philippines was the same all over the world. I had grown up seeing the Church defend the poor and commit to protecting the ecological heritage of our country, but that elderly woman helped me understand that the Church had been part of the system that enslaved thousands of Africans forcibly transported to Brazil, that the Church owned slaves, and that churches had been built by slaves. Yet she was a Catholic and active in the Church. She effectively undermined the image I had of the Church; she made real for me what in fact I had already heard previously. That encounter has helped me be critical of myself as regards my contribution to mission, to question my own way of doing things and also the choices that I have made. One might say that she challenged in me any tendency towards missionary arrogance that may have colored my attitude to others.

In Peru I met another most impressive woman. Mary Nieto, originally from the Andean mountain area, was a member of the team that in 1991 started a project to recycle domestic garbage. In 2006, I took on the role of coordinating the Columban Justice and Peace work as well as the management of the recycling project.

Mary embodies for me the image of a lay person in the Church in the World. She never studied at a university, but the knowledge she has accumulated about everything related to recycling is amazing. She is also committed to the social outreach program of her parish here in Motupe Montenegro (Our Lady of Peace Parish). She is most precise and demanding in all related to accounting for institutional funds. Now in her early 40s, she continues in the recycling project and is most grateful to the Columbans for all we have done to train and facilitate lay leaders.

Recently the recycling project was named as one of the outstanding projects in the country by the Ministry of the Environment. Mary has at times worked in the project for a small wage but not at the moment. There has always been a strong emphasis on it being community work so, even when funds are running low, those involved still do what is necessary to make things happen. During the past five years we have collected and recycled more than 400 tons of domestic garbage from 200 homes. This project has helped me keep my feet on the ground as it is something practical and concrete in which I am involved. We had nearly 1,000 visitors come to inspect our project last year as it is the only project of its kind in Lima. It has shown me that people can change; people can learn to classify garbage.

This project and others related to some of the most pressing ecological issues in Peru helped me get in touch with the Peruvian civic movement that deals with climate change—MOCCIC. Columbans were involved in the founding of this umbrella organization that helps a variety of groups develop a network, inform each other and at times do things together. When I attend meetings I feel pushed to get on top of the science of climate change; I felt inadequate and uncomfortable with so many people who seemed to be much more knowledgeable than I. Eventually I felt more at home and accepted within the group and made friends with some.

Some wondered why the Church was involved at all. However, all are aware of the conflicting images of Church that are constantly being projected by two leading churchmen[10] and so realize that at least a sector of the Church's leadership does not want to see the Church on the fringe of the debate about significant social issues. This umbrella group is not just for talk but also for organizing marches and conferences, getting our message out to the country more effectively. Neither the central government nor the municipalities have a long term plan to tackle the ecological concerns of the populace so for now this informal grouping of voluntary organizations is the voice of civic concern in that area.

By the time this goes to print I will have left Latin America to take up a new mission assignment with lay missionaries in my home country, where I return grateful, renewed and inspired to continue working in the vineyard of the Lord.

Link to our tradition:

Seventeen years' experience as a lay missionary in Brazil and Peru has had a major impact on John Din, who has completed his term in Latin America and has recently returned to his native Philippines. He has also done as Paul the Apostle said of his own missionary work: "Since, then, we have the same spirit of faith, according to what is written, 'I believed, therefore I spoke,' we too believe and therefore speak, knowing that the one who raised the Lord Jesus will raise us also with Jesus and place us with you in his presence. Everything indeed is for you, so that the grace bestowed in abundance on more and more people may cause the thanksgiving to overflow for the glory of God." (2 Corinthians 4, 13-15)

## Connecting to Country

### By Columban Employee Anne Lanyon

"Country" is a word that means different things to different people. Australia is a new country now populated by people from hundreds of overseas countries. But for the first Australians, "country" means something much deeper, and all Australians have much to learn about what it is to be a person of the land. This is an opportunity for interfaith dialogue, especially in a multi-religious urban setting.

Australia has hundreds of Aboriginal countries. Aboriginal woman Oomera Edwards explains that she is from Darkinjung Country, her spirit home. To her people it is spiritual being.

---

[10]   The present Cardinal Archbishop Juan Luis Cipriani of Lima takes an Opus Dei line of non-involvement in grassroots social protests and retired Jesuit Bishop Luis Bambaren has always been involved in social matters and continues to speak out on key issues, often in disagreement with the Cardinal.

As spiritual beings, we are custodians of country. We need to be disciplined and honorable beings, and this requires a lifetime. When you mature, you see the whole world and concepts at deepening levels, so you respect more. Aborigines over eons learned to sing and talk to the country in the language of that country. Connections with country include a web of relationships through kinship systems. We need to be in tune with the whole web of natural relationships, but the main actor is country itself. We are bit players!

The steps to connecting to country are about firstly understanding that such a relationship is possible. Find a place in the land where you feel comfortable. Just sit and listen to the birds, the bush and feel the wind. This takes you out of your chatterbox head. You'll feel the country. You'll go out of your head and into the stillness of body!

This lesson on Aboriginal spirituality from Oomera was part of a series of seminars in Sydney organized by the Faith Ecology Network (FEN) on the theme, Earth: Our Common Home. Over the three sessions, people from Anglican, Buddhist, Baha'i, Catholic, Hindu, Jewish, Muslim and Uniting Church traditions spoke about teachings on what most call Creation. At these seminars, the dialogue also included environmental activists. At other events organized by FEN, ecologists, academics and professional experts have been included as well as people of no particular faith. By engaging in this form of listening and learning, the presence of God in different ways has been brought to the attention of the participants.

The Faith Ecology Network (FEN) began in 2003 when an interfaith conference on the theme "Wonder and the Will to Care" was organized by the Columban Center for Peace, Ecology and Justice. Since then a public event has been held annually on a common area of interest: water, climate change, food. A small planning group does most of the organizing with the administration remaining with the Columban Mission Institute. Sharing mutual appreciation of religious traditions regarding ecology is one of the aims of FEN. The other is to discern and foster religious reasons for advocacy about care for the earth.

The network operates through an e-group where members from across the state and beyond exchange information and insights with openness and in a non-confrontational way. Through hearing about the activities of other groups, there is further building of networks and learning from others' perspectives. There is great religious and cultural diversity with about ten faiths represented. Members feel supported and nourished in their common interests. The message about faith and ecology is getting out to many groups, including secular groups, and other organizations. And it is reaching around the globe!

Pope John Paul II called all people to an ecological conversion and this has been reiterated by Pope Benedict XVI. But Oomera talks about it in an Aboriginal way:

Australians have an opportunity to begin learning about this land and to eventually find a place of belonging within it. This process of connecting will be different for each individual and it will take time, but eventually all Australians will become people of this Land in the proper sense.

We should not be surprised to realize that connecting to country and ecological conversion are the same thing in different languages. Through the FEN activities, many people from different faiths have been able to articulate for the first time what "country" means to them. The ongoing challenge for those already on this journey is to then engage members of our own faith communities in this crucial mission.

Link to our tradition:
Let the earth bless the Lord; praise and exalt him above all forever.
Mountains and hills, bless the Lord; praise and exalt him above all forever.
Everything growing from the earth, bless the Lord; praise and exalt him above all forever.
You springs, bless the Lord; praise and exalt him above all forever.
Seas and rivers, bless the Lord; praise and exalt him above all forever.
You dolphins and all water creatures, bless the Lord; praise and exalt him above all forever.
All you birds of the air, bless the Lord; praise and exalt him above all forever.
All you beasts, wild and tame, bless the Lord; praise and exalt him above all forever. (Daniel 3, 74-81).

## A David and Goliath Case

By Columban Fr. Pat Cunningham

Whether or not it would be good for South Korea to build a naval base on Jeju Island is an issue that is hotly debated among the citizens of this country. The central government is pushing ahead with the project but those who disagree with what is happening will not be easily silenced. All who take an interest in local politics have an opinion for or against the construction of the naval base. The overwhelming majority of the residents of Ganjeong village have manifested their opposition to the construction of the naval base.

I am a Columban missionary priest from Ireland and have been working in South Korea for 20 years or so. I have a particular interest in issues related to justice, peace and ecology. Our missionary mandate insists that we take up such issues and do so in solidarity with the poor and those on the margins of society. It is from that point of view that I wish to reflect briefly on what is happening on Jeju Island in regard to the naval base project.

Recent historical events on Jeju Island have left a deep mark on the psyche of the island's residents. In the words of Jeju Island's Catholic Bishop, Peter Kang Woo-il, who is also president of the Catholic Bishops' Conference of Korea: "Many Jeju residents . . . feel disillusioned with the South Korean government . . . . It's similar to the sadness they felt after the April 3 uprising in 1948—that sense of being utterly trampled." In 1948 more than 30,000 people were killed as villagers and communist radicals alike were imprisoned in internment camps under the policies of the central government. A government sponsored group repressed "communist sympathizers" with a campaign of raping, torturing, and killing hundreds of islanders. At that time, mainland officials treated islanders as if they were nothing.

Bishop Kang went on to say, "I think that even their ability to get angry over this has been crushed by the sense of abandonment by the central government when Jeju was a place of exile in the past, and the sense of shame over the lack of any kind of healing or apology process for this from the government for the past sixty years."

"At the same time, they have been stripped of their freedom, since most of the residents who actively protested against the naval base were arrested or charged and fined and would have to pay millions of won if they showed their face again," Kang added.

There are ways things are done in a totalitarian dictatorship, and there are ways things should be done in a democracy. I and many others stand with the residents of Jeju Island in their quest for a way to feel free to participate in the decision making process around the naval base project. They remember being crushed by vicious totalitarian tactics in the recent past. They, together with their supporters, will do all we can to ensure there is no repetition of past abuse.

Even officials of the previous government that planned the naval base have publicly recognized their mistake. In August and September 2011, lawmaker Jeong Dong-young and senior adviser Moon Jae-in, both former senior officials in the previous government, apologized in Jeju for their decision to construct the base: "This construction was planned under our administration, as I look back on it, I see that it was a mistake."

The process of standing in solidarity with the residents of Jeju Island is complex. We join in marches; we celebrate Mass in the street to ask God's support and make known our position; we join in demonstrations; we speak out in the media. The support group is quite diverse, and I am sure that our reasons for participating are as varied as we are. For me, the words taken from the last paragraph of the introductory part of the conclusion of the Synod Bishops, held in Rome in 1971, sustain me in my conviction that our work for justice in all its forms is at the heart of announcing the Good News of Jesus Christ:

"Action on behalf of justice and participation in the transformation of the world fully appear to us as a constitutive dimension of the preaching of the

Gospel, or, in other words, of the Church's mission for the redemption of the human race and its liberation from every oppressive situation."

I strive to engage with the issues related to justice, peace and ecology in the spirit outlined in Pope Benedict XVI's encyclical letter, *Caritas in Veritate*, #51:

"The Church has a responsibility towards creation and she must assert this responsibility in the public sphere. In so doing, she must defend not only earth, water and air as gifts of creation that belong to everyone. She must above all protect mankind from self-destruction."

Link to our tradition:

"For this we toil and struggle, because we have set our hope on the living God, who is the savior of all, especially of those who believe." (1Timothy 4, 10) "Jesus cried out in a loud voice, 'Father, into your hands I commend my spirit'; and when he had said this he breathed his last.'" (Luke 23, 46) Trust may not be easy but Jesus insists upon it: "Do not let your hearts be troubled. Trust in God; trust also in me." (John 14, 1)

## Getting at the Root of the Problem

### By James Dass

What matters is to evangelize people's culture and cultures, not in a purely decorative way, as it were, by applying a thin veneer, but in a vital way, in depth and right to their very roots in the wide and rich sense, . . . always taking the person as one's starting-point and always coming back to the relationships of people among themselves and with God. (Evangelii Nuntiandi, Pope Paul VI, 1975, No. 20)

I have been active in Raiwaqa parish (Fiji) for many years and was parish chairman in 1987 when Columban Fr. Tom Rouse, our parish priest, was asked to leave the country by the leaders of the military coup against whose act of violently usurping the reins of government he, with others, were protesting. From the time of independence in 1970, we had attempted to develop a multi-ethnic democracy but a series of military coups as from 1987 points to our failure.

I am Indo-Fijian and many of my race left Fiji as they saw little future for themselves and their children in a nation divided along ethnic lines. However, many Fijians, both ethnic Fijians and Indo-Fijians, are searching for ways to rebuild democracy in our country. We know that it is not simply a matter of having elections. We need to find ways of changing the "them and us" mindset that seems to condition many of our countrymen and women. As long as this mindset endures, unscrupulous politicians will be free to stir up fear, mistrust and division along ethnic lines in order to establish self-serving power bases.

Since 2004 I have been active in The Social Empowerment Education Program (SEEP), one of four programs established, under the umbrella of the

Fiji Council of Churches, by the Ecumenical Center for Research, Education and Advocacy (ECREA) in 2001. SEEP works towards increasing the participation of women and youth in community decision-making processes in some rural areas. We became independent of ECREA in 2009 as the bureaucracy seemed to curtail the flexibility we felt we needed to move ahead with our project.

We wanted to help rural community leaders move away from both the traditional and modern styles of leadership, which tend to concentrate power in the leader. We began to enter with our program via villages but now we enter via provincial councils. We present them with an outline of our program and also explain the reason for our work. To date, we have found them most cooperative.

In this transformative education process we deal with two types of leaders: hereditary Fijian leaders and modern leaders who are appointed and paid by either churches or government. We do a review with them of their style of leadership, and it is usually clear from the review that there is little or no consultation with those affected by the decisions (unless it be with a small group of cronies who are happy to agree with the leader).

A culture of silence hinders questioning from below but when we raise the question of exclusion of women and youth, we hear the standard answer that the women's place is in the kitchen and the youth are there to do as they are told. We avoid confrontation but point out that women and youth do most of the work to put the food on the table, so does it not follow that they should share in the decision making? Generally in the workshop with both types of leaders, traditional and modern, participants end up agreeing on what we are proposing.

However, once they go back to their communities change can be slow. It seems to me that the root problem in many cases is that the leaders are quite insecure. They have grown up with a way of doing things, a way that has never, in their memory, been seriously challenged. A fundamental framework of their lives is stability, not dynamic flexibility. In some cases participants return to their villages and share first at the clan level and may gradually work up to village level. This program got under way in 2002 and continues to this day. At this stage we have the top leadership in three provinces accepting change, which they are introducing gradually.

While I am at present chairperson of the board of SEEP I never go out with our teams to the rural communities as I am Indo-Fijian. All our grassroots workers are Fijian.

There is much to do at the grassroots level as in our rural communities there is little opportunity for personal development for youth or women. They are almost like unpaid workers. But, things are improving with ever more recognition of the importance of education for young people who want to move away from rural village life. Families are usually large, and the arable land is limited so many in each generation have to move out.

In 2009 we began a workshop with women and youth as we realized that we needed to do something to break down the culture of silence. At first it was a painful exercise for the women as they had never been asked to tell their stories. However, we could see that we were making progress, that leadership style in a number of cases was changing and so too was the mindset that underpinned the concentration of power style of leadership.

Having advanced in the leadership area, we began to tackle the land issue in 2008. For rural Fijians the land is their main resource, and so administering it intelligently for the benefit of all is an ongoing challenge. They are about to face the challenge of dealing intelligently with major mining companies who come with the backing of the government. For many years ethnic groups in many parts of the world have been doing this with varying degrees of success. We plan to continue developing our "See, Think & Act" approach for collective leadership as rural Fijians continue to work out what is best for them and their main resource— their land.

Link to our tradition:

Jesus empowers those with whom He has shared His life. He does not leave them lost and focused on the past:

When they had gathered together they asked him, "Lord, are you at this time going to restore the kingdom to Israel?" He answered them, "It is not for you to know the times or seasons that the Father has established by his own authority. But you will receive power when the Holy Spirit comes upon you, and you will be my witnesses in Jerusalem, throughout Judea and Samaria, and to the ends of the earth." (Acts 1, 6-8)

## Passion for Justice and Peace

By Columban Fr. Peter Woodruff

Columban Fr. Pat Cunningham and I traveled from the Columban house to Gimpo airport on the subway, a journey of an hour and fifteen minutes with just one change. On the flight south to Jeju City, I pushed Fr. Pat for clarification of the arguments against the building of the naval base on Jeju Island. I realized after a while that while I was attempting to address the matter with the dispassionate logic of one who is not involved in the struggle, Fr. Pat engaged in the conversation with both logic and passion. Where passion informs logic and vice versa homing in on the heart of an issue requires more than a merely logical perspective. I decided that I needed to get in touch with the passion of some of those involved in this struggle.

Protesters gathered before and after the Mass in the local peace center. We got off the bus that had brought us half way around the island from Jeju City and

Fr. Pat greeted people at the center and told me a little about each one. Meeting a few activists and being present at the regular open air Mass outside one of the gates of the naval base construction site, let me feel some of the passion driving activists opposed to this military project.

People committed to the cause sustain each other by being together at various kinds of protests. The rock that is being destroyed has a spiritual significance dating back centuries. Local people have not been able to enact their ancestral rites at the rock for five years.

Fr. Pat tells me that he comes away from sharing and celebrating at this place with a renewed energy. The religious services of various kinds keep alive the spirit. The services are not in competition with each other; rather, all serve to support those involved.

There was Regina Pyon who has for many years worked in organizations of the Catholic Church that promote human rights—the Justice and Peace Commission of the Bishops' Conference and the Catholic Human Rights Committee. She is also a member of an NGO (SPARK—Solidarity for Peace and Reunification in Korea) whose offices were raided early this year in connection with their support for the protest against the naval base construction in Jeju.

Regina told me about the "street priest," Fr. Mun Jong Hyen, who for over a year has been living in the village of Gangjeong to be in solidarity with the residents, the majority of whom do not want the naval base to go ahead. This priest now in his 70s, with his younger brother who is also a priest, is a member of a priests' organization committed to working for social justice. Both brothers have been involved in numerous justice issues over the years. When Fr. Mun moved to Jeju the local bishop gave him a motor scooter to help him get around.

A young auxiliary bishop from Kwangju led the concelebrated Mass with over 50 priests. Bishop Wok spoke of the state unleashing excessive state power to impose this naval base against the wishes of the locals. He recalled a previous occasion in 1948 when thousands of islanders were massacred by government forces, also using excessive power to crush a popular social protest against police abuse.

Protest marches by trade unionists, religious celebrations and protests by Buddhist, Catholic and Protestant groups, round the clock sit ins at the two main gates, swimmers and kayakers attempting to enter the port area from the sea, acts of civil disobedience, such as cutting through perimeter razor wire, a media team located in a center in the village to put the word out nationally and internationally, and more, all point to a powerful passion that urges men and women from Korea and other countries to join in the resistance to the construction of this naval base.

After the Mass, participants processed down to the harbor to the edge of the construction area where they were met by a phalanx of police and a barrier of police buses. Police are on duty around the clock outside the construction site. Many are mobilized to contain the protests. On this occasion the police came in at least twelve buses. Throughout the procession protesters sang and prayed; there was no violence.

Link to our tradition:

[Jesus] said to them, "Because of your little faith. Amen, I say to you, if you have faith the size of a mustard seed, you will say to this mountain, 'Move from here to there,' and it will move. Nothing will be impossible for you." (Matthew 17, 20)

## Organic and Sustainable Agriculture

### By Columban Fr. Brian Gore

### Background

We are promoting a program of subsistence farming in the parish of Oringao, the Philippines, where I worked from 1975 to 1984. I no longer work as parish priest but coordinate any parish related matters with the present parish council. We are doing now what we started many years ago when we had 56 communities spread around the hills of this mountain parish. In those days we were able to organize rallies of up to 10,000 community members determined to protest abuses by the military, government officials and landlords. We were seen by the Marcos regime as a threat to established power. Seldom before on Negros Island had the poor found a way to stand up to the wealthy and powerful.

In the early 1970s the price of sugar began to rise, prompting major sugar-cane growers to make a grab for more land by moving on the land of subsistence farmers around the foothills of the mountains. They would attempt to pick off the small farmers one by one by taking out an eviction order and having it enforced by the police or the military. However, on the day of the eviction each community in our parish would send up to 20 members who would join in the communal work on the farm affected. They created a festive atmosphere, despite the fear they felt, and the military did not know how to take on unarmed farmers. Our non-violent tactics together with the ability to convoke so many local residents to a rally constituted a power, which the military were not able to control. So, up to the highest echelons of government and military hierarchy, we were seen as a threat that had to be eliminated.

After Pope John Paul II's 1980 visit to the Philippines the establishment in Negros declared war on the Church. The Pope had said publicly: "The Church should never hesitate to be the voice of those who have no voice."

On March 10, 1982, the mayor of Kabankalan was ambushed and killed along with four others. At the time he was out on bail having being charged, along with the military, of the murder of seven farmers from our parish. In September of the same year Niall O'Brien RIP, Vicente Dangan RIP, six lay workers (Conrado Muhal RIP, Lydio Mangao, Peter Cuales, Geronimo Perez, Jesus Arzaga and Ernesto Tajones) and I were charged with the murder of the mayor and his four companions. We were jailed and later dubbed the Negros Nine by the then Senator Michael Tate during his visit to Negros. We were released 14 months later after the judge ruled that there was not enough evidence to convict. After the Negros Nine refused a pardon a deal was worked out that all charges were to be dropped against all of us and that Niall and I would leave the country within 30 days of being released. The six Filipino lay workers would be free to return to their families without reprisals.

President Marcos was defeated by Cory Aquino in the 1986 snap election but the new president was unable to control right wing elements in the military, who unleashed a reign of terror on the Christian communities involved in social issues. The army used para-military forces to destroy the networking and the non-violent power of the Christian communities. The U.S. had recently pulled out of the conflict in Vietnam and was frightened of losing their considerable military and economic influence in the Philippines.

Also, the bishops began to back a less confrontational form of Christian communities, which were not built on organizing around social issues. They called them basic ecclesial communities, which were less conflictive as they were built on the promotion of intra-ecclesial ministries with very little involvement in the social issues of the day.

## The Pastoral Challenge Today

In 2007 I renewed contact with people I was forced to say goodbye to in 1984. With parish workers and community members I was committed to a life giving mission that was thwarted for many years, and I am seeing what I can do to retake the basic thrust of our project even though the times and circumstances are quite different. However, the lot of the poor is maybe even worse than in the 1980s. Those of us involved with the rural communities today wish to ensure that the sacrifice of those who were martyred for their commitment to live their faith, proclaiming justice and protesting injustice, might neither be forgotten nor be in vain.

Generating large networks of communities committed to shaping a more just society is no longer a major thrust in the Church's pastoral ministry in the Philippines, which limits our engagement to a more supportive role. Consequently, we are putting our energy into the development of sustainable agricultural methods, a more efficient approach to marketing and the promotion of a producer/consumer cooperative. Of course there are still plenty of abuses and injustices and, in coordination with the local parish, we do what we can in that area. However, most of our energy is going into creating, with the communities, a viable way of remaining on the land. Otherwise thousands of small, subsistence farmers and their families will simply swell even more the poverty stricken squatter settlements on the fringes of our cities.

### Facing the Challenge of Making Subsistence Farming Viable

The cooperative is an essential part of our work with the farmers. No matter how efficient farming methods may be, without some control of the marketing of their produce, the small subsistence farmers cannot progress economically. They are forever squeezed by those in control of the marketing as they have no power to negotiate. Working together in marketing their produce is the only way for them to get ahead. Also, we hope that through the cooperative the various experimental agricultural projects of the Negros Nine Demo Farm will be replicated in the farms of its members.

I don't feel we are starting from scratch, because the parishioners do not forget what we worked on many years ago. Some of the young adults tell me that I married their parents. I am in a familiar place, but many faces are different. A new generation has grown up here with a different experience of life from that of their parents. Electricity, cell phones, internet and computers have all happened in this part of the world since I left in 1984. The basic Christian communities, which were at the heart of the diocesan pastoral program, are now one of many forms of Christian community supported by the diocese. The grassroots church has ceased to be seen as a place of formation for social engagement, but there are exceptions. So, in a sense, I am beginning anew.

There are now 53 communities in the parish, three of which were started since we came here in 2007 and seven of which surround our experimental farm and reforestation project. With financial support from Columban benefactors we bought land to start an experimental farm and are well on the way to showing results that should help local farmers improve their farming methods. We have also bought land above us on the mountain where we are maintaining the indigenous trees, shrubs, vines and grasses. Where necessary we have planted new trees as much of the forest had been destroyed by logging and slash and burn farming.

Our patch of forest protects the water catchment, and the spring that allows us to irrigate our farm and provides water for our nursery, the vermi-culture project, the fish pond, the vegetable garden, various animals and domestic purposes. We are experimenting with contour farming to control the erosion of the soil and rejuvenate the soil's fertility by crop rotation and various forms of composting.

The farming system of the traditional farmers is slash and burn, but that has led to soil erosion and degradation and so, over a period of forty to fifty years, the land has lost its productivity. Some farmers are forced to sell or lease their holdings. Then the land is planted with sugar-cane, which grows because the new owners have the capital to buy chemical fertilizer. The original owners and their children then have to look for a future in the cities. Due to their lack of resources many of their children cannot go to school and end up in even worse poverty. So, despite a variety of obstacles, we feel that we must make farming a viable option for the subsistence farmers of these hills. The alternative for them would be to move even further down the spiral of abject poverty.

Link to our tradition:

Deuteronomy 15, 11 states: "The land will never lack for needy persons; that is why I command you: 'Open your hand freely to your poor and to your needy kin in your land.'" Jesus of Nazareth reached out to the poor and needy; sometimes he fed them and often he healed and empowered them: One man was there who had been ill for thirty-eight years. When Jesus saw him lying there and knew that he had been ill for a long time, he said to him: "'Do you want to be well?' The sick man answered him, 'Sir, I have no one to put me into the pool when the water is stirred up; while I am on my way, someone else gets down there before me.' Jesus said to him, 'Rise, take up your mat, and walk.' Immediately the man became well, took up his mat, and walked." (John 5, 5-9)

## Rooted in the Earth

### By Columban Fr. Charles Rue

My "green" experience has been a step by step affair. Evangelization has been at the center of my life as a priest and a missionary, whether it has been running a parish, teaching liturgy or promoting social justice.

It all began on our family farm in Canowindra. I remember the childhood fun of running around the shearing shed, of being out with Dad in the paddocks or exploring the creek. I remember the curiosity aroused in me by my grandfather as we went around his rather large vegetable garden. As a youth, I was often on the tractor plowing at night. I can recall the aroma of the soil as it was turned over, and see—hear, really—the chatter of a myriad of stars. Twinkle is too weak a word to describe the experience. But the hard realities of sheep dying in the drought, and negotiations with the bank manager were also part of my farm experience. I was a member of the Junior Farmers Club where I had my first real taste of applied science. We learnt about documenting experiments, farm management and husbanding nature to get the desired outcomes in breeding.

As a priest in South Korea, unjust conditions in factories became my main concern. My farm experiences as a youth stayed in the background until the writings of fellow Columban priest Sean McDonagh revived them in the 1980s. From the Philippines, he wrote about the clear-fell logging of tropical forests and manipulative practices of the international agricultural-chemical companies. Along with many Columbans I became convinced about the link between environmental problems and social injustice, care for the poor, care for the land.

I was appointed to Australia to give feedback to the local church from churches overseas. My focus combined love of the YCW methodology, see-judge-act, with environmental campaigning. I started a group in Melbourne focused on transport but it failed. Members were more interested in using ecology for personal healing rather than in campaigning to change the way we live on earth.

Not wanting to be dismissed as a "do-gooder priest" if I talked environment, from 1988-90 I built on my Sheep and Wool studies as a youth to do a Masters in Environmental Planning at Macquarie University (Australia). Other students tried to hide their surprise at having a priest in their class. I gradually found out that many were Catholics and were pleased to have a priest among them taking their line of work seriously. With newfound skills, I asked for and gained a column, titled Greening the Gospel, in Sydney's Catholic Weekly during 1990.

After that I volunteered for the Columban mission team in Jamaica, where I joined the Royal Jamaican Conservation Society, which campaigned to preserve ocean reefs from over fishing and to create marine parks that gave an alternative living for the fishermen. In 1992 our parish celebrated 500 years since the first recorded European discovery of the Americas by Columbus. We built a Stations of the Cross in the church grounds. For Passion Sunday the text and songs we created focused on reconciliation with exploited former slaves and with the abused earth.

Returning to Australia in 2001, I submitted a doctoral thesis on the Columban contribution to the theory and practice of mission. One chapter focused on the role we played over three decades in making environmental concerns integral to preaching the Gospel within the local Australian church.

This role continued when Columbans helped the Australian bishops establish Catholic Earthcare Australia (CEA). In 2001 we hosted an initial exploratory meeting at North Turramurra. CEA was formally set up the following year and published a DVD, The Garden Planet. In 2005 CEA organized a Climate Change Conference in Canberra, and I was invited to write an initial draft which evolved into a statement endorsed by the Australian Catholic Bishops' Conference.

Columban Society leaders often set the agenda for local social action. In line with the World Council of Churches, Justice, Peace and the Integrity of Creation (JPIC) was the title given to such works. This title derives from the insight that one cannot be effectively addressed without reference to the others.

The mixed attitudes of Catholics towards the environment puzzled me, as the Catholic faith and the Church's social teaching offer a clear framework plus strong motivation for environmental work. Trinity, a dynamic communion of love, gives the basis for the communion of all things. Incarnation offers a theological basis for combining the material and the divine. Sacraments, beginning with Baptism, provide the ritual experience. Convinced of the need for further education in the area, in 2006 I wrote Catholics and Nature: Two hundred years of environmental attitudes in Australia.

I initiated an inter-faith group to work on environmental issues. Eleven faith groups participated in an initial meeting under the banner Wonder and the Will to Care. The science of ecology provided the common language and neutral space where disparate faith groups could dialogue. An ongoing group was formed called Faith and Ecology Network (FEN). It has held at least twice yearly gatherings ever since focusing on an aspect of ecological insight. In 2012 FEN set up its own website.

Convinced also that religiously motivated people needed to join with those with other motivations, I joined other environmental groups—NSW Nature Conservation foundation, Sydney Food Fairness Alliance, GM Free Australia—and cooperated with Gene Ethics, Friends of the Earth, Climate Institute's ARRCC, and Lock the Gate. I was privileged to meet many inspiring people in secular organizations, who added excitement to my ecological journey.

A JPIC campaign to expose the sinister side of biotech companies' plans was initiated worldwide in the early 2000s. These biotech conglomerates are anti-farmer in their manipulation of seed and chemical supplies, using international agreements and local patenting laws; anti-consumer, as they lobby to keep transgenic foods (GMOs) unlabeled and regulations lax; anti-health, in that the long-term effects of eating GMO derived foods are not publically researched; anti-nature, in that unplanned gene transfers threaten bio-diversity. I believe they aim to control the food chain, also the medical chain, through the manipulation of share prices, scientific research and government regulators.

In 2005 I commissioned a DVD to stimulate debate on the dangers of GMOs and biotech companies. Crop prices, labeling and health provided entry points. I called on the contacts I had made in the eastern states to do interviews with farmers, scientists and campaigners. We produced Unjust Genes—Life and Death for Sale. Often drawing on CEA contacts, or ecumenical groups such as the Earth Bible, I toured most Catholic dioceses on the east coast to sell the DVD and gave talks. Producing the DVD was costly, and these costs were not recouped.

Refocused on the climate change issue I wrote, Let the Son Shine, in 2009 and self-published 2000 copies. Again I traveled to dioceses on the east coast to give talks and sell the booklet, which resulted in JPIC making a profit. In 2013 an updated version of the booklet titled, Between Calamity and Hope, was made available online.

My environmental journey began as a social justice one but became a spiritual one. God looked different—God with skin on, as a child once said. I found God present in ever new ways. I reclaimed those experiences of nature in my earlier life as spiritual ones. I now like to say I belong along Emu Creek at Canowindra and believe I have some appreciation for what Aboriginal people feel about Country. I plan to be buried in Canowindra. Earth is now fixed in the dialogue of my missionary life.

I am ever grateful to the scientists who have shared their ecological insights convinced that they help reveal the face of God to us. I find courage in the example of committed environmentalists and the prophetic quality of their work. I find a source of prayer in taking a more humble posture towards the Earth and living within its wonder. I experience something of the mystery of God present in the natural world, and so I pray.

Link to our tradition

Certain elements of today's ecological crisis reveal its moral character. First among these is the indiscriminate application of advances in science and technology. Many recent discoveries have brought undeniable benefits to humanity. Indeed, they demonstrate the nobility of the human vocation to participate responsibly in God's creative action in the world. Unfortunately, it is now clear that the application of these discoveries in the fields of industry and agriculture have produced harmful long-term effects. This has led to the painful realization that we cannot interfere in one area of the ecosystem without paying due attention both to the consequences of such interference in other areas and to the well-being of future generations. (Message of Pope John Paul II, World Day of Peace, January 1, 1990, # 6)

# A Man Who Has Lived for His Family

By Columban Fr. Frank Ferrie

Redressing injustices perpetrated by the Korean State during a period of extreme social tension

The Korean peninsula has been a hotspot since the Soviet Union and the U.S. agreed to divide it after defeating and driving out the Japanese colonial administration in 1945. The Soviet Union imposed its system on the part to the north of the 38th parallel, while the U.S. imposed its system on the southern part. One result of this superpower agreement at the end of World War II has been a supersensitive attitude from both states to public expression of support for ideas and policies similar to or in some way leaning towards the ideas and policies of the other part of Korea.

In the south this led to the promulgation of laws aimed at protecting national security. Draconian national security laws were put in place during the presidency of Park Chung-hee (1961-79). These laws remain on the books but, in recent times, have not been applied as drastically as in the past. The following is the story of a man whose life was unjustly ruined by the harsh application of these laws during the period of the cruel Park dictatorship and his struggle to live and rehabilitate his name for the sake of his family.

Lorenzo worked as a civil servant in the municipality of his home town. He could speak and read both Japanese and Korean; he could read Chinese characters. These were skills that stood him in good stead in his job as records going back 200 years were written in these languages and their corresponding scripts. Prior to the Japanese colony, during the first half of the 19th century, Chinese was the official recording language in government offices. Then there was a period of Japanese and since 1945 Korean has been in use. Lorenzo did his job well and as a token of recognition he, along with other civil servants, was offered a trip to Japan, ostensibly to see how the Japanese run their civil service but in reality it was a junket.

Lorenzo's half-brother had been active in local Jeju politics and belonged to a party similar to a western labor political party, but he was not a communist. When he realized that the government was going to crack down on all dissent he left Jeju and went to Japan. However, his name and that of many more was put on a Korean government wanted list. Of course, no one in the family knew this so on arrival in Japan Lorenzo contacted his half-brother. Then on his return to Korea he was arrested for illicit association with a communist, and therefore an enemy of the state.

The national security law allowed the government to go ahead with a summary trial, sentence Lorenzo to thirteen years in prison, and deny him any right of appeal. Once in prison he was subjected to further torture to elicit more information. His health deteriorated, and he contemplated suicide. A relative in Kwangju (on the mainland), who was a Catholic priest teaching in the diocesan seminary, visited him regularly and persuaded him to live for his family and forget about suicide.

While he was in prison his wife had a mental breakdown. Lorenzo and his wife had five children. His wife was able to feed them from the farm, but it was his sister, Maria, who helped with their education and other support. She used her wages from her work with the Columbans.

On completing his prison sentence Lorenzo returned home to a great welcome. His fellow workers in the municipality recognized the injustice done to him, but they could not give him a job with all the benefits of a civil servant. Having been found guilty of a crime against the State and sentenced to prison he was no longer eligible for a government job. The municipality hired him informally to take on his old job and paid him out of a slush fund. Lorenzo's case is typical of many in Korea, and there are groups who are working towards redressing this situation. This is very important for Lorenzo as his immediate family is also denied access to a government job. He has to go through the legal process of rehabilitating his name.

This takes time and anyone in Lorenzo's position requires support. I know of two groups that are involved in this matter nationally: the Korean Association of Priests for Peace and Social Justice and a group of committed lawyers. The legal case is for compensation, which does not really concern Lorenzo, but the lawyers in charge of his case have to be paid. However, more importantly it's about restoring his name so that there is no longer any legal impediment preventing him or his immediate family members from taking a government job. Righting the wrong done to his family has kept Lorenzo going for so many years. It is a privilege to count him and his family as my friends.

Link to our tradition:

Doing what one feels to be right is not necessarily a guarantee of personal wellbeing. For Moses, on one occasion it was not but on a second it was:

"On one occasion, after Moses had grown up, when he had gone out to his kinsmen and witnessed their forced labor, he saw an Egyptian striking a Hebrew, one of his own kinsmen. Looking about and seeing no one, he struck down the

Egyptian and hid him in the sand. The next day he went out again, and now two Hebrews were fighting! So he asked the culprit, 'Why are you striking your companion?' But he replied, 'Who has appointed you ruler and judge over us? Are you thinking of killing me as you killed the Egyptian?' Then Moses became afraid and thought, 'The affair must certainly be known.' . . . Moses fled from Pharaoh and went to the land of Midian. There he sat down by a well. Now the priest of Midian had seven daughters, and they came to draw water and fill the troughs to water their father's flock. But shepherds came and drove them away. So Moses rose up in their defense and watered their flock. When they returned to their father Reuel, he said to them, 'How is it you have returned so soon today?' They answered, 'An Egyptian delivered us from the shepherds. He even drew water for us and watered the flock!' 'Where is he?' he asked his daughters. 'Why did you leave the man there? Invite him to have something to eat.' Moses agreed to stay with him, and the man gave Moses his daughter Zipporah in marriage." (Exodus 2, 11-21)

## Doing Christianity

### By Columban Fr. Bob Brennan

Campaigning for housing rights of urban poor in Seoul

When I first arrived in Seoul, three million people lived here. By 1980 there were twelve million residents. Rural families hoped to find a better future in the big city, at least for the children via education and possibly business. The rural to city migration created massive problems as regards housing, transport and employment. I wish to describe briefly how the poorest of the rural migrants fared in the scramble for housing and the role of the local Church in seeking justice for these people.

Many hills ring the city of Seoul. The city owned the land, but with no one using it, poor families needing housing moved in, built their homes on the slopes but never acquired legal title to the land. In the late 1970s the city began to implement a policy of redeveloping the illegally occupied land on the sides of the hills and along some riverbanks. The injustice they planned to perpetrate was to remove thousands of poor families from their homes without due compensation.

They dealt with the matter piecemeal and in 1982 arrived at the place where I was parish priest. Residents had already been violently dislodged from other slum areas and had begun to organize and protest the city's policy of redevelopment. Our area was next to go. This was in preparation for the 1988 Olympic Games due to be held in Seoul.

Local leaders approached me to ask for the use of the church for meetings as there was no other place large enough. About 50 leaders representing a few thousand residents began to meet. My only role at the time was to be present and offer support. In due course the church would also become a place of refuge for protest leaders being sought by the police who would not enter the church to arrest them but surrounded the building in order to capture them as they left. Despite protests the government achieved their objective and those who lost their homes received little or no compensation

Six years later I was living and working on a hillside in another part of Seoul. Private companies engaged by the city to clear slums and rebuild multi-story apartment blocks employed a variety of nasty tactics to wear down residents. Many families left one by one for a variety of reasons, such as fear, the shame of the children who felt they could not invite their friends to their home, the accumulation of rubbish as houses were left vacant, etc. When it came for the moment of the definitive eviction gangs of thugs entered the area accompanied by bulldozers. As soon as the thugs had dragged family members from their home the bulldozers flattened the house. Over a 20 year period, my home was bulldozed four times.

However, the residents' organizations gradually won the right to various kinds of compensation, but this more comprehensive approach to residents' rights was not legally finalized until the year 2000. Some residents owned their houses, but most were renting and the economic loss incurred by both groups was eventually acknowledged and compensated, at least in part. It was a long struggle and even though the so called slum clearance has now finished there is still much to be done in the housing apostolate. To develop this pastoral outreach in a coordinated way, in 1987, Cardinal Kim, Archbishop of Seoul, set up the City Poor Apostolate.

A North American Jesuit and university lecturer, John Daly, with a Korean layman, who was a bricklayer, initiated the work of church solidarity with slum residents seeking their rights. Subsequently, other Jesuits, Columbans, Franciscan Missionaries of Mary and lay people joined the struggle and continue to organize under the umbrella of the City Poor Apostolate.

Locally we might organize ecumenically as was the case in my second hillside parish, where I collaborated with the local Presbyterian minister and residents. The minister called a meeting in his church where we elected a coordinating committee. I was elected to carry out and present a monthly audit of our funds.

There were four neighboring areas that were similarly affected by the city's redevelopment plans at the time, each with its own internal organization. In two of the four areas the construction company's pressure tactics resulted in all the residents leaving before demolition of their homes. In the other two areas we organized successfully for a compensation fund (in the case of our area, $700,000) to build temporary housing further up the hill at the back of the construction site. However, in our area, by the time we were ready to relocate, only 50 out of 170 families were still living in the area zoned for redevelopment.

We thought we would be in temporary housing for about three years, but it turned out to be five. There the 50 families worked at community development. We developed a friendly village-like spirit among residents. We set up a credit union and ran courses on human rights. We helped residents grow in confidence and in their ability to grip the reins of their lives and not be pushed around by bullies, whether they be employees of government or big business.

After more than 20 years involvement in City Poor Apostolate one thing remains clear. For all the changes in society over these years, "the poor we still have with us," and will have for the foreseeable future. Presently I am living and working in a small community of such people.

My involvement with these people gives me a feeling of doing what the Gospel proclaims. Together with others, what we live and do gives witness to our faith in Christ. Our involvement makes it clear to others that the Church is not simply about prayer and religious celebrations. Our neighbors and others can see that we of the Church are interested in the issues that affect their lives.

Link to our tradition:

Following a Synod of Bishops on the topic of Justice in the World, Pope Paul VI in 1971 published a challenging document on the topic. One key statement in the document (Paragraph 6) reminds us of our Christian duty in the face of injustice: "Action on behalf of justice and participation in the transformation of the world fully appear to us as a constitutive dimension of the preaching of the Gospel, or, in other words, of the Church's mission for the redemption of the human race and its liberation from every oppressive situation." Clearly, such action is not an optional extra!

## Awards All Round

### By Columban Fr. Alo Connaughton

#### A Permanent Visa?

People who work "on the missions" are very familiar with the inside of visa departments for "foreign nationals." Korea is one of the better places so, last year, New Zealand Columban Fr. Bob Brennan decided to apply for a permanent residence permit, an item which is these days, finally, being made available to non-Koreans. After 47 years in the country he thought he stood a fair chance. The lady in the office was a bit officious—long-term visas aren't there just for the asking. Could he produce any evidence, religious duties aside, why he might merit it?

#### Working for Justice

When he mentioned this setback in the area of Seoul where he works the local community decided to provide the missing evidence—and even suggested that he should be awarded a prize. There was indeed plenty of material—but was it the right stuff? Would official eyebrows be raised at the mention of his activities during twelve years in the diocese of Wonju? The Bishop, Daniel Tji, was a courageous defender of poorer people. It was a time of the military dictatorship of Park Chung Hee, father of Korea's recently-elected female president. Economic development was taking place, but at a price. Movements for a freer society were ruthlessly crushed; workers were exploited in factories; arrests, torture and disappearances were common. The Bishop, because of his support for the struggles of his people was framed, arrested and accused of treason. A group of people had already been detained and accused of being North Korean collaborators. Seven of them were tried and executed. The bishop was accused of giving them financial support; he got a 15-year prison sentence. All priests and religious in the diocese were drawn into the conflict and treated with suspicion. Bob's two-year visa was now reduced to a four-week one, dependent on the will of the government ministry. They were difficult times. Many years later the "collaborators" got a new trial and were completely cleared. They were simply a group campaigning for justice.

### Living Among the Poor

In the early 1980s the rural population was moving to the cities. At the same time, Columban policy changed; a presence among the people in the poor areas around Seoul was now seen as a more urgent priority. The recent arrivals had lost their rural roots and needed help to create new supportive communities. Fr. Bob was assigned to Mok Dong in the southwest area of Seoul; a place that was, as yet, surrounded by rice fields. A small river of highly-polluted water from the nearby factories ran through the area and along its banks were thousands of squatters who had been evicted from the city center. Originally most of them were victims of the Korean War (1950-1954). Korea's joy at hearing that it had been awarded the 1988 Olympics was bad news in the riverside shacks. The city authorities decided that the new highway from the main airport to the city center would be built through the area and that the eyes of the visitors should not be offended by ugly slums. The parish priest was drawn into the wars again as he supported the people in their fight to have a place to call home. Over two-thirds of Catholics in the parish were from the squatter area. Visits and strong words of warning from police and other officials were frequent.

### Fighting for Property Rights

After a six-year stint (1985-91) as rector of the Columban seminary in Seoul Fr. Bob was appointed to another area north of the city, where poor people lived, but again, without property rights. Powerful construction companies were coming in, demolishing houses and building high-rise apartments. The pattern was familiar. Once again the people fought for a place to live and resisted eviction. As years passed and campaigns continued the official attitude slowly changed. Builders of luxury apartments were finally obliged by law to include flats with affordable rents for local people in their projects. Later other new laws favorable to poorer people were passed.

Official Recognition

How would all this activity appear to official eyes looking at a curriculum vitae sent to the immigration department as a backup letter for a permanent residence permit? The letter was submitted and to Fr. Bob's surprise a reply came back much sooner than expected. A first letter notified him that he was among those awarded a prize for his contribution to the welfare of people in Seoul. A second letter informed him that, of the ten recipients in 2012, he would receive the Grand Prize, the Number One, so to speak. Then came an announcement that he had been approved for honorary citizenship of the city—an honor conferred by the Mayor of Seoul, Park Won-soon, at a luncheon in October 2012. In November the Korean Ecological Foundation awarded him a prize "for making the world a brighter place." A television program about his work was screened several times on a national station in January. As his theme song for 2013 he might well choose a song of that other Bob—Bob Dylan—"The Times They Are a-Changin'."

Link to our tradition:

We have to move from our devotion to independence, through an understanding of interdependence, to a commitment to human solidarity. That challenge must find its realization in the kind of community we build among us. Love implies concern for all—especially the poor—and a continued search for those social and economic structures that permit everyone to share in a community that is a part of a redeemed creation. (Romans 8, 21-23) (*Economic Justice for All*, Pastoral Letter on Catholic Social Teaching and the U.S. Economy, 1986, United States Catholic Bishops #365)

# Questioning Voices in South Korea

By Columban Fr. Peter Woodruff

Reflections on a democratic state that fails to include the full political spectrum

During my five week visit to South Korea to gather material for Columban mission magazines I scoured the English version of the daily newspapers in an attempt to understand the local political scenario. I asked fellow Columbans about the policy difference between the major parties, and it soon became clear that left of center did not exist. South Korea's conflict with communist North Korea has engendered a fear of and resistance to any public political discourse that even hints at mildly socialist policies. Consequently, those who may disagree with the present economic model of development have little impact of the direction of the country. However, all seems to be calm for now as economic growth continues to open up opportunities for most sectors of the workforce.

But there were also signs of concerns simmering below the surface. I heard about the protests against the construction of a naval base on the south side of

Jeju Island. I accompanied Fr. Thomas Nam, a Korean Columban with whom I had worked in Peru, to a demonstration of protest outside the Samsung headquarters in downtown Seoul. A few priests led a concelebrated Mass on the footpath, where about 60 men and women, holding lighted candles, joined in with prayer and song. A branch of Samsung Heavy Industries has the main contract to build the new naval base.

The average South Korean supports security measures against any attempted incursion from North Korea and welcomes the backing of U.S. military forces in this regard. However, many might question (if they felt free to do so publicly) building military installations whose primary purpose seems to be supporting U.S. military strategy to contain an expanding China. They would maintain that the better course for Korea would be neutrality when it comes to choosing a position between rising and declining superpowers.

With such thoughts in mind I flew from Seoul to Jeju City with Columban Fr. Pat Cunningham who is heavily involved in the campaign protesting the construction of a naval base on the south side of the island. I had been advised that since this South Korean government project was set in motion in 2007, there had been protests from many quarters, especially from residents of Jeju Island. They feel imposed upon by the central government, and they don't want their island to become a military target, which is what it will be in an international conflict once the naval base is operational. Many residents and anti-base activists from the Korean mainland see the naval base as a future outpost for the United States Navy to project its power against China.

Then I heard that the local Catholic Bishop, Peter Kang, has spoken against the base project since it was first proposed by the central government. Recently he said at a public meeting: "The central government has recognized the administrative autonomy and independence of Jeju Special Self-Governing Province. It is unacceptable for them to simply disregard it when the governor, provincial council head, and even the provincial ruling and opposition party chairs have expressed the view that we should hold off for now on the construction to ensure a fair re-examination." The bishop continued, "The government is acting like it hasn't heard and is going ahead with what it's calling a 'national project' but the argument that a project is justified simply because the state is carrying it out is something you would have expected in the era of totalitarianism. In a democratic government, you can even stop or turn back on a national project you've started if there is resistance from citizens or objections from a lot of people."[11]

Priests, Sisters, laity and some bishops are standing in solidarity with a broader national and international campaign to stop the construction of the Jeju naval base. The Catholic Church has respect within Korean society as it has been seen

---

[11]    Catholic bishop reflects on the tumultuous story of Jeju By Huh Ho-joon, Jeju

to stand with the people in times of crisis and hardship, especially since World War II and the Japanese colonial occupation. Bishop Kang argues on the basis of inadequate consultation of residents most affected by the base project, and it is this basic lack of respect for the people of the island that resonates with many island families, who only 60 years ago suffered at the hands of outsiders who decimated the population.

Political conflict between left and right led to vicious slaughter of about 29,000 islanders, mostly from poor rural villages in the center of the island. In the name of national security villages were wiped out and the population that survived was moved to towns close to the coast. From 1948 to 1951 Cold War politics were played out on the island as the U.S. and the former Soviet Union moved into a phase of deadly but not openly armed conflict, fostered by a spirit of mutual mistrust and superpower brinkmanship. The Korean War left over three million Koreans dead and a people was left divided along lines of political ideology. A long term consequence has been the lack of genuine political process and an unwillingness to work with all shades of political opinion. All this has left deep scars in the psyche of many island families and for that matter of Koreans the length and breadth of the peninsula.

Divisions were similarly reinforced in Gwangju in the south west of the Korean peninsula in 1981 when the military were ordered to viciously put down a student rebellion. Two generals responsible for the overkill were eventually tried and convicted of the crimes committed. However, the national political discourse has as yet not found a way to integrate the whole political spectrum. Laws are still in place that would allow the government to deny basic human rights in the name of national security and conduct police-state style investigations and trials. Those who dare to see events and policies from a perspective left of center must continue to be cautious about how they express themselves. In fact, democracy seems to be very much a political project rather than a reality of the body politic of South Korea.

Link to our tradition:

We may be tempted to allow fear not love govern our approach to complex social challenges. "Christian love of neighbor and justice cannot be separated. For love implies an absolute demand for justice, namely, recognition of the dignity and rights of one's neighbor. Justice attains its inner fullness only in love. Because every person is truly a visible image of the invisible God and a brother or sister of Christ, the Christian finds in every person God himself and God's absolute demand for justice and love." (Pope Paul VI, Justice in the World, 1971, No. 34.)

## Beacons of Hope

By Columban Fr. Bobby Gilmore

Sometime after returning from Jamaica I ran into a friend in Dublin, Ireland, whom I hadn't met for a number of years. His greeting was, "You still in London?" I replied that I had left London eleven years ago. Then he said, 'Where are you now?" Jokingly, I replied, "Here in front of you." Assigning particular spaces to people is a common mental tactic that facilitates daily interactions.

But in modern Europe it has much more sinister overtones, particularly in relation to foreigners and outsiders. When Europeans see people of difference on their high streets, generally, they see them as out of place even if they are nationals of countries in which European colonists did not see themselves as out of place while residing there. This European attitude is the basis of institutional racism that permeates European society. This attitude also prompted me, together with few collaborators, to establish The Migrant Rights Centre Ireland in 2000. We believe that our efforts are sowing a seed of justice that will bear fruit beyond our immediate focus. Undocumented immigrants who are helped towards regularization by immigrant agencies carry with them an appreciation of the support they received and are more prepared to be active in seeking justice and equality for others. The God of the Bible pitched His tent with those who were excluded, vulnerable and outsiders. It is with those that the Strategic Plan of the Migrant Rights Center directs its resources.

The Jamaican poet, Grace Nichols, writes of a Jamaican woman immigrant, undocumented and separated from her children.

A crisis of papers unfixed,
> Two jobs as a domestic
> And weathering the cold,
> The barrel in her kitchen-corner
> A ship's hold, constantly
> Waiting to be filled-
> This time with bargain clothes,
> Employers' cast-offs
> For the children back home.
> The children waiting for her
To find a survival-kit
> That would lead to citizenship.
> Waiting for her to clear
A sky of fog, a path of snow,
> So that they could follow.

When we opened the Migrant Rights Center in Dublin the first callers were undocumented immigrants. They were people who had been invited through the work permit system to come to work in Ireland. But due to a variety of reasons they had fallen out of the system. They were left with no option but to return home or be returned by the agency that brought them to Ireland under the auspices of government policy. At that time the immigration department of the Irish government had no mechanism to rectify this situation. The work permit holder was tied to the employer who held the permit. Immigration department officials, though sympathetic, were hidebound as to solutions. Thus began a campaign by the Migrant Rights Center to prevent an immigrant becoming undocumented.

Irish government ministers saw no contradiction in lobbying the United States government to have Irish over-stayers regularized. So, the Migrant Rights Center began to make comparisons between undocumented at home and away. Government officials kept up the mantra; "We don't do amnesty." Our reply was: "We are not seeking amnesty; our clients have broken no law." They were confused and had to negotiate.

After World War II, Europe sought sources of cheap labor and deployed the "guest worker system." The thinking underpinning the system was: import workers, not people, for as long as they are needed and then dispose of them. The guest worker system precluded the possibility of settlement, family reunification, health, education, welfare, holiday and other allowances.

Immigrants in the guest worker systems began to organize themselves and use the emerging rights legislation to seek rights of residency, marriage, family reunification, education, health and other benefits that the indigenous population had access to. Leaders of industry in which these guest workers were employed began to highlight the difficulties they were experiencing. They had invested in the training and skilling of these guest workers but were having to send them home after a few years in order to fulfill government regulation. Gradually, government lobbying by industry brought about changes in regulation regarding residency, family reunification and other rights.

In the past, post-colonial governments pretended to be embarrassed when they failed to give their people the quality of life promised by independence. Now, these same governments unashamedly prepare, promote and export their people as commodities. The people trade is most lucrative for governments and private recruiting agencies. What has emerged is a new slave trade, which returns remittances to their countries of origin totaling up to $250 billion per year.

Recently, MRCI has worked closely with Mohammed Younis[12] who is from a small village in Pakistan. He is married with nine children; all now aged over 15 years. He has worked in different jobs and different countries in order to provide

---

[12]    For further information visit: *http://www.mrci.ie/our-work/forced-labour-trafficking/*

for his family. He worked as a chef in the army for many years; he opened up a small grocery shop in his local area and he also migrated to Dubai to work as a laborer. In 2002, Mr. Younnis was asked by his cousin to come to Ireland to work for him as a tandoori chef. Mohammed Younnis was told he would come to work under work permit conditions and that this would be renewed for the duration of his time in Ireland. He came to work in Ireland in 2002 so that he could earn money and send remittances back to his family.

Unfortunately, he found himself in modern day slavery, deceived and coerced by unscrupulous employers. This is a growing problem in Ireland and globally. Over the last six years MRCI has dealt with some 180 cases, which is only the tip of the iceberg. Forced labor occurs mainly in unregulated, low-paid employment.

Mohammed Younnis' employer failed to renew his permit which left him undocumented in Ireland. For many years he was paid 55 cent per hour, received no day off, no holidays, his passport was withheld, and he was threatened by his employer. Any money that he earned he sent back to his family. He was merely existing and not living. He felt many times that he was living in "a deep black hole" with no way out of the situation. Other workers and the MRCI helped Mohammed Younnis leave his employment and assisted him in taking a case for non-payment of his full wages to the employment courts. He was awarded €92,000 by the Labor Court in compensation for years of severe exploitation.

Unfortunately, Mohammed has not yet received a penny of this. His ex-employer took the matter to the High Court that ruled in favor of the employer, arguing that Mohammed as an undocumented worker cannot seek redress under labor law as the employment contract has no legal standing. Mohammed is appealing this ruling to the Supreme Court.

Mohammed Younnis is one of the key leaders who worked on the Forced Labor Action Campaign with Migrant Rights Center Ireland to criminalize modern day slavery in Ireland. He took on this role so that other workers would not have to suffer like he did.

Maybe migrants will give Europe a heart!

> "Beyond workers we need to speak to every person;
> Beyond individuals, we need to respect the family;

And beyond rights, the dignity of each human being,

> Migrant or citizen, working or not.

Globalisation will only be fair, and work decent

> If rather than allowing workers to be destroyed, thrown away,
> We raise our structures, our laws, our leaders and ourselves fully
> And unrelentingly to the calling of human dignity."[13]

---

[13]   John K. Bingham, ILO Forum on Decent Work, 2002.

Link to our tradition:

The seventh commandment forbids acts or enterprises that for any reason—selfish or ideological, commercial, or totalitarian—lead to the enslavement of human beings, to their being bought, sold and exchanged like merchandise, in disregard for their personal dignity. It is a sin against the dignity of persons and their fundamental rights to reduce them by violence to their productive value or to a source of profit. St. Paul directed a Christian master to treat his Christian slave "no longer as a slave but more than a slave, as a beloved brother, . . . both in the flesh and in the Lord." (The Catechism of the Catholic Church, 1993, #2414)

The Apostle, Paul, writes to his friend, Onesimus, about Philemon, a slave of Onesimus:

Perhaps this is why he was away from you for a while, that you might have him back forever, no longer as a slave but more than a slave, a brother, beloved especially to me, but even more so to you, as a man and in the Lord. So if you regard me as a partner, welcome him as you would me. (Philemon 1, 15-17)

## Climate Change Campaign

### By Ellen Teague

Ellen Teague has worked with the Columban UK JPIC Team for the past 22 years.

### My Own Beginnings

One conversation stands out for me from the time I spent as a young lay missionary in the northern Nigerian city of Kaduna 30 years ago. Over a beer one night, an elderly neighbor, Baba Kofi, was asked about the changes he had seen in the city. "You know, when I first came to this place it was just a few houses in a forest clearing, and I could hear the hyenas and other wildlife at night" he said. I could hardly believe there had once been a forest in a region which was now so dry and desert-like. Within one person's lifetime, the settlement from which people walked into the forest to meet their daily needs for food had become a vast city of several million people teeming with shanty-towns. It was that conversation that began my interest in the links between development and environment.

### Renewing the Earth

It was around five years later that I recalled that conversation again. Based in London, I was now the campaign coordinator for the Renewing the Earth campaign of CAFOD, the Catholic development agency in England and Wales. Columban Fr. Seán McDonagh had been brought in as a consultant. The issue of global warming had been treated in his recently published book *To Care for the*

*Earth*, and the Irish missionary with twenty years of experience in the Philippines urged that climate change should be one of the key campaign issues.

Drought and disruption of food patterns had been a significant factor in the 1984 Ethiopian famine, but climate change was not being taken seriously. Despite a growing number of scientists suggesting that humans were having an impact on the global climate, most people refused to believe it. Another two decades would pass before CAFOD and other Catholic agencies featured climate change in their campaigns.

## Columban JPIC

However, the Columban Justice, Peace and the Integrity of Creation (JPIC) network, backed by the expertise of Fr. Seán McDonagh, had been lobbying all that time, from the mid 1980s. These are dedicated JPIC Columban teams in the sixteen regions where Columbans are based. They were warning about climate change for twenty years before the scientific consensus finally proved that it was happening. At a JPIC gathering in Manila in 2007, Columbans in China and Korea warned of the increasing quantities of dust as the Gobi Desert spread and expanded due to global warning. Those from Peru reported that 22% of Peru's tropical glaciers had melted away in the previous 25 years. The meltwater from those glaciers provide the water supply for major urban centers like Lima.

## Climate Change Campaign

Climate change has been one of our five primary objectives of Columban JPIC in Britain for some years, along with Water, Migration, Mining and the Patenting of Life. Our team in Britain, Columban Frs. Peter Hughes and Frank Nally and myself have spent a significant amount of time on it. We have planned and supported a religious lobby of Parliament on climate change. "The Wave" demonstration, in December 2009, brought 60,000 marchers onto London's streets demanding action at the Copenhagen Climate Summit. In advance of that march, there was a service attended by 2,500 Christians which the Columbans helped to organize. We now support the annual climate service and march in London every December. Our strategy has led us to take every opportunity to join with others. We played our part in the lobby of the UK Government to introduce the world's first Climate Act and establish a Green Climate Fund through our web work, printed materials and advocacy. We promoted an internet lobby of British MPs ahead of the Rio+20 Earth Summit in June 2012, asking them to sign up to the Rio-UK Declaration ". . . that the UK should lead the world in the transition to a fair and green economy, reduce greenhouse emissions and protect biodiversity."

## Advocacy Work

Two weeks before Rio+20 in Brazil, we promoted and attended a meeting with Caroline Spelman MP, Secretary of State for the Environment, Britain's representative at Rio. She acknowledged that the Churches had an important role in advocacy work on behalf of sustainable development. Religious leaders and agencies in Britain used Ash Wednesday of last year to call all Christians to repent for the "shrug culture" existing towards climate change and Operation Noah, a Christian climate change lobby, released its Ash Wednesday Declaration.

I find that exciting and challenging initiatives are to be found in the alliances we have formed with other Christian denominations and with secular agencies, plus the contacts we are building up with social media.

Link to our tradition:

God also said: See, I give you every seed-bearing plant on all the earth and every tree that has seed-bearing fruit on it to be your food; and to all the wild animals, all the birds of the air, and all the living creatures that crawl on the earth, I give all the green plants for food . . . . God looked at everything he had made, and found it very good. (Genesis 1, 29-31)

For creation awaits with eager expectation the revelation of the children of God; for creation was made subject to futility, not of its own accord but because of the one who subjected it, in hope that creation itself would be set free from slavery to corruption and share in the glorious freedom of the children of God. We know that all creation is groaning in labor pains even until now; and not only that, but we ourselves, who have the first fruits of the Spirit, we also groan within ourselves as we wait for adoption, the redemption of our bodies. For in hope we were saved. Now hope that sees for itself is not hope. For who hopes for what one sees? But if we hope for what we do not see, we wait with endurance. (Romans 8, 19-25)

## Solidarity with the Poor on His Own Turf

By Columban Fr. Bill Morton

Ruben Garcia, a native of El Paso, Texas, has dedicated his life to serving
undocumented migrants and asylum seekers

Since arriving in the U.S./Mexico border area of El Paso, Texas, and Ciudad Juárez, Mexico, I have been inspired by Ruben Garcia, a native of El Paso who is now in his mid-sixties. Ruben talks about growing up with friends and family on both sides of the border. They crisscrossed the border with ease and spoke English and Spanish from childhood. Today border crossing from the U.S. to Mexico continues to be easy but from Mexico to U.S. control is strict. Despite the best efforts of a high fence, constant border patrols and vigilant passport checks, many undocumented migrants find a way to cross.

After finishing high school Ruben went to the Jesuit run Rockhurst College in Kansas City and subsequently studied theology at Gonzaga University in Seattle.

He then returned to El Paso to take up the post of coordinator of the diocesan youth ministry.

One of the highlights of this period for Ruben was the visit of Mother Teresa of Calcutta in 1976 to address a congress of 5,000 youth who had been brought together by the diocesan youth ministry. When Ruben consulted with his team about who might be the keynote speaker at the diocesan youth congress they urged that he invite Mother Teresa. Two international phone calls later Mother Teresa had accepted the invitation.

Her visit had a major impact on his search for a way in life. He spoke to her about going to India to work among the poor, but she told him that his work would be with the poor in the U.S./Mexico border area.

Subsequently, for about a year he and a few friends of around the same age met regularly to discuss, discern and pray about what might be for them a meaningful path in life. They concluded that the poor were the key to their search, so Ruben asked the bishop for the use of part of a building that had been vacated. However, along with the request was the condition that the bishop not interfere with whatever he and the group might decide to do.

The bishop agreed and in 1978, Ruben with four friends moved into what would become the first part of the Annunciation House project (set up to announce the Good News to the poor). Ruben and his friends were still discerning; they were not sure what they would do. They were in part of a building, located a few blocks from the city center. The building had been used for Catholic Church services for many years, so was known as a place where needy people might find assistance of some kind.

On the evening of the day Ruben and his friends moved in two men from Central America knocked and asked for shelter. When asked why they had not gone to the known shelters for the homeless, they explained that they had no documentation, a requirement for entry into the regular shelters at that time. That moment marked the end of the initial discernment process. Ruben and his friends decided they were called to give shelter to the undocumented.

Ruben continues to work as director of Annunciation House, which has evolved constantly in response to the needs of undocumented migrants and in more recent times to asylum seekers. He was recently awarded the 2012 Teacher of Peace Award from Pax Christi U.S.A., a national Catholic peace organization. His strength lies in his personal integrity and his deep commitment to work with others towards a compassionate society. All of us who are in any way associated with him know that we have so much to do; we are a long way from being a compassionate society.

Ruben often says, "Hospitality is not something that we do; it is who we are." He also insists that everyone should "have a place at the table." Annunciation House has always been financed by private no strings attached donations. The project has never allowed itself to become dependent on any government or corporate support.

For me, it has been a privilege and a joy to collaborate with Ruben and his team at Annunciation House. In fact, I have been on the project's board of directors for the past five years. Ruben has been a keynote speaker at our annual Companions on Mission meeting.

Our Columban Border Team coordinates exposure programs with Annunciation House, focusing on undocumented immigrants, asylum seekers, violence in Juárez, drug use and drug trade, the exploitative system of the *maquilas* (free trade zone factories on the Mexican side of the border that pay Mexican workers low wages—about $50 a month). We collaborate closely in developing programs of border awareness education in the light of Catholic social teaching (one of our best kept secrets). We attempt to leave our visitors with the question: "How can I stand with the poor where I live?"

Link to our tradition:

No doubt Jesus is there at our side in the poor but do we recognize him? Ponder Luke 24, 13-31: "Now that very day two of them were going to a village seven miles from Jerusalem called Emmaus, and they were conversing about all the things that had occurred. And it happened that while they were conversing and debating, Jesus himself drew near and walked with them, but their eyes were prevented from recognizing him . . . . beginning with Moses and all the prophets, he interpreted to them what referred to him in all the scriptures. As they approached the village to which they were going, . . . they urged him, 'Stay with us, for it is nearly evening and the day is almost over.' So he went in to stay with them . . . . while he was with them at table, he took bread, said the blessing, broke it, and gave it to them. With that their eyes were opened and they recognized him, but he vanished from their sight."

## La Monja

By Guadalupe Perez, friend of Columban Fr. Kevin Mullins, who lives in Juárez, Mexico.

Two months ago *Los Federales* (the Federal Police) broke into our house and arrested my youngest brother. First, they accused him of stealing an auto, then later of exporting arms and finally of importing arms. Instead of protecting us they do us harm. This was the third time *Los Federales* had broken into our home at night. On the first and second occasion they simply came to rob and destroy.

They came by night and forced in the door, entered without a warrant, destroyed much of our furniture, physically attacked the men of our family and insulted the women. Then they took what they thought they might use or sell.

They act this way in many parts of Juárez, and residents are afraid to protest. The police abuse their authority with impunity, and no officer admits to being in charge of the operation.

After the second police incursion into our homes (our extended family lives in seven adjacent houses on one block of our barrio; other neighbors were treated the same way) I denounced publicly and judicially what they had done. After that the police came and took my brother away.

My brother was in prison for three days where he was tortured with electricity and other methods that left him traumatized. He is afraid to open the door of the house when someone knocks and has an incredible fear of the police. Yet he is determined to meet them face to face and say what they did to him. Despite their intimidation he will not give in; he is only 18 years old.

Our initial reaction to the police abuse was fear. Some neighbors left the area. We also thought of leaving. We did not know how we might effectively protest against the state. We know that the police and other state institutions, such as the judiciary, are together in this. They look out for the well-being of each other, not that of the citizens.

Initially we made no progress with our case against the police. We were merely forced to deal with more abuse as they arrested, accused and tortured my young brother. So, we organized a public protest with placards outside the law courts. I have a large extended family and a few neighbors also joined us even though many were afraid to join with us. Still it was an important step, and we got coverage in the press.

I suppose the police never expected us to push ahead with the protest and, even though we live in hope, have much faith in God and find lots of support in our Church community, we cannot be sure that our protest will prosper. The matter is being dealt with by the judiciary. The police case hinges on their assertion that they arrested my brother with a gang in another part of town. We maintain that they took him from our home. Each side must present evidence to the court, which is due to hear our case soon.

I feel that God is with me in this struggle in a variety of ways. My husband, Juan, is like a rock. He does not talk much but I feel such strength knowing that he is with me. After the second police incursion into our home, Columban Fr. Kevin sent me to a diocesan human rights course where I learnt about our rights and what we might do to protect them. In fact, while I was participating in the workshop on human rights, I decided to organize the public protest in front of the law courts. I also met men and women from other parishes in Juárez who encouraged me and promised support in our struggle.

Economically our family has suffered; my father lost his job as he was frequently absent from work attending to my young brother's case. However, as time has passed we have found ever more support in our community and in our Church. I really feel that God is with us.

I don't have any special qualifications, nor does my husband. As well as driving a truck he can fix anything, so he is always ready to give a hand around the house and also in our chapel of San Juan Bautista. We have four children and one granddaughter. I look after the home while my husband earns the money necessary to keep our family. We came together as a couple fifteen years ago and then five years ago were married in the Church. I have always been very religious but only since we have had this trouble with the police abuse have other family members begun to take an interest in our Catholic faith. They ask me about the rosary, the Bible and many other things as they find ways of making our faith their own. My family has always nicknamed me *la monja*, the nun.

Link to our tradition:

Guadalupe found a way to counter injustice thanks to her faith in God, family support, especially her husband, and Christian community solidarity. St. Paul faced the hardships of his mission in a similar fashion: "We had been there several days when a prophet named Agabus came down from Judea. He came up to us, took Paul's belt, bound his own feet and hands with it, and said, 'Thus says the Holy Spirit: This is the way the Jews will bind the owner of this belt in Jerusalem, and they will hand him over to the Gentiles.' When we heard this, we and the local residents begged him not to go up to Jerusalem. Then Paul replied, 'What are you doing, weeping and breaking my heart? I am prepared not only to be bound but even to die in Jerusalem for the name of the Lord Jesus.' Since he would not be dissuaded we let the matter rest, saying, 'The Lord's will be done.'" (Acts 21, 10-14)

## Human Trafficking in the Philippines

### By Jerome Seballos

I work with the Negros Nine Human Development Foundation[14] or NNHDF at Kabankalan City, situated at the southern part of Negros Occidental, the Philippines. NNHDF was founded in the year of the Great Jubilee (2000), to continue the work of human development started over 30 years ago during

---

[14]     In 1983 three priests including Columban Fr. Brian Gore and six lay workers from the island of Negros were charged with multiple murder. Over the next 14 months of trial and imprisonment they became known as the Negros Nine. On July 5, 1984 all charges were dropped and they were freed. These trumped-up charges were meant to stop the work of the Basic Christian Communities in Negros, which was non-violent transformation of Negros society through integral human development.

the intense struggle of the Filipinos to be free from the chains of the Marcos dictatorship.

We also wanted to keep in our hearts and minds the memory of all who suffered and died for the cause of justice. We are determined to continue their struggle and keep the torch of freedom embedded in the hearts of every Filipino.

Ours is not a Church organization, but one that is deeply rooted in Gospel values and principles and grounded in the experience of the poor striving to live their lives according to the teaching of the Christian Gospel.

One of the programs of the Foundation is the Prison Ministry. I provided legal assistance and facilitated the release of minors in conflict with the law. We are helping poor people with problems on legal procedures and help them to get out of jail.

One of the members of Kristianong Katilingban (Christian Community) in Oringao asked assistance from us to find his son missing for two years. A case of illegal recruitment was then filed by the family against the suspected recruiter, but it was dismissed in court for lack of jurisdiction—filed in the wrong court! We went to Dumaguete City, Negros Oriental, to re-file the case of illegal recruitment against the said suspected recruiter. I attended the hearing, and to this date we are waiting for the promulgation of the decision.

We have another case of a young girl from a small village who had been missing for three years. We filed a case of qualified trafficking against the person involved and eventually found the girl in Manila, where she was working as a domestic servant. We were able to bring her back to her family and also have the trafficker arrested in Caloocan City, Manila. The trafficker was brought to Kabankalan City Jail, where she is now incarcerated. The case has been heard at the Regional Trial Court of Kabankalan City, and we are now waiting for the conclusion of the case. If the trafficker is convicted, this will be the first conviction of human trafficking in the whole of the Western Visayas region.

We have also taken another case of two sisters (12 and 14 years old) from Himamaylan City, Negros Occidental who were recruited to work in a bar serving male customers. We rescued them and put them into a temporary shelter for psychological and personal assessment. Later we sent them back to their families and enrolled them in school. Recently, the elder sister graduated from primary level. The suspected trafficker was arrested and imprisoned. We filed a case of qualified trafficking at the Regional Trial Court of Himamaylan City.

To this date, even with the prevalent issue of human trafficking in the entire Philippines archipelago, only thirteen convictions have been handed down by the judiciary.

The four primary reasons why traffickers are not arrested are: first, lack of interest from the family of the victims due to poverty, second, lack of support from the local government units, third, lack of awareness from the community, and fourth, the stigma of the victim in facing the perpetrators during court proceedings. Because of these reasons the perpetrators become more aggressive in their illegal activity.

Internationally, human trafficking is considered a very serious crime. It is a crime against the human person. In the Philippines, trafficking is considered a heinous crime, and if proven guilty the perpetrators will suffer life imprisonment for trafficking of minors and 20 years for trafficking of adults.

In our effort to dissuade them to continue their illegal activities, we have launched publicity campaigns, conducted forums and seminars in every local government unit in the southern part of Negros Occidental.

Traffickers generally operate as part of a syndicate. Within the syndicate there are financiers, who assign quotas to their recruiters. These recruiters are paid according to the number recruited by them. The rate paid ranges from 1,000 pesos to 5,000 pesos ($23.07 to $115.35 U.S.) per person, Philippine currency.

For every 20 minors recruited, the head-hunter has a minimum take-home pay of P20,000.00 (equivalent to a managerial salary) or $461.41 U.S. The recruiters, known as head-hunters, most of whom are acquaintances, friends or relatives of the victims, go to the villages, check out the possibilities of persuading families to release their children into their care, then make their pitch by promising a good job and money. They even give an advance payment of 500 to 1,000 pesos or a small radio to the family in order to allow their son or daughter to work away from home. The head-hunters do not, as a rule, kidnap their victims, but deceive them with false promises of better working conditions and a good paying job. These head hunters, are considered traffickers by the law. Because of poverty, especially in the countryside, head hunters are able to lure their victims with the pretense of helping them and their family.

After persuading the parents of the victims to let them go, they will be taken to a safe house in a nearby city and transported to Manila. Usually, they travel by ferry or bus. The minors are kept below the decks and out of sight of the other passengers.

The traffickers go to the Department of Labor Office and declare that they are taking a number of 19 to 20 year olds to Manila for a variety of jobs, which is the second part of the deception. Upon their arrival in Manila, the victims will disembark from the back of the boat and will be loaded into vans and taken to a house where agents will come to pick the boys and girls according to their requirements—domestic service, factory work or prostitution. Their wages are withheld for a year or more, supposedly to cover the cost of recruitment, travel, food and lodging.

Without money and no one to turn to they are afraid to run away from their captors.

The Negros Nine is working with the communities from where these boys and girls are recruited. We focus on education and advocacy. In the major cities we have forums and meetings about trafficking. We campaign publicly to inform and encourage the citizens to work against this organized criminal activity. We also work with government departments, the public prosecutor's office, schools, Church social action groups, concerned NGOs and the police to raise awareness about human trafficking in this part of our country. Since the victims are mostly poor children from the mountain villages, the better off residents of the bigger towns and cities in the area are unaware of such trafficking of people. We do all we can to raise awareness of this criminal activity and to at least minimize the problem of trafficking in our province. Our concerted efforts will hopefully make a big difference in the lives of the victims.

Jerome Seballos, married and father of one daughter, is a former Columban student for the priesthood. He has been working for the Negros Nine Human Development Foundation since 2008.

Link to our tradition:
Exodus 21, 16 states: "A kidnaper, whether he sells the person or the person is found in his possession, shall be put to death." This teaching is repeated in Deuteronomy 24, 7: "If anyone is caught kidnapping a fellow Israelite, enslaving or selling the victim, that kidnapper shall be put to death. Thus shall you purge the evil from your midst." By teaching us to pray, "Our Father, . . ." Jesus assures us that we are sons and daughters of God and so should treat each other accordingly.

## Witnesses of a Long and Continuing Struggle

By Columban Frs. Sean Martin and Frank Nally

### Mining

The year 1995 saw the introduction of a new Mining Act with a bias in favor of major foreign mining companies, and so began the rush of big foreign mining companies to get licenses from the Philippine government. A legal challenge in the Supreme Court by tribal groups put a halt to mining progress. However in 2004 the Court reversed an earlier decision and ruled in favor of mining companies getting 100% ownership even though this is patently unconstitutional.

The Philippines is an archipelago of some 7,107 tropical islands and seas in the highly mineralized "Ring of Fire" which encompasses an arc running through Latin America and the South Pacific Islands. The Philippines is a mega-bio-diverse country with a great diversity of species of plants, animals, birds, fishes and of course humans. Of the 90 million inhabitants, 15% are tribal peoples. There are 171 different languages. While Christianity accounts for 80% of the religious belief, tribal peoples find their God in the cathedral of nature where the sounds of the forest, the air and the ocean praise their Maker. Here we Columbans rediscovered God as Creator.

We learned from the indigenous peoples that breaking the relationship and balance of nature unleashes floods, creates erosion, paves the way for landslides and contributes to climate change. Trying to end the illegal logging took time, effort and subjected us to death threats. After that battle was won came the miners. They were going to cut the remaining forests to get to the minerals underneath. Those who lived there were referred to as "surface dwellers," who could be moved out of the licensed areas that were legally handed over to local and foreign mining companies. Overseas investors and their Manila-based agents knew nothing of life in Mindanao. Their only concern was how much profit they would make. Large scale open-cut mining was about to destroy fragile ecosystems where thousands of poor lived by subsistence farming. They were told they would become rich, but they knew otherwise. Without healthy watersheds and forests, without their rivers and irrigation waters, they would go hungry.

When mining companies are required to mitigate mining damage of large holes in the ground and having to dispose of mining waste of 50,000 to 100,000 tons a day in an environment with heavy monsoon rains, earthquakes and deforestation, they know from tragic experience that if they allow this they are doomed. Our Bishops spoke out warning the nation about the dangers of opening up the whole country to large scale mining.

In 1996, there was a meeting in Pagadian City between the mining company CRA of Australia and its UK partner RTZ-Rio Tinto, and people came from nearby towns and villages to discuss the implications of the proposed mining venture for 600,000 hectares of local land. The local people were determined not to allow the mining company representatives talk them down. They were on their guard, more so than me. When time for serving refreshments arrived the company employees were passing around drinks and snacks and I took what was offered, but was immediately prodded in the back by Columban Sister Margaret, who, with a stern look on her face, indicated that none of the Subanens present, who had eaten little or no breakfast, had taken a snack or drink, and here was I, after a hearty breakfast, accepting whatever was offered.

That was just the beginning of the struggle with the mining interests. CRA was taken over and together with RTZ became Rio Tinto of London and Rio Tinto of Australia. An Australian director working with their Philippine company, which was disguised as Tropical Exploration Philippines Incorporated (TEPI), told us that his father received the Columban magazine and that they would like to be friends with us. Someone suggested that if they were to pack up, go home and leave us to work out how best to develop our forests and land, we could indeed be friends.

The Columban international network allowed us to present our case to the Rio Tinto AGM in London where a statement of the Bishop (see 1988 RP Bishops' Pastoral Letter on Ecology and 1995 RP Bishops' Statement on Mining) was read out to the shareholders, putting pressure on the company. Also, we went well prepared to local meetings after investigating the company's record with indigenous communities and the environment in other parts of the world. We knew what mining would do to our land. We learned how it had destroyed vast areas of natural forest, polluted rivers and seas, and ruined peoples' livelihoods in Papua New Guinea and Bougainville. We had people who could argue the case against mining, and we also did the same in London through our partners there. Bringing back short reports published in our magazines were most encouraging for the people here. They could see that there were people out there who cared for them.

It was about 1999 when Rio Tinto withdrew from the Philippines. However, other companies rushed in to fill the gap. Mining interests with Philippine government support continue to press for access to the mineral wealth beneath the vital forests. Watersheds and rivers have no value to them. However, the Church and the people have continued to protest and challenge proposals for mining.

Also, in recent years, local government has echoed central government support for mining, logging and large plantations of biofuel crops as a path to development. So, it is ever easier for the mining companies to operate despite local resistance. Even though there is more income locally from agriculture and home-grown industries and fisheries, this does not count with those in government, who often receive kickbacks from the big companies. However, there are a few local governments that have made sustainability the center of their development agenda, and we hope that they will be able to sustain their brave stand as they take on the power of the national government, the interests of international capital and pressure from the Foreign Chambers of Commerce.

## Corruption

The National Government of the Philippines, through the Department of Budget and Management, disperses a fund called the Internal Revenue Allotment to Provinces and Municipalities. This considerable Central government finances for local government is meant to reach the village level and is primarily for basic services and infrastructure. Towns and cities around the country are rated from class one through class five. The salaries of local officials vary according to the class. In this province of Zamboanga del Sur, in western Mindanao, 19 of the 25 municipalities are using this money to pay salaries according to a class one pay scale, when in fact they should be paying according to a class three, four or five scale. Little is left for development of services and infrastructure. Despite endless efforts in Midsalip to fight corruption, even through the court, this abuse continues. Those who are supposed to deal with the protest also benefit from the excessive salaries.

Our political system at the moment seems to have little concern for the rule of law. It's all about money, contacts, and cronies, who everybody knows are doing deals in their closed circle. It's as if the vast majority of citizens exist for the benefit of the few who govern, rather than vice versa. The person in charge has, to a very large extent, become the law. Some have their own militia too. Despite the facade of democracy the style of political leadership in Philippine society is becoming even more feudal than it used to be.

## Illegal Logging

Soon after arriving in Mindanao I met Fr. Jack Bartlett, a Columban working in Midsalip, and Vin Hindmarsh in the next parish. Jack told me that a company was going to start logging again in Midsalip and that it would be detrimental to the environment. It would affect the last of the mountain forest in the province of Zamboanga del Sur and beyond. Despite local protests, logging started in 1977. I was appointed to San Jose Parish in 1979. The logging was still getting established, and they had a temporary camp way up in the hills. But then the loggers built a base a few miles from Midsalip and wanted it blessed. I consulted the parish council, and they insisted that we could not bless a sin, which the logging was. All of us thought that the timber was there for the good of everyone and that the logging company was harming the locality and its people, so we decided not to bless the new center.

The logging people were annoyed and angry and said they would look for someone else to do the blessing. I told the neighboring parish priest what was going on and asked him not to come up and bless it as it was the decision of the parish council.

At this time some of the influential people from Midsalip asked the logging company for timber to help with building the church, and the logging company left some cut tree trunks along the side of the road for the church. Then one Sunday near the end of Mass a truck came along with a loader and took the logs to another site to help build a high school to compete with the Catholic High School in Midsalip.

In the early 1980s I went up the hills to where they were logging. They destroyed everything as they chopped and dragged the logs. It was all just mud now. What they were doing was against the forestry laws, but they were not checked by government officials. It was as if no one in authority cared. During the rainy season the road out of Midsalip was not passable for four months or so. During most of the dry season about ten trucks made the trip out of the forest with logs each day. Then, under an agreement between the Philippine and Australian governments, an Australian company built roads in the area. Roads as such are neutral but, in this case, it turned out that they helped the loggers more than the local people, as the trucks were each able to make as many as three trips a day with loads of logs taken from the forest. I knew that the Australian lads working on the road project wanted to benefit the local people, but circumstances in this case favored the logging interests.

The times were tough for other reasons too, such as the generalized poverty of the area and, from around 1984, the intensification of the conflict between the military and the communist rebels. The ordinary people were often caught in the crossfire. Also the conflict worsened due to the authorities not listening to the people in the villages who told them where it was dangerous for the military to go. Despite the warning the military insisted on going and were ambushed. In the ensuing conflict with the rebels the villagers were also branded as rebels, even though they had no choice but to give food to any group carrying guns when they asked for it. There were many armed encounters and killing of innocent civilians, some deliberate and well planned.

Each village had two representatives on the parish council and the two sections of the town had two each, so everyone had a way of making their voice heard. The system of representation prevented the townspeople from dominating those from the villages. Some community representatives would have to walk six to eight hours to get to meetings. They would bring a ration of rice, and we would provide fish. They were always thin; there were no overweight people.

We trained locals to run liturgical prayer services and organize the catechetical programs. The people really felt that it was their Church, that it was on their side, that they could have their say and challenge the opinions of those who were accustomed to calling the shots. We ran seminars in the villages to help people be more aware of the ways in which they might be fooled by those who wanted to exploit or take advantage of them. In the 1980s there was great hope here as the people felt that all were working towards self-governing, self-supporting and self-sustaining communities (as endorsed by the Mindanao Sulu Pastoral Conference). They felt part of the exciting process of shaping both society and Church.

Fr. Peter Leonard and other Columbans in Ozamiz (the major city in the area) organized a live-in seminar that ran for five weeks, and one or two participants were chosen to attend from each parish on a regular basis. The agenda included topics such as personal development, leadership training, community-based healthcare and creative theatre. When participants reintegrated in their communities they would give feedback from the five weeks, which was a new thing, and build vibrant ecclesial communities. People were used to doing what the priest told them, presuming that he got the message straight from God, but those who had been to the five week seminar had acquired a habit of evaluation and the confidence to speak their mind in meetings.

Some struggled to set up a cooperative. I felt tempted to put my hand in my pocket and give them what they needed to get the cooperative off the ground, but we found that those that struggled most to get started lasted longer than those who got an easy start. In Midsalip there were only three or four cooperatives, but in Dumalinao, where I began, there were up to a dozen. That was part of self-governance learning from experience. As well as praying to God there were practical steps to move things along towards helping the neighbor, but all that was hit on the head when all the troubles with the communist rebels and military came along. After that life was all about survival.

At one stage locals with Columban support set up a picket to stop the logging trucks coming out of the hills. The police chief of the time, Major Paulino Alecha, supported the move as he could see the importance of the forest for the local villagers and his own farm. The protesters used a small hut previously used by the police as a check point. The so-called People Power Picket (PPP) was manned from there beginning on Sunday, October 11, 1987. It was the only entry point into the town of Midsalip and the tropical forest. Many joined in the rotation to maintain the picket 24 hours a day. They had to be fed and supported in a variety of ways. The local diocese of Pagadian supported us by strengthening the Diocesan Synod meeting of priests. Sisters, parish workers and program coordinators were now asked to attend every meeting too. Many Sisters, priests and lay people from the other parishes joined the picket at different times and for Sunday Mass at the People Power Picket site in Midsalip.

When the picket began the logging company began a nursery for seedlings as it should have done in accordance with the law. Everything they did until then was illegal. The Forestry Act was very beautiful. The laws to protect the tropical forest were well defined. But the reality was very different. Corruption was rife in the Bureau of Forest Development (BFD). The people joked that it was the bureau of forest destruction.

During the picket the provincial police with Lt. Col. Meravite as commander and head of the Provincial Law Enforcement Council (PLECC) authorized the local police chief, Major Paulino Alecha, and the PPP to undertake an ocular survey of the forest and document their findings. With photographic evidence and using the forestry law as the basis of their report, widespread disregard for the law was documented. Miravite signed the report which was delivered to the Department of the Environment and Natural Resources in Manila. Miravite's support for the picket led to him being reassigned and a replacement put in his position, but after a month he too saw the light. The politicians, who were behind the logging, had to lie low for a while. The report was buried like the logs in the forest for a time in the DENR, but in the end it was brought to light and used as evidence finally to cancel the company's timber license in December 1988.

Fortunately no civilians were killed at the picket despite being attacked by paramilitaries and having their banners and posters forcibly removed at gun point. It was then that the provincial police assigned five police to keep the peace and order at the picket site, but three police constabulary were killed on February 21, 1988, when the local military attacked. The military had been getting money from the illegal logging as were the local rebels. The deaths of the police led to the immediate suspension of the timber license agreement (TLA) of the logging company, Sunville Timber Products Incorporated (STPI). The picket was disbanded on February 27, 1988.

However, even during martial law conditions the protesters succeeded in blocking the logging. I think it was a miracle that they stayed with it, that it was effective and that there was no civilian killed. The picket was sustained for just over four months (October 1987-February 1988) when the logging license was suspended. However, some locals have continued chopping down the trees, which they turn into charcoal and bring down to the town to sell for domestic fuel. However, what we treasure is the experience of sharing the faith driven commitment of so many people. They showed us a face of God, Creator of their beautiful home in the Philippine mountains of Mindanao; God, fount of wisdom transmitted by a Subanen indigenous tribe that encouraged the Church and the community of St. Joseph's Midsalip to put their lives on the line to protect mother earth for future generations.

Link to our tradition:

James is scathing in his warning to the rich (James 5, 1-6): "Come now, you rich, weep and wail over your impending miseries. Your wealth has rotted away, your clothes have become moth-eaten, your gold and silver have corroded, and that corrosion will be a testimony against you; it will devour your flesh like a fire. You have stored up treasure for the last days. Behold, the wages you withheld from the workers who harvested your fields are crying aloud, and the cries of the harvesters have reached the ears of the Lord of hosts. You have lived on earth in luxury and pleasure; you have fattened your hearts for the day of slaughter. You have condemned; you have murdered the righteous one; he offers you no resistance." Jesus highlights the depth of human attachment to wealth in Luke 16, 19-31, concluding the passage with a fearful punch line: "Then Abraham said, 'If they will not listen to Moses and the prophets, neither will they be persuaded if someone should rise from the dead.'"

## Fr. Jim[15] the Editor/Fr. Jim the Pastor

### By Columban Fr. Peter Woodruff

Fr. Jim Mulroney, a Columban missionary priest who grew up in Adelaide, Australia, worked for a time in Japan and then in Australia, and has been the editor for some years of the Sunday Examiner, the English language Catholic weekly newspaper of the diocese of Hong Kong. I presumed that job was his primary interest and commitment. It is certainly what calls him to the newspaper's

---

[15]   This is how Jim Mulroney signs his editorial column in the Sunday Examiner.

office each day. It allows him to introduce himself to men and women in many walks of life. It's a job that requires him to keep his finger on the pulse of events in Hong Kong and elsewhere. Jim likes to be in touch with what's happening and with those who profess to know all about such matters. He always struck me as the ideal person for such a job.

Then something happened that prompted me to rethink Jim. Fr. Tommy Murphy was showing me around the sights of Hong Kong. We caught a taxi to the cable car station with the intention of riding up to the peak, but the queue was long, and we decided to move on. We walked down the hill, visiting sites on the way; Tommy knew something about each place, and I knew nothing, making our leisurely walk a win-win experience for both of us.

Near the bottom of the hill, Tommy sighted the small eighteen story building where the Catholic Center was located, so we went to see if it was open. Being a Sunday we had our doubts. The chaplaincy was closed, but some Philippine women told us there was a party on upstairs. They showed us the way, and we opened the door to a crowded noisy room with a party in full swing. Philippine domestic workers were happily celebrating a saint's feast day, part of which was a dance competition. Much to our surprise, Fr. Jim was seated with two others forming the panel of judges. It was about the last place I might have expected to find Fr. Jim.

There are over 130,000 Philippine women working as domestics in Hong Kong. Most have Sundays off, and they meet on the streets of the city. They take over a number of public places, form groups, sit on the ground, chat, listen to music and eat and drink what they have brought with them. My guess is that there are more picnics happening in Hong Kong on Sundays than in any other place in the world.

Many, if not most, have left the Philippines in search of a solution to some family or personal problem. They definitely have not journeyed to Hong Kong to enjoy the sights of this Special Administrative Region of the People's Republic of China. Life for the domestic workers of Hong Kong may not be as demeaning as it is in many parts of the world, but it is far from easy. Life away from family, friends and the familiarity of one's own country cannot be faced alone. The Sunday gathering of Philippine domestics on the streets of Hong Kong has to be one of the main social supports of these young women who have temporarily left their native land to earn money and, in many cases, find some personal space.

They also find space in The Sunday Examiner, especially on the page titled, The Notice Board, where their letters and reflections on life are posted. Christine Valdez, who found help from a nun, a doctor and some priests to deal with her thyroid cancer, writes[16]: "Being away from my family was not easy for me. Living

---

[16]   Sunday Examiner, 10 October 2010.

in a strange country, where you can depend upon no one, but yourself, was also tough for me. I cannot imagine how I survived and adjusted to everything. Now I live like I am at home in this country." Lynn Salinas writes of an experience in the Love of God Prayer Group[17]: "The Love of God Prayer Group celebrated its eighth anniversary on September 19. The mission of the group led us to the Shui On Elderly Centre in Yau Tong. We were warmly welcomed by the staff and residents. I was assigned to lead an opening prayer. We shared our love and time with elderly people giving them a bit of entertainment . . . . We would like to thank our Chinese friend, Tammy Yan, who kindly facilitates and supports us in our apostolic work." They use the notice board to share their faith, how they express their faith in action and how God has been good to them, especially in times of crisis. Fr. Jim is so pleased to be able to support them in the little things of their lives.

He is also alert to the poor's struggles for justice in their homeland. In the north of the southern island of Mindanao and across the visayas immediately to the north mining companies are doing all they can to open up mines that will destroy the way of life of those living in the areas affected by environmental destruction. The mining would totally transform the environment, and thousands would become ecological refugees displaced from their homeland and condemned to living in misery on the periphery of some big city. Fr. Jim sees that the Hong Kong Sunday Examiner regularly carries stories[18] of miners' plans and the corresponding protests and resistance of those who reject their unwanted incursion.

On moving behind Fr. Jim's executive façade one discovers the down to earth hands-on pastor who can take people where they are and be with them in the ordinary things of their lives. He also finds a way to open up the bigger picture issues as he gives publicity to the business ventures that will prejudice the lives of the families of people such as the Philippine domestic workers of Hong Kong. He has learnt how to stay in touch with the small picture agenda of life and simultaneously publish a critical view of the big picture agenda that is vitally relevant to the lives of the poor in the Philippines.

Link to our tradition:

Both Jesus and His early followers clearly stated and lived out their solidarity with the poor: "He came to Nazareth, where he had grown up, and went according to his custom into the synagogue on the Sabbath day. He stood up to read and was handed a scroll of the prophet Isaiah. He unrolled the scroll and found the passage where it was written: 'The Spirit of the Lord is upon me, because he has anointed me to bring glad tidings to the poor. He has sent me to proclaim liberty

---

17    Sunday Examiner, 17 October 2010.
18    Sunday Examiner, 24 October 2010, 7 November 2010.

to captives and recovery of sight to the blind, to let the oppressed go free, and to proclaim a year acceptable to the Lord.' Rolling up the scroll, he handed it back to the attendant and sat down, and the eyes of all in the synagogue looked intently at him. He said to them, 'Today this scripture passage is fulfilled in your hearing.'" (Luke 4, 16-21) James echoes Jesus' focus on the poor: "Listen, my beloved brothers. Did not God choose those who are poor in the world to be rich in faith and heirs of the kingdom that he promised to those who love him?" (James 2, 5)

# Migrant Ministry

### By Columban Fr. Peter O'Neill

#### Working Globally

William Wilberforce led a campaign against the British international slave trafficking business just a few hundred years ago. About 150 years ago a vicious civil war was fought in the U.S. over a way of life that had institutionalized the slavery of Africans who had been trafficked like animals to many parts of the Americas since the 16th century. Over the centuries, national and international campaigns have done much to change attitudes to slavery. However, modern forms of the same evil continue to rear their head in most countries despite being rejected by our laws and the moral sensitivity of citizens. Working nationally and internationally to prevent human trafficking continues to be a major challenge to all who believe in the United Nations (U.N.) charter of human rights.

As the Hsinchu diocese migrant and immigrant chaplain I was invited to be a member of the Migrant Forum in Asia (MFA) delegation to the 99th International Labor Conference (ILC) and the U.N. Human Rights Council in Geneva in early June 2010. At the ILC we discussed the draft report on the U.N. Convention on Decent Work for Domestic Workers. We lobbied government members to support a clear and robust convention. I had the task of lobbying the governments of Australia, New Zealand and the U.S. It was considered too sensitive for me to lobby the Chinese government as I was an NGO delegate from Taiwan. The week-long process tried the patience and negotiating skills of the tripartite members of workers' and employers' organizations and governments as they battled it out on the conference floor debating each word in the draft report.

On day three of the ILC the employer members requested a recorded vote to have recommendations only without a convention. It is quite rare at the ILC to have a recorded vote so early in proceedings. Of the 109 government members' names called 62 voted against the employers' proposal (57%); 13 voted for the proposal (12%); 4 abstained (4%); and 30 were not present (27%). In response to this historic moment the worker members and NGO delegates erupted with applause. Asia was the only continent where the majority of governments supported the employers' position. The battle had just begun as we lobbied governments to make sure the convention substantially protected the human rights of domestic workers.

We have a long road ahead of us.

December 18, 2010, (U.N. International Migrants Day) is the 20th anniversary of the U.N. Convention on the Protection of Migrant Workers and Members of their Families. So far only 43 governments have ratified this Convention and sixteen governments are signatories to the Convention. No receiving government has signed the Convention. We highlighted this anniversary and the U.N. Convention for Domestic Workers at a press conference in Taipei on International Human Rights Day, December 10, 2010.

Working Locally
Exorbitant Cost of Migrating

In 1989 Taiwan began to welcome documented migrant workers. Prior to that there were an estimated 100,000 to 200,000 undocumented migrants in the country. Today there are approximately 370,700 migrant workers in Taiwan, who work as fishermen (1.9%), in domestic service (0.6%), as carers (48.7%), in construction (0.9%) and manufacturing industry (47.9%). The migrants come from the Philippines (76,725), Vietnam (78,858), Thailand (64,342) and Indonesia (150,767). The present system allows migrant workers to come on a two year contract renewable for one more year. They can renew their contract for a maximum total of nine years after leaving the country for at least one day after each three year period. All migrants need to have a job arranged before arrival. It is around that need that government bureaucrats and the private sector weave a web of abuse and exploitation.

The sending country has placement agencies and Taiwan has brokers. They coordinate with each other and both charge the migrant worker a fee. Philippine migrants can pay up to U.S. $3,800; Thais up to U.S. $3,500; Indonesians up to U.S. $4,000; Vietnamese up to U.S. $9,000. In my view, the cause of this abuse is massive corruption at high government level in both Taiwan and the countries of origin. With a system of government to government direct hiring the cost to the migrant workers could be reduced to about U.S. $450, plus the cost of the airfare. The Taiwan Government has agreed to adopt this system for all Philippine migrant workers as from January 2010. This advance towards fairness has come as a result of constant campaigning and social pressure over a period of years.

The struggle is not over. Other sending governments continue to support exploitive migration systems. Also, carers and domestic workers generally cannot use this method first time around as employers don't know them, but they can use it for subsequent two-year work contracts, a practice which is allowed by the Indonesian government.

Wage Discrimination

The Taiwan government allows factories to employ 30% migrant labor who are paid the legal minimum wage, which was raised 1% in 2007 after no rise for ten years. Taiwan workers are on a higher graduated wage scale with increases being determined by each company's wage policy. This is clearly unjust and discriminatory. It seems to me that the local government does not want more factories moving their operation to other countries so collaborates in whatever way it can to keep companies' wage bill down. This of course only applies to blue collar workers.

In 1986, the Columbans founded the Hope Workers' Center in the Hsinchu Diocese to assist local Taiwanese workers and migrant workers. The workers began to frequent the center soon after. I went to work there in 1995 and worked as the center's director for eight years. In 2006 I became Migrant and Immigrant Chaplain of the Hsinchu Diocese and at this time, Sister Doris Zahra, originally from Malta, was director of HWC. In January 2009, in coordination with the local bishop the Columbans decided to place HWC under the auspices of the diocese. There are also two other centers dedicated to working with migrant workers, which also function under the auspices of the diocese.

These centers engage in the following activities in favor of migrant workers:

Crisis management-counseling,
Lobbying and advocacy,
Proactive education,
Community enhancement,
Sheltering victims of trafficking and abused migrant workers,
Reintegration programs for their return home,
Religious services.
Workers' and Carers' Rights

This group suffers the most abuse and exploitation. They are not covered by any labor law, only by the terms of their contract. Even then, unless they know how to stand up for themselves and protest, they often end up without a day off despite the stipulations of their contract. This is frequently the case with the Indonesians and Vietnamese. However, the Filipinos are generally more confident and better educated, so they usually do know how to stand up for their rights. The Thai Government refused to let Thais migrate as carers and domestic workers until they were covered by Taiwan labor law. We are convinced and work untiringly towards ensuring that the U.N. Convention for Domestic Workers will be a firm basis for insisting on upholding their rights.

Link to our tradition:

Ancient Hebrew law indicates that abuse of the foreigner has been going on for a long time: "Thus says the LORD: Do what is right and just. Rescue the victims from the hand of their oppressors. Do not wrong or oppress the resident alien, the orphan, or the widow, and do not shed innocent blood in this place." (Jeremiah 22, 3) "You shall have but one rule, for alien and native-born alike. I, the LORD, am your God." (Leviticus 24, 22) The letter to the Hebrews puts a positive spin on the matter: "Do not neglect hospitality, for through it some have unknowingly entertained angels" (Hebrews 13, 2); so too does Matthew: "For I was hungry and you gave me food, I was thirsty and you gave me drink, a stranger and you welcomed me." (Matthew 25, 35)

## Standing with Our People in a Foreign Land

By Columban Fr. Peter Nguyen Van Hung

Nguyen Van Phuc died on May 30, 2007, in an accident on a construction site in Taiwan. He paid U.S. $7,000 as a broker fee to a broker agency in Vietnam for the chance to be a migrant worker in Taiwan for three years. His work contract bonded him to an employer for a specific job for an initial period of two years, with the option of renewing his contract for another year.

Taiwanese law then requires the migrant to leave the country for at least one day thus making him or her ineligible for a permanent resident's visa. The worker may then reapply for two more renewals of the original visa, which would allow him or her to remain in Taiwan for a maximum of nine years. The system is open to abuse and exploitation in both Vietnam and Taiwan. Each time the migrant worker applies for a working visa, he or she has to pay another huge amount of broker fee, ranging from U.S. $5,000-U.S. $7,000.

In December 2010, I accompanied Nguyen Van Phuc's 26 year old widow, Nguyen Thi Thuy, to court. I acted as her translator and as the representative of her father-in-law. I helped her obtain a visa to enter Taiwan to help with the claim for compensation from the company that had employed her husband.

The deceased's father is a Catholic and knew about the work of our Center. He contacted us after his son's fatal accident and came to Taiwan for three months to begin legal proceedings for compensation. Labor insurance, plus the cost of the funeral is paid by the government and is forty five times the basic wage (45 x $570 = U.S. $25,650). Without the help of an NGO such as ours that would be the total compensation received. Our Center helped seek compensation from the employer claiming negligence that caused death. In this case the family was awarded U.S. $15,000. We also helped the family of the deceased apply for a condolence gift of U.S. $3,000 from the local labor bureau.

There are nearly 80,000 Vietnamese migrant workers in Taiwan. This is just one of hundreds of tragic cases brought to our attention each year. With the support of the Columban Taiwan Mission Unit and the local bishop, in 2004 I set up the Vietnamese Migrant Workers and Brides Office (VMWBO) in the buildings of the Eucharist parish complex in which I work in Taoyuan city, a little south of the capital, Taipei. With the founding of the Center I began to put organizational shape on work with abused migrant workers in which I had been engaged since 1988.

In our Center we give up to 50 Vietnamese workers a home for as long as they are in litigation involving claims of human trafficking, of a workplace accident and of abuse (of many kinds). So many aspects of the international migrant worker phenomenon are viciously unjust. Initially those who help him/her organize their trip to another country put both the worker and their family into debt, with the family property being collateral. On arrival, the worker is often assigned to work in a dangerous situation and the worker has no freedom to choose his/her job for fear of being repatriated.

Clearly, the system in place today effectively enslaves thousands of workers as it allows employers to treat them as if they were their property. While we certainly need to respond to the immediate needs of so many abused and suffering people, we also need to work locally and globally to challenge the injustices of this migrant worker system and change the laws and attitudes that allow this abusive system to remain in place.

When workers can no longer endure the abuse and exploitation they often run away from their job and so become undocumented. With the permission of the local National Immigrant Agency (NIA), we take them into our shelter on a humanitarian basis. We finance this work with what we have been able to save from other funding and donations. We offer shelter, counseling, accompaniment and translation service in court, and we request government permission for the worker to remain in our shelter legally. Our Center helps identify victims of human trafficking, sexual abuse and workplace accident. We also offer lodging and support for pregnant women and women with small children.

At the International Conference on Strategies for Combating Human Trafficking from Southeast Asia to Taiwan, held in Taipei in November 2005, I met the representative from the U.S. and invited him to our Center to meet migrant workers and hear the real story of abuse and exploitation. The Taiwanese Law against Human Trafficking was passed in January 2010 and applied from June 2010. A coordinated local and international campaign helped this happen. This law provides us with a legal basis with which to challenge employers and the government in court. However, to be fair, I must say that we have a very good relationship with the Taiwanese government authority that deals with migrant worker affairs.

Initially our Center received funding from the Columbans. We also received help from Vietnamese in the U.S., Canada, Australia, Europe and other countries. I traveled the world to explain the plight of migrant workers and ask for support. We continue to look for private donations, but now most of our funding comes from the Taiwanese government, which gives us a fixed amount per day per person receiving shelter. The Taiwan Legal Aid Foundation, which is financed by the state and private donations, provides lawyers for migrant workers in litigation.

I could not have done any of this without the support of many friends in other parts of the world, especially the overseas Vietnamese. I also have a great team of collaborators who see to the efficient and effective running of the services that our Center plans to offer migrant workers for as long as it may be necessary.

Link to our tradition:

In 1952, well into the world's biggest refugee crisis following the ravages of World War II, Pope Pius XII wrote the Apostolic Constitution, *EXSUL FAMILIA NAZARETHANA* (The Migrant Family of Nazareth), which is akin to a charter for Catholic Church work with migrants and refugees. The Pope draws on history to make his case: "Let us recall what the great St. Ambrose did and said when that illustrious Bishop of Milan succeeded in ransoming the wretched captives who had been taken after the defeat of the Emperor Valentine near Adrianopolis. He sacrificed the sacred vessels in order to protect the destitute ones from physical suffering and to relieve them of their pressing spiritual dangers which were even a greater hazard. 'For who,' said Ambrose,' is so callous, unfeeling, hard-hearted and cruel that he does not want men saved from death and women from barbarous attacks worse than death? For who is not willing to rescue girls and boys or little children from the service of pagan idols, into which they have been forced under pain of death? We have not undertaken this work without reason; and we have done it openly to proclaim that it is far better to preserve souls for the Lord than to preserve gold.'"

## Recovering What We Have Lost

By Columban Fr. Don Hornsey

No one dies of starvation here (rural Peru), but malnutrition and its long term consequences are common. This is common in small children and expectant mothers. Doctors, nutritionists, in fact anybody who understands the need for a healthy diet, knows that the way many families in the area eat is unhealthy. There is a very high level of gastric infection in the population. There is also a major dependence on fried food. However, the roots of this problem are complex, as are the ways in which it is being tackled.

Subsidized communal kitchens have been functioning for many years and have been a major help to many poor families during hard times. Often the aid arrives in the form of bulk food, which has been produced in another part of Peru or of the world. Powdered milk, wheat flour and rice are three prime examples. Many people have become accustomed to the imported foods, and consequently much locally produced food has become a cash crop rather than for the consumption by those who have produced it.

In recent times, especially in the rural areas, there has been a growing emphasis on the use of local produce to solve the food needs of the poor. However, the common diet of potatoes, maize and broad beans continues to be inadequate. While well-established emergency food aid programs continue to serve the poor, other kinds of projects, born out of a different vision of social development for this part of rural Peru, are helping many of us rethink some of our ways of being in solidarity with the poor.

Faustino Arminta, with the support of his parish priest in Checacupe, just ten minutes up the road towards Cuzco, has been busy setting up a project designed to recover ancient knowledge and habits relating to food production that have been lost over time. Faustino grew up in Checacupe and studied engineering at the university in Cuzco. He took seven years to complete the course since he had to work to cover his living and study costs. Even though his specialty was in food transformation he also understood and was interested in food production as he grew up on the land.

From when he first began his university studies in 1996 he was developing his dream of a different, locally sustainable approach to food production, but ideas and dreams have to become projects, which in turn require funds. Faustino's parish priest, Fr. Bernardo (from France), helped find the funding. Sadly, Bernardo died recently, but the project continues and now we in Combapata are taking the initial steps towards implementing something similar. Following Bernardo´s death I was asked to add the administration of the Checacupe parish to my pastoral responsibilities.

In Checacupe Faustino had taken a plot of parish land and divided it into ten by two meter lots. Families participating in the project may take on one or two lots. The project provides them with seeds or seedlings, according to the crop, and the families are responsible for the care of their lots. The project runs courses to teach the families how to use the vegetables in a variety of dishes. All this is hands-on with people actually doing the cooking and eating what has been prepared. They are then encouraged to prepare similar dishes in their own homes. This is monitored lest the project degenerate into a scheme for getting cheap greens for the family's animals (mainly guinea pigs) or for selling in the local market.

The project also challenges the use of chemical fertilizer and is showing farmers how things can be grown without access to such aids. The practices of composting and developing humus are integral to the new agricultural vision being proposed.

One of the key elements of the project is the use of small hothouses made of light, transparent plastic sheeting. Crops that would not otherwise grow in the area, because of frosts, are now doing very well. During the dry months of the year from March to October the night temperature can go down to below minus eight degrees Celsius, even though during the same day it may go up to over plus twenty five degrees Celsius.

I am not a farmer, but I do come from a rural background in New Zealand. My family is from the Waikato dairy farming region. So, while I personally don't have the skills needed to help develop agricultural projects, I do want to help extend people's agricultural skills to horticultural enterprises. I see the organic garden as a key element in this, so I have asked Faustino to help us here in Combapata develop our own gardens, the center piece of which would be a plastic sheeting hothouse on a strip of vacant land along the side of our parish church.

We plan to target the young people of our parish, invite them to take on a small parcel of land in our hothouse and learn to grow a variety of crops. We hope they will continue by creating small gardens at home with seeds and plants that we will provide. We will also teach them about a balanced diet and, through the work of our communal kitchen, show them what that means. Re-education in this area is a major need here as many families are happy to eat rice and pasta and leave aside vegetables and fruit.

Our communal kitchen regularly feeds up to 150 primary school children. Their families contribute some produce; the municipality pays the wages of three cooks. The Columbans contribute ingredients not grown locally, such as cooking oil. The children are from poor families, many of whom are subsistence farmers in the outlying communities. They walk into town to go to school with a handful of toasted corn. We send them home well fed. We also run educational programs to help parents appreciate the value of a good diet and how to prepare tasty meals with ingredients that are available but often not in common domestic use.

We plan to work closely with Faustino, and here in the parish we have good rapport with many families dedicated to subsistence farming. We hope to help introduce them to the project's proposals for growing and including vegetables in the family diet. As Faustino insists, it is not really about something new but rather the recovery of ancient knowledge and skills. We know that it is difficult to grow many crops at higher altitudes (even with the aid of the plastic sheeting hothouse), but we believe that can also be solved by retaking an ancient tradition, namely trading along the length of our Andean valleys, from the highlands to the lowlands. In the sharing of crops and animals our people will once again have access to what they need for a balanced diet.

We realize that this project in itself will not motivate families to change their eating habits. We also need to educate and persuade residents. We know that in the communities in the Salcca valley up to 40% of the children less than six years old are undernourished. We are aware that a major factor is poverty, but even within the poverty there are bad habits that could be eliminated. We believe the vision being pioneered by Faustino could help bring in major changes favoring the health of the families of this valley.

Link to our tradition:

In a rural zone in the south of Peru a few men and women are collaborating with each other to combat malnutrition. They take up the challenge of the mandate from God stated in Genesis 1, 27-30: "God created mankind in his image; in the image of God he created them; male and female he created them. God blessed them and God said to them: 'Be fertile and multiply; fill the earth and subdue it. Have dominion over the fish of the sea, the birds of the air, and all the living things that crawl on the earth.' God also said: 'See, I give you every seed-bearing plant on all the earth and every tree that has seed-bearing fruit on it to be your food; and to all the wild animals, all the birds of the air, and all the living creatures that crawl on the earth, I give all the green plants for food. And so it happened.'"

## Solidarity in the Ongoing Struggle for Justice for the Poor

By Sandra Oblitas (in collaboration with Columban Fr. Peter Woodruff)

My mother, who is from Chile, always maintained that it was better to have sons than daughters. I had three elder brothers and an elder sister who died a few years ago. All of us were born in Chile but brought up for the most part in Peru. The boys considered it their duty to look after me and that meant I could not go anywhere alone and, against the better judgment of all, I played so-called male sports. I was brought up in a socialist, non-religious family in Lima, Peru. My Dad was a life-long member of the Peruvian Communist Party (PCP), but he was buried with a Requiem Mass, referred to as the spiritual aspect, as well as the civic aspect, namely speeches by his socialist friends. Dad was also a great friend of a Jesuit priest who lived beside a central church in Lima and, while Dad did not profess any religious belief, he certainly did not reject those who did. He used to say to his Jesuit friend that they really did the same thing, as both were dedicated to helping the poor get justice.

Through my family connection with the PCP I got a scholarship to study medicine in Bulgaria, where I spent seven happy years. On returning to Lima I went to work in San Juan de Miraflores, a poor area to the south of the city. I soon discovered that my approach to patients was not getting results. They did not buy the medicines that I prescribed, because they did not have enough money. So, like many other medical personnel, I chose to give priority to developing a system of preventive medicine and focused on this for two or three days a week. After a year in the area I had prepared a reasonable diagnosis of local health needs, plus actual and preferred responses to the situation. I did all this through my work with local women's organizations, such as soup kitchens, a number of civic organizations and some non-government organizations. However, I could not get used the cumbersome ways of the state bureaucracy and decided to look for work with a non-government organization (NGO).

After completing the required one year of service with the Ministry of Health in a poor urban or rural area, I got a job with FOVIDA. During the 1980s the socialist mayor of Lima, Alfonso Barrantes, had developed ways of working with a free milk distribution program for children. There were also networks of soup kitchens and medical clinics in the poor barrios of Lima. The work with FOVIDA, my socialist family background and my experience of life in Bulgaria combined to convince me of the importance of tackling the medical issues of the poor by working closely with the local community. FOVIDA was financed through particular projects, and I stayed in that job for six years.

The projects ran their course, and I found myself back with the Ministry of Health in 1992 and worked for some months in local medical centers, but soon tired of that because the Ministry delayed our wages for periods of up to three months. I went to work for another NGO, Flora Tristan, which financed an itinerant medical team for detecting and treating cervical cancer. In just one poor district we checked 1,600 women and discovered six cases of cancer. I did the follow-up work with those women during the next four years.

Flora Tristan is a feminist NGO where I received my intellectual formation in feminism—quite a change after the macho formation at home, where even as a youngster I remember challenging the macho ways of my family by answering back and playing the so-called male sports. In Flora Tristan the organizers provided plenty of opportunity for reflection and discussion on relevant feminist issues. Once again I moved on because the project I had worked on was completed.

I returned to the Ministry of Health, but this time to a clinic on the eastern slopes of the Andes Mountains. In Mendoza we were just a little higher than the flat land of the Amazon jungle. Our medical team in the clinic worked in primary health care, and when I arrived all were busy coping with a yellow fever epidemic.

The rural people live a different kind of poverty from the city. They don't seem to be motivated to strive for anything beyond the routine of country life, so tend to be super laid back. They work their small farms, have a basic diet of root vegetables, bananas and other tropical fruits, get together to celebrate baptisms, birthdays, weddings and funerals, but even then it all depends on whether the family concerned has money for the party.

The place is beautiful and the people are so kind and welcoming but the unchanging routine of daily life, with no stimulus to do anything but quietly fit in, was too much for me. I returned to Lima even though the pay was good. Also, from a medical point of view, I lost heart after a group from our local clinic went to lots of trouble to transfer a patient suffering from tuberculosis to the main town, which had a hospital. Through negligence the hospital doctor and staff simply let him die.

Once back in Lima a friend invited me to work in a similar kind of clinic in the Huarochiri area, in a small town in the mountains a few hours to the east of Lima. There were about 5,000 residents in San Damian, all of whom made a living working the land and/or running a small business. There was no electricity and little social life, but I could return to Lima each week to see my children.

After nine months in San Damian I found another job with an NGO, Doctors without Frontiers, who were running a project to combat family violence, child abuse, and sexual and reproductive health for adolescents (unwanted teenage pregnancies among the poor were increasing). From there I moved to my present job in the clinic, run by the Sisters of Mercy from Australia (North Sydney). So much of what I learnt in the previous jobs I've done in various parts of Lima and in rural areas has prepared me for this job. Most of those I work with are from rural Peru who have come to Lima in search of a better life.

I do the basic doctor-patient consulting but, in this clinic, the patients can buy the subsidized medicine that we sell in our pharmacy. I also draw on my experience of work with other local communities to develop our preventive medicine projects. We have 25 health promoters whom I supervised up until a year ago. I now join in the monthly meeting with the health promoters and meet regularly with the team (a nurse and a social worker) that supervises them. The health promoters do follow-up visits with needy cases, especially the elderly and physically disadvantaged. They give talks on health,

The Columbans have been pastorally responsible for the area where the Sisters work since 1952, when it was still under cultivation. The urban sprawl of Lima began to take over the farmland in the 1980s and the Columbans led the development of what is now the parish, The Holy Archangels. In 1994, Sister of Mercy, Jackie Ford, who was working in Santiago de Chile, came to look at one of the poorest parts of the parish. I was parish priest at the time and took Jackie to a small hill more or less in the middle of our parish jurisdiction. It was a good place from which to get an overview. I told her that we were building a small chapel for the local community and that the patron saint would be recently named Chilean saint, Saint Teresa of the Andes. Jackie took that as a sign from God and returned to Chile to prepare for the move to Lima. She arrived in Lima on February 14, 1995. Sisters Joan Doyle and Patricia McDermot completed the team in May and July 1996 respectively. The three Sisters belong to the Australian North Sydney group. A couple of years ago Sr. Jackie returned to Australia after more than 20 years in Latin America. Srs. Joan and Patricia returned to Australia in 2013, after handing over responsibility for the projects to lay teams with support from the Missionaries of the Sacred Heart. The parish priest of the area is Fr. George Hogarty, a Columban from Australia. (Fr. Peter Woodruff) in particular on malnourishment in children and also help publicize what we do in the clinic.

I'm happy working with the Sisters. We understand each other and share goals and objectives in our work together. We may differ in some of our beliefs but, after working in this clinic with the Sisters for eight years, I've found them open and flexible in their attitude towards the issues we must face in our work. We don't like others trying to impose their view of things upon us. As in the case of my Dad and his Jesuit friend, I can say that we are doing the same thing since all of us are dedicated to helping the poor get justice.

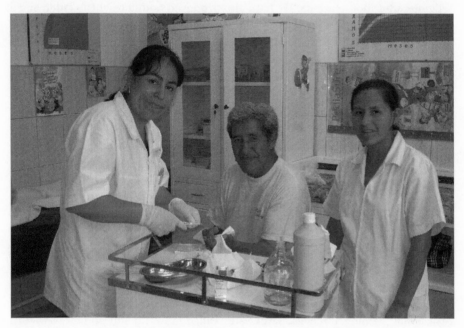

Link to our tradition:

"If a man is just—if he does what is right, . . . if he oppresses no one, gives back the pledge received for a debt, commits no robbery; gives food to the hungry and clothes the naked; if he does not lend at interest or exact usury; if he refrains from evildoing and makes a fair judgment between two opponents; if he walks by my statutes and is careful to observe my ordinances, that man is just—he shall surely live—oracle of the Lord GOD." (Ezekiel 18) "If someone who has worldly means sees a brother in need and refuses him compassion, how can the love of God remain in him? Children, let us love not in word or speech but in deed and truth." (1 John 3, 17-18)

# Planting the Seed

By Columban Lay Missionary and Columban JPIC Coordinator in Pakistan Gloria Canama

The issue of the integrity of creation is very low profile in our local church, and few personnel work in the area. Yet, most are open to the topic. We would like this topic to be an integral part of the religious education curriculum and, with this in mind, we have been running workshops on the integrity of creation with religious education teachers. We have also produced both a teacher's guide and a children's workbook on the topic.

We decided that we needed to do more in order to make some impact on the school, so we developed a module to be worked with the whole staff and asked for four to five hours to run a workshop with them. This included teachers of both primary and secondary school levels, Muslims and Christians. The teachers responded in a variety of ways; one teacher, Mrs. Shabana Samson, responded with enthusiasm.

The two immediate grassroots problems from an ecological perspective are littering and leaving the tap on (faucet open). People take care of their own space but feel no responsibility for public space; that is the job of street sweepers and cleaners (the lowest rung in the social order). As regards leaving the tap on, people generally think there is plenty of water so why bother turning the tap off! We believe that the lack of a sense of responsibility flows from a lack of understanding and appreciation of the interconnectedness between everything.

Perhaps the best way to change our way of seeing things is to do practical things that challenge our perception. If we understand better how plants and trees are a source of life for us we might feel motivated to plant a tree, and then we realize that planting a tree also saves water, which in turn might prompt us to turn off the tap.

We encouraged the students with their teachers to create a green corner in the school grounds and they transformed a small barren patch of earth into a varied garden of plants. We helped them prepare and present dramas about the inter-relatedness of creation. We encouraged them to celebrate various earth days—environmental day (June), earth day (April) and water day (March). We have produced a CD with songs written by our teachers, and which was put to music and sung for recording by professionals.

Recently we asked two teachers and their students for feedback on our work with them at St. John's Girls' High School. There are about 500 girls at the school in both the primary and secondary sections. The Sisters of Charity of Jesus and Mary run the school but most teachers are lay employees, Christian and Muslim. The school is located in the suburb, Youhnabad (place of John), a poor suburb where most residents are Christian (of many denominations, Catholic being the largest in number). This is what students and teachers had to say:

"Most of us have small pot plant gardens at home and help by watering the plants, but our parents care for them. We have learnt that we should take care of all creation. We understand better the importance of air, light, soil and water for all forms of life. We are more aware now that we take so much from plants—food, flowers, medicine, wood for our furniture, etc. Some of us feel that we should have more plants at home. We teachers now have a clearer concept of creation and feel more motivated to keep the classroom clean. We realized that the students were quite excited when they were working on developing the green corner. The experience has helped us reflect on the current situation of the environment in Pakistan. We may be busy about many things but we don't forget what we have learnt."

During the course of the workshops the students participating shared their experience with other students and generated interest throughout the school. Also, the exhibition and presentation before the whole school of student commitments at the end of the workshop helped many get some insight into ecological issues that had never been brought to their attention.

We scattered seed. May others nurture what we have sown.

Link to our tradition:

Raising Ecological Awareness and Commitment in Catholic Schools in a Poor Suburb in Lahore, Pakistan, may be likened to planting a seed. "In the morning sow your seed, and at evening do not let your hand be idle: For you do not know which of the two will be successful, or whether both alike will turn out well." (Ecclesiastes 11, 6) "[Jesus] spoke in a parable, 'A sower went out to sow his seed. And as he sowed, some seed fell on the path and was trampled, and the birds of the sky ate it up. Some seed fell on rocky ground, and when it grew, it withered for lack of moisture. Some seed fell among thorns, and the thorns grew with it and choked it. And some seed fell on good soil, and when it grew, it produced fruit a hundredfold.' After saying this, he called out, 'Whoever has ears to hear ought to hear.'" (Luke 8, 4-8)

## Caring for what Has Been Entrusted to Us

### By Aqif Shahzad

Growing into the Role of Responsible Stewards of Creation in Pakistan

We are called to care for and nurture creation as we are part of it and, since everything is inter-related, everyone benefits if we act as stewards.

Six years ago Gloria Canama (Lay Missionary who is Columban JPIC Coordinator in Pakistan) invited me to translate articles on ecology from English to Urdu. I soon began to take an active interest in the project of the Columban JPIC team. In the beginning we focused on awareness-raising among Christian religion teachers in Catholic schools. We were inviting them to develop their perception of creation from something that is simply there for us to use as we wish, towards a vision of our duty to be good stewards of creation.

We developed workshops for Catholic schools. Each workshop consisted of three sections: first, developing awareness of what the Bible, especially the Book of Genesis, tells us about our relationship with Creation; second, highlighting what we have done to the earth, especially in recent centuries; third, working out with participants some practical steps for restoring creation.

In the beginning we had to persuade schools to invite us to do a workshop with their teachers and students. Initially, we used only Biblical texts to provide a basis for our vision so, when we were invited to schools where most of the students and teachers are Muslims, we found we had to rethink our approach, using texts from both the Bible and the Koran. After a couple of years we became quite busy, and many schools, youth and Sunday school groups began to invite us to work with them. Some religious congregations also invited us to share our experience.

As we broadened our scope we networked with other NGOs, most of which are staffed by Muslims. They sometimes help out with resource people when we need a speaker for a mixed group of Muslims and Christians and also when we launched an Urdu version of the book, "Care for the Earth" by Sean McDonagh[19], which we distributed to those interested in the ecological challenges facing us.

For two years we have given priority to climate change and global warming. We help people be in touch with what is happening on our planet. Many Pakistanis think everything is simply God's will, but we propose that God has given us responsibility to care for the earth. The irresponsible destruction and misuse of the environment is our will and is contrary to God's will.

We have supported national campaigns of tree planting in August and September. Now some groups plant trees of their own initiative. Regularly there are national days to celebrate some aspect of environmental care, and we have been producing liturgy outlines, posters and information about the occasion, which we send to schools, parishes and religious congregations. Some bishops have written and thanked us for sharing our material.

Our basic workshop program is constantly evolving. Recently we were invited to run a three day workshop with the catechists of the diocese of Hyderabad. All the catechists are mature men who have had three years formal preparation for their role in the Church. However, neither our national seminary nor our catechetical institutes include in their syllabus the ecological challenges of our times. In this workshop we help the catechists integrate the ecological dimension with their understanding of the Christian Gospel. In a few months we plan to run a second phase workshop at which we will examine the catechists' evolution in this regard.

We began by inviting the participants to describe and draw an image of where they come from and what it is like. We then focused on the duty of catechists to help others become aware of their responsibility to care for the earth, which includes humans, all types of creatures, plants and the earth itself. We then reflected together on the Book of Genesis' message for us about the present ecological crisis in our world and, in particular, in Pakistan. We had a liturgy in which we recognized the harm done to our earth and asked forgiveness. We recalled the sensitivity of Jesus to His environment, how He was so aware of the plants, the birds and animals and referred to all with loving care, especially in His teaching. We then moved on to the teaching of the Church as regards our ecological responsibilities, which in turn is reinforced by the teaching and example of saints, such as St. Francis of Assisi and St. Columban. Finally, we discussed the challenges of our ecological calling, our vocation in this regard.

We hope and trust that the second phase of our workshop will help participants deepen their commitment to care for the earth.

---

[19]    There is very little literature on this topic in Urdu, but this is changing as a number of
        groups who are working on the topic publish for local readers.

Links to both Christian and Muslim traditions:

## Ecological references in the Holy Bible

Genesis 1, 1: In the beginning, when God created the heavens and the earth

Genesis 1, 30-31: and to all the wild animals, all the birds of the air, and all the living creatures that crawl on the earth, I give all the green plants for food. And so it happened. God looked at everything he had made, and found it very good. Evening came, and morning followed—the sixth day.

Genesis 2, 1: Thus the heavens and the earth and all their array were completed.

Genesis 2, 15: The LORD God then took the man and settled him in the garden of Eden, to cultivate and care for it.

Genesis 9, 8-15: God said to Noah and to his sons with him: See, I am now establishing my covenant with you and your descendants after you and with every living creature that was with you: the birds, the tame animals, and all the wild animals that were with you—all that came out of the ark. I will establish my covenant with you, that never again shall all creatures be destroyed by the waters of a flood; there shall not be another flood to devastate the earth. God said: This is the sign of the covenant that I am making between me and you and every living creature with you for all ages to come: I set my bow in the clouds to serve as a sign of the covenant between me and the earth. When I bring clouds over the earth, and the bow appears in the clouds, I will remember my covenant between me and you and every living creature—every mortal being—so that the waters will never again become a flood to destroy every mortal being.

Deuteronomy 19, 30; Isaiah 11, 1-11; Psalm 24, 1; Job 12, 1-12; John 1, 1-5; John 10, 1-10; Colossians 1, 16-18; Mark 16, 15; John 15, 1-10; Revelations 3-4.

## Ecological references in the Holy Koran

Surah 2: Al Baqarah 116: To him is due. The primal origin of the heavens and the earth: when He decreeth a matter, He said to it: "Be" and it is.

Surah 6: Al Anam 1: Praise be to Allah, who created the heavens and the earth, and made the Darkness and the Light.

Surah 6: Al Anam 95: It is Allah who causeth the seed grain and the date stone to split and sprout.

Surah 24: Al Nur 35: Allah is the Light of the Heavens and the earth.

Surah 76: Al Insan 1: Has there not been, over man a long period of time when he was nothing, (not even) mentioned?

Surah 6: Al Anam 73: It is he who created the heavens and the earth, according to a plan and with a purpose. Whatever He wills to 'be', it evolves into 'Being' his words turn into reality.

Surah 7: Al Araf 129:—surely the earth belongs to God, and He bequeaths it to such of His servants as He pleases . . . .

Surah 30: Al Rum 41: Corruption has appeared over land and water on account of what man's hands have wrought.

Surah 35: Fatir 9: It is God who looses the winds that set the clouds in motion, and we drive them on to a land that is dead.

Surah 24: Al Nur 45: God created every animal out of water: of them there are some that creep on their bellies, others walk on two legs and others on four.

Surah 6: Al Anam 38: There is not an animal on earth, nor a bird that flies on its wings, but they are communities like you . . . .

Surah 16: Al Nahl 68: And your Lord revealed to the bees: Make hives in the mountains and in the trees, and in human habitation.

Surah 40: Ghafir 60: Your Lord says: Call Me and I shall answer . . . .

## Sowing Seeds of Hope

By Rosemary Noel[20]

A Pakistani Christian Woman Describes Her Work for Women's Rights

Participating in the women's struggle for our rights in society, family and Church has changed my life significantly. I realize that my work with women has become my passion, and I feel that this is my vocation. I constantly raise the question: what is lacking in our culture, families and church as regards the role

---

[20]    Rosemary has a Master of Arts degree in comparative religions, has graduated in law and awaits her license to practice from the Sindh Bar Council.

and identity of women? The injustices and inequalities inflicted on women leave me with so many unanswered questions. And yet I feel that I have grown more in the value of my very own being, the value of being a woman, the value of being valued.

I started my work for Women's Rights in 2001 in the Catholic Diocese of Hyderabad. I was working with the National Commission for Justice and Peace (the person with overall responsibility being Bishop Max J. Rodriguez of Hyderabad). We organized parish based women's groups and met with the women to run workshops and seminars on issues related to women's rights in Pakistan. We also ran activities and prayer services for women on days related to our struggle for basic rights. Columban Sisters Rebecca Conlon, Roberta Ryan and Marie Galvin were always a great support to me in my work, as they were already involved in working with and for women in several ways.

I felt we should be doing more than just awareness-raising, something practical. I shared with my Bishop that many women come to me seeking help in legal matters, but with limited resources I was not able to help them. The Bishop took up the matter at the Bishops' Meeting and the bishops decided to start an organization for Catholic Women in Pakistan. The Catholic Women's Organization (CWO) was launched in 2006, and the coordinators were recruited from all seven Catholic Dioceses of Pakistan. The National office of the CWO ran the initial orientation for the staff in January 2007 in Lahore.

I represented Hyderabad Diocese, and in 2008 I was appointed Deputy National Coordinator tasked with helping the National Office design our project and taking care of three dioceses in the south of the country (Hyderabad, Karachi and Quetta. In January 2009 the Board of Directors and the Chairperson (Archbishop Lawrence Saldanha) contracted me as the National Coordinator for CWO, where I worked until April 2011.

I was already in contact with Columban Fr. Tomás King and Ms. Gloria Canama, the Columban lay missionary responsible for coordinating the Columban JPIC Office. Gloria told me she was looking for a woman to join the team. I contacted her and successfully applied for the position.

For the last ten years, I have been working for women's rights (focusing on Christian women) at the Justice and Peace office and the Catholic Women's Organization Pakistan. I have worked especially in fostering the development of women's groups, running training workshops and seminars, and providing women with legal aid and paralegal assistance.

I have delved into the teachings of the Bible and the Church on women. My question is simple: "What do the Bible and the Church teach us about women?"

I wonder why God is presented in the Bible as Father and not as Mother. I feel it is so strange that God is the creator of all that is; God has given life to all that is and yet God is not proclaimed as mother. I wonder why the roles for women in the Church are so restricted. What has made the Church treat women as inferior to males when we know that all of us, men and women, were born equally in the image and likeness of God?

I go back to the Bible, conscious that the Bible has always been so full of meaning for women. Yet our macho culture and religions have explained it solely from a male perspective. I realize that I need new eyes, the eyes of the source of all life, a creator woman, to understand the stories, prayers and teaching of the Bible from a female perspective. I trust that just as Jesus' mother had been close to Him in his joys, sorrows, death and rising again so too can we women of today.

All things considered, I have had a good life with equal opportunities and equal rights within my own family. Now I am living an independent life in Pakistan and that is something I value a lot. I appreciate that the formation a girl receives within her family matters a lot. The way she is treated outside the family circle also contributes to her very being, to the way she lives, behaves and responds to life's challenges.

I rely on all that I have learnt to push ahead with my work for the dignity of women—my experience and struggle for women's rights, my law studies, my understanding of God as mother, as the source of all life, as the model for women who wish to bring forth and nurture life in their own right, who wish to grow as the God of Life calls them into being the image and likeness of our Creator.

I can see more clearly that God first chose me to be a woman and then prepared me for this sacred mission and has led me along this path. I push on convinced that God calls me to solidarity with women in our struggle for justice.

Link to our tradition:

In Luke 13, 16 (This daughter of Abraham, whom Satan has bound for eighteen years now, ought she not to have been set free on the Sabbath day from this bondage?) Jesus calls a woman he cures a daughter of Abraham, thus implying that she had equal status with sons of Abraham. Many women were present at Jesus' execution—Mark 15, 40-41: 40: "There were also women looking on from a distance. Among them were Mary Magdalene, Mary the mother of the younger James and of Joses, and Salome. These women had followed him when he was in Galilee and ministered to him. There were also many other women who had come up with him to Jerusalem." According to John's Gospel, Jesus' mother was also present—"Standing by the cross of Jesus were his mother and his mother's sister, Mary the wife of Clopas, and Mary of Magdala." (John 19, 25)

# Comments on the Experience of Being a Prison Chaplain in Lima, Peru

By Columban Fr. Noel Kerins

It was a hot day and humid. The jail is isolated and surrounded by sand. The prisoner's name was Peter. He was twenty two. I asked him his name; he looked at the ground. His face was sad. He had just been baptised, and his mother and two sisters had arrived for the ceremony. Peruvians have a cultural faith, much like the Ireland of my youth. I had embarrassed him, as having known his name was Peter, I asked for his father's name. In Peru I would be called Noel Kerins Fitzgerald. Both the father's and mother's surname figure in the name, of the child Peter's response—"my father never recognized me" was a double loss of face. Not only did he have only one surname, but now he had lost his honor, as if to say I am an illegitimate child. And that in front of a foreign priest. And today was a special day in his life, a day of fiesta. And his family had come a long way to be present.

Perhaps this episode might seem trivial, even irrelevant. Eight years as a prison chaplain in Lima has taught me otherwise. The vast majority of those in prison—in all three thousand six hundred—are victims before they victimize. In Peter's case, his single mother was the bread earner of his home. His mother worked a twelve hour day for ten dollars a day. His sisters, who were only five and three years older than him, "looked after and nourished him from the outset." Need I say more? Attempt to walk in those shoes for twenty two years. I honestly believe I would have fared a lot worse than Peter.

Briefly, an overview of the prison situation in Peru, and more specifically of the two jails in the diocese of Carabayllo, Lima North, where we work.

We are thirty three pastoral agents who voluntarily, visit the jail once a week for three hours, a morning or an afternoon weekly.

More generally, there are 57,529 prisoners in Peru's 66 jails. Two thirds of that total have not received a sentence. On being accused they are jailed as a "precautionary measure." This injustice is inherent in an unjust penitentiary system. It means in practice a prisoner can be four, five or six years in jail, while being innocent. One of the tasks we do—a tedious and painstaking task—that requires, time, patience and dedication, is to locate the piece of paper (called *expediente*) so that legal proceedings may begin. If the prisoner is not from Lima, it implies travel. Even having found it, legal proceedings are painstakingly slow. At each step payment is required. The partner is generally poor and trying to look after two or three children, quite often, earning only $8.00. Over half of the total prison population is imprisoned in Lima. Though not in either of the two prisons we serve, overcrowding is the norm. Prison capacity is 28,689. Total prison population presently is more than 60,000. Consequences within the prisons I leave to your imagination.

Three other indicators I emphasize, given their importance, however briefly:

1.  Corruption: From the smallest simple fact, e.g. where a bed is placed, to the key fundamental underpinnings—severity and extent of a sentence are influenced by who I know and how much I am prepared to pay. A prisoner I got to know quite well put it succinctly to me one day as we spoke: "with $10,000.00 I am out of here in two weeks."

2.  Nutrition: A prison ombudsman certified after due process that the food served in the jail we attend is not fit for human consumption. To move from that fact, which is verified by the competent authority, would require, time. I don´t know how long. Three years? Perhaps. In political will, a lot more than exists at the moment. In fact family members nourish the prisoners. Hundreds of kilos of food are brought to the prison each day there are visits.

3.  Health care: In the two jails we serve there are in total, three thousand six hundred prisoners. Of that total five hundred are women. In both jails there is technically, a small office for health care. It exists, but in practice, it is nominal. I state the real problem, by way of illustration, in personal terms. I had two operations regarding the same health problem within the last four years. I received the best of care. That notwithstanding I was recuperating with medication post op for a period of six weeks. In the prison I came across one prisoner who suffers from the same condition. Not an aspirin! God help us all! To get clearance to be operated on in a small local clinic he needs authorization from a *junta medica* (team of specialists). The paper work (*tramites*) to actually get the team to the jail takes a year and a day. The same goes for tuberculosis, AIDS or anything else.

The picture I paint is bleak. So, in this bleak scenario what do we do? In summary:

a)  We are a voluntary team of thirty three members. There is one salaried coordinator.

b)  Each team member, in pairs, attends the jail a morning or afternoon a week.

c)  We are a human face within an inhuman system. We talk about "normal" life happenings—a birthday, a visit from a friend who came from afar, a family member who brought food, a parent who died.

d)  We share a reflection, for those who wish, of the words and actions of Jesus, and the human dignity that each one of us have.

e)  We assist the poorest prisoners, and 95% are from Peru´s poor, to locate the *expediente*—the document which committed them to jail in the first place. I emphasize that two thirds are jailed without a sentence. Hence the importance of this document to start the legal process.

f) We celebrate the Eucharist on important occasions, Holy Week, Christmas, death of a relative, and on significant feasts.

g) We assist the more extreme health cases.

h) Together with another institution (IRFA) we facilitate an education program which has an official department of education recognition. A four month program has the value of a nine month (one school year) primary and secondary education year. We trust this will motivate some to continue their basic primary and secondary education.

i) We do a screening, once annually, to detect the number of victims of tuberculosis and AIDS, with the professional contribution of a clinic and medical team.

j) The pastoral team is a church presence to witness events as they unfold. Periodic reports inform about and advocate change.

k) A team member teaches the prisoners reflexology.

I have never read in the Gospel pages where Jesus, though He shared the table with those who were despised and considered outcasts, visits a jail in His homeland, then part of the Roman Empire. Yet He reminds us as the final curtain falls, "I was sick and imprisoned and you visited me." Matthew 25, 36.

A sobering thought!

A link to our tradition:

[Solidarity] is not a feeling of vague compassion or shallow distress at the misfortunes of so many people, both near and far. On the contrary, it is a firm and persevering determination to commit oneself to the common good; that is to say, to the good of all and of each individual, because we are all really responsible for all. (On Social Concern [*Sollicitudo Rei Socialis*], Encyclical Letter of Pope John Paul II, 1987, #38)

## Bus Ride

### By Columban Fr. Tomás King

On a recent Sunday afternoon I was sitting in a bus at the bus stand of Mirpurkhas city, in interior Sindh, Pakistan. The city and its surrounds are famous for their luscious mango orchards, as well as countless NGOs, some of which contribute much to the welfare of the local people, while others exist only on paper. There were very few passengers on the bus, so the driver and conductor waited for more passengers before they would eventually set off for Khipro, a town 75 minutes journey away. Since it was a hot day, a vendor boarded the bus, carrying a jug and two glasses, hoping to sell a cold drink to passengers. From his appearance, I surmised that he was a Sindhi Muslim who was working hard to eke out a subsistence living.

In the seat just in front of me sat a man and his daughter who looked to be around six years old. To me, they looked like Parkari Kohli, or members of a tribal people outside the accepted caste system, who live in Sindh. When the girl asked her father to buy her a cold drink, he requested one from the vendor. In response, the vendor put the two glasses, which he held in his hand, down on an empty seat, and reached into his pocket to take out an aluminum tumbler. Then pouring the cold drink into it, he handed it to the child. When she had finished, her father ordered a drink for himself and was given the same tumbler. Then, when he had satisfied his thirst, he paid the vendor. The aluminum tumbler designated the low status of this father and daughter in their society. Even so, the vendor, who considered himself of superior status to them, had no qualms about accepting their money. The story, and many similar incidents, confirms that the caste system continues to shape people's lives, even though society, which is predominantly Islamic, theoretically rejects it.

Since time immemorial human beings have, in part, described their identity by excluding others whom they perceive as different. One of the most insidious forms has been the caste system. Historically in the Indian sub-continent, the core dynamic in social relations is caste, which is lived out within a social organization that is feudal and patriarchal. While the language of caste may not be used much nowadays in Pakistan, the prejudice and discrimination it embodies are still very much part of people's daily reality.

The Christian community is an "outsider," because of its religious status, ethnic status, caste status and socio-economic status. The marginalization they experience because of their status is accepted within the wider society and in some cases is enshrined in the law of the land. Even though Pakistan is predominately Muslim, the caste mentality and the practices that stem from it continue to persist.

This system of social organization can be traced back at least 5,000 years to the Aryans who colonized the Indus Valley Civilization, which is located in present day Pakistan in northern Sindh. The caste system was legitimized and perpetuated by Brahmanism which is the antecedent of a variety of later religious traditions which go under the name of Hinduism, which also legitimates the caste system. Buddhism, which came later, struggled to shed caste ideology. Islam and Christianity, relative newcomers to the sub-continent, have also found it difficult to unravel the tentacles of the caste mentality, which is a deeply internalized phenomenon among all people. "If you are human, you have caste. If you don't have caste, you are not human," is a succinct statement of how people understand and articulate their internalized world view and their understanding of what it is to be human. This is central to understanding why those in positions of power and leadership are not motivated to help the poor and marginalized in their midst.

Below the surface of present day Pakistani society lies centuries of internalization of caste sensibilities deriving from the Hindu caste system.

Classical Hinduism is divided into four racially-based castes. A person has the same caste as his or her parents had. Each caste provides an overall framework that facilitates classification and hierarchical ordering. Also, each caste observes certain rules of purity.

The four castes are: the BRAHMINS, who are at the top. They are the priests and the scholars. Their role is to learn the Vedas plus other sacred texts, prayer, study and teaching. Then there are the KSHATRIYA who are the kings and warriors and understand themselves as people who are born to rule. They are followed by the VAISYA who are the merchants and agriculturists. Finally are the SUDRA who are the tradesmen, artisans and craftsmen, workers and service providers.

Underneath all this is a fifth major caste which is considered so low that it does not even qualify to be included in any of the four castes. They are the "Untouchable" caste, because its members are forbidden to touch anyone who belongs to one of the other four castes. If a Brahmin priest touches an untouchable, he must go through a ritual cleansing. Untouchables do all the most unpleasant work in south Asia, like clearing up human waste. They are forced to live on the outskirts of towns and villages. As the story above illustrates the vestiges of the caste system continues to impact greatly on the lives of those people who are considered untouchable.

It is among these untouchable people that Columbans live and work, primarily because this is the background of the vast majority of Christians in Pakistan. The largest group of these ethnic peoples are Punjabi, and they make up 98% of the Christian community in Pakistan. They are traditionally the people who swept the streets and cleaned the sewers. Their ancestors began what became known as a mass movement into Christianity beginning in the 1870s at the height of colonialism and which continued into the 20th century. The main reason for doing so was a search for a new identity and a place where they would be accepted.

It was not until the 1940s that the first Parkari Kohli became Christian. The Parkari Kohlis are one of several Hindu tribal peoples, mostly living in Sindh, who work mainly as bonded laborers for feudal landlords. Traditionally they have also been considered untouchable. In the ensuing decades, small numbers from the Parkari Kohlis, Kutchi Kohlis and Bheels became Christian. Again, a large part of the motivation was a search for an identity and a sense of belonging and acceptance.

But these untouchable castes and ethnic peoples themselves have, historically, had very little social interaction and also have their own hierarchical system. For example, the Parkari Kohlis, who are mainly landless peasants working as indentured laborers for big landlords in Sindh, consider themselves superior to Punjabi Christians who have traditionally been sweepers, i.e. cleaning the streets and the sewers and are seen as unclean and untouchable even though they may be economically better off.

This indicates a major Gospel contribution to the culture and social interaction of Sindh. In a number of parishes, including those in which Columbans work, there are untouchable groups of various ethnicities coming together as one Christian community. It has not always been easy, and there have been struggles and difficulties along the way. Now, every Sunday in the Columban parish of Badin three separate ethnic groups pray and worship together. Parkari Kohlis, Sindhi Bheels and Punjabis sing each other's hymns. All common meetings, programs and liturgies at the parish center are in the Urdu language, so facilitating understanding among the various ethnic groups within the one parish community. In everyday life they eat and socialize together. They also live in the same colony. This was not always the case. It has taken a lot of hard work, patience and the seizing of moments of opportunity, arising from the many crises, to make the necessary emotional and psychological breakthroughs, as well as in thinking, understanding and action.

While there is still a long way to go in mutual acceptance, these developments show that it is possible to change values and ways of thinking that have been internalized in people and ethnic communities for millennia. Our common humanity is stronger and deeper than the differences that divide us.

Link to our tradition:

Jews and Christians eventually gave up on slavery, even though, up until relatively recent times, slavery was an accepted fact of life that had Biblical support. [Colossians 3, 22-4, 1; Exodus 21, 21] St. Paul sent the slave, Onesimus, back to his master, Philemon, with the following plea: "I urge you on behalf of my child Onesimus, whose father I have become in my imprisonment, who was once useless to you but is now useful to [both] you and me. I am sending him, that is, my own heart, back to you. I should have liked to retain him for myself, so that he might serve me on your behalf in my imprisonment for the gospel, but I did not want to do anything without your consent, so that the good you do might not be forced but voluntary. Perhaps this is why he was away from you for a while, that you might have him back forever, no longer as a slave but more than a slave, a brother, beloved especially to me, but even more so to you, as a man and in the Lord. So if you regard me as a partner, welcome him as you would me. And if he has done you any injustice or owes you anything, charge it to me." (Philomena 1, 10-18)

# CHAPTER 4

## The practice of interreligious dialogue

In Christian mission there has always been dialogue, but when missionaries are associated with an intimidating colonial enterprise, they inevitably collude with foreign imposition in some way. Such has been the case for the past 500 years as European colonial enterprises moved into the Americas, Asia, Oceania and Africa. Unravelling the damage wrought by the Christian Churches' alliance with European colonial enterprises still has some way to go but, it can be claimed that many if not most of today's Christian missionaries strive to avoid such disastrous compromises of an era that is now part of history.

However, despite grave errors in perception and practice, dialogue in Christian mission has been a constant throughout the ages. From early times missionaries have gone out to peoples who have not yet heard the Good News of Jesus of Nazareth announcing, "We have something for you. Might you be interested?" Some simply preached the Good News of Jesus; some went with a non-religious gift, such as writing and schools, agricultural expertise and manufacturing skills.

In the 9th century Cyril and Methodius were sent from Constantinople to the Slav peoples and did much to help develop an alphabet suitable for the Slavonic languages, which then allowed the liturgy to develop in the language of the Slav peoples. They stood with the Slav peoples against cultural colonization of the Slavs by the Germanic peoples, who at that time ruled in much of northern and central Europe. In more recent times in Mexico, the first Franciscans to arrive adapted Nahuatl and Mayan to the Roman script and so made it accessible to all via catechisms and Bible translations. However, the Spanish language as an integral part of Spanish colonization eventually won the day.

Mateo Ricci, the Italian Jesuit, went to China as a missionary in 1583 and took with him much of the new scientific knowledge emerging in renaissance Europe; he is still honored by the Chinese state for his contribution to China. Such missionaries went with the Gospel message, adapted to local customs and entered into a dialogue from a standpoint of respect.

Dialogue in mission became official policy of the Catholic Church with Paul VI's encyclical, "Ecclesia Suam," 1964. It was taken up by Vatican II in *Nostra Aetate* and later by The Secretariat for Non-Christians in: "The Attitude of the Church toward Followers of Other Religions: Reflections and Orientations on Dialogue and Mission," May 10, 1984. Dialogue was a key concept in Paul VI's encyclical, which used the word dialogue 81 times. Of course, dialogue was at the heart of the encyclical's message:

73. The dialogue of salvation sprang from the goodness and the love of God. "For God so loved the world that he gave his only Son." (John 3, 16) Our inducement, therefore, to enter into this dialogue must be nothing other than a love which is ardent and sincere.

74. The dialogue of salvation did not depend on the merits of those with whom it was initiated, nor on the results it might achieve. "Those who are healthy do not need a physician." (Luke 5, 31) Neither, therefore, should we set limits to our dialogue or seek in it our own advantage.

Just as we Catholics believe with conviction and commitment so too do people of other faiths believe, an existential situation that requires us to respect each other and desist from an agenda, overt or covert, of conversion to our respective beliefs.

In 1984 The Secretariat for Non-Christians further clarified and emphasized dialogue in Christian mission; it described "The Dialogue of Life" in the following words:

Before all else, dialogue is a manner of acting, an attitude; a spirit which guides one's conduct. It implies concern, respect, and hospitality toward the other. It leaves room for the other person's identity, modes of expression, and values. Dialogue is thus the norm and necessary manner of every form of Christian mission, as well as of every aspect of it, whether one speaks of simple presence and witness, service, or direct proclamation. (CIC 787, n. 1) Any sense of mission not permeated by such a dialogical spirit would go against the demands of true humanity and against the teachings of the Gospel. (The Attitude of the Church toward Followers of Other Religions: Reflections and Orientations on Dialogue and Mission, No. 29)

Dialogue between parties holding distinct beliefs need not be vague nor need it undermine the conviction of either participant. In *Ecclesiam Suam*, No. 81, Paul VI outlines four characteristics of healthy dialogue:

1) Clarity before all else; the dialogue demands that what is said should be intelligible . . . . It is an invitation to the exercise and development of the highest spiritual and mental powers a [person] possesses . . . .

2)  . . . What gives it its authority is the fact that it affirms the truth, shares with others the gifts of charity, is itself an example of virtue, avoids peremptory language, makes no demands. It is peaceful, has no use for extreme methods, is patient under contradiction and inclines towards generosity.

3)  Confidence is also necessary; confidence not only in the power of one's own words, but also in the good will of both parties to the dialogue. Hence dialogue promotes intimacy and friendship on both sides . . . .

4)  . . . The person who speaks is always at pains to learn the sensitivities of his audience [to which] he adapts himself . . .

The rest of this chapter is made up of mission stories illustrating the above paragraphs. After each story or, in some cases groups of stories, there is a link to our religious tradition, which, for the most part, is taken from the Bible but, also from teachings of the Popes, General Councils and Episcopal Conferences.

## Christian/Muslim Dialogue in Mindanao, Republic of the Philippines

By Columban Fr. Paul Glynn, Amina Mambuay and Nathaniel Mambuay

Paul Glynn is a Columban priest. Nathaniel and Amina Mambuay are a Muslim couple with whom Paul has worked for a number of years.

The Columbans have a long history of working in the area of Muslim/Christian relations in the prelature of St. Marys, Marawi, Mindanao, the Philippines. Actually two of our priests were killed or martyred in Marawi prelature, Columban Fr. Martin Dempsey in 1970 and Columban Fr. Rufus Hally in 2001. The late Monsignor Des Hartford, SSC, who was the apostolic administrator of Marawi, gave most of his life to building relations between Christians and Muslims. During his time a group, made up of bishops, imams, priests, pastors and ulama from the Lanao area, was established and they would meet once a month in order to promote peace, solidarity and mutual understanding between Christians and Muslims. The group has faithfully met each month since 1992. It is not just a talk shop, but rather there is a constant search for practical ways of doing something about peace and understanding at the grass roots.

### Peace Building Workshops
One of the fruits of this process was a group of us being trained by the Uniting Church of Australia as "Young Ambassadors for Peace." We were trained as facilitators of peace building workshops. From 2006 to 2010 we conducted twelve, seven-day, live-in, peace-building workshops, mostly for Christians and Muslims at the grassroots i.e. from both rural and urban communities throughout

Mindanao. The workshop style is interactive and participative, with most of the activities being in the form of games in which young and adult Muslims and Christians participate. After the game they reflect together on their experience, all of which engages the participants in a more holistic experience that they would miss out on in a lecture-based seminar. The workshop dynamic helps participants imbibe the values of peace and cooperation.

Many have come to these workshops with strong fears and deeply ingrained biases. Muslims and Christians may want to trust each other, but we don't. We have to learn to undo the mistrust we have inherited, that has been instilled in us by family and a warped understanding of our history. The first part of the workshop helps break down the prejudices through games and sharing. Many have described themselves as having been transformed through these workshops. They are definitely venues for empowering people to be advocates for peace and tolerance among Christians and Muslims in Mindanao.

### Islam and Violence

For us moderate Muslims, we understand that suicide bombing is against the Qur'an because there is a verse in the Qur'an that says that if you kill one person it is as if you have killed the whole of humanity and if you save one person it is as if you have saved the whole of humanity.

Qur'an 5:32: . . . if any one slew a person—unless it be for murder or for spreading mischief in the land—it would be as if he slew the whole people: and if any one saved a life, it would be as if he saved the life of the whole people.

This is totally contrary to the teaching of some Muslim fundamentalist extremists that when you go on a suicide bombing you will go to heaven. But heaven is not a place for criminals but rather for good people. So, if you really read the Qur'an you will see that there is nothing written there that being a martyr by killing someone else is rewarded by going to heaven. That is merely a teaching of some leaders taking advantage of uneducated Muslims. If such leaders really think that is true, why don't they go first? Why do they use people who are living in poverty and indoctrinate them with a spurious belief? Why don't they themselves, who do understand Islam, do the suicide bombing?

### Sharing Moments of Celebration

In response to an atmosphere of mistrust and misunderstanding between Christians and Muslims, Catholic, Protestant and Muslim leaders in Cagayan de Oro City have established an interfaith forum. We see the huge importance of ordinary people being able to see that pastors, priests and imams can meet and work together. This is symbolically very important for reinforcing the idea that it is possible for Christians and Muslims to do things together.

In 2008 the interfaith group, on realizing that Christmas Day and the Muslim feast of Id'l Adha[21] were about to fall at the same time, decided to organize an activity for children in a poor area of the city where Muslims and Christians lived together. We organized a Christmas and Id'l Adha party so that Christians and Muslims could celebrate the two feasts together, emphasizing the aspect of sharing. All the members of the interfaith group brought gifts—Christmas and Id'l Adha presents.

One of the activities was a quiz for the children and prizes, so Ustadz Aliasa Alinog and I made out the questions, he for the Muslim children and me for the Christian children. There is one area of this city called Nazareth, so the first question I asked the children was: where did Jesus Christ grow up? Did he grow up in Cogon (the Cogon market is the main market in the city) or in Nazareth? One of the Christian children thought long and hard and then replied: "Cogon." All the Muslim kids around me said: "No, that's not true. Jesus grew up in Nazareth because there is a movie called Jesus of Nazareth." It was the first time I witnessed a group of Muslim children teaching a Christian child about her religious faith.

We also organize gestures of solidarity during our respective fasting seasons. Christians show support for fasting Muslims during Ramadan by bringing fruit to the mosques at the hour of Iftar (breaking of the fast at 5:45 p.m.). Muslims reciprocate during Lent. In a recent sharing between Catholics, Methodists and Muslims in a Methodist church, the Muslim representative urged Christians to take the Lenten fast seriously because of the benefits of fasting, one of which is that if one feels hunger it is easier to have compassion for the poor who go hungry all the time.

### The Birth of Jesus in the Qur'an

This first story happened on Christmas Eve 2008, in Cagayan de Oro City. Not only are Christians making the effort to reach out to Muslims during their feasts, such as Ramadan, but Muslims are reaching out to Christians in a similar way, especially at Christmas. Amina Mambuay, one of the Muslims who visited the Nazareno Parish in Cagayan de Oro for the Christmas Eve Mass in 2008, relates the story.

We (Amina Mambuay, Ombra Gandamra Al Hajj—director of the office of Muslim affairs, Mohammad Gondarangin—president of the largest mosque in Cagayan de Oro City) were invited by the parish priest of Nazareno, Monsignor

---

[21] This is the feast of sacrifice during the Hadj, that commemorates the occasion of Allah asking Ibrahim (Abraham) to sacrifice his son but then, at the last moment before executing the sacrifice, he was told not to sacrifice his son but a sheep instead. Today Muslims celebrate this feast by killing a sheep, goat or even a cow and eating it together, and so it is also a day of sharing like the Christian celebration of Christmas.

Ray Monsanto, to the Christmas Eve Mass. After Monsignor Ray spoke about the birth of Jesus Christ, as related in the Bible, towards the end of the Mass Ombra Gandamra stood directly in front and spoke about the birth of Jesus Christ as written in the Holy Qur'an.

The following is an edited version of the story as presented in the Holy Qur'an:

| | |
|---|---|
| Behold! The angels said: | So she conceived him, |
| "O Mary! Allah hath chosen thee | And she retired with him |
| And purified thee—chosen thee | To a remote place. |
| Above the women of all nations. | And the pains of childbirth |
| Behold! the angels said: | Drove her to the trunk |
| "O Mary! Allah giveth thee | Of a palm-tree: |
| Glad tidings of a Word | She cried (in her anguish): |
| From Him: his name | "Ah! would that I had |
| Will be Christ Jesus. | Died before this! Would that |
| "He shall speak to the people | I had been a thing |
| In childhood[3] and in maturity. " | Forgotten and out of sight!" |
| She said: "O my Lord! | But (a voice) cried to her |
| How shall I have a son | From beneath the (palm-tree): |
| When no man hath touched me?" | "Grieve not! for thy Lord |
| He said: "Even so: | Hath provided a rivulet |
| Allah createth | Beneath thee; |
| What He willeth: | At length she brought |
| When He hath decreed | The (babe) to her people, |
| A Plan He but saith | Carrying him (in her arms). |
| To it, 'Be', and it is! | They said: "O Mary! |
| "And Allah will teach him | Truly an amazing thing |
| The Book and Wisdom, | Hast thou brought! |
| The Law and the Gospel, | But she pointed to the babe. |
| "And (appoint him) | They said: "How can we |
| A messenger to the Children | Talk to one who is |
| Of Israel | A child in the cradle?" |
| Qur'an 3 | He[6] said: "I am indeed |
| Relate in the Book | A servant of Allah: |
| (The story of) Mary, | He hath given me |
| When she withdrew | Revelation and made me |

From her family
To a place in the East[4].
She placed a screen
(To screen herself) from them;
Then We sent to her
Our angel, and he appeared
Before her as a man in all respects.
She said: "I seek refuge
From thee to (Allah)
Most Gracious: (come not near)
If thou dost fear Allah[5]."
He said: "Nay, I am only
A messenger from thy Lord,
(To announce) to thee
The gift of a holy son."
She said: "How shall I
Have a son, seeing that
No man has touched me,
And I am not unchaste?"
He said: "So (it will be):
Thy Lord saith, `That i—Easy for
Me: and (We
Wish) to appoint him
As a Sign unto men
And a Mercy from Us':
It is a matter
(So) decreed."

A prophet."
"And He hath made me
Blessed wheresoever I be,
And hath enjoined on me
Prayer and Charity.
"So Peace is on me
The day I was born,
The day that I die,
And the Day that I
Shall be raised up
To life (again)"!
Such (was) Jesus the son
Of Mary: (it is) a statement
Of truth, about which
They (vainly) dispute. Qur'an 19

1   God is referring to Prophet Muhammad.

2   From the very childhood, Mary was so purified
and such a devout worshipper of God that
a lot was cast among her people as to who
should be charged with the care of Mary.

3   When, after the birth of Jesus, people came to
know the matter, they suspected Mary. Mary,
knowing full well that it was useless telling
them that her son was born miraculously
without a father, and knowing that her son was
not an ordinary one but a messenger of God,
only pointed to the baby, and immediately
Jesus started speaking in support of his
mother's chastity and to the fact that he was
sent by God to the people of Israel to call
them to the right path.

4   Mary used to worship God in a Synagogue
somewhere in the eastern part of Jerusalem.

5   When suddenly the angel appeared in the
form of a man in that solitary room, Mary
naturally became afraid thinking that he
might have evil designs.

| | 6 | Here infant Jesus started speaking to the accusers of his mother in support of her chastity. This is the incident that is referred to in the previous set of verses by "He shall speak to the people in childhood". This incident of Jesus speaking from the cradle is not mentioned in any of the four Gospels. |
|---|---|---|

The church was packed, and people were quite amazed at the similarity of the stories in the Bible and the Qur'an. After Mass many came up to thank us for sharing with them, and they shook our hands. We were moved by the response of people because we are aware that Christian Filipinos have a strong prejudice against Muslims. In the past and maybe in some places even today, parents or grandparents threaten misbehaving children with kidnapping by Muslim monsters.

### Walk for Peace

Every year in Cagayan de Oro we celebrate the Mindanao week of peace, beginning on the last Thursday of November until the first Wednesday of December. We have one activity called, Walk for Peace, in which Muslims, Christians and Lumads (indigenous peoples) come together in the provincial capitol building to walk to the kiosk in the center of the city. Bishop Ledesma has participated along with a variety of religious and civic leaders. Something similar has also been organized with students in other cities of Mindanao. We walk together in the hope that we might gradually learn to live together.

Link to our tradition:

Cross cultural dialogue was also part of Jesus' life experience; see Mark 7, 25-30: "Soon a woman whose daughter had an unclean spirit heard about him. She came and fell at his feet. The woman was a Greek, a Syrophoenician by birth, and she begged him to drive the demon out of her daughter. He said to her, 'Let the children be fed first. For it is not right to take the food of the children and throw it to the dogs.' She replied and said to him, 'Lord, even the dogs under the table eat the children's scraps.' Then he said to her, 'For saying this, you may go. The demon has gone out of your daughter.' When the woman went home, she found the child lying in bed and the demon gone."

# High Mountain, Flowing Water

By Columban Fr. Dan Troy

In the late 16th century, Matteo Ricci, an Italian Jesuit priest and missionary, founder of the modern Chinese Church, wrote and published a small book in Chinese, titled, "On Friendship: One Hundred Maxims for a Chinese Prince." His book was published in China in a number of editions and was popular with the literary class. The book's success was of course due to the skill of its author but maybe even more so to the topic he chose. An appreciation for deep friendship has been at the heart of Chinese culture since at least the first millennium before Christ.

On a number of occasions I have visited a memorial park in Wuhan, where I live and work, which celebrates the Chinese story illustrating the beauty and wonder of friendship. The park known as the Gu Qin Tai, located at the foot of Tortoise Hill, Hanyang, was first built in the fifth century. The present platform was built in 1957 in the style in which it had been restored by Emperor Guangxu, the reforming Ming emperor of the late 19th century.

Recently I had the chance to speak at length with Mr. Wu Chuqi, director of Gu Qin Tai. I asked him about the expression, high mountain flowing water, and its relationship to the place of friendship in Chinese culture. He recalled the story of the origin of the expression, reminding me at the same time that there are a variety of versions of the story but all revolve around the same theme of deep friendship. The tradition goes back many years as the qin instrument (pronounced, chin) dates to 1,500 B.C., and Confucius wrote about it over 2,500 years ago.

Mr. Wu talked to me about the musician, Bo Ya, who was very skilled with the ancient Chinese instrument, known as the qin (akin to a harp). Bo Ya always found others unable to comprehend his music until one day he met a poor man, Zhong Zi Qi, who listened secretly at a distance. A string broke on the instrument, and Bo Ya immediately concluded that someone was listening secretly. Zhong Zi Qi came forward. Bo Ya played a tune and asked his audience of one what image it brought to mind and he replied, "High mountain." "Correct," he said, and then played another tune and asked Zhong Zi Qi the same question, to which he responded, "Flowing water." Bo Ya was elated because he had at last found someone who could understand his music.

Zhong Zi Qi and the musician were in harmony, and they became soul friends. Nature contemplated and reflected in the arts of writing and music had drawn two men together in deep friendship. The massive stability of the mountains, and the gentle movement of the river found expression in the artistic hearts of two men. While it is true that people like stability, it is also true that the more open person also likes to see and participate in movement. Such are the insights of Confucius, which were conveyed by Bo Ya with his qin instrument and recognized by Zhong Zi Qi. When Bo Ya heard later that Zhong Zi Qi had died he smashed his qin instrument, declaring that it was of no further use to him as now there was no one to appreciate his music.

In his work as director of the Gu Qin Tai, Mr. Wu Chuqi takes every opportunity to promote the idea of friendship between people and between nations. He has books about qin music for specialists and an array of DVDs for all who may be interested. He himself plays the qin instrument with great skill and is most patient with foreigners who may not speak Chinese quite as well as he does. Mr. Wu Chuqi pointed out that, "Friendship between two people promotes friendship between groups, which promotes friendship between nations. Friendship between nations is the cornerstone of peace in our world."

Link to our tradition:

Jesus rated friendship highly. See John 15, 12-15: "This is my commandment: love one another as I love you. No one has greater love than this, to lay down one's life for one's friends. You are my friends if you do what I command you. I no longer call you slaves, because a slave does not know what his master is doing. I have called you friends, because I have told you everything I have heard from my Father."

## Chinese Friends Welcoming Me to Mission

By Columban Fr. Warren Kinne

I came to China fourteen years ago, settled into Beijing to learn Mandarin for three years and then came to Shanghai. Mrs. Cecilia Tao Bei Ling, whom I met about 20 years ago in Manila, the Philippines, where she was studying to improve her English had suggested that I might be able to help her translate books at Guang Qi Press. Along with our friendship, two practical matters influenced my decision: my need to find a way of being on mission in China and perhaps Cecilia's need for someone who might check the accuracy of her translations or at the least explain what the English meant. I began going to her office each day, and with the help of Chinese friends I gradually found my way into other jobs.

Four churches in Shanghai now have Masses for the English speaking community, and I help out with these Masses in two places. As is the custom with many priests, I greet worshippers at the church door after Mass, and through such contacts I have made a few friends who have helped me move deeper into my missionary commitment in a variety of ways, beginning with a concern for the life of the Church itself. I see it as an ongoing dialogue with the local Church. I've taught a bishop, priests and Sisters English, and I am ready to help in the translation of documents or in polishing up English translations. I do what

I can to help in the pastoral care of the large and scattered expatriate Catholic community in Shanghai. I have a good relationship with Bishop Jin who was born in 1916 and who has supported me in my life here. On some occasions I join in the celebrations in the cathedral at significant moments in the local Church's life, such as ordinations and anniversaries.

During my second year in Shanghai, Cecilia spoke to Evelyn and Jim Whitehead about me, and they spoke to the Fudan University authorities in the school of philosophy. They are consultants in education and ministry who serve university programs and other institutions throughout the United States and internationally. The University sent out Rachel Zhu Xiao Hong to see whether I was worth talking to. I then met Professor Zhang Ying Xiong who invited me to teach a course the following semester. I have now been teaching there for nine years. At the moment I now only teach one philosophy course to post-graduate students each semester. This university was founded over 100 years ago by Ma Xiang Bo, a former Jesuit. It is one of the top universities in China with an enrolment of around 50,000 students.

The comments and questions of the students often allow me to introduce ideas and perspectives quite unfamiliar to them. In one paper a student wrote: "Those who lived in the Age of Enlightenment gradually cut the doctrines of Christianity out of their brains. They then filled them with scientific knowledge." I then in response remarked that, "Such an imbalance led to the greatest slaughter of human beings in the 20th century wars and revolutions," which of course prompted a lively discussion. On the topic of the Renaissance one student wrote: "On the one hand it (the Renaissance) releases man from the bondage of religion, on the other hand it makes later generations have a bad obsession with individualism and money worship." This opened up a similarly good discussion. On the topic of religious faith and science, one student wrote: "Just as science gives us the eyes to perceive the physical realm, faith grants us the eyes to discern the spiritual realm. Science and faith are not mutually exclusive," a position that flies in the face of so much of what they have been taught that has colored all their formal education in this communist context, although one must always add "with Chinese characteristics." On the topic of Jesus of Nazareth, the thoughts expressed in student papers are many and varied: "The deed of Jesus reminds me of those communist party members and warriors who died in wars for a new China. Just like Jesus, in order to make people have a happy life, they sacrificed their precious lives." One can always find a reason to explain some of the basics of Jesus' teaching and its Sacramental celebration when you get comments like: "According to Christian Gospel, it is the salvation when Christians eat the bread and wine, which represent Jesus' body and his blood. But it is so disgusting that we absolutely can't understand and accept it in Chinese culture." One too can follow through with a lively discussion with the class when someone writes: "But in Chinese tradition, it is different, because there is not a superior God beyond human beings."

Rachel, the university's scout who first contacted me became much more than a fleeting one-time encounter. We were teaching in the same department, got to know each other and became friends. The whole family has in fact become Catholic. Then, once it was clear to them that I intended to remain in China for some years, they invited me to be godfather of the younger son. On returning from study in the U.S. where their second son was born, they had a hard time in the university due to their breach of the one child policy, but that has passed and I generally have dinner with the family once a week.

About five years ago I was talking to friends about the difficult lives of internal migrants in this city of 20 million inhabitants, six to seven million of whom are migrants. By "internal migration" I mean people who have moved to the big cities but were born and brought up elsewhere in one of the 32 Provinces outside Shanghai Province. With a concerned group of Catholics, both expatriates and Chinese, I began to put some practical shape on our shared concern and eventually the You Dao Foundation was formed.

We felt we were responding to a need that no government, individual or organization would be able to solve alone. Every day each one of us saw migrants sleeping rough on the street or on building sites and in makeshift shanties. We researched the matter professionally with the help of Audrey Leung, a well-qualified business executive with a Kellogg's MBA and also an attorney at law, who came onto our Board. We formed an NGO, which we then registered in Hong Kong. We would prefer to register in mainland China as it would permit us to regularize our way of working and so make many things easier. However, very few charities have been able to do so as the government is slow to allow what it does not fully control. An observer may wonder why we put so much effort into doing so little in the face of such a massive challenge, such as the injustices suffered by the millions of migrants in Shanghai. My response can be summed up in the saying: "Better to light a candle than to curse the darkness!" the origin of which is uncertain but some maintain that it is derived from a Chinese proverb.

## Comments from Fr. Warren Kinne's Students in Shanghai, China

I think this class has been very inspiring for me in that it has provided a superb platform for me to shape my own questions and my own perspective in the realm of philosophy . . . I have been trained to discover valuable questions, which can provide a good direction for further research and thinking in a given context . . . Besides, the study of class has also provided me with a new attitude toward the academic quest.

. . . I used to assume that any two languages in the world can be mutually translated into each other. As in the case of English and Chinese, as long as there is a sufficient command of vocabulary and knowledge of grammar in the mind of a translator, any word, expression or sentence can be translated. However, I come to a frustrating experience which helped me to reflect on the basis of such a seemingly natural assumption . . .

I also acquired a new way to conduct my learning and research. "Life is too short for endlessly quoting others!" This is the most impressive teaching in the class for me. These words draw me out of the endless repetition and hopeless imitation in the history of philosophy. Professor Kinne teaches us that we have to make a try in shaping our own mind towards the specific questions facing humanity in the contemporary time. This teaching has brought a realistic dimension to my study, and I think it is very helpful for me to discover the real meaning of philosophy, which is beyond the mere composition of word games.

As a Chinese philosopher, we ought to find solutions to current social problems in China and also a way out of the human crisis. To try to understand China and her problems, we should rethink the so-called "development." In China, "development" is more like material progress. Every time we talk about development, we exhibit solid statistics to prove our economic achievement with pride. But is such kind of development really worthy of being aspired after? What about social justice, what about morality and humanity? If material progress is achieved at the cost of justice and morality, it is not admirable, and even accusable . . .

The second aspect I want to mention here is that we should hold a more multidimensional attitude toward religions. Religion, as an essential part of culture, exists almost in every corner of the world and every period of history. It is not simply one of the dispensable cultural phenomena, or an artificial invention of a hierarchy with no essential relation to our basic existence. It roots in religious emotion and ultimate need of humans . . . . Another important idea is that we should always form our own opinions, for life is too short to repeat others . . . . Moreover, repeating others can not bring about solutions to new problems that are ceaselessly emerging. We should trust our own minds, develop out judgment, and form opinions of our own. Properly, if we do so, mistakes are inevitable. But without making a mistake, we have no opportunity to correct it, not to say to gain original thoughts.

The role of religion should never be ignored in the study of the West, especially for our Chinese, who are especially prone to forget this . . . Professor Kinne often asked us to think independently and hold our own opinions. His words that "You are graduate students" are provoking.

. . . the spirit which is specially highlighted during the whole semester, the spirit of "think for yourself," I have also learnt to reflect over our own culture in comparison with the rational thinking of the western philosophers and with the religious thought of Christianity . . . ."

What impresses me most is the professor kept telling us to form our own opinion. There is no doubt that life is short and keeping on repeating the thought and the speech of others exhausts our own life. But I have to say this requirement to form a personal insight may be a little difficult for us Chinese students to accept, especially for students majoring in philosophy in this specific university.

Philosophy is a science of wisdom . . . . it concerns with reality. So, as a philosophy student, we should also be concerned about China and our surroundings, but also know the tense relations between the North and South Korea, the living conditions of mankind in the third world and the crisis of capitalism in Europe and America etc. which are called general knowledge.

In middle school, we are taught that socialism and capitalism are incompatible with each other and the result of their conflict is that the former will replace the latter at length. As the result of this education, we are prone to make extreme judgments when we have grown up. We are inclined to judge every view to be either totally correct, or absolutely ridiculous. My attitude towards the relationship between reason and religion is a good example of this. Originally, I held that there was a fierce conflict between religion and reason and each form of religion was simply a kind of superstition. Through this course, I have changed my thought and I become more tolerant. What is more important is that I start to realize that the need for beliefs is rooted in the bottom of human hearts.

Your urgent asking that we should have our own thought is very impressive and it really moved me. And we are really overlooking the changes happening in China.

More specifically, I'd like to talk a little about my part in our group's work. We picked up the topic on Jesus' words and deeds. It is not an easy one . . . For my part, I've chosen to talk a little bit more about Jesus' crucifixion and the influence it left to some mystics . . . I have to admit, it was really a wonderful semester to enjoy with my classmates a brilliant, clear and unforgettable journey of practicing English. All my gratitude!

One important thing of this turning-back process for me is to ask one question, the question that we once raised during the course, and that is: Do humans today have more wisdom than traditional people?

This wonderful training further has freed the brain of victims by the Chinese education . . . Through the course, I came to use critical thinking to free myself from the "worship of authority."

Indeed, people in the 21st century have more knowledge about science and themselves than people who were in the middle ages. However, we are in another form of darkness. Nowadays, most people in the world are pursuing money, no matter what nations and faith.

Not only have I improved my ability of reading, writing, listening and speaking through this course, but also change my mind about religion, especially Christianity. The form of the class is colorful . . . Half century ago, we believed in Communism under the leadership of Chairman Mao, but nowadays in a certain degree we lose our belief and direction in the spiritual world. While the economic conditions get better and better, we live in the environment of poor mind.

The biggest challenge is that I know very little about religion. I usually think that religion is such a private matter that I hold the wrong conception of religion which is unworthy of serious study . . . . I have bought an English version of the Bible and read a few lines before sleep . . . . I read the Bible every day as part of my time listening to God and my spirit become clear.

I did as you suggested: I began to read some general introductory materials related to the topics we discussed during our classes, and particularly I read the four Gospels to know more about Christianity, about which I had been quite ignorant before. I read the birth of Jesus and the aim of it, the death of Jesus and the aim of it and also the revival of Jesus which means death has been defeated by Jesus. What a great victory it will be if it is true!

Nicomachean Ethics . . . what Aristotle really wants to say was although I love my teacher, I do have the absolute obligation to follow the truth.

The most impressive thing is the professor insisted we should have our own viewpoint all the time . . . It's more important for us to tell people where we stand than just repeating what other people said. We should have our own standpoint and try to explain it clearly.

I appreciate the teacher freestyle way of teaching, also very advocate academic freedom. The course has stimulated my interest in English and reinforced my conviction that faith is important to so many people.

Link to our tradition:

"We know that all things work for good for those who love God, who are called according to his purpose." (Romans 8, 28) [God] destined us for adoption to himself through Jesus Christ, in accord with the favor of his will, for the praise of the glory of his grace that he granted us in the beloved." (Ephesians 1, 5-6) The Christian vocation may lead us along unexpected paths!

## Interreligious Dialogue with Candomblé

### By Columban Fr. Colin McLean

"I believe that we are all walking towards the divine along parallel paths, and that one day our paths will converge and we will walk the final distance together."—Mae Stella of Oxossi, priestess/ medium of a Candomblé terreiro in Salvador, State of Bahia, Brazil.

In 1999, I was privileged to be at a history-making meeting of the Black Priests, Bishops and Deacons of Brazil here in Salvador. The meeting is an annual event, but what made this one so special was the presence for the first time of Mae Stella, the most prestigious figure of Candomblé in Salvador.

Candomblé is a widely-followed Afro-Brazilian religion, the origins of which are found in the "religion of the orixas" located in the tribal Yoruba regions of Nigeria and Benin today. The orixas are Yoruba spirits brought across the Atlantic Ocean in the fetid holds of the slave ships during the 350 years in which Brazil received 40% of the Atlantic slave traffic. Each of the orixas (spirits created by the All Supreme deity Olorum) has divine attributes associated with ecological and cosmological forces, and all human beings have a guardian orixa, whose presence is often gauged from the personality of the individual person. The faith experience of millions was confined to secret celebrations under the cover of night until in the 1880s three Nigerian women founded the first official terreiro (sacred space where the spirits—the orixas—could be honored and invoked) in Salvador. Throughout decades of repression (Candomblé was only legitimized by the government in 1976), faith in the Yoruba orixas was channeled into the figures of Catholic saints so as to preserve it. Hence, Xango, Yemanja, Iansa, Oxossi, Oxum and Ogum, to name but a few, all have their equivalents among Catholic saints (St. George, the Immaculate Conception, St. Barbara, St. Sebastian, Our Lady of the Candles, St. Anthony, etc.) and elements in nature—lightning and thunder, sea, tempests, the forest, fresh water, iron and steel.

The government repression of Candomblé and other forms of it, which today we refer to as Afro-Brazilian religions, was, of course, sanctioned and promoted by the Church (the government being nominally Catholic), and many of today's "purist" Brazilian Catholics still have trouble seeing these religious expressions as anything other than sects, or, worse still, devil worship. Yet a great majority of

Catholics would have some belief in, if not fear of, Candomblé practices. We refer to it as *dulpa pertença* or "double belonging." Due to the abominable history of African slavery, an ever-growing number of priests, bishops, nuns and lay Catholics today would understand and be tolerant of this phenomenon and see it as a necessary part of our interreligious dialogue. Fortunately, the CELAM conferences (the various bishops' conferences of Latin America and the Caribbean) have finally come to specifically deal with the cultural and religious experiences of peoples in the Americas of African and Indigenous descent, both of whose traditions were formerly seen as little more than superstition. "To recognize the cultural values, the history and the traditions of Afro-Americans, to enter into fraternal and respectful dialogue with them, is the first important step in the evangelizing mission of the Church." Document of the CELAM conference in Aparecida, Brazil, 2007 (paragraph 532; see also paragraphs 237-238).

I still remember well my first meeting with a Mãe-de-Santo (priestess/medium), Mãe Mildete, back in 1988. The reverence she was accorded by her followers, and her quiet dignity and personal warmth when I was introduced made a deep impression on me. Today, I still feel the quiet dignity that mães-de-santo and pais-de-santo (priest/mediums) seem to possess. The wholehearted participation of the Candomblé initiates, the deep reverence for nature in the *terreiros* (sacred halls where the rituals occur), the warm welcome accorded people visiting the *terreiro* for the ritual, and the fact that everyone present partakes of food offered after the ritual are things that have impressed me. Candomblé is not a "religion of the book" as are Judaism, Christianity and Islam. It is an oral tradition, and the presence of the orixás in those who go into trances conveys to the congregation that the spirits are still with us today, so all is well. They are good points of entry for dialogue.

Back to Mae Stella. Given this background, it was so moving to see Mae Stella seated on the same level between the Cardinal Archbishop of Salvador, Dom Geraldo Majella Agnelo, and his auxiliary bishop, Dom Gilio Felicio. Dom Gilio, the first black bishop appointed to Salvador (his arrival at the airport in 1998 from the south of Brazil was greeted like a mini-version of Nelson Mandela's arrival in 1991), was the person responsible for this historic meeting. During his all-too-brief five years in Salvador, Dom Gilio made strong inroads towards dialogue with Candomblé, visiting all the major Candomblé terreiros and meeting with the Ialorixas (women priestess/mediums) and the babalorixas (men priest/mediums). Personnel from Mae Stella's *terreiro*, Ile Opo Afonja, told us afterwards, of her (and their) unease at participating for the first time in such an official Catholic Church meeting. They would be wary of the Catholic Church's possible use of the term "interreligious dialogue" as a tactical weapon to win over and control Afro-Brazilian religions.

The meeting was ground-breaking, but, unfortunately, failed to see any official follow-through on the part of the Church. An attempt was made to form an archdiocesan commission for Interreligious Dialogue with Candomblé in Salvador (myself and Marcelo Batista, one of the married deacons from our parish, were invited to be part of this commission), but it lacked real direction from the appointed coordinator, and, finally, floundered. Once again, it was left to us, the foot-sloggers to take it further, even at the risk of official Church sanctions! Fortunately, for those of us in the Brazilian Black Priests, Bishops and Deacons' Conference, inroads have been made due to the strong participation of the black Jesuit, Fr. Clovis Cabral, whose mother Mae America, was a recognized Mae de Santo ("mother of the saint"—the Portuguese title given to Candomblé ialorixas, who regularly "receive" a particular orixa). All of Clovis' brothers and sisters (with the sole exception of himself) have been initiated into Candomblé. I am a close friend of their family, since Antonio Cabral, one of Clovis' brothers, was the administrator of our Cena Um theater project.

A year after their mother's death, I was invited to participate in a closed ritual of the commemoration. It was a great honor, and started to get really interesting, but, unfortunately, most Candomblé rituals, especially the closed ones, take place very late at night and continue until the early hours of the morning. Since the next morning was Sunday, and I had a couple of early Masses in parish communities, I had to excuse myself in the middle of the celebration. Since I am a good friend of Antonio, I can only hope my leaving was not considered insulting by the presiding Babalorixa, his brother, Balbino. Other more regular Candomblé festas that are open to the public do not occur on a weekly basis like Christian liturgies, but are celebrated during a cycle of dates that are considered important to the various orixas/spirits. And therein lies the problem! If we are really serious about dialogue, how can we liberate people for it, or are we talking about what we can do in our spare time?

# More Than Ecumenism

By Columban Fr. Peter Woodruff

Spanish colonizers left many enduring customs with the people who live in the southern Andes of Peru. In the major towns horse racing is part of the celebrations in memory of the town's foundation and also during the celebrations in honor of the town's patron saint. Then there is cock fighting, which like the horse racing comes hand in hand with lots of betting. I heard that in one town it is being advertised that the prize for the champion cock will be a new pick-up truck. Finally, of course the bull fight has become a central moment of the anniversary festivities or those in honor of the patron saint.

The Spaniards also made their version of Catholicism an integral part of life in a large part of Latin America, including the southern Andes of Peru. However, despite the efforts of some zealous church leaders they did not entirely eliminate a number of significant Andean religious beliefs and related practices.

In Tinta, a town on the Vilcanota River, a few kilometers along the valley from Combapata where Columban Fr. Don Hornsey, is parish priest, I had the opportunity to speak about religious traditions with Valerio Mamaní and Orlando Sotteccani Cardenas. Both were born and grew up in the region so their mother tongue is Quechua. Valerio has worked with the Catholic Church in a number of parishes, including his own where Columban Fr. Paul Prendergast is parish priest. Orlando is a teacher.

I asked them how, in their experience, Spanish Catholicism and grassroots Andean religion have in some ways intertwined and complemented each other in the religious practice of local residents. Since they live the mixed religious heritage from birth it has become an accepted part of their lives. They don't feel the need to analyses or justify it, so I had some difficulty moving into a conversation on the topic. They seemed bemused at my attempts to unpack what I saw as an issue. I felt it was similar to a situation in which friends are discussing an issue and one among them just cannot see that there is an issue.

The feast of the Holy Cross on May 3 brings together elements of both Catholicism and ancient Andean religion. Crosses have been placed on the hills surrounding the towns and villages and are brought down to the parish church for the celebration of Mass. They usually come down and return in procession with devotees accompanying. On the hills the crosses occupy the place where stone monuments dedicated to the spirits of the hills (Apus) were placed.

When the cross is being removed devotees place three coca leaves near the hole from which the cross has been removed and pray for whatever their personal intentions may be. They pray to the Apus and to almighty God. Valerio and Orlando insisted that Catholics, who are the vast majority, recognize God as the supreme being but they also continue to look to the Apus for protection, much the same way as they might pray to the saints and the angels. Also, on the way to and from the church devotees stop to rest and drink chicha, the first glass of which and/or a little of each glass served is poured into the earth in recognition of the spirit within.

Having been an agricultural people for millennia, the peoples of the Andes have a sense of life in the hills and rivers of their land. From there generation after generation they have drawn sustenance for their lives. Their ancient beliefs indicate a sense of spiritual power within the earth that can either work for or against them. And so, they developed religious rites and symbols to placate the spirits of the land.

The rite of *pago a la tierra* (payment to the earth) has continued to this day as an important religious rite for all. Prayers of the rite invoke the Holy Trinity and the saints. Part of the rite also includes praying aloud the Apostles Creed, the Lord's Prayer and the Hail Mary. This rite is also directed towards the spirits of the earth, especially the *Pachamama* (earth mother).

It is celebrated especially around February and March at harvest time and also in August at the beginning of the sowing season. A person who knows the rite and is respected in the community leads the rite. As often as not this ritual leader is a Catholic, who sees no conflict between their role in this ancient practice and the Catholic faith.

The ancient Andean religious rites that continue to be part of community life among the rural people of this part of Peru seem to complement the Christian approach to the earth. They recognize the need to work at harmonizing with the earth, and they make it clear that the people involved see and feel the earth as a source of life for themselves. The Catholic faith of these people does not debate with another religious tradition but rather draws on what speaks to their own experience of life to praise, beseech and worship God.

Link to our tradition:

The conclusions of CELAM[22], Aparecida, 2007, encourage interreligious dialogue, cases of which are described in the previous two stories from Latin America:

The following two paragraphs are quotes from the conclusions of the Aparecida meeting:

No. 237: Interreligious dialogue, particularly with the monotheistic religions, is based directly on the mission that Christ entrusted to us, and it calls for wise articulation between proclamation and dialogue as constitutive elements of

---

[22]  The meeting of the bishops of Latin America and the Caribbean, held in Aparecida, Brazil.

evangelization. With that attitude the Church, "universal sacrament of salvation," reflects the light of Christ which "enlightens everyone." (John 1, 9)

No. 239: In addition to its theological character, interreligious dialogue has a specific significance in the building of the new humanity: it opens unexplored paths of Christian testimony, promotes the freedom and dignity of peoples, stimulates collaboration for the common good, overcomes violence motivated by fundamentalist religious attitudes, and educates in peace and civic tolerance: it is an area of the beatitudes which are promoted by the Church's social doctrine.

## Asia on Mission to Asia

By Columban Fr. Pat Colgan (with Tony Kavanagh)

Reciprocation between the Fiji Hindi Catholic community and the Catholic community in Pakistan

Columbans have moved between the Fiji and Pakistan missions since we first went to Pakistan in 1979. Columban Fr. Pat McCaffery was working in Fiji when he volunteered to join our first group of missionaries in Pakistan. Columban Fr. P.J. Kelly came later to look after the Columban house in Lahore. Columban Fr. David Arms worked in Pakistan on two occasions, first in the Sindh around 1983 only to discover after arriving that he would be duplicating linguistic work already being done by another Christian Church and later with the Parkari Kohli tribal group to work on a dictionary and grammar of their language. Columban Fr. Sean Rainey came around the mid-1980s and did a lot of work in St. Elizabeth's Hospital as a chaplain and English teacher. Columban Fr. Tony Kavanagh came to Pakistan from Fiji in early 1995. Columban Fr. Vincent Ratnam, an Indo-Fijian, and Columban Fr. Palenapa Tavo, from Tonga, worked briefly in Pakistan while still seminarians and returned as priests but for a very brief time. Columban Fr. Feliciano Fatu, from Tonga, took up an assignment in Pakistan after he was ordained a priest.

Many of these missionaries arrived in Pakistan with certain advantages from their experience with the Fiji Hindi community. However, they discovered that there are major differences between the two countries. First, I will mention some advantages that I see and then certain difficulties arising from differences between the two countries.

The Hindi and Urdu languages share a common basic grammar and have mutually enriched each other, so Hindi and Urdu speakers can communicate quite easily with each other. Consequently a fluent Hindi speaker from Fiji is off to a good start when it comes to learning Urdu, Pakistan's national language. However, the written forms of the two languages are quite different.

The Catholic communities of both Fiji and Pakistan are small minorities and so assert their Catholicism in the case of Fiji and their Christianity in the case of

Pakistan as a core aspect of their identity. Both have a sense of hanging in there in a difficult socio-religious-political atmosphere. Their liturgies and songs, which are at the heart of bonding them as communities, are similar in the Sindh, but the Punjabis tend to be more boisterous and follow the Roman rite, except in the singing of the psalms, which is uniquely Punjabi and resonates with the people and their culture. In the rural areas there is more scope for adapting the liturgy to the local culture. There is an earthiness about the liturgy here that is not so prominent in Fiji, especially in the use of symbols from nature such as earth, water, plants, fruit and light.

The friendliness of the Fijian sparks on meeting with the curiosity and friendliness of Pakistanis. Also, Fijians understand the significance of extended family networks, which are a key part of a way of life. In both countries respect for the elderly as revered members of the extended family remains a basic value.

Both Fijians and Pakistanis are very religious. God is part of life, ever present and constantly invoked. For the Muslims there is the regular call to prayer by the Muezzin, for the Hindus the bells ringing in the temples at the time of prayer and for the Christians the bells or the beating of the carved out lali tree trunk (in Fiji).

However, the differences are vast. The poverty of Pakistan is so much greater; it is shocking and stark, not to say that there is no poverty in Fiji, but it seems to be manageable. Also, the overwhelming presence of Islam in Pakistan at times oppresses Pakistani Christians, especially when the Blasphemy Law is used against them.

In a sense I feel that Fr. Pat McCafferey sums up in his person the link between the Catholic communities of Fiji and Pakistan. Fr. Pat began his mission work in Fiji in 1968. He then volunteered to be in the first group of Columbans who went to Pakistan in 1979. He then returned to Fiji after about 20 years to resume ministry with Indo-Fijian Catholics.

From the early 1980s inter-church dialogue was very much part of religious life in Fiji. Fr. Pat took the initiative to help his Indo-Fijian community open up to interfaith dialogue, an experience he initially had in Bradford in the Christian-Muslim dialogue. Their monthly meetings included members of the Fiji Muslim League. The success of this work prompted Pat to return to Pakistan to initiate a similar dialogue where such work is more difficult but also more important.

While visiting two Fijian lay missionaries in the north of Pakistan, Fr. Pat suffered a heart attack and died. The Church of Lahore gave him a send-off in accord with the way he had entered their lives. The first part of the funeral service in the cathedral was very orderly; the second part in the parish where Fr. Pat had worked was more people oriented, reflecting in a way his approach to life. Fr. Pat for me is a symbol of how these two mission experiences feed off each other.

Link to our tradition:

This story highlights the ingenuity required of missionaries as they strive to open the door to God's kingdom: "The kingdom of heaven is like a treasure buried in a field, which a person finds and hides again, and out of joy goes and sells all that he has and buys that field. Again, the kingdom of heaven is like a merchant searching for fine pearls. When he finds a pearl of great price, he goes and sells all that he has and buys it. Again, the kingdom of heaven is like a net thrown into the sea, which collects fish of every kind." (Matthew 13, 44-47)

## Dialogue of Deeds

By Columban Fr. Liam O'Callaghan

Muslim/Christian Dialogue in a Recently Established Lahore Parish

Our dialogue does not involve religious discussions but rather reaching out compassionately to those in need regardless of their religious faith. The explicit form of interfaith dialogue has become rather problematic in recent years as the increasing violence in society has engendered a narrowness that makes many very defensive about their religious beliefs. However, despite the reports of many acts of violence committed for a variety of reasons we see a lot of good things happening in our neighborhoods, many of which might serve as the basis for an article on interfaith dialogue. However, in the following paragraphs I will limit myself to the dialogue that has been happening in the area of healthcare in our parish.

In recent years we have been developing a parish healthcare project. In some ways it has been planned, even though not in a detailed way, but to a large extent it has emerged through our response to the needs of parishioners and other neighbors in need. We presently coordinate with three local medical institutions, an NGO run orthopedic hospital, an NGO run eye clinic and a government run hospital.

We have found ways of helping people in need access low cost (or free) high quality medical care. Through contacts on the staff of these institutions we are now able to help many in need of treatment and have surgical procedures done free or at low cost.

In 2005 a major earthquake that wreaked havoc in the mountains ten hours' drive to the north of Lahore forced thousands to abandon their ruined homes and come to the city to be with their men folk who were already here for work reasons. This was the only way to have a roof over their heads during the winter. Many arrived in Lahore with serious medical problems, in particular broken bones.

Before the earthquake we were taking patients to the orthopedic hospital, but infrequently. In the emergency situation after the earthquake that began to change. On one occasion I was visiting earthquake victims in the hospital when one patient told me that his family lived near the parish center. I visited his family, and they introduced me to other families with ill family members in need of treatment. Because I knew the hospital staff I was able to help many be admitted to the hospital in what we call here "Category E," which ensures the patient will receive treatment free of charge.

For many who had fled their villages I was the right person in the right place at the right time. Due to the emergency the whole system was overcrowded so often those in need of treatment could not access it. We had established good rapport with a doctor who attended in the hospital twice a week. As numbers increased he had a meeting with us in which it was decided that once a person was confirmed as an earthquake victim he or she would be eligible for free treatment.

At this time I was visiting the hospital with a catechist, George, and we got to know all the hospital staff and cemented a good working relationship with them. All the doctors and administrative staff are Muslims, but I am sure they came to respect us during the emergency period as all of those from the mountains whom we helped were also Muslims. By the end of winter we were taking about 20 injured people per week to the hospital; they kept coming out of the woodwork. Once the earthquake refugees returned to their villages in the spring, our relationship with the staff stayed in place.

The poor we take these days are mostly Christians. Administrative staff, nurses and doctors trust us; all know that we ask for assistance only for patients who need serious treatment. As long as we are careful not to abuse the system, they class such patients brought in by us as Category E. Two Muslim women who are social welfare officers have been responsible for having most of our patients placed in this category.

These days we help twelve to fifteen patients a week. As long as we can get them into Category E, all we need to find is the money for medicines and George's salary; he works for the parish part time in this ministry.

I believe that it is in the everyday interaction between Muslims and Christians that the dialogue happens. It is a grassroots dialogue of life which progressively builds mutual respect and, in some cases, genuine friendship. In the many and varied experiences of working together to lift up or empower people we share and reinforce our common humanity. Working together communicates an idea of a common humanity and harmony that all of us strive and wish for.

I believe that relationship is the heart of mission and in that context dialogue happens. Also, interreligious dialogue is truly prophetic only when it strives for the betterment of all. This happens for me when people with diverse belief systems come together to respond to basic human needs.

Link to our tradition:

"As the human sciences have emphasized, in interpersonal dialogue one experiences one's own limitations as well as the possibility of overcoming them. A person discovers that he does not possess the truth in a perfect and total way but can walk together with others toward that goal. Mutual affirmation, reciprocal correction, and fraternal exchange lead the partners in dialogue to an ever greater maturity which in turn generates interpersonal communion. Religious experiences and outlooks can themselves be purified and enriched in this process of encounter." (The Attitude of the Church toward Followers of Other Religions: Reflections and Orientations on Dialogue and Mission, No. 21, Secretariat for Non-Christians, May 10, 1984)

## Friendship, God and Hope

### By Columban lay missionary Gloria Canama

The headline of one of Pakistan's national newspapers announced another distressing, even fearful, news item: "Blasphemy law claims another life," referring to the assassination of Salman Taseer, Punjab Governor. Minorities of Pakistan found a defender in Taseer, an appreciation expressed in a message circulated following his death, "Salman Taseer was the most courageous voice after Benazir Bhutto on the rights of women and minorities . . ." There may be mixed responses to this tragic event, but all peace-seekers, both Muslim and Christian, shared sadness with another hope dashed, another deep wound of division and intolerance.

It's very easy to be judgmental, to be depressed and even paralyzed with fear and hopelessness especially when we focus on what's being reported in the news. My emotions are heightened when I hear sensationalized news. I personally need to seek and hold on to signs of hope to keep me going. There were moments when I painfully struggled to find meaning and reasons in my continued missionary journey in Pakistan. Yet, I don't have to look far to find signs of hope. My daily encounters here are filled with experiences of the goodness and hospitality of Pakistanis, both Christians and Muslims. All people have dreams and aspirations in life. Dreams of peace, security and a full life cross boundaries of culture and belief. Moreover, it's humbling to learn and experience the truth, goodness and beauty of the other.

Naseem's family has been part of my journey here since I arrived in Pakistan twenty years ago with my lay missionary companions, Pilar Tilos and Emma Pabera. Experiencing their goodness, we thought they were Christians! Likewise as they experienced our goodness, they thought we were Muslims like them.

I am always filled with joy and gratitude remembering moments with the whole family who accepted, supported and shared their lives. Baji Farida, the mother, also showered me with the same care and concern as she did her own family. All through the years, they let me feel part of their growing family in diverse, humbling ways. I'm always invited to join their family celebrations of weddings, birthdays and Muslim feasts. They remember me in times of sickness and death in the family. They always ask me about the well-being of my family back home, especially of my own mother and father.

During the early years, my visits were for two or more days, definitely not just for a few hours. As I got busier with my ministries, my visits became less frequent. Like a prodigal daughter, I always find Baji Farida and all family members with their arms open for a warm welcome, lavishing me with their hospitality and care. Yes, a feast of delicious Pakistani food always followed my homecoming with the mutual sharing of stories, of the joys and difficulties we have experienced in life. During a recent visit, I shared the expectant joy of the family as they await daughter Sarah's college graduation. She's the youngest. Like many families this time, they too are filled with apprehension about what the future might hold for the young generation. The country seems to be in endless mess, with crisis after crisis! "God is Great and merciful. In God we put our hope and trust," Baji Farida said as she fixed the duppata, or long scarf, covering her head. I say Amen.

Once again, Naseem's family rekindles my hope and trust in the goodness and beauty of all people. Times with them are always moments of grace. With these people whose religion and culture is very different from mine I experience love and the sacred.

Link to our tradition:

Did the Syrophoenician woman move Jesus to care for non-Jews?

From that place he went off to the district of Tyre. He entered a house and wanted no one to know about it, but he could not escape notice. Soon a woman whose daughter had an unclean spirit heard about him. She came and fell at his feet. The woman was a Greek, a Syrophoenician by birth, and she begged him to drive the demon out of her daughter. He said to her, "Let the children be fed first. For it is not right to take the food of the children and throw it to the dogs." She replied and said to him, "Lord, even the dogs under the table eat the children's scraps." Then he said to her, "For saying this, you may go. The demon has gone out of your daughter." When the woman went home, she found the child lying in bed and the demon gone.

## Her Own Woman

### By Columban Sister Marie Galvin

Bernadith or Berna, a Parkari Kohli, has been with us on the Kunri parish school staff for nine months. She is in charge of the nursery class in one of the three branches of our school. She is a Catholic, originally trained as a midwife but did not like the job so tried her hand at teaching, which she does very well and enjoys.

Berna was married two and a half years ago and moved to our parish. She was teaching in the local Church of Pakistan school at the time we were looking for a replacement in our nursery department. Since joining our parish school staff the enrolment in the nursery class has risen from around 10 to 33. Most of the children are Parkari Kohli, and the fact that Berna speaks their language is a real advantage. I have noticed that in the classroom she is firm but kind, and the children like her.

Like most of our teachers Berna has had no formal training as a teacher. When hiring teachers we insist on their having completed secondary school, review the family background and evaluate any previous work experience. Finally, there is the interview. In my search for a new nursery teacher I had basically two criteria—that the new teacher be a woman and a Parkari Kohli. These criteria I considered to be important for the sake of good rapport with both parents and children.

Even though most of our teachers do not have formal teacher training, with the support of the Catholic Board of Education, we have developed a program of ongoing in-service training for the teachers who staff the four schools of our parish.

Berna has shown great initiative and creativity in her class preparation and is reflected in her attractive classroom. She has brought color and life into the teaching of the three Rs. Her husband works at ZONG, a Pakistani telecommunications company, and Berna was able to lay her hands on unused advertising posters which she used to display tables of numbers, the alphabet, animals, vegetables and so on. I have been in teaching for many years, and I must say that I am both amazed and very impressed at the skill Berna has spontaneously demonstrated in creating a child-centered classroom where learning and teaching at a rudimentary stage are happening.

Our teachers come from both the Punjabi and Parkari communities The Punjabis tend to be generally more aggressive than their Parkari Kohlis peers. However, the fact of their working and regularly meeting together helps break down prejudices and other barriers. I have the impression that Berna is asserting a certain moral leadership in our group of teachers that transcends ethnic differences. To cite one example: At a recent meeting of teachers a male Parkari teacher suggested that that students' copy books be paid for from school funds as, in his opinion, the students could not afford to buy them. However, Berna questioned this attitude of always holding out the begging bowl and received the support of the other teachers who knew that the students could and would pay for their copy books. Clearly, she is game to voice her opinion at the risk of being put down and has won the respect of both the Parkari Kohli and the Punjabi teachers. In such ways she is helping cement a united faculty for the four parish schools and challenging her peers toward mutual dignity and equality.

After school Berna runs a literacy program with Parkari women.

Link to our tradition:

They were exceedingly astonished and they said, "He has done all things well. He makes the deaf hear and [the] mute speak." (Mark 7, 37) Rarely but occasionally a missionary is heartened when she meets a person who seems to have this gift of being able to "do all things well" that Jesus demonstrated in an amazing way.

## Waqt ki Awaz—Call of Today

### Muslim/Christian Dialogue via Radio Pakistan in Lahore and Pindi
### By Raza William

The name, William, identifies me as a Christian in a predominantly Muslim society. It is part of my identity and is on all my official documents. I have had the opportunity to work as a Christian actor and get to know some of the best artists in the country in the course of my work in radio and television for over 25 years. I began working in special programs for Christmas and Easter and was subsequently invited to act in social dramas for transmission on Pakistan national television.

Columban Fr. Colm Murphy came into my life soon after he arrived in Lahore. Prior to that, from 1981 to 1994 he had been Secretary General of

UNDA (International Catholic Association for Radio and Television).[23] He had an in-depth understanding of radio and television media, and he began to get to know our local scene. Our Bishop at that time, Armando Trindade, knew of Fr. Colm's work as he had helped Wave Studio acquire state of the art equipment. With this we were well equipped to produce Urdu programs for a Catholic radio broadcaster in the Philippines. Our bishop was not satisfied with what our local Catholic Broadcasting Association was producing so, in 1998, he put Fr. Colm in charge of the Association.

Fr. Colm formed a board or team with which he could work. With Fr. Colm, there were six of us. Fr Zacharia Ghouri, a Pakistani priest, me, Cecil Chaudhry, a retired air force group captain, Rana Faheem, a musical director, and Gloria John, a script writer. We planned and worked together very well for nearly five years.

Fr. Colm insisted that we remain on medium wave in Lahore. Less than 30% of the people of Pakistan could read, and he wanted to reach illiterate listeners in the remote villages where they would be most susceptible to fundamentalist influence. He was convinced that the high rate of illiteracy makes radio a powerful influence. We found it impossible to find out how many were listening, and of course the illiteracy did not help.

Fr. Colm made friends with many who worked in the world of mass media, most of them being Muslims. When we were casting for what we expected to be a high rating program Fr. Colm insisted that we choose our actors professionally. As a result, we were the first Catholic group to include a Muslim actor in a Christmas drama broadcast on Pakistan national television. Muslims were very happy to have a Muslim acting in our Christmas presentation, as they too have a most reverent attitude towards Jesus of Nazareth, whom they recognize as a prophet.

We were moving into the area of Christian/Muslim dialogue and some local priests were not altogether happy with that. Also, they did not like to see Muslim actors in Christian programs. Then there was the way we presented the Christmas and Easter stories. We did not merely offer a traditional presentation. Rather, exasperated with the usual repetitive Easter and Christmas presentations, we attempted to point to the relevance of both Christmas and Easter to the issues of our society. Our move away from what some understood as traditional Catholic presentations disturbed some Catholics.

I recall on one occasion, at the end of Ramadan, the Columbans made another gesture towards Muslim/Christian dialogue, which had nothing to

---

[23]    SIGNIS was founded by merging two organizations that had existed since 1928: OCIC, the International Catholic Organization for Cinema, and UNDA, the International Catholic Association for Radio and Television. It is recognized by the Holy See as an International Catholic Organization, and is a member of the Conference of ICOs, and as an NGO it has consultative status with UNESCO, Ecosoc and the Council of Europe.

do with radio or television. Fr. Pat McInerney (the Columban coordinator at the time) took the initiative to invite the neighbors along the street where the Columban house is located to come to break their fast (Iftar) at the Columban house. We organized it together, and I did most of the work. The first year we just had the simple breaking of the fast after saying the final prayer of the Ramadan fast, but in the following year we started having a full meal afterwards. Subsequently, the neighbors took it in turns to invite each other, thus fostering a communal spirit in the street.

In 2003, while Fr. Colm was out of the country, our opponents within the Catholic Church managed to persuade the new bishop to put another person in charge of the Catholic Broadcasting Association. Without any consultation we were relieved of our role on the board of CBA and Fr. Colm was replaced by a local Pakistani priest and formally thanked for his services in the Lahore diocesan newsletter.

Many of those in the world of media with whom we had worked were quite upset about the decision. An influential radio program manager, Zulfiqar Kazim, invited us to work on other programs. Sadly, Kazim died while Fr. Colm was still here with us, but not before he and Fr. Colm toured England in 2001, recording experiences of Muslims in England where they were a minority. They stayed in Columban houses, and Kazim claimed to be the first Muslim Columban. They got some excellent interviews which Kazim broadcast when he got back and then again later in the year after 9/11. His sudden death was a terrible loss.

Because of budgetary restrictions we initially looked at the possibility of Christian/Muslim programs on radio. We wrote to the Director General of Pakistan Radio in Islamabad, and he encouraged us to go ahead with our proposal. And so, we launched the Pakistan interfaith harmony programs. The name we chose for our program was Waqt Ki Awaz (Call of Today).

We were breaking new ground; we produced four programs a month, two being discussions among Christian and Muslim representatives and two being dramas. We broadcast thirteen programs on an experimental basis. These were the first programs broadcast about Muslim/Christian relationships on government radio. Since we got positive feedback from both government and private organizations we decided to continue to produce our interfaith dialogue program in which we involve people from all sectors of society—wealthy and not so wealthy, Muslims, Christians, Sikhs, Hindus, etc.

The Lahore Station Director of Pakistan Broadcasting Corporation, Khalid Waqar, wrote in a letter to us, dated December 3, 2010: "Program Waqt Ki Awaz has been broadcast on every Friday from PBC Lahore . . . . It is the need of the hour that we should concentrate more to develop brotherhood and tolerance in the society. Interfaith Harmony can only be promoted and survive if we have commitment and passion. I commend the achievement of Program Waqt Ki Awaz."

Of course, we did all this independently. Fr. Colm helped and continues to help us obtain finance to keep our work going. I don't know where he gets the money. Paying wages in the media industry tends to be costly.

We began to record our radio discussion programs for Catholic cable television, and a Catholic channel run by a local priest broadcasts these programs. The basic question that we constantly address in varying ways is: How can we achieve harmony in Pakistan?

Fr. Colm sowed a seed, and we have been able to help it grow. The Columbans have continued to support us personally, up until recently with the accompaniment of the recently deceased Fr. Pat McCaffrey, and now with that of Liam O'Callaghan, and also financially.

Link to our tradition:

"Dialogue thus becomes a source of hope and a factor of communion in mutual transformation. The Holy Spirit directs the carrying out of God's design in the history of the individual and of all humanity until the time when God's children who are dispersed by sin will be reunited as one (cf. John 11, 52). God alone knows those days, he to whom nothing is impossible, he whose mysterious and silent Spirit opens the paths of dialogue to individuals and peoples in order to overcome racial, social, and religious differences and to bring mutual enrichment. We live in the age of the patience of God for the Church and every Christian community, for no one can oblige God to act more quickly than he has chosen to do." (The Attitude of the Church toward Followers of Other Religions: Reflections and Orientations on Dialogue and Mission, Secretariat for Non-Christians, Nos. 43-44, May 10, 1984)

# A Church with Room for All

By Columban seminarian Joseph Li Jiangang

My village of 800 residents is 100% Catholic. My Christian name was chosen for me by our parish priest when he baptized me. Our village is in Shaanxi Province, sixteen hours by train south west of Beijing, China. As a young boy I always went to church with my grandmother even though I did not really like to. I preferred to be playing with my friends. On one occasion, during my primary school years, I went to see an open air movie at Mass time.

The Franciscan Missionaries of Mary Sisters (FMMs) worked in our village and ran a medical clinic. In junior high school one Sister got us together in summer holidays for religious education and at age eleven years I began to know more about God. I was born after the Cultural Revolution so much religious practice had ceased. I used to sit at the back of the church when I went alone, but when I joined the youth group we would sit at the front. As a youth I went of my own free will to church.

I was timid and afraid to read in public. I became an altar server, and at age twelve I was leading the congregation in half an hour of prayers before Mass. I liked that and on returning from school I'd drop my bag and head for the church.

When I was sixteen my father's cousin, who is a priest, wanted me to go to the minor seminary so I went, but because I wanted to. My father had the idea that since he had two sons offering one up to God was a good thing. I was only there for two months, and the government shut the seminary as it was run by the underground (illegal) part of the Church. I returned home and my father told me to just wait and see what might happen. In the meantime I enrolled at the local junior high school.

I remember one day there was a total eclipse of the sun and heavy rain. I was returning from school, climbing a hill about twenty minutes away from my home. Suddenly I was afraid that I would die. It was raining so heavily; it was dark and slippery; I found it hard to breath and started crying out to God. It was such a relief to get to the top of the hill.

After middle school I got a job as my family was poor. I worked for one year and then returned to the reopened minor seminary. I felt that the community atmosphere of the seminary helped me draw closer to God. During this time I lived with a Catholic family from Monday to Friday and on weekends returned to the seminary. Since the family I stayed with knew the school principal I was able to attend the local high school (which was not in the residential zone of my family), paying lower fees.

At age 23, in 2005, I began to think about being a missionary. I used to help out in the church during summer with catechetical programs with children. That is when I realized that many in other villages were not Catholic, and I remembered that Jesus had said that the Gospel is for everyone. I noticed that youth who said they had no faith also talked about being lonely and having feelings of emptiness in their lives. At this time I was 24 and was already in the seminary having completed high school when I was 22.

I left the seminary but began to rediscover my vocation, and a diocesan priest who had studied in Ireland for four years on a Columban scholarship connected me with Columban Fr. Kevin O'Neill. I found a job after leaving the seminary and was living in Xi'an where I became involved with the local church and youth group.

When I try to answer the question: "Why be a missionary?" I do my best to answer this question out of my experience in China. Three points occur to me. First, since my youth I grew up as a Catholic and want to share my faith, both in China and overseas. Second, it is good that the Church offers opportunities to help youth come together and share their search for meaning in life. My experience in China prompts me to think that possibly youth in other parts of the world are also searching for meaning in their lives. Third, there should be space in the life of the Church for all, not just Christians; there should be a welcome for all. Here in China I have learnt of the importance of dealing with people who are not Christians; we need to reach out to them too, and also to those in other parts of the world who struggle to find meaning for their lives and have had little chance to hear the Christian message.

Link to our tradition:

A young man whose Christian faith is rooted in family and village tradition wants others to have the chance to know Christ, a missionary spirit that echoes that of Paul the Apostle. See 2 Corinthians 12, 2-9: "I know someone in Christ who, fourteen years ago (whether in the body or out of the body I do not know, God knows), was caught up to the third heaven . . . and heard ineffable things, which no one may utter. About this person I will boast, but about myself I will not boast, except about my weaknesses . . . I refrain, so that no one may think more of me than what he sees in me or hears from me because of the abundance of the revelations. Therefore, that I might not become too elated, a thorn in the flesh was given to me, an angel of Satan, to beat me, to keep me from being too elated. Three times I begged the Lord about this, that it might leave me, but he said to me, 'My grace is sufficient for you, for power is made perfect in weakness.' I will rather boast most gladly of my weaknesses, in order that the power of Christ may dwell with me."

# Soon to Go on Mission

Rafael Ramirez Salazar is from Temuco, Chile, just over 500 kilometers south of Santiago; he is in the seventh year of a ten year initial Columban formation program.

All of us have a call from God, and each one is different. I feel that I have a call to mission, in particular to Asia. From when I was a child their way of life has fascinated me, probably because I saw it as so different from ours.

Asia seemed to me like another world, one that has been shaped by very different religious and philosophical systems, and one whose history over thousands of years has had little or nothing to do with our history in this part of the world.

My preference would be to enter into dialogue with a country who, I think, are more in touch with nature and lead a simple life, quite unlike that of the major urban centers of the world. My mission would be to share my experience of God with them, and they with me. Our dialogue would be an experience of mutual enrichment. I would like to become part of their lives and, in some way, walk the path of life together.

I feel that both God and the mission call me. I cannot identify precisely the source of this call. It comes from deep within me, and I experience it as one call to mission. I don't think it is simply my own desire or curiosity. There is definitely more to it than that. It exercises a mysterious power over me; it draws me on. It's more than just motivation, more than invitation; it's an interior force with power to shape my life.

Jorge Vargas Saboya is from Lima, Peru, and is in the seventh year of ten year initial Columban formation program.

For me the heart of mission is meeting with others who, like me, have their own particular way of seeing life and God. This meeting with others does not necessarily need to be with people from another country or culture. However my Columban experience has opened up for me the possibility of friendship and dialogue with people from other cultures.

I have lived in a mixed nationality community; I have studied in Chicago where I had the opportunity to meet young men and women from many countries. I would like to go on mission to a people of another culture in order to broaden my horizons, to share, to be enriched and to enrich others with all that is my experience and vision of life. For me, the preferred place to meet others at a meaningful level is their home.

I look forward to spending my life doing this but I am not focused on any particular country or part of the world. I feel that I can be missionary anywhere. A Peruvian priest once quoted me the following saying: *Personas que viven a Dios las encuentras en todas partes.* (You find godly people everywhere.)

For me the differences between cultures are of minor importance in comparison with what we have in common. The fact that all of us are sons and daughters of God is far more significant than all the differences that may divide us. However, I am aware of the need to recognize our differences in order to enter into a dialogue of life.

Gonzalo Borquez Diaz is from Santiago, Chile, and is in the sixth year of the initial Columban formation program.

My missionary interest was initially focused on China; my dream was to go there on mission. I realize that perhaps that may happen but not necessarily so. In fact, being a Columban seems to include much uncertainty about the future, so I feel that it is important to live the mission here and now. However, I continue to dream of living out my mission in Asia.

I want to be with God, walk with God here and now, and that is for me being mystical. I want to see God present in each person, in each moment of my life.

It seems to me that being a Columban is like walking along a ridge with a great chasm on either side. Then, at some stage one has to leap either left or right and trust in God. Faith is, in a way, a leap into the abyss. Such trust in God's love guides the heart of a mission spirituality.

However, a Columban needs to be clear about where he comes, where he is in his life at the present moment, and where he is heading. Abandoning oneself to God does not imply forgoing the responsibility to know oneself.

Not only does a Columban missionary leave his country but is also expected to leave himself, to move beyond his own needs and preferences. To be part of this missionary enterprise it seems to me that one cannot afford to be focused primarily on what he may want or prefer, and this is a permanent challenge for the missionary.

At the end of the day, no place is home.


Link to our tradition:

Columban students in our initial formation program in Santiago, Chile, share their dreams of life as missionaries. Their hope brings to mind he parable of the "mustard seed." "He proposed another parable to them. 'The kingdom of heaven is like a mustard seed that a person took and sowed in a field. It is the smallest of all the seeds, yet when full-grown it is the largest of plants. It becomes a large bush, and the birds of the sky come and dwell in its branches.'" (Matthew 13, 31-32)

# Adapting and Learning

By Columban associate Fr. Huang Joo Won Miguel (Diocese of Uijeongbu Corea del Sur)

A Korean diocesan priest reflects upon his experience of entering into the lives of Peruvians in his missionary work as an associate with the Columbans in Peru.

In a parish in Korea everything is well ordered. The diocesan plan includes programs for sacramental preparation, Biblical study and catechism. The parish priest organizes and directs everything. Lay people collaborate but are directed by the parish priest, who nominates those he wants to take on positions of responsibility in the parish. On the other hand, in a parish in Peru, at least in my experience with the Columbans, there is a variety of religious programs. Also, the lay people, among themselves, come to an agreement about who will coordinate the teamwork, be it in catechesis, a Biblical program or a social program.

In Korea parish work has been thoroughly systematized and is limited to religious programs, that is, to catechesis, Sacraments and Bible. A priest who works in a parish can take on a social commitment but that would be over and above his parish work. On the other hand, in the Peruvian parish there is a variety of parish groups that focus on social needs. Also, at diocesan level the bishop promotes the social apostolate.

In Korea what happens within the parish depends entirely on the parish priest, and the assistant priest has to ask permission to take pastoral initiatives. The parish priest coordinates everything, and the assistant must work within the parameters determined by the parish priest. On the other hand, in Peru the assistant priest has more freedom to become involved with the community and does not need to worry about administration. In this situation, at times it is better to be an assistant priest as one has pastoral freedom and no administrative obligations.

In Peru, there is less formality in relationships. In Lima the youth call me, Michael, but not so much in the rural area. It seems that there is still a certain respect for traditional social norms in the rural area. However, one does notice certain things in the rural area that are not so frequent in Lima. For example, more lay people lead liturgical celebrations, probably because there are more small communities in each parish, and each community has its patron saint, its chapel and its traditional celebrations. Community members also expect baptisms and marriages to be celebrated in their own chapel.

The vertical vision of things and the corresponding vertical organization are typical of both Korea and Peru, but there are also some differences. The Peruvian likes to have a voice and a vote; he or she likes to participate in every type of election, but at the same time expects the person in charge to know how to give orders. Within the Church the Peruvian lay person has little chance of taking on an autonomous leadership role, unless it is within an independent lay organization. One could say that there are shoots of democracy within the Church but, at the same time, church leaders are on the alert lest matters get out of hand. In Korea the independent voice of the laity is little more than a whisper.

During the past ten to fifteen years there has been a lot of change in the Korean political system as regards ever greater acceptance of the rules of a democratic system. This is having a big impact on the youth, who use the internet to both inform themselves and express their point of view. Before the advent of the internet, one way of limiting lay initiative and leadership was by controlling information and the mass communication media.

I would say that my experience of having lived and worked outside my country for eight years has allowed me to learn a number of things that help me in my missionary work and in the following points I mention just a few that occur to me:

In my country religious celebrations are solemn affairs, are according to indications written in a book and show considerable respect for hierarchical order. In Peru there is more an attitude of equality and flexibility. The priests, in many cases, sit with the lay faithful; it seems to be a more open Church.

In Korea, even among the clergy, the hierarchy of age or position is quite noticeable (the age or position of a person determines the form we use to speak to them). This is an aspect of a culture formed by Confucian thinking, but here, even though it is true that is some kind of hierarchy, in many situations there is more a tendency towards a culture of equality.

In Korea the age of the person is always taken into account in conversation and in social gatherings. In Peru the older person is respected, but the manners of social courtesy are not as strict as in Korean culture.

The formality of social life is stronger in Korea. For example, in Peru I have learned to give my opinion regardless of who may be present at a meeting, but according to my Korean culture one does not express an opinion in the presence of his elders. Also, if one goes to a meeting with a bishop in Korea, one dresses formally but here not necessarily so.

Finally, I would like to say that here with the Catholics of Peru I have learned something quite significant about my way of living the Christian faith. In my country the celebration of Mass is very solemn; it is an interior moment and that is fine. In Peru the Mass is happier and, in a sense a little chaotic, as the people sometimes arrive late, they chat during Mass. They do the same at a retreat. All this makes me think that the Lord is among us in the things of our lives, but in my country the predominant idea is of the Lord present in what is solemn in the Mass and the retreat. In Korea what is emphasized is the Lord present in the religious, but in Peru the emphasis is on the Lord present in life.

Link to our tradition:

Ephesians 4, 1-6 sets out the basis of church unity in diversity: "I, then, a prisoner for the Lord, urge you to live in a manner worthy of the call you have received, with all humility and gentleness, with patience, bearing with one another through love, striving to preserve the unity of the spirit through the bond of peace: one body and one Spirit, as you were also called to the one hope of your call; one Lord, one faith, one baptism; one God and Father of all, who is over all and through all and in all."

## Finding Ways to Be Who I Am

### By Columban Fr. Gabriel Rojas

Urdu is the language of the central Punjabi region and is one of many languages spoken in Pakistan but, at the time of the formation of Pakistan in 1947, it was declared the official language of the country. Many might link success in mission with proficiency in the local language. I did my best to learn Urdu, but I knew that I was not a natural linguist. However, I was determined to make a contribution to our mission in Pakistan with or without proficiency in the Urdu language.

My prime interest was and still is work with youth. I put together a simple booklet titled, "Follow Me," to support my work with 120 youth from the 30 communities of our parish. It contained three parts: first, prayers by famous Christians who have been significantly relevant to our Church's pilgrimage over the ages—Oscar Arnulfo Romero, San Francisco de Assis, Don Bosco, San Ignacio de Loyola, San Columbano, Teilhard de Chardin, Thomas Merton, Lancelot Andrews and others; second, catechetical themes such as, self-worth, God, my personal story, my vocation, the sacraments, who is Jesus Christ, the Holy Spirit, and so on; third, reflections about life—an eight day retreat with Jesus. Pakistani friends helped with the Urdu text. Following the publication of "Follow Me" I went on to prepare two more small booklets for my young Pakistani friends: one on how to celebrate the sacraments, and another with outlines of lay-led liturgies for various occasions. These small publishing jobs were for me a way to contribute to our mission. I could go out and meet others socially, but I still had plenty of time to spare. My job as such was not very demanding so I needed to find ways to use my time creatively.

I went on to refocus on my musical interest. I write, sing and play instruments, but not at a professional level, but good enough to publish and informally share with others. To date I have published two CDs of songs that I've written and am preparing a third. Most of my songs are in Spanish, but there are also some in English and Urdu. All are basically about my personal journey so some reflect what was happening for me during my seven years in Pakistan.

Painting also became part of making a new life in Pakistan. It was another way of expressing myself. I was determined not to simply close in on myself and become depressed. I was aware of my own limitations, but I was also aware of my gifts and talents. My life situation in Pakistan challenged me to develop my God-given gifts.

In due course my early pedagogical studies also stood me in good stead. As a seminarian I had studied pedagogy but did not get a chance to make use of what I'd learned until I was appointed to a parish with a parish school. I really got to like working with the school team and the children.

In the midst of striving to find a way to be missionary in a creative way, what moved me most was being immersed in a culture so like that of Jesus of Nazareth. This experience has helped me see things as He might have. Just as Jesus prayed in public for all to see, so too do the people of Pakistan. The shepherds also walk ahead of their sheep that follow along. I have seen day workers in the local town plaza waiting to be hired. Just as in the time of Jesus, blasphemy is a major sin and crime. These are just a few examples of similarities that I have noted.

In the midst of steady progress as regards my missionary contribution I also had some bad luck. I got around on a small motorbike and was in at least ten accidents. Most would say that Peruvian traffic is chaotic, but I assure you that it is even worse in Pakistan. Even now injuries from those accidents continue to affect me, and I cannot walk without some discomfort or pain. All this was for me quite traumatic, changing my way of seeing myself and helping me see others, with whom I shared my life, as my brothers and sisters. This in turn moved me to go and wish the Muslims well on the occasion of their major religious celebrations. I did not want to stand by and passively allow our religious differences be a barrier between us. For a time I wondered whether to stay or leave as I was the only Columban in Lahore. I decided to stay.

Thanks to the grace of God I've been able to return to Peru alive. I did not die in a traffic accident or in a terrorist attack. It could have happened easily as there is so much violence in Pakistan. On returning to Peru I sensed I was in a strange country. Pakistan changed me so now I see and feel Peru in a different way.

However, I continue with my preference for working with the youth. My job in Peru is to help young men discover whether or not they might want to become Columban missionary priests, and I know that this will surely challenge me. If I can help some of my fellow Peruvians see life and its challenges from a different perspective no doubt I will contribute to a renewed zest for life in those with whom I meet and work, and maybe some of these young men will join us.

Link to our tradition:

Searching for ways to be missionary in both Pakistan and Peru is essentially about discovering ways of entering into dialogue with others. As in the case of Paul the Apostle in Athens, not everything one attempts is as successful as one might wish. See Acts 17, 22-34: "Then Paul stood up at the Areopagus and said: 'You Athenians, I see that in every respect you are very religious . . . .' When they heard about resurrection of the dead, some began to scoff, but others said, 'We should like to hear you on this some other time.' And so Paul left them. But some did join him, and became believers. Among them were Dionysius, a member of the Court of the Areopagus, a woman named Damaris, and others with them."

## Traipsing from House to House

### By Columban seminarian Kurt Zion V. Pala

It was already about five in the afternoon, but I had told my host father that I would be home by around one so I told them I have to leave because it was getting dark. I often get scolded for coming home late. But I always have my good reasons. "Been traipsing around from house to house?" my host mother asked. I just put on my best smile and greeted them. I lived with an Indo-Fijian family, Uncle Bhola and Auntie Mary, for almost five months. Right after my Hindi class with Master Gyan, I walk back home from the Mission House. But before reaching home I have to climb a hill and on the way pass through about ten houses. On any given day people would call out for me to have some tea or yangona or on some special days even get free lunch of goat curry, rice and dhal. This is what I enjoyed most when I was living in Paharkhaala, in Naleba, Labasa, Fiji, not just the food but also the people.

"Hello, Grandad and Grandma!" I greeted the Muslim couple that I never miss seeing on my way home. Aji never fails to greet me when she sees me and says every time, "Go slowly my son, go slowly." She's fond of children and that includes me because her children are not with them anymore.

From on top of the hill, I could see the girls waiting for me. I sometimes help them out with their homework. "Greetings, Brother!" I heard them greeting. Aunty Jyoti asked me to have lunch first. Sitting on the veranda I saw Grandad Bara Babu riding on something driven by two big bulls. I knew what it was so I exclaimed, "Grandad is this your tonton?" Nana just laughed and told me that it is called tamtam (ox cart) and not tonton. After revising their homework I told them I had to go.

Just a few steps, is Auntie Almelu's place. I saw her sitting under the tree and so I called out, "Auntie, how are you?" Almilu Attha is my host father's older sister. Before I could say no, she had already set a cup of tea and pudding cake before me. I told her I will be celebrating my birthday with the children this coming Sunday. I finished my tea and left. I decided to see the parents of the children and asked them if the children could come to my small birthday party. All the children came in their best dress. I was surprised to see Guddhi and Dennis wearing shirts—they usually run around half-naked. The children enjoyed the games and sweets, but I guess I enjoyed the day the most.

I tried to visit, as much as I could, all the families in the village not just the Catholics. Grandad Boss, a devout Hindu, invited me to his place. I learned that he owns two milking cows, and so I asked him if I could come and learn to milk the cow. Early next day, I went back to his place and saw him tying the two hind legs of the cow. He showed me how to do it, and I just started milking the cow. I went home happy with two bottles of fresh milk.

If you ask me how I spend my day, I would say, "Traipsing from house to house!" and that is how I learned more about the language, culture, and every aspect of life in an Indo-Fijian village. I grew to love the people and became a family member to them from being a stranger when they started to call me beta (son), natin (grandson), bhaeni (nephew), and anna (elder brother). And I will never forget this one little girl who calls me Brother-Mama (Uncle Brother). Thank you Naleba! I hope I brought you some joy—as much as you have brought into my life. May we become missionaries of joy to every person we meet, regardless of their faith or color.

Link to our tradition:

Jesus also sent out his first followers to learn what being a missionary might be about for them: "He summoned the Twelve and began to send them out two by two and gave them authority over unclean spirits. He instructed them to take nothing for the journey but a walking stick—no food, no sack, no money in their belts. They were, however, to wear sandals but not a second tunic. He said to them, "Wherever you enter a house, stay there until you leave from there. Whatever place does not welcome you or listen to you, leave there and shake the dust off your feet in testimony against them." (Mark 6, 7-11)

# CHAPTER 5

## Efforts of Inculturation

Inculturation means the transformation of authentic cultural values through their integration in Christianity and the insertion of Christianity in human cultures. Inculturation of the Christian Gospel happens when a cultural group embraces the Christian faith and gradually puts their cultural stamp on the practice of that faith. Inculturation is a slow journey which accompanies the whole of missionary life. It involves those working in the Church's cross-cultural mission, the Christian communities as they develop, and the bishops, who have the task of providing discernment and encouragement for its implementation. Today we recognize the result of this process as we refer to English Catholicism, Irish Catholicism, German Catholicism, Spanish Catholicism, the many forms of Latin American and African Catholicism, and so on.

The split between the Gospel and culture is without a doubt the drama of our time. Cultures have to be regenerated by an encounter with the Gospel. Humanity's cultures need to be evangelized (not superficially, but in a vital, in depth way—i.e. to their very roots), always taking the person as one's starting-point and always coming back to the relationships of people among themselves and with God. The reign of God which the Gospel proclaims is lived by men and women who are profoundly linked to a culture, and the task of building up of the reign of God inevitably borrows elements of humanity's cultures.[24]

The missionary is not the only one responsible for the inculturation process, but he or she might help or hinder it. Over the centuries many missionaries have done their work under the protection and with the explicit support of the secular power. They often failed to contribute to the process of inculturating the Gospel. In fact, much missionary work attempted to impose European ways on the conquered. The destruction wrecked by the arrogant brutality of rapacious soldiers and those who profited from their conquest, together with the long-term

---

[24]   Evangelii Nuntiandi No. 20 and Redemptoris Missio, No. 52 are the main source for the content of the previous two paragraphs.

belittling of both the languages and cultures of colonized peoples must rate as one of the biggest systemic crimes in the history of the human race.

However, some missionaries did provide wonderful tools, which helped the people to whom they were sent to inculturate the Gospel in due course. These tools include a methodology for writing the local language and providing access to an education that ensures that at least the young will learn to read and write. Such tools ensure that a cultural group might continue to affirm and live out their own identity in the modern world. Men and women of the modern missionary movement have provided thousands of schools and teachers for those to whom they were sent as messengers of the Good News.

At times the inculturation process has happened, and will probably continue to happen on the fringes of missionaries' efforts. The conquered peoples of Latin America put their particular stamp on the Christian faith through the appropriation of the Catholic devotion to the saints. Soon after the European conquest and colonization, the Mexican peasant, Juan Diego, was caught up in a mystical experience with Mary, the mother of Jesus. The image that resulted from this experience is known as Our Lady of Guadalupe. Similar experiences happened in many parts of Latin America and became the basis of the Christian religious practice of the conquered peoples of the continent. There was always a story or legend associated with that foundational moment. The saint involved became patron of the village or the whole people and is venerated in a special way each year on the anniversary of the initial mystical encounter. At the heart of the devotion is the belief in the miraculous power of the patron in favor of his or her devotees.

The rest of this chapter is made up of mission stories illustrating the above paragraphs. After each story or, in some cases groups of stories, there is a link to our religious tradition, which, for the most part, is taken from the Bible but, also from teachings of the Popes, General Councils and Episcopal Conferences.

## Recreating Andean Identity

### By Columban Fr. Paul Prendergast

Quechua is the language of the people and integral to their identity and culture.

Columban Fr. Paul Prendergast's pastoral vision for parishes in the southern Andes of Peru is one among many initiatives that are like building blocks in the recovery and re-creation of an Andean culture that was mostly destroyed by the Spanish invasion and colonization of the Andean region nearly 500 years ago. Quechua is the first language of most of Paul's 25,000 parishioners who live in about 100 villages and hamlets scattered over this mountainous region (ranging between 3,500 and 4,500 meters above sea level) in the south of Peru.

He has been doing his best to promote Quechua in the liturgy and catechetical programs in the parishes in which he has worked for over the past 25 years. Even though he has received little support, he believes he is swimming with the current. At one time, he may have been a voice crying in the wilderness, but no longer.

When Jesus of Nazareth saw the need to ensure the continuity of his vision he chose 12 men and spent time preparing them for the mission they would eventually assume. Thousands of institutions around the world have emerged from the vision of one person or a few people. In recent decades in the predominantly Andean countries of Latin America (Ecuador, Peru and Bolivia) a recovery of Andean identity has been having an increasing impact. Ever more politicians of Andean background have been coming to the fore; Evo Morales, an indigenous politician identified especially with indigenous interests won the presidential election in Bolivia in 2005.

Rural Andeans swarmed to the cities, and did their best to educate their children, many of whom have moved into positions in business and the professions achieving a place in society that they would never have dreamed of 100 years ago, or even less. Non-government organizations, representatives of indigenous groups, people within the Catholic and other Churches, sectors within national and local government have been promoting the importance of indigenous languages as a significant means to retain and enrich cultural identity.

Teachers, doctors, nurses, lawyers and judges who work in this part of the country are expected to master the rudiments of Quechua in order to speak to, or at least understand the locals when they speak their own language. Many local professionals grew up speaking Quechua and don't forget their roots. In another region of Peru, civil servants are expected to be able to attend citizens in either Spanish or Quechua. The State Education Department is developing new initiatives for teaching Quechua in schools. Even so, teachers often meet resistance from parents who want their children to learn Spanish in order to get on and have choices in life beyond the back-breaking labor in the fields.

In the parishes of Peru's southern Andes each village has a catechist who is in charge of what happens in the local Catholic community. The catechists coordinate with the parish priest and attend monthly meetings to prepare themselves to oversee and run the catechetical programs in their home communities.

Over the years Paul has developed a number of texts to help the catechists but he insists that there is still so much to do, in particular for youth and children. I was at his 73rd birthday celebration and he was telling me how he is looking at new ways of continuing the project he initiated years ago through the development of the Quechua Center.

Like others with a vision, he wants to form an institute to promote the use of the Quechua language in the Catholic Church of this part of Peru, but his vision is not restricted to the Church. He does not spell out all the details but hopes to become aware of new possibilities as he goes about his missionary work with the people of his parish. One thing he does want to do is to recover the personal history of the older generation whose way of life is quickly disappearing; better roads, television, the internet and mobile phones have brought the world in all its variety to the hills of the southern Andes. At the same time, he wants to record the myths and legends of the local people.

If young people are cut off from the memory of the way of life of their ancestors, if they have no chance to appreciate the myths and stories that describe the life-meaning framework of their parents, grandparents and great-grandparents, they will not be able to recover and recreate their cultural heritage in the rapidly changing circumstances of the modern world. Paul wants to do his best to ensure that the youth of today have the means to live in cultural continuity with their ancestors. At this stage of his life he feels that the best he might be able to do is provide the initial impetus in the hope that others will carry on the task.

Link to our tradition:

Inspired by no earthly ambition, the Church seeks but a solitary goal: to carry forward the work of Christ under the lead of the befriending Spirit. And Christ entered this world to give witness to the truth, to rescue and not to sit in judgment, to serve and not to be served . . . . To carry out such a task, the Church has always had the duty of scrutinizing the signs of the times and of interpreting them in the light of the Gospel. Thus, in language intelligible to each generation, she can respond to the perennial questions which men ask about this present life and the life to come, and about the relationship of the one to the other. (Vatican II, The Church in the Modern World, Nos. 3-4)

## Poetry Has Shaped My Life

### By Columban Fr. Kevin O'Rourke

After arriving in South Korea in 1964 my group studied Korean language for a year, worked pastorally for two years and then studied language again for another year. At that time there were over 150 Columban priests in Korea. I decided that there was more to be learned than taught and there were already more than enough to do the teaching. Also I realized that our role in the parish apostolate was fast coming to an end as the local seminaries were full and many young Koreans were being ordained and looking for parish appointments. It seemed to me that we had done our part in this area and it was time to move on.

To prepare myself for another way of being missionary in Korea I enrolled in graduate school at a local university in 1968 and completed the studies for a

Master of Arts degree in Korean language and literature in 1970. I applied for a teaching post at Kyunghee University and soon obtained tenure but was advised from the beginning to get a doctorate in order to guarantee permanency in my job. Putting together a doctoral thesis in Korean on Korean poetry was hard work and it took me until 1982.

I believed that an important cultural contribution we, as a missionary society, could make was to introduce Korean culture to the west. As I delved into the vast field of Korean literature I worked first in the modern period: my MA dissertation was on naturalism and the Korean short story of the 1920s. Subsequently I specialized in modern Korean poetry for my Ph.D. and subsequently in the poetry of the classical period, Shilla and Koryŏ (600 to 1392), and Choson (1392 to 1910). To date, I have published more than 20 books of modern fiction and poetry and Korean classical fiction and poetry.

Zen Buddhism is the heart of the poetry of the Shilla and Koryŏ periods; it is a poetry rooted in awareness of the moment. Confucianism was the framework for the poetry of the subsequent Choson period; the new ruling class rejected Buddhism and so attempted to eliminate passion and feeling from local literature. Yet the poetry of both periods sought to promote self-cultivation and the freedom of the human spirit. Zen strove to reveal what was beneath the appearances. Poetry in the Confucian period focused on inculcating moral values.

In the 1920s when Korea was a colony of Japan, Korean students in Tokyo were exposed to poetic forms popular in Europe during the late 19th century. They were taught to imitate a poetic style that had never been part of their own cultural tradition. However, So Chongju (1915-2000), the greatest poet of modern Korea, returned to the classical period in search of what a modern Korean poet might be. He sought especially to recreate the spirit of Shilla and Koryŏ. So Chongju imbibed classical poetry in the spirit of the following short verse:

Small Lotus Pond by Hyeshim (1178-1234) [The original text was written in Chinese characters as the Korean alphabet did not come into use until the 16th century]

No wind, no swell;
a world so various opens before my eyes.
No need for a lot of words,
to look is to see.[25]

The Confucian approach is illustrated in the following verse by Yang Saŏn (1517-1584):

---

25    *The Book of Korean Poetry*, translated and edited by Kevin O'Rourke, University of Iowa Press, 2006, p. 76.

The mountain may be high,
but it is still below heaven.
Climb and climb again; everyone can reach the summit.
Only he
who never climbs insists the mountain is high.[26]

I would like to mention an interesting difference that I have noted between western and eastern poetry. If Hopkins, for example, were to write a poem about a dandelion he would home in on what makes this dandelion different from every other dandelion in the world, whereas a Korean poet would focus on what this dandelion has in common with all other dandelions. Hopkins begins in the particular and ascribes everything to the glory of God. The Korean poet begins in the universal and inculcates moral values. Differentiation is Hopkins' way; harmonization is the Korean way.

During the early years of my work on Korean literature I focused primarily on making the riches of the Korean poetic tradition available to the English speaking west, but I was always interested in reading Korean poetry for what it told me about myself and my life. I always told my students to study poetry for what it tells them about themselves. In later years I ponder more and more on what I have learnt through forty years of reading, research, translation, writing, and teaching.

I continue to believe that what I have done in making Korean literature more available to the west is an important missionary contribution. However, I suspect that what Korean literature has taught me about myself and my life in Korea is of even more fundamental importance. I actually date my love of poetry to a class on 12th century Gaelic poetry (called Fenian poetry) in secondary school in Ireland. We composed poetry among class members and were encouraged by our teacher to play with words and the poetic form. I taught English poetry in Korea for thirty years; I read Chinese poetry in translation and Korean poetry, hanmun (Koreanized form of literary Chinese and the official literary language of medieval Korea) and the vernacular in the original. Now in retirement I continue to write poetry, translate and teach others the joys of poetry.

Link to our tradition:
"But it seems to Us that the sort of relationship for the Church to establish with the world should be more in the nature of a dialogue, . . . this method of approach is demanded nowadays by the prevalent understanding of the relationship between the sacred and the profane. It is demanded by the dynamic

---

[26]     *The Book of Korean Shijo,* translated and edited by Kevin O'Rourke, Harvard-Ewha Series on Korea, 2002, p. 58.

course of action which is changing the face of modern society. It is demanded by the pluralism of society, and by the maturity humanity has reached in this day and age. Be a person religious or not, his or her secular education has enabled them to think and speak, and conduct a dialogue with dignity.

Moreover, the very fact that they engage in a dialogue of this sort is proof of their consideration and esteem for others, their understanding and their kindness. They detest bigotry and prejudice, malicious and indiscriminate hostility, and empty, boastful speech." (Ecclesiam Suam, Pope Paul VI, 1964, Nos. 78-79)

## Shudh Hindi and Fiji Hindi

### By Columban Fr. David G. Arms

A discussion about the use of the appropriate language in prayer and liturgy among Indo-Fijian Catholics

Over the years there have been discussions, both among Indo-Fijian Catholics and Indo-Fijians in general, about the relative usefulness of Shudh Hindi and Fiji Hindi. Sometimes the discussions become quite heated, particularly as efforts are made to promote the use of Fiji Hindi.

At the outset, it is important to acknowledge the attributes of both forms of Hindi. Shudh Hindi is an important world language with many speakers (including in the Indian diaspora) and an extensive literature. It provides a very dignified atmosphere to formal occasions, both civil and religious. It is also the language generally used in the media.

For its part, Fiji Hindi is the language spoken by the people of Fiji as their everyday means of communication. It is something which Indo-Fijians can be rightly proud of, as it is something that has been developed by them and their forefathers right here in Fiji over the last century or so. Being the language of daily use however, it is not regarded as appropriate for formal occasions. This is where the arguments start, for an increasing number of people feel it should be respected and used rather more widely than it is at present.

Fiji Hindi is not an inferior language or a pidgin. Several linguists have taken a good look at Fiji Hindi, and all agree that it is a proper language, has a full grammar, and should not be regarded as in any way second-rate. True, it has very little by way of a literature. There are also areas of vocabulary which are not well developed, but Fiji Hindi in such circumstances, like any other true language, borrows from another language or creates vocabulary items to suit. Fiji Hindi can also be written, just as Shudh Hindi is, in Devanagari, Roman, or even Arabic (Urdu) script.

How does all this affect us in the Catholic Church? The move for greater acceptance of Fiji Hindi has led to the publication of religious materials in it. There is the Fiji Hindi New Testament with the title Nawa Haup (New Hope), and a DVD about the life of Our Lord with the title The Pathfinder. However, some feel that Fiji Hindi is not suitable for such religious material.

Presently, when Indo-Fijians pray in a formal or semi-formal (e.g. mandali) setting, Shudh Hindi is used. But when an Indo-Fijian spontaneously turns to God in prayer, (even mental prayer without pronouncing out loud the words), what language is used? When speaking from the depth of one's soul to God about something very near and dear, is Shudh Hindi all that can be used? In that case, what about the many Indo-Fijians who don't know Shudh Hindi well? Are they cut off from speaking to God?

God is indeed almighty, glorious and most holy. But God is also our Father, and that is the term Jesus told us to use. "So you should pray like this: Our Father in heaven, . . ." (Matthew 6, 9). Similarly, when Jesus gave Mary to us on the cross through the apostle John, he did not say, "This is your Queen", but "This is your Mother" (John 19, 27). Children usually speak to their father and mother in familiar rather than honorific language. Wouldn't that imply that using everyday language in at least some of our prayers would be fine, even normal? Not that Shudh Hindi should be abandoned, but rather there should be a place for Fiji Hindi too. And perhaps its role should become greater rather than less.

It is certainly possible for people to have excessive regard for Shudh Hindi. I once heard with my own ears an Indo-Fijian parishioner saying, "Father's homily today was really good. I barely understood a word, but it sounded so nice!" To some, this may seem an extraordinary comment, but the attitude it reflects is not limited to Indo-Fijians. In the English-speaking world too there are those who like elevated language for their religion, and those indeed who prefer Latin—a different language altogether—as sounding nice and being something special for God. They seem to seriously downplay the value of understanding what is said.

I have been in mandalis where the scriptures are first read in Shudh Hindi. Then people are encouraged to ask about any word they don't understand. Yet some participants, especially the younger generation, read an English version instead in order to understand immediately what is being read. The use of Shudh Hindi in this sort of circumstance seems to be pushing people out of Hindi altogether to the use of another language. If they need English to help them understand the scriptures, are they not likely to simply use English from the beginning and save themselves bother? And might not the same attitude take over for the recital of prayers?

People are likely to have quite different responses in wanting on the one hand to respect the sacred, and on the other hand to be practical. As Catholics though, perhaps the matter should be discussed in mandalis and at district and even national level. There are likely to be those who feel Fiji Hindi should have a greater role.

The problem will come, of course, when it comes to using Fiji Hindi in practice. Toleration and some willingness to experiment should be encouraged.

While on the one hand it would not be good to force Fiji Hindi prayers and texts on an unwilling community, it would not be good either to presume that using Shudh Hindi suits everyone. Quite a few of the faithful don't know Shudh Hindi well, but may feel embarrassed about saying they do not understand what has been read or said. In all cases the overall objective would be to improve the quality of our prayer, the understanding of our faith, and the sharing, within the Indo-Fijian cultural setting.

Link to our tradition:

Jesus offers us brief advice about prayer: "When you pray, do not be like the hypocrites, who love to stand and pray in the synagogues and on street corners so that others may see them. Amen, I say to you, they have received their reward. But when you pray, go to your inner room, close the door, and pray to your Father in secret. And your Father who sees in secret will repay you. In praying, do not babble like the pagans, who think that they will be heard because of their many words. Do not be like them. Your Father knows what you need before you ask him." (Matthew 6, 5-8)

St. Paul recognizes our inability to know and say what is in our heart: "In the same way, the Spirit too comes to the aid of our weakness; for we do not know how to pray as we ought, but the Spirit itself intercedes with inexpressible groaning. And the one who searches hearts knows what is the intention of the Spirit, because it intercedes for the holy ones according to God's will." (Romans 8, 26-27)

Psalm 139, 4 suggested something similar long before Paul wrote his letters: "Even before a word is on my tongue, Lord, you know it all."

## Post-parish Mission Era

### By Columban Fr. Pat McMullan

Some joys and challenges of working on mission in Korea now that foreign missionaries are not needed to establish and develop parishes

Now that Columban priests do not arrive in Korea expecting to be appointed to a parish we see a different kind of flowering of talent and dedication. Korean language poses a serious challenge to English speakers, and yet many English speaking Columbans take on jobs that require advanced language skills. Missionaries today often plough a lonely furrow as we search for and take on jobs that allow us to witness to Gospel values. In this context of search and commitment we develop friendship networks.

I don't see our life and work here as heroic, but it does demand that we have the confidence, courage and faith to have a go. It would be a lot easier to be doing what we do in our country of origin. The fact that we have chosen to be here engaged in missionary work of this kind speaks to me of a powerful energy in each one and in our missionary group.

While forging a life as a missionary priest outside the parish framework does pose its own set of challenges and difficulties, it is also a release from a form of constant pressure. The Korean Church of today is based to a large extent on adult baptisms, a fact indicating that many Korean Catholics have deliberately chosen to be members of the Catholic Church. Consequently we have an active and searching adult laity. At times cradle Catholics tend to be indifferent as regards active involvement in the Church's mission. So, not being caught up in the intense dynamics of urban parish life leaves us space and energy to be missionary in another way.

I have found that there are many people of goodwill who gladly give us a hand to find our way. Korea is a religiously alive country, perhaps one of the under-studied countries in the world as regards religion. For the past 40 or so years this country has gone down the modernization and development path without simultaneously moving into a process of secularization. Here, religion and personal religious conviction would be considered normal aspects of life; religious belief is not the exception. In Korea I would rarely be asked the question, "Is there a God?", but rather, "Who is God for you?"

Perhaps this seemingly innate religious curiosity of Koreans in general eases the way for a priest missionary in Korea. Koreans are clear that we are not here to teach English or to do business. Accordingly, many offer us entry into their personal and family lives. I feel that we have privileged entry; we are trusted, which of course becomes the basis for friendship and sharing our mutual quest for life.

While it is inevitable that I have opinions about what might be the most suitable ways of being missionary in Korea today, I must say that I am impressed by the dedication of other missionaries who may not see things quite as I do. I see them engaging with this society with energy and love. My decision to walk a different path does not imply that I not take my hat off to them.

I feel that a major challenge of being a foreign missionary in Korea today is living with the feeling of insecurity. There is no such thing as a career path to help focus our energies. We need to be open to allowing things to evolve without having a project well mapped out. I have found that trust has been and still is a huge challenge for me—trust in myself, trust in others, trust in God. At the end of the day, it is impossible to even think of myself as the self-made man. I am thoroughly networked with others, and God is there in the midst of it all.

On one occasion, I was in an elevator in a multi-story office block when I met a woman who worked in the Church history research office. I was working on the floor above hers doing a series of 150 twenty minute television shows for the diocesan media office. We chatted briefly, and she asked me whether I would help with some translation from Korean to English. My commitments allowed me to respond positively to her request, which opened up further possibilities to me.

Much of my life here has been like that. Being a foreign missionary here demands an ability to go with the flow, to be ready to respond without being one hundred percent sure that you can do the job, confidant that there will be a way around any problem that may arise.

There definitely is scope for the foreign missionary in Korea. To date I have worked in the parish apostolate, been a seminary professor (lecturing in Korean), done an annual series of lectures (20 night sessions) for laity on one of the Gospels, written short articles for one of the Seoul Catholic weeklies and translated books and articles from Korean to English. At the moment I am engaged in university chaplaincy and am chaplain to a home for seriously intellectually disabled men. I am also looking at doing post-graduate study at Seoul National University. What might be next? God knows!

Link to our tradition:

Faith is the realization of what is hoped for and evidence of things not seen . . . . By faith Abraham obeyed when he was called to go out to a place that he was to receive as an inheritance; . . . By faith he received power to generate, even though he was past the normal age . . . for he thought that the one who had made the promise was trustworthy. So it was that there came forth from one man, himself as good as dead, descendants as numerous as the stars in the sky and as countless as the sands on the seashore. All these died in faith. They did not receive what had been promised . . . By faith Abraham, when put to the test, offered up Isaac, and he who had received the promises was ready to offer his only son, . . . let us . . . persevere in running the race that lies before us while keeping our eyes fixed on Jesus, the leader and perfecter of faith. For the sake of the joy that lay before him he endured the cross, despising its shame, and has taken his seat at the right of the throne of God. (see Hebrews 11, 1-12, 2)

## Helping the Korean Church Grow

### By Columban Fr. Jeremiah J Cotter

A protest against the dictatorship of President Park Chung-hee went slightly wrong. In Korea at that time people were being kidnapped, tortured and imprisoned; some simply disappeared. Fr. Jim Sinnott, the Maryknoll vicar general of the diocese of Incheon where I was working, had preached a fiery sermon about the need to resist dictatorship at a peace Mass in Incheon cathedral. He recalled that because Hitler was not effectively opposed in the beginning we ended up with World War II and the Holocaust.

The young Korean priests present prepared to lead a public protest; they wanted the support of the foreigners but asked us to leave the frontline to them. As we processed out of the cathedral the Korean priests with anti-Park placards took the lead. The riot police appeared and tried to block us from continuing to the main street. In all the pushing and shoving we foreigners ended up in the frontline.

I tied a handkerchief around my face for protection against pepper gas. However the police took photos and friends told me later that my photo with face covered was on the wall of local police stations. A few months later when I was leaving to go on home leave (1975) I was refused a re-entry visa.

I was appointed to do vocation promotion work in England, and there I got to know about "houses of affirmation," which were recently established to help priests and religious with emotional and spiritual problems. I was taken by their holistic approach to the issues that clients wanted to address. I wished such places had existed when I was 20 years younger.

I returned to Korea in 1980, the year after Park Chung-hee was assassinated, and the new government adopted a less drastic style. I went to work in a Seoul parish for four years and was pleasantly surprised at the changes in the local church since I had left in 1975. There had been many new converts, new priests and a lot more university graduates coming into the church. However, growth and change were putting a lot of pressure on priests.

I thought it would be great if they had something like the "houses of affirmation" to help them cope with pressures resulting from the rapid rate of change and the new challenges. I campaigned for something to be done about training someone, but my colleagues turned it back on me. I resisted but then in 1985 I went to do some study in the U.S. and Canada. The studies helped me hone skills in the areas of counseling and spiritual direction, and in 1987 I returned to Korea.

I wanted to work with others who were properly trained in these fields so I talked with people I thought might be interested. Eventually a group came together to talk about the project. Teresa Wang, who had studied in Manila and spent seven years counseling university students, expressed interest in the project; she wanted a change. Some bishops were vague in their response to my proposal and others expressed support. Cardinal Kim (Seoul) was supportive. His auxiliary, Bishop Peter Kang, came on board with practical suggestions.

Originally I thought that the Bishops' Conference might take responsibility for the project. However, Bishop Kang told me that I would be waiting a very long time for that to happen. He suggested beginning in Seoul but with the backing of the Columbans and other religious orders; each (the archdiocese, the Columbans, other religious orders) would put up one third of the cost.

We set up in an office in the Seoul Diocesan Center and began to see clients. It was a trickle at first but then more and more began to come. At that time in Korea people would generally resist considering receiving the kind of help we offered; they might feel ashamed. Most of our clients have been Sisters, some lay men and women and regrettably only a few priests. As client numbers grew so did our staff, who were for the most part Korean religious, all of whom had the required professional training. They were mostly part time employees of our center.

There was no professional counseling service open to the public in Korea at the time we started. Gradually counseling became more acceptable in Korean society and other similar services were started. Over the 20 years that I worked with the center the perception of counseling changed and more professionals qualified in our field, so services increased. I feel grateful for having had the opportunity and the support to pioneer a field of service that is now well established in Korea.

Link to our tradition:

Establishing the first modern, professional counseling service in Korea was a work of charity in line with similar initiatives in the early Church. See Acts 6, 2-6: "So the Twelve called together the community of the disciples and said, 'It is not right for us to neglect the word of God to serve at table. Brothers, select from among you seven reputable men, filled with the Spirit and wisdom, whom we shall appoint to this task [distribution of food to widows in the community], whereas we shall devote ourselves to prayer and to the ministry of the word.' The proposal was acceptable to the whole community, so they chose Stephen, a man filled with faith and the Holy Spirit, also Philip, Prochorus, Nicanor, Timon, Parmenas, and Nicholas of Antioch, a convert to Judaism. They presented these men to the apostles who prayed and laid hands on them."

## In the Church in the World

### By Veronika Rausuvanua

As St. Paul makes clear in 1 Corinthians 12, the members of the Christian community have many and diverse talents, all of which we should be grateful for and ensure that they are put at the service of the community and the Church's mission.

To each individual the manifestation of the Spirit is given for some benefit . . . . But one and the same Spirit produces all of these, distributing them individually to each person as he wishes.

My life experience to date confirms for me that God has entrusted me with a gift of leadership, which I have been constantly asked to exercise in both the Church and civil society.

My family roots are in the Solevu parish in Vanua-Levu (main north island of Fiji). We came to live in Raiwaqa in 1975. My late Dad was an inactive Methodist, and my late Mum a strong Catholic so all of us were brought up Catholics. Dad eventually joined the Catholic Church in 2000. He worked as a medical orderly looking after leprosy patients in a state run hospital.

I went to Catholic schools and enjoyed joining in the youth activities in our sector of the parish (the parish is divided administratively into 11 sectors). Then in 1994 the elders in our sector urged the younger group to participate in the sector leadership. One Sunday I went to the parish youth meeting as substitute for our sector youth leader. I was quite surprised to be elected interim parish youth president at that meeting as I had not attended parish meetings. We were so busy with sector youth activities that we hardly ever went to parish meetings.

In my new role I was required to attend Parish Pastoral Council meetings. I soon became vice chairperson of the PPC and later the chair person. My sector also made me sector leader, not just the youth representative.

Something similar happened for me when I went as parish youth representative to our regional youth meetings, which drew together youth leaders from seventeen parishes. I was elected to the regional leadership and our meetings were a great educational experience as we rotated them around the parishes, and so got to see and understand better the reality of the youth in many places.

From these diverse experiences I discovered the need for good planning. People were happy to participate when things were well planned and they were given prior advice of the plans and their role in them. I saw clearly that good communication fostered participation and encouraged collaboration. In fact, I might go further and say that an inclusive, collaborative process encourages all to come prepared to play their part. Sharing responsibilities allows all to own a project or program.

All this transfers smoothly to my present workplace in the Ministry for Health where I head a section responsible for supporting technical staff, that is, nurses, doctors, paramedics, dental technicians and so on. We are in charge of providing clear terms of reference within the workplace. We see that all comply with work ethics, rules and policies as established. Our job requires that we get the technical staff to collaborate and we do, but not in a dictatorial way. My grassroots church experience has taught me a much more effective approach, one that emphasises teamwork and consultative leadership.

Perhaps my most significant experience of belonging to the Church that has a direct bearing on my present workplace is that of having shared with a great variety of people in parish life and, I suspect, the most significant component of that sharing has been listening. This has helped me so much in my work in the Ministry of Health.

I also must say that it is not just the workplace that has benefited from my parish experience, but the parish is also benefiting from my workplace experience. We have brought a health awareness program to our parish and the program's outreach includes both Catholics and non-Catholics. This program develops awareness about non-communicable diseases (NCDs) i.e. life-style diseases, and proposes ways of preventing their spread. It is especially important for many Fijians as obesity and some of its more glaring consequences, such as diabetes and heart disease, are causing the early death of many people, in particular, men. Our parish has set the pace for others who have now become involved in the preventive health program.

Link to our tradition:

There are different kinds of spiritual gifts but the same Spirit; there are different forms of service but the same Lord; there are different workings but the same God who produces all of them in everyone. To each individual the manifestation of the Spirit is given for some benefit. To one is given through the Spirit the expression of wisdom; to another the expression of knowledge according to the same Spirit; to another faith by the same Spirit; to another gifts of healing by the one Spirit; to another mighty deeds; to another prophecy; to another discernment of spirits; to another varieties of tongues; to another interpretation of tongues. But one and the same Spirit produces all of these, distributing them individually to each person as he wishes. (1 Corinthians 12, 4-11)

## Mission, a Constant Opportunity

By Columban Fr. Bob Mosher

How one Columban has searched for and found varied opportunities to live out
his vocation

My life as a missionary began and grew where new ground was being broken,
as I worked within the familiar structures of parishes but took on the principal
missionary challenges of other contexts. Let me explain.

Even though, during the military dictatorship of 1973 to 1990, the parish
constituted the backbone of the local Church in Chile, the Church in the western
zone of Santiago came up with a four-stage plan of evangelization, titled "working
class apostolate." This plan proposed a new way of being church, not in opposition
to the parish but as a complementary alternative. It sought to establish Christian
communities where the Gospel was generally unknown, and had not taken root in
people's lives.

The first stage consisted of a friendly presence. Another Columban and I
moved into a small house in a local "población", or neighborhood, and we joined
community organizations, gradually becoming accepted by the community.
Neighbors would regularly drop in for a cup of tea and a conversation in the
afternoon. Often in the course of the years we spent there, they would wait for
us to return from a Mass, wedding or baptism in the neighboring parish before
beginning a local community activity or celebration. Such was life for us once we
were accepted as part of the local community. We had no chapel in the area, nor
did we yet attempt to form any Christian communities.

The second stage blossomed as the neighbors began to wonder why we were
there. They would ask us about our decision to live among them, and about our
intentions or plans. Such questions provided us with the opportunity to talk about
Christ, and the faith, and of our experiences of God's presence and work in the
lives of those who lived the Gospel. In the context of the brutal dictatorship Chile
suffered under in those days, our dialogues ran deep into the night as we explored
the implications of living as Christians in dark times of violence, torture, secret
police surveillance and death.

From that period of dialogue emerged a third stage, in which we offered
interested parties the chance to get to know more about our way of life. We
offered meetings for formal instruction in the faith, looking at what the Bible or
Church documents had to reveal about the real-life situations of unemployment or
sickness that people lived through. We invited them to form a community that met
regularly to share, pray and search.

Finally, the community would arrive at a mature state, and develop into a
fully-fledged Catholic community enjoying a sacramental celebration of their faith.
In this way, we put the sacraments at the end of the process rather than at the

beginning. We did not use them as a way to get people interested in our Catholic faith. Rather, our communities learned to experience the sacraments as a source of spiritual sustenance for their daily lives.

During this time I also worked as a house painter for a few months, and met other men and women who never came near any churches or Christian communities. Yet they knew well how to form communities, and trade unions, of which Chile has a long history. I found myself learning many skills from them, both as a painter and as a member of their vibrant community. On one occasion I was arrested by police for participating in a peaceful street protest against torture, and then had trouble explaining to the investigating officer that this Catholic priest was also a painter. No, I said, not a painter of portraits or landscapes, but a painter of walls and ceilings. He angrily dismissed me, not quite ready to believe that the Church could be that close to the life of the working poor.

In 1987 I was asked to suspend this apostolate and work in our program for preparing young Chilean men for the Columban missionary priesthood. It was a new venture in Chile, which was part of our changing missionary emphasis around the world. For years since our foundation in 1918 we had dedicated our human and material resources to establishing and building up parishes, putting down the basis of the diocesan Church. We then decided to prioritize helping the local churches in which we worked to become more missionary. Inviting Chileans to join us as Columban missionary priests has been one response to that priority.

In 1990 I went to Rome for further studies, which equipped me well for the next stage of my missionary journey. I became director of the formation program in Chile, but also became the Director of the National Commission for Ecumenical and Interfaith Dialogue. Each year we centered our activities on the Week of Christian Unity that ended on Pentecost Sunday.

At an interfaith level we had significant dialogue with Muslims (both Shia and Sunni), Jews (Sephardic) and Buddhists (Tibetan). All had been in Chile for a long time, even several generations in some cases, and had adapted to Chilean ways. We allowed a variety of religious traditions to gain some appreciation of each other and demonstrated that there are Catholics who are open to discovering the religious riches of other faiths.

Ecumenically, our primary aim was to establish a commission with similar objectives in each of the 28 dioceses of Chile. However, perhaps our major achievement was an agreement about Baptism with a number of other Christian churches, which took two years of debate and agreement to compose. Since the signing of the Chilean agreement at least a dozen countries have achieved a similar coming together of various Christian Churches.

Chilean Christians (Catholic, Orthodox, Lutheran, Methodist and some Pentecostal Churches) recognized the validity of each other's Baptism, an agreement that was fundamental for the cause of Christian unity. How could we hope to effectively proclaim our faith to others while doing nothing about the sad divisions among us? The Chilean cardinal in charge of the Vatican's Congregation for Liturgy in Rome backed us, and so did the vast majority of the Chilean bishops, led by Cardinal Errázuriz of Santiago. We celebrated the signing of the agreement during the Jubilee Year 2000. This agreement about Baptism brought together two currents of ecumenical work, one based on dialogue about doctrine and another based on doing things together pastorally, resolving tensions regarding the enrollment of children in Catholic schools, or in the process of marriage preparation of Christians from different traditions. In order to reach agreement we stipulated two conditions: the use of water, and the words of the Trinitarian formula to impart the sacrament.

Then before leaving Chile in 2009 I was involved in setting up a mission center to help the local Church become more missionary. The idea behind that center has inspired us to develop something similar in El Paso, Texas, considering the needs and challenges of this part of North America.

Link to our tradition:

"Inspired by no earthly ambition, the Church seeks but a solitary goal: to carry forward the work of Christ under the lead of the befriending Spirit. And Christ entered this world to give witness to the truth, to rescue and not to sit in judgment, to serve and not to be served . . . . To carry out such a task, the Church has always had the duty of scrutinizing the signs of the times and of interpreting them in the light of the Gospel. Thus, in language intelligible to each generation, she can respond to the perennial questions which men and women ask about this present life and the life to come, and about the relationship of the one to the other. We must therefore recognize and understand the world in which we live, its explanations, its longings, and its often dramatic characteristics." (See Vatican II, PASTORAL CONSTITUTION ON THE CHURCH IN THE MODERN WORLD, GAUDIUM ET SPES, 1965, Nos. 3 & 4)

## Post Vatican II Renewal in Labasa Parish

### By Josefa Vasakula

Lay men and women discover and take on their role in the mission of our parish.

In 1984 Archbishop Petero Mataca invited Fr. Nicholas, an Irish Jesuit working in Japan, to do three Post Vatican II workshops in Lautoka, Suva and Labasa, Fiji. Along with ten others from our parish I participated in the Labasa workshop, the basic purpose of which was to help us discover the role of lay men and women in the Church's mission.

Prior to these workshops most of us Fijian Catholics had presumed that our role was to do what the priests told us to do. In the course of the workshop I, along with others, learned that by Baptism we have a right and a responsibility to participate intelligently in our Church's mission. So began a new way of being a Catholic in the parishes of Fiji, as all of us belong to one archdiocese.

The workshop helped us appreciate that lay people have an active role in the Church's mission; we came to a clearer understanding of what that role might be; we were helped to see the difference between our role and that of the priest; the workshop helped us see how the role of the priest and that of the lay person might complement each other. We gained enough understanding to move ahead with confidence.

This parish had been established in 1963, with Fr. Dick O'Sullivan as our first parish priest. I arrived in the parish in 1972. At that time the parish was divided into four sectors; now we have eleven. Once the Post Vatican II workshop of 1984 gave us the green light to move into a more proactive evangelisation role, we became interested in personal renewal programs. I found that Marriage Encounter and the Charismatic Renewal gave me and other members of our parish new life.

Couples began to do things together; they clearly loved each other. Participation in the Charismatic Renewal seemed to make people more open, and being open to one another we were able and ready to take on new initiatives. Even informally, chatting over the kava bowl, we felt freer discussing our religious beliefs. We also moved into areas of the parish where previously there had been no formal church presence. In fact, the parish committee did wonders to our community by organizing a great variety of renewal activities, all of which helped the laity discover and exercise our role in the task of evangelization.

One of our first initiatives following the workshop was to organize youth groups in each sector. We invited the youth to be part of parish life, and soon they were involved in everything in the parish-liturgy, choir, St. Vincent de Paul and so on. In those days it was easier to communicate with the youth but things began to change in the mid-nineties. More youth moved out of our area; others influences from outside entered via internet, television and mobile phones. Our island world changed considerably. We still have active youth in each sector, but these days less participate in the Church. In addition, they seem to think quite differently from the youth who joined our groups in the 1980s.

About this time we began the RCIA program (Rite of Christian Initiation of Adults), and a small but steady stream of people have participated and requested to be members of our Catholic community. The numbers joining the program have varied over the years but, after the boom of the 1980s with up to fifteen being received into the Church in 1985, we have had from two to eight asking to join our community each year.

Sharing with other religions did not begin until about 2004, and in 2008 we formed a Bible discussion group with representatives from other Christian churches. However, interest is limited, and we have not met for about two years.

However, liturgically we might share but perhaps not in a planned and organized way. People may feel interested, particularly during Holy Week or Christmas, and when welcomed they participate.

During this period of Post Vatican II renewal our parish community has also been a small seedbed of vocations to the priesthood, the religious life and the role of parish lay catechist. Three young men have been ordained priests; three young women have become Sisters, and we now have six catechists, where as previously we had only one.

Our participation in the Church's mission has never been restricted to internal parish community activities. We do have to build up our Church, which in turn has a mission to our world. It sends us out to proclaim the Gospel by deed and, as St. Francis said, if necessary by word. Our parish community has developed three organizations that respond in different ways to needs in our society, namely, The Catholic Women's League, The St. Vincent de Paul Society and The Ecumenical Center for Research, Education and Advocacy. The members of these organizations work to help improve our local society, to make it a more human and just place in which to live. They act in the spirit of the words of Jesus, "I have come that you may have life and have it to the full."

Link to our tradition:

Brief excerpts from Vatican II's decree on the Church's missionary activity, *Ad Gentes*, promulgated by Pope Paul VI, 7 Dec 1965:

The pilgrim Church is missionary by her very nature, since it is from the mission of the Son and the mission of the Holy Spirit that she draws her origin, in accordance with the decree of God the Father. #2

. . . by the very necessity of mission, all the baptized are called to gather into one flock, and thus they will be able to bear unanimous witness before the nations to Christ their Lord. #6

This missionary activity derives its reason from the will of God, "who wishes all people to be saved and to come to the knowledge of the truth." #7

## Yes, I Can Be a Missionary

### By Columban Fr. Jude Genovia

Becoming a Columban missionary began for me in 1986 soon before I was due to finish high school. Two Columban priests, Fr. Dick Pankratz from the U.S. and Fr. Charlie Meagher from Ireland, came to our school to talk to the boys in the final year. They introduced themselves and explained why they had come to the Philippines and told us where they were working. I was impressed by Fr. Charlie's deep, strong voice and even more by the fact that both priests spoke to us in our own language, Cebuano. Hearing about their mission and that they had come from so far away started me thinking. Then Fr. Dick followed up with five of us, and after a short test we were down to three. He then helped us to attend a weekend where we had more discussions and tests. Fr. Dick kept at me and wanted to see my parents.

My mother realized that I was on the same track as my elder brother who had been in the Redemptorist seminary for three years, but had decided to leave. She laughed and told me that I would not persevere. Still, my parents supported my decision. Religious vocation was nothing new in our family. My mother's sister and my cousin are nuns. My mother's three brothers and two of my cousins entered the seminary for a time, but left before ordination. Other members of the family were also in the seminary for a time but chose another path.

I was in the Columban house in Cagayan de Oro for the night before leaving on the ferry for Cebu City (on a neighboring island) where Columban students did college studies. Bishop Paddy Cronin was there and that was the first time I realized that our local bishop was a Columban. He was so warm and encouraging.

Leaving for college in Cebu was another step along the path of my Columban missionary journey. It all really began from Manticao, Mizamis Oriental, the small village where I was born and brought up. It's been a story of gradually moving further and further away—after Cebu, to Manila and then on mission in Japan and Korea. Moving on and meeting new people and facing the challenges before me has helped me grow in appreciation of my missionary vocation. I grew in confidence in myself, in conviction as regards my faith, and in passion as regards my calling to share this faith with others.

My few years in Japan allowed me to arrive at the firm belief that I could and wanted to take on the missionary vocation. For a Filipino, Japan poses a number of challenges. First, Christians are in a minority whereas in the Philippines we are the majority. Second, the Japanese language is quite difficult. Third, Japanese culture is quite different from ours. Then too, there is the cultural bias of the Japanese against Filipinos; they tend to look down on us, see us as a lower class of people. All of this was like a maze I had to find my way through in order to be able to communicate my faith to the Japanese whom I might have the opportunity to meet and get to know.

At first, the Japanese youth I met could not understand why I was in their country. It made no sense to them talking about wanting to share my faith, of working as a missionary of the Catholic Church, of entering into dialogue with them about life and its meaning, etc. In fact, the one word that seemed to make some sense to them was, volunteer. They would be slow to accept me. Of course, they would be polite, but I was aware that I was on the outside. How was I to get into the inside?

Part of our initial introduction to life in Japan was living with a Japanese family. I had the good fortune to be received into the home of a family of Japanese artists of national renown. Bit by bit they took me into their confidence; I was courteous and patient and eventually came to feel like part of the family. In fact, one of the most poignant moments for me was listening to the mother of the house, who was at that time in her early seventies, talk about the issue of Japanese soldiers forcing thousands of women in the countries Japan invaded in World War II, including my own country, into bondage as comfort women. She apologized to me for what they had done, and I was so moved.

I came to feel accepted as my family and also the youth of the parish began to invite me to family functions. This did not happen overnight, but I realized that it was important to wait patiently. I knew I needed their acceptance to even begin to share what I had come to share with them, namely my Christian faith. Clearly, there could be no dialogue before there was mutual acceptance. In time, especially the youth, came to accept my Filipino way of greeting with a hug. The Japanese are so non-tactile in their way of relating but we Filipinos like to hug; it's our way.

I could relate many instances of being affirmed by my Japanese friends. Their affirmation helped me believe that I could be a missionary in a foreign land. As I learned from them they too accepted my insights into life. They may have had the impression that Filipinos are basically troublemakers, which for them is quite unacceptable as they are quite focused on harmony. In coming to know me they also realized that there are Filipinos with other values that they could appreciate.

Now I am in my own country once again, charged with the task of inviting young Filipinos to share their Christian faith with other peoples. Young Filipino Catholics are not lacking in zealous enthusiasm, but at times they may need to be persuaded that they may have a role to play beyond the borders of our own country. I can tell them of the joy that I experience as a missionary; I can persuade them that they too might be up to the challenge. I tell them that they can find God too and share their faith with other peoples. We Filipinos are deeply spiritual and know that our way of being might help other cultures in some way.

We have the base of a vibrant though imperfect Church. Many young people participate enthusiastically in spreading the Gospel message through involvement in religious and social organizations. Recently, 5,000 priests attended a national conference of the clergy held in Manila, and the younger group outnumbered the older group, a basic sign of life among the clergy. Part of being Filipino is being on the move, going from one island to another, as if mobility were an innate characteristic of our people. Filipino Catholics give generous support to the Church and its works.

In recent years, quite a few religious orders have come to work and recruit, although some do little work other than recruiting and training. However, it is a sign of recognition of the generosity of our Catholic youth. There are also many lay missionary sending organizations, some of which send out well prepared Filipino professionals.

Our Church is active in social issues, especially those related to the environment and honesty in our government and electoral processes. However, in general our prophetic role leaves much to be desired. We are slow to tackle some of the major issues of injustice that ensure a huge gap between the wealthy and the poor in this country and allow the poor to be used as pawns in an economic chess game played in the interests of a small but powerful local and international elite.

I know we have a lot to do here in the Philippines in order to be faithful to Christ's invitation, but I believe that we have the faith and our Church has sufficient depth and vibrancy to recruit and send missionaries to other lands. I feel privileged to be part of that Gospel enterprise.

Link to our tradition:

"The Good News proclaimed by the witness of life sooner or later has to be proclaimed by the word of life. There is no true evangelization if the name, the teaching, the life, the promises, the kingdom and the mystery of Jesus of Nazareth, the Son of God are not proclaimed . . . . In fact the proclamation only reaches full development when it is listened to, accepted and assimilated, . . . In a word, adherence to the kingdom, that is to say, to the "new world," to the new state of things, to the new manner of being, of living, of living in community, which the Gospel inaugurates. Such an adherence, . . . reveals itself concretely by a visible entry into a community of believers . . . . Finally, the person who has been evangelized goes on to evangelize others. Here lies the test of truth, the touchstone of evangelization . . ." (*Evangelii Nuntiandi*, Nos. 21-24, Pope Paul VI, 1975)

## Last Man In and Last Man Out

### By Columban Fr. Peter Woodruff

Spanish Augustinian friars founded the town of Lingayen, the Philippines, in 1614 and established the parish in 1616, naming it, *Los Tres Reyes* (The Three Kings). In 1740 the Dominicans took over the parish. They were obliged to leave the parish after the successful Filipino revolt against Spanish rule in 1898, and Filipino priests served in the parish until 1933, when the Columbans were invited to staff and develop the parish. Soon after in 1939, the Columban Sisters arrived to work in the catechetical apostolate and in education.

The massive adobe church with its imposing bell tower dates from around 1700 and has gone through many stages of construction and reconstruction, the latest of which was the rebuilding after World War II bombs destroyed most of it. It was officially reopened in 1965, but is now called the Parish of the Epiphany of Our Lord, as there is no mention of three kings in the Bible.

Lourdes de Guzman, my guide for the visit to Pangasinan Province, grew up in Lingayen. She knew many Columbans who worked in the parish of her hometown. She wanted me to put on record some of the achievements of the Columbans in the province and also parishioners' memories of Columbans. The last Columbans to work in Lingayen left in 1981, so I did not expect to find many whose memories went back beyond that date.

We drove into the church courtyard and the first person Lourdes met was Salud Puzon, now 88 years old, has been active in the parish since 1939. She told me how she was first introduced to the Sodality of Our Lady by the Columban Sisters when she was in high school. The Sisters also asked her to teach catechism to the primary school children. In 1943 the parish priest brought the Legion of Mary to Lingayen; it was the first presidium in the Philippines outside Manila. The Legion flourished for many years, with numerous groups of adults and youth. Now there is only one group of elderly members. However, Salud is undaunted. She told me that the basic ecclesial communities now do much the same as what the Legion used to do. For her, the bases continue to be covered despite all the changes she has seen.

She and her friends told me about parish social outreach initiatives. In 1947 the parish primary and secondary school was established, and in 1960 the college level was added. It is now called St. Columbans Academy. The Lingayen Catholic Credit Cooperative was founded in 1964 and was declared the most outstanding cooperative (nationwide) in 2001 by the Cooperative Development Authority. It now has assets of around $4.6 million and has over 8,000 members. In 1971 a parish clinic was started for the indigent, but since the local state hospital opened a few years ago the clinic does little more than hand out free or low cost medicine to the poor.

Natividad Crisostomo, a companion of many years of Salud in the parish community, was also active in religious and social issues. She told me of her work as a teacher at St. Columbans Academy where she met her husband, Fernando. She showed me her house built of local hardwood over 100 years ago, long before the days of air conditioning; her pride and joy is a shrine to the Sacred Heart in the sitting room of her home. Fernando died seventeen years ago and was also active in the parish community. He donated land to the Columban Bishop, Harry Byrne, for a building to be used for the apostolate to the Aetas, the indigenous who lived in the nearby hills of Zambales Province, Fernando's home territory.

If I could meet two such people coincidentally in the space of an hour I am sure there are many more I did not meet, others who might have told me more about how the Columbans of years past helped them form a vibrant parish community that gave witness to the Gospel in a variety of ways. Nor did I meet the many parishioners of other parishes in Pangasinan that were subsequently staffed by Columbans. Lourdes took me to where Columbans worked in six other towns along the road from Lingayen south west to Zambales Province—Domalandan, Labrador, Sual, Dasol, Eguia Dasol and Infanta.

One Columban continues in Labrador, one of the poorer parishes of the province, and we met briefly as I was whisked from place to place. Fr. Jim Sheehy, despite over 80 years old, continues to lead a busy parish. He had no advance warning of our visit as we did not have his phone number, nor did I know we were heading his way until the morning we went. Being Palm Sunday, Fr. Jim had been busy about many things since 6:30 a.m. It was Palm Sunday, and then he had a house blessing, and later a family came looking for a baptism, and after that a parish group was getting their act together to go camping, and then Lourdes and I arrived with two friends plus a driver.

Fr. Jim insisted we stay for lunch, and he ordered in some take away. He showed us the church, especially the Stations of the Cross that had recently been renewed by a parishioner who had recently returned from a visit to the U.S. They begin with the last supper and end with the resurrection. He talked about the parish cooperative and other projects that are helping neighbors use their talents productively and so improve the family income.

Whatever matters Fr. Jim may be involved in these days I know I met a contented and lively missionary priest in the Labrador parish house on Palm Sunday 2010. He is the last Columban to be appointed to Pangasinan Province and will be the last man out.

Link to our tradition:

"[T]he Holy Spirit is the principal agent of evangelization: [the Holy Spirit] impels each individual to proclaim the Gospel, and . . . causes the word of salvation to be accepted and understood. [The Holy Spirit] is the goal of evangelization [who] stirs up the new creation, the new humanity of which evangelization is to be the result, with that unity in variety which evangelization wishes to achieve within the Christian community. Through the Holy Spirit the Gospel penetrates to the heart of the world, for it is [the Holy Spirit] who causes people to discern the signs of the times . . . which evangelization reveals and puts to use within history." (*Evangelii Nuntiandi*, No. 75, Pope Paul VI, 1975)

# Getting into the Nuts and Bolts of Life

### By Columban Fr. Oliver McCrossan

I first arrived in the Philippines in 1976, was assigned to Mindanao and worked first in Pagadian. At that time there were more than 150 Columbans in five dioceses. In those days the main emphasis in our local church was the development of basic Christian communities; it was all about the development of lay people. There was a communist rebellion going on at the time, and some believed the Church was infiltrated. I worked in five parishes in the diocese of Pagadian, all of which have now been handed over to Filipino diocesan priests. Parish leaders and friends were killed. Along with many others in our parish communities, I was involved in human rights issues. I drew great courage seeing others stand up for their rights, as they experienced their faith as a liberating experience. I was inspired by ordinary people facing up to a very tough situation.

When I came back many years later (2000) I was moved by a cab driver who had been affected by polio as a child. I began to get involved with other drivers as well. There was a small credit cooperative that had been started by a local priest in 1969, and I discussed with its leaders the possibility of doing something to help the pedi cab drivers. The manager showed interest, so we drew up a proposal and asked for seed money, which we received through the Columbans. In 2006 we launched our "Pedi cab-to-live" project.

What moved me on from the parish based work of my first sojourn in Mindanao was that most Columbans had moved out of parishes. I looked for another way of supporting those in need, those on the periphery, the handicapped, the pedi cab drivers, etc. In short, those who were not being taken care of in the parish system. I have been involved with these people and to a certain extent with prisoners. I felt that neither the local church nor the government responded adequately to these groups in society. Also I attended a conference in England at the Schumacher College, which is very much into environmental studies and care for the earth. A lecture on microfinance and strategies for helping people to be responsible for their own lives had a major impact on me. I believe that if people improve economically they often grow in dignity and capacity for involvement and decision making beyond mere survival.

All these factors came together to help me find my way, and I believe that in some way the Lord is in there looking after and guiding me. I also grew up in a family where our house was always open and I remember the travelers coming around selling things and others begging. My mother was always kind and welcoming to strangers. My father, who came from a farming background, had a small business. He had a small truck. My family background has had a lot to do with my interest in the promotion of small income-generating projects.

Many missionaries focus more on education in some form or other, but in large part, because of my background, I tend to prefer more practically oriented projects. I'm just more into doing. I think my particular gift is in the line of relating to ordinary people. I get a buzz out of listening to others and hearing how they are doing in their family and work. With the pedi cab drivers I like to hear how they are going with their payments, how they are managing to make ends meet, and so on. I think I've found my niche helping others in their work and giving them a wee bit of encouragement and support in any way I can.

Before I came back here in 2000, the circumstances of parish life did not allow me the time to get into anything other than what the parish demanded. However, I always did have an interest in new development ventures that people were setting up. The people I stay in touch with in the parishes are into practical income-generating projects, such as planting this or that crop or type of tree. I never could get into being a teacher; it is just not my style, even though I recognize it as important and an essential aspect of our mission work. I've accepted that I'm inclined to a more action based approach.

I've been lucky finding some NGOs in Ozamis City in which I've been able to become involved. It may be small time stuff but it's what our lives are about—small time stuff. I'm always on the lookout for income generating activities.

I've seen people grow in confidence in themselves, especially in the case of the pedi cab drivers. They have so little schooling and have to really struggle to make ends meet. I see them learning to be part of an organization. They struggle to pay back the loan to the cooperative, but they are proud to do just that since fulfilling their contractual obligation gives them a certain sense of dignity.

"But you will receive power when the Holy Spirit comes upon you, and you will be my witnesses in Jerusalem, throughout Judea and Samaria, and to the ends of the earth." (Acts 1, 8)

# Managing a Cooperative for the Poor

### By Fuly Procianos

I am the manager of this cooperative. We have 4,000 members. We support small farmers and are producing organic fertilizer as the commercial fertilizer is very costly. Columban Fr. Oliver McCrossan also gave us money to help set up a small nursery. Most of our members are very poor and many look as if they have no hope in life. We screen the prospective members; we make sure they are not drinkers or irresponsible in some way. So far it's working for us.

Fr. Ollie came to our cooperative to finance the pedi cab project. Right now 80 pedi cab drivers are members of our cooperative, and about 40 have completely paid off their loan. They pay 50 pesos a day, 25 of which goes into their savings account in the cooperative. Fr. Ollie also helps us send one child per family to school and helps cover the cost of a medical check-up for the children.

Most of the pedi cab drivers have plenty of children. We try to run the diocesan natural family planning project with them, but it does not work. At the moment we are releasing one unit (pedi cab) per month. We know that it's very difficult for many of the families living along the shore, because when the waves come up they flood the houses. Last year some of the children almost drowned. So, we developed low cost housing for the pedi cab owners. It is similar to the project Habitat for Humanity.

## Undaunted and Determined

By Rick Vincent Duma

I am 35 years of age, married with three kids and a polio victim since nine months of age. My handicap is almost normal for me, and it does not hinder me from pushing ahead. Still, I have to make a real effort to achieve my dreams, which seem a long way off. However, I can see some daylight now, as I will begin fourth year of law school in June and hopefully next year I will be taking the bar exams. I am so grateful to Fr. Ollie for the scholarship to study, not only for myself, because I hope to be able to help other disabled people.

We have an organization called STAND (Strategic Alliance for Networking on Disability). Most of our members are on crutches or in wheelchairs, but it is open to others. Most are mobility impaired. We try to lobby the government to pass laws for the benefit of the disabled sector. I used to be president, but my studies obliged me to hand over to someone else with more time to do the job, which entails writing lots of letters and trying to persuade authorities to implement the access laws for the disabled so that we might have greater freedom of movement.

My scholarship began in 2007, and I'm the only one in university on this scholarship. The scholarship program also helps others in primary and secondary school. I also work as a clerk in the municipality, and with what I earn there I am able to cover family expenses.

Link to our tradition:

"And whoever gives only a cup of cold water to one of these little ones to drink because he is a disciple—amen, I say to you, he will surely not lose his reward." (Matthew 10, 42)

# Interview with Roweena Cuanico, Coordinator of the Columban Lay Missionary Program in the Philippines

By Columban Fr. Peter Woodruff

Why do you think the Columban lay mission program in the Philippines has continued to attract new LMs?

The lay mission program was initially set up with the active support and involvement of Columbans who were involved at the grassroots level with Basic Ecclesial Communities and their leadership. These men had the experience of forming lay leaders and seeing them in action, so they knew how to work with lay initiative and leadership locally and simply applied their knowledge to the broader challenge of developing a lay missionary movement for work overseas. They knew that, if given the right conditions, lay leaders would blossom. They were also working with the confidence that Vatican II supported and encouraged what they were implementing with the laity locally and internationally.

How are the lay missionaries sustained in their missionary commitment?

We are now about to send out the 18th group from the Philippines. They are going to work in Birmingham, U.K. One third of all those who have been sent out since the beginning of the program in 1990 are still on mission. Being on overseas mission has given so many an opportunity to find themselves, grow into their missionary vocation and develop their initial commitment. The continuity of a significant group in the program has given us stability and offers a degree of security to new lay missionaries.

We have received constant support from Columban leadership and Columbans in general in both the Philippines and the countries to which we have been sent. We experience their support in nurturing the lay mission vocation, in the stage of preparing for overseas mission, and also in our missionary commitment as they open doors for us with mission opportunities that they help us find and take on.

We have also grown into an attitude with its corresponding habitual process of review that allows us to constantly find ways of improving how we go about our mission. Each lay missionary has two personal reviews every three years. We have a monthly meeting of lay missionaries at which suggestions are welcomed and discussed. We also having an annual meeting that involves review and planning. There is a genuine commitment to reflect on our lives and mission work and improve what we are doing.

Recently we decided to have a two day bi-monthly meeting. The first day will be for prayer and reflection and the second day for business. At our annual meeting, we begin with a two day workshop on intercultural living, followed by two days of reflection prayer in silence, then two days of business, and finishing with a one day outing.

What has the experience of international, cross-cultural mission meant to you?

First, it has allowed me to discover myself in terms of God, my family and my own person. It helped me become so much more aware of who I am and to grow as a person.

My eight years in Fiji was a humbling experience—learning a new language, being told what I could and could not do because of cultural and religious traditions. I may have had great ideas when I left the Philippines in 2000, but found that I had to rethink everything in Fiji. The new reality into which I had thrown myself challenge so much of what I had previously taken for granted.

I am so grateful to God for being able to let go of my own agenda and respond to others according to their needs.

A defining moment for me was the experience of living with a Muslim family in Fiji for four years. I was deeply moved by their openness and acceptance of each other, and introduced to a friendship that was born and nourished by living together. I had my own room and kitchen, but all of us shared the same house.

My own faith was nourished by their faith—their dedication to prayer and fasting. Their way of living their faith made me want to be sensitive to their religious beliefs. I realized that, through my friendship with them and a few Hindu families, even though there are differences among us we have so much in common. I have learned to recognize and be grateful for what we have in common. My faith has deepened and been nourished by others whose faith is different from mine. This experience of mission in Fiji added so much color and meaning to my life.

In conclusion, let me say that I now firmly believe that forming and living relationship is at the heart of mission.

Link to our tradition:

"It is necessary, then, to keep a watchful eye on this our world, with its problems and values, its unrest and hopes, its defeats and triumphs: a world whose economic, social, political and cultural affairs pose problems and grave difficulties in light of the description provided by the Council in the Pastoral Constitution, *Gaudium et Spes*. This, then, is the vineyard; this is the field in which the faithful are called to fulfill their mission. Jesus wants them, as he wants all his disciples, to be the 'salt of the earth' and the 'light of the world' (cf. Matthew 5, 13-14). But what is the actual state of affairs of the 'earth' and the 'world', for which Christians ought to be 'salt' and 'light'"? (See Christifideles Laici, No. 3, Pope John Paul II, 1988)

## Anita, a Peruvian Lay Missionary in the Philippines

### By Columban Fr. Peter Woodruff

Anita grew up in what used to be a Columban-run parish in the northern suburbs of Lima, Peru. Her barrio was first settled by migrants from the provinces in the 1960s. From her family and her personal life experience she learned about poverty, solidarity and struggle. Anita joined the Columban lay missionary program and in 2008, with three companions, arrived in the Philippines.

In Cagayan de Oro, the Philippines, Anita was introduced to the local St. Vincent de Paul conference, Alliance of Two Hearts, whose president, Fe Jaquilmac, knew the Columbans from the days when Columban Archbishop Paddy Cronin was her boss in the social action program in the early 1980s. The St. Vincent de Paul Society had arrived in the Cagayan de Oro in the early 1980s, thanks to the concern and initiative of a Filipino diocesan priest. However, some of those in charge of the conference misappropriated funds, and when Fe was asked to take on the presidency she first had to put the house in order. Fe has been president of the archdiocesan conference since 1988, but finds she has to push to get local support for the work. People may have goodwill, but then they also seem to be so busy about whatever may be the hectic nature of their lives.

Fe was so pleased to be able to help Anita find a way of being with and supporting the poor with whom the local conference worked. As Fe explained to me, the focus of their work is to enable the poor and, in the context of this task, help them discover the person of Jesus Christ. Their projects do require funding, but it all happens in a context of supporting the efforts of the poor to stand on their own feet. Progress is slow, and some do not make it. The poverty of the poorest is grinding and can leave its victims devoid of hope and so lacking in the determination to take hold of the reins of their lives. The gentle accompaniment of the St. Vincent de Paul workers, such as Anita, encourages families, often headed by women, to push ahead.

The St. Vincent de Paul Society also has other projects such as a consumer cooperative that offers loans for house repair, small businesses and tuition. The size of the loan given to a member depends on the size of their capital build-up. Those who do not build up their capital are asked to leave the co-op. There are also three small grocery stores and a massage clinic under the umbrella of the conference's works.

The place I visited was a day-care center run by the women of the group who rotated to look after the many small children I met running about at will. Rotating the job of caring for the children allows the women to work and so earn a living. The group I met have a small workshop where they make candles, for which there is a constant demand due to regular brown-outs as the local electricity supply cannot always keep up with the demand, even more so when there is drought since the generators are water driven.

Anita had taken me to meet her friends in one of the poorest places I have ever seen. They welcomed me with joy and a courtesy that I had noticed seemed to be typical of Filipinos. After taking a few photos, which the children absolutely revelled in, we settled down to chat and watch the children playing their games.

I left the day-care center and the candle making workshop knowing that most of those I had met will spend the rest of their lives in poverty but, at the same time, they gave me heart.

Link to our tradition:

This group of women recalls a friend of Jesus who 'did it her way' (John 12, 2-7): "They gave a dinner for him (Jesus) there, and Martha served, while Lazarus was one of those reclining at table with him. Mary took a liter of costly perfumed oil made from genuine aromatic nard and anointed the feet of Jesus and dried them with her hair; the house was filled with the fragrance of the oil. Then Judas the Iscariot, one [of] his disciples, and the one who would betray him, said, 'Why was this oil not sold for three hundred days' wages and given to the poor?' He said this not because he cared about the poor but because he was a thief and held the money bag and used to steal the contributions. So Jesus said, 'Leave her alone. Let her keep this for the day of my burial. You always have the poor with you, but you do not always have me.'"

## Subanen Ministry

### Intelligent Use and Defense of Land
### By Richardo Tolino

I began work in the Subanen Ministry in Midsalip in 1991 when I was still a high school student. I have since qualified as an electrical engineer, and in 2001 began to work here fulltime. I speak Subanen and Visayan (and of course Tagalog, the official national language). Both my parents are Subanen.

I am one of five staff in the farming program of the Subanen Ministry. We teach the farmers how to contour their land. Between the contour edges farmers plant fruit trees as well as vegetables, sweet potatoes, ginger, beans and peanuts. The fruit trees begin to bear fruit after six years, but need to be maintained constantly until then.

We have carried out agro-forestry projects in seventeen villages. There are now 600 families involved in the program. One obvious result that we already see is that the children are better nourished.

Upland rice (grown in dry soil) and corn are the Subanens' main traditional crops, but we are also beginning to teach them to develop and work rice paddies. Even though they now live mainly in the hills, there are places they can plant and grow rice as long as there is irrigation.

Along with these sustainable agriculture projects we need to constantly educate our people about the harm that slash and burn agriculture does to the land and forest. We also try to persuade people to stop chopping down and burning trees to produce charcoal over a slow fire. This is difficult because there is a demand for the charcoal for domestic fuel in the lowland towns.

We also campaign to stop open cut mining ventures coming into our land and destroying all we have. The people here in Midsalip protested the logging for years and had some success, so we are not new to the business of defending our ancestral land, which is essential for our way of life.

Once again, we believe we can successfully defend ourselves in the face of seemingly overwhelming odds. It is true we are up against big business interests, local and central government authorities and possibly the military. However, our national constitution and our laws support our cause.

Recently I went to the Mines and Geo-sciences Bureau in Manila and was told there that as long as the indigenous people oppose the mining they will not release a mining license. According to IPRA (Indigenous People's Reform Act) it would be illegal for mining to go ahead on our land if we oppose it. However to make the law effective we must continue to make our voice heard, promote another path of development and convince our own people that this is the way to preserve our identity and culture.

## Valiant and Respectful Women

### By Columban Fr. Sean Martin

I was reassigned to Midsalip, the Philippines, in 1994 and attempted to learn some Subanen, but made little progress. However, I did learn to say the parts of Mass that don't change each day and, in the process, was alerted to what is going on among the Subanen people. There was a chap called Jimmy Tindao who helped me a lot in the meetings, where I would sit and pick up this and that and miss a whole lot, but every now and then he would stop and summarize what was going on.

At that time the Columban Sisters were learning Subanen, which prompted the locals to rethink their attitude to their children learning their own language at school. They had considered it a waste of time since what young people seemed to need to get on beyond the confines of their country village was Visayan and English. The Sisters learning Subanen seemed to me to be a huge step towards helping the Subanens appreciate and value their own heritage.

The Sisters were looking for ways to adapt to their culture. With the support of the bishop, they shaped the Baptism ceremony according to Subanen customs. Baptism now takes place along a river, because they are the people of the river, as suba means river or stream in their language. They line up along the river and make a small altar. It's very much like our own baptismal ceremony, but there are some significant differences in that they use some of their own symbols. They use something like incense and also put a small cloth around their head. Sister Ita showed me a bowl, and I thought we might use it to pour the water but she explained that would not be possible. In fact, using that bowl for Baptism would be for the Subanens something like us using the monstrance in a parade. It is something to be revered, not used.

I found a practical way of giving a hand by participating in a tree planting venture. A team working with the Sisters in the promotion of farming—Danilo, Richardo, Terso, Mario and Lucio—would give a hundred or more fruit trees of a number of varieties to a small landowner and he and his family would have to see to the planting. What I did not understand in the beginning was the allowance that the Sisters also gave the farmers who received trees. The reality of the Subanen in the hills was harsh; they lived from hand to mouth; they had no free time, no reserves of food. If they did not work they did not eat. If they were to find time to plant the trees they needed money for food that day. For each tree they had to dig a hole, one meter in diameter and about 80 centimeters deep. Most of their land is on steep mountain slopes so working it, in whatever form, is arduous. The trees needed to be planted to survive the long dry season so the farmers had to care for them two or three times a week until they took root.

Visayans own most of the richer land and Subanens tend to be in the poorer mountainous parts of the peninsula. At the end of World War II most of the land on the coast and in the hills was probably owned by Subanens, who have traditionally held the land in a communal way. No individual had title. Also, they farmed a piece of land and then moved on leaving it fallow but expecting to return to farm it again. However, when the Visayans began to arrive they bought the fallow land at a very low price and remained but also registered their purchase in the municipal titles office in Pagadian. The Subanens would have expected the purchaser to move on after a year or two but that did not happen. The Subanens did not want conflict so pulled back further and further. They also became increasingly impoverished, a condition that also makes it harder for them to value their traditions, language and way of life. Today there are about 300,000 Subanens in this peninsula.

The Sisters have started pre-schools in some of the more isolated villages. They are training teachers to teach the children in their own language. This way the children get a good start. Before they could not understand Visayan nor English and so did not know what the teacher was saying. Many dropped out, perpetuating the cycle of poverty into which they have been trapped. These pre-schools get the children on to the educational ladder. This early introduction to school in their own language gives them a better chance to push ahead.

Subanens are traditionally animist. For the most part, they have not been invited into the Catholic Church. For the Sisters, if a person wants to know about the Catholic faith they have an introductory program. However, their emphasis is helping the people value themselves, their culture and traditions and find a way ahead, especially with the help of education. They work on literacy, a community based health program, translation of the traditional stories into Visayan and English and translation of parts of the Bible.

The Sisters do not ride rough shod over their customs and traditions. They don't proselytize, but rather respectfully walk with their Subanen friends in search of a more dignified life for all.

## A Leader's Vision

### By Columban Sister Kathleen Melia

I feel that I have been enriched by the Subanen sense of the sacred and so feel a commitment to care for the whole planet. I feel impelled to search for a way forward for ourselves, to discover how we might live simply in a context of caring for this earth that is both our home and our responsibility.

Ours is a mission of accompaniment of the Subanens in their struggles, as an indigenous group of people, to live in peace on their ancestral lands and to live according to their ancestral customs, and to participate in decisions which affect their lives, their future and traditions. Adult education attainment is quite low. A majority of parents are illiterate. Services are very poor, and politics are quite corrupt. Their struggle is very hard and has been basically about protecting their ancestral lands, where they have lived for centuries in the shadow of their sacred mountain, Mt. Pinukis.

First they were up against big logging interests and organized to struggle against their intrusion during the 1980s and, as from 1996, major mining companies, such as Rio Tinto, have been looking for ways of moving in to begin open-cut mining, which would totally destroy their habitat. While Rio Tinto seems to have stepped back, other international mining companies have taken their place. More recently Chinese companies are looking at moving in, and we expect them to be a lot harder to deal with as they don't even respect the human rights of their own people in China.

We want to continue to be involved in the protection of the forests, which are vital not just for the Subanens but for lowland farmers and fishermen. The remaining forests on the Midsalip mountains are a very rich bio-diversity area, which is the water catchment area for Midsalip. We focus our energies in various fields of sustainable development, such as better farming methods, better healthcare and better education. We push ahead with all this in coordination with our partners Subanen.

However, the mining companies are like a weight around our neck; they hold us back as we have to divert energy and time into the struggle to stop them moving ahead with their open-cut mining plans. Still, we are aware that we have to keep the two aspects of the struggle going. The whole area is a series of interconnected volcanic mountains, two of which are inactive volcanoes.

We understand mission as dialogue, and we spent four years listening to the people, learning about their struggles. Since it was a time of severe militarization and our home was in the mountains, we evacuated along with our neighbors and returned with them. Through this the bonds of friendship grew closer. From the Subanen people I have learned to live lightly and respectfully on the earth. They have ritual for all aspects of their lives; they don't take their environment for granted.

Also, we see the worst of the consumer culture moving in and clashing with the traditional Subanen culture. The young people cannot live in isolation from what is happening in the rest of the world, but they are constantly challenged to keeping their own integrity in the face of strong external cultural influences. Parts of their culture have gone, in large part because of poverty.

However, if the forest is taken from them, then their culture will disappear. They will be unable to go to their sacred mountain; the trees they need for their sacred rituals will no longer be there. The wood for the musical instruments will not be available. If the mining comes the culture cannot survive. On the other hand, if the Subanens choose to adapt to modernity that's fine, but not so if others intervene and cut off any chance of them continuing to cherish and nurture what is theirs, a unique culture, a gift from God.

## Health Care and Education

### By Manuela Patiño

I began work with the community in 1985 when we had to help 70 families from five villages near Midsalip who had to leave their homes because of the conflict between the NPA (New People's Army) and the military.

In 1986 I joined the Subanen Ministry team, doing home visitation with Sisters Glenda and Kathleen. I knew the people, and they knew me so my presence helped the people trust the Sisters, allowing the Sisters to make headway.

At that time the Sisters wanted to learn about the Subanen people's rituals, their musical instruments and how they worked the land.

The Subanen Ministry began in 1983 with arrival of the Sisters in Lumpunid in the Midsalip area; here they learned the language. In 1984 they went to Cumarum in the hills to learn the life style of the Subanens, and also to learn what were the needs of the people. In 1988 they came down to Midsalip because of militarization.

We got to know the local leader (Timuay) of each village who came down to Midsalip for meetings about a variety of needs that were not being met in their villages, especially problems related to the sicknesses of both adults and children, and low productivity from the land. The group that worked on improving farming dealt with land issues. Anita and I were members of the health team.

We organized nutrition seminars on health, focusing on good nutrition, how to avoid common sicknesses and how to treat them with traditional herbal medicines. Eventually the women in the barrios organized themselves into groups. Now there are twenty groups of women who make medicine on a regular basis. This, together with improved nutrition because of the farming program, has led to an improvement in the children's health, with a lesser mortality rate and fewer children needing to be admitted to hospital.

At first many had little confidence in themselves as regards finding their way about a hospital, so we were available to accompany them and also help them obtain the medicines, the costs of which were covered by the Subanen Ministry. Now they manage quite well, but Anita continues to visit Subanens who are in hospital.

Of course, if we can avoid having to use the hospital we do too. It costs 900 pesos ($23.00) to take a seriously ill person in ambulance from Midsalip to the hospital in Aurora, and that would be equivalent to about eleven days' wages. A few years ago a so-called hospital was built in Midsalip. However the doctor only visited for a few years, on two to three days a week. There is little medicine, so the majority of patients go to the hospital in another municipality.

There have been times when we have had to deal with serious emergencies. In 1992, in a village about 30 kilometers from Midsalip, 30 children died of measles in six weeks. It was near the end of the dry season, and the children were malnourished and dehydrated. Dehydration is common due to the local belief that when children have diarrhea they should not be given water to drink. In the case of the measles the villagers were closing the windows of their houses, even though it was quite hot, and then they would also wrap their children in cloths. There are now, thank God, very few deaths from measles.

In 2002, in another village, fifteen adults died from capilliariasis, an ailment from eating contaminated fish. One parent who succumbed to capilliariasis was Aben who left seven children, and now only four are still alive. Because the victims of this disease were mostly adult men, and the Subanen livelihood is almost entirely from farming, the effects of the failure to care for the people is still being felt by victims' families.

## The Seeds of Our Own Education System

### By Wilma Tero (Wing Wing)

I like my nickname; it helps me feel that I go easily from place to place, that I negotiate life gracefully. I was born in the Hacienda Margarita of Negros Occidental, the Philippines, so was to be called Margarita. My Uncle Andress insisted on Andresa, and so it came to pass, but often when I was called Andresa I got sick, so my parents changed my name to Wilma, but Wing Wing is fine.

I started working with the Subanen Ministry as a part time typist, then later in a health program with herbal medicine and helping the sick get into hospital. The Columban Sisters, who run the Subanen Ministry, gave me a scholarship at St. Columbans College in Pagadian where I took a course in business administration, which I completed in 2000 and have worked here since then.

I coordinate the IPEA (Indigenous People's Education Program), which establishes and runs pre-schools in Subanen villages in the hills. At present we have nine schools. The Assisi Foundation funded our work for six years. The rest of the budget comes from private donations and a grant from the Irish government.

The pre-school program is conducted in Subanen, and the children are introduced to Visayan and Tagalog in order to give them a better chance of adapting to mainstream education. We aim to help the children be proud of our culture and capable of standing up for themselves when taunted or otherwise given a hard time by students from the majority Visaya culture. We also want the parents to appreciate the importance of mainstream education for their children.

We teach the children communication arts, writing, music, arithmetic, science, social science and values. They learn about defending our ancestral land with its sacred sites, especially Mt. Pinukis, the source of the three major rivers of the Zamboanga Peninsula—the Salug, the Ecuan and the Labangan. We teach them why it's important to resist the entry of mining companies into our territory.

Consequently those in favor of mining our hills oppose our education project. The mayor of Midsalip, in league with the supervisor of education in Midsalip, wants to close down our education programs. We are told that we are not qualified to teach, which is true in the sense that our teachers have not completed the formal program for teacher training. However, the Constitution of the Republic of the Philippines and the IPRA (Indigenous Peoples' Rights Act) affirm our right to set up our own indigenous peoples' education program.

In addition to two-day monthly trainings, and a longer training during summer, our teachers are trained by the Assisi Foundation in live-in courses in Davao, Cagayan and Bukidnon, twice a year for one week each time. They have also assisted at a two day training course in the Montessori method. There are nine teachers, and all are Subanens. The majority of the children who graduated from our program are doing very well in elementary school. Many children are the first in their family to have had the opportunity to attend school.

We have good support in the broader community, especially from donors locally and abroad. Columban Fr. Vinnie Busch facilitated training on how to make a small book and also helps some of our young women continue their education in high school and college in Ozamiz.

Sr. Patty Andonaire, a Columban Sister from Peru, accompanies us in the preschool program and Sister Kathleen Melia, a Columban Sister from Ireland, is the overall coordinator of the Subanen Ministry, including our education program and has been serving our people for 27 years.

Paulino, First Midsalip Police Chief, now a retired colonel

I was the first chief of police of Midsalip and held the job for 30 years, retiring in 1996.

With Fr. Frank Nally I was involved in the campaign against illegal logging. We had some success. Now, as a retired policeman, I continue to support the campaign to defend the Subanen lands against destruction, this time by mining companies.

All those mountains will be destroyed by the mining, not just here in Midsalip but the whole of the Zamboanga Peninsula. The soil will be washed away, and there will be massive landslides.

The government does not support us. We are just ordinary people who organize and struggle. We count on the support of the Columbans and others who are aware of the justice of our cause.

We are coming up to elections, and we are urging people to elect candidates who are anti-mining. All that we have would be in danger of destruction if mining were to begin here.

We file cases in the local court and even in the Supreme Court. We have three cases running at the moment. Even if our cases are dismissed we must continue to try whatever we can. We know we have to fight corruption in the courts and the bureaucracy.

Link to our tradition:

". . . [Vatican II] insisted on the unique character of their (laity) vocation, which is in a special way to 'seek the Kingdom of God by engaging in temporal affairs and ordering them according to the plan of God'(14) . . . . Through Baptism the lay faithful are made one body with Christ and are established among the People of God. They are in their own way made sharers in the priestly, prophetic and kingly office of Christ. They carry out their own part in the mission of the whole Christian people with respect to the Church and the world.'" (*Christifideles Laici*, No. 9, Pope John Paul II, 1988)

See also John 15, 1-8: "I am the true vine, and my Father is the vine grower. He takes away every branch in me that does not bear fruit, and everyone that does he prunes so that it bears more fruit. You are already pruned because of the word that I spoke to you. Remain in me, as I remain in you. Just as a branch cannot bear fruit on its own unless it remains on the vine, so neither can you unless you remain in me. I am the vine, you are the branches. Whoever remains in me and I in him will bear much fruit, because without me you can do nothing. Anyone who does not remain in me will be thrown out like a branch and wither; people will gather them and throw them into a fire and they will be burned. If you remain in me and my words remain in you, ask for whatever you want and it will be done for you. By this is my Father glorified, that you bear much fruit and become my disciples."

## One Church, Two Communities

### By Columban Fr. Kevin O'Neill

There is one Catholic Church in China, and this Church is in communion with Rome and thus loyal to the Pope. Within this one Church there are, however, two communities.

The Chinese government approves of Buddhism, Taoism, Islam and the two Christian Churches, Catholic and Protestant. The Religious Affairs Bureau of the government monitors the activities of these approved religions.

The "open" community of the Catholic Church, also referred to as the "registered" community or the "official" community, in that it is registered with the government and in the eyes of the government it is official and legal, is monitored by the Religious Affairs Bureau. The vast majority of dioceses in China belong to the "open" community.

The "underground" community of the Catholic Church, also referred to as the "unregistered" community or the "unofficial" community, in that it is not registered with the government, in the eyes of the government it is an illegal community. The "underground" community only exists in a small number of dioceses in China.

The Patriotic Association is an organization established by the government as a link between the open church and the Religious Affairs Bureau of the government. The Patriotic Association advocates self-elected and self-ordained bishops. Neither the open nor the underground communities advocate this. The Association exists in most dioceses in China. In these dioceses the "open" community has to cooperate with the Association. In a few dioceses the Association is very strong and controls the church. The "open" church community would rather work directly with the Religious Affairs Bureau and have the Patriotic Association dismantled.

The "underground" community has a number of different realities. In some dioceses, where the local government is more tolerant, the "underground" community is allowed to have churches where Catholics can worship regularly, while in other dioceses, where the local government does not tolerate the "underground" community, the underground community is very clandestine and so does everything on the quiet. Catholics in these dioceses meet in each other's homes. These clandestine communities only exist in a few dioceses in China. In these few dioceses there is conflict between the "open" and "underground" communities. In most dioceses that have both communities the relationship between the two communities is harmonious.

Link to our tradition:

"I, then, a prisoner for the Lord, urge you to live in a manner worthy of the call you have received, with all humility and gentleness, with patience, bearing with one another through love, striving to preserve the unity of the spirit through the bond of peace: one body and one Spirit, as you were also called to the one hope of your call; one Lord, one faith, one baptism; one God and Father of all, who is over all and through all and in all." (Ephesians 4, 1-6)

## My Passion as a Missionary

### By Columban Fr. Hugh MacMahon

For 45 years I have lived and struggled with the following question: How might I help the people to whom I was sent to come to faith in Jesus Christ and put their particular cultural stamp on living out that faith?

Before coming to Hong Kong in 1995, I worked in Korea for 30 years. The Church was growing there, and in some ways the Korean people were putting their own distinctive shape on their Christian faith.

Nearly 400 years ago, Korean scholars had journeyed to China to learn more about the new religion that Europeans had recently brought to Asia, and so the Koreans themselves were the first to bring the Christian message to their country. Subsequently, many died for their faith as rulers forbad the practice of the "foreign" religion. In times of persecution, Korean laity also learned to practice and pass on their faith without the ministry of priests.

Long before that, Koreans had imbibed basic aspects of Confucian thought, such as an orderly society and clear instruction on how to behave. In the hierarchical structure and doctrinal approach of the Catholic Church, they found a mirror image of that Confucian cultural conditioning. Order and clarity can be positive, but an over emphasis on these aspects may lead to an oppressive and marginalizing Church, which tends to ostracize the poor and those on the fringe of society. However, I realized that no matter how much I may protest there was little chance of successfully challenging such a deep rooted cultural force.

Yet I did discover another basic component of Korean culture into which I could creatively put my energies. Koreans are doers with little interest in the subtleties of doctrinal distinctions. They like to get on with whatever may be the business at hand. They tend to ask, "What do we need to do to be good Christians?" and would not lose much sleep about the finer points of what they might need to believe.

This made it easy for me to promote participatory community in the parishes in which I worked. During my years in Korea thousands, maybe millions migrated from the country to the city, where they flocked to places that offered a welcome and a chance to actively join in community life. Consequently, so many of our parishes grew rapidly.

One of my most memorable moments was celebrating Mass in a daycare center in a shanty town area in the capital, Seoul. There was not much space, but all would sit on the floor Korean style, more or less squashed together. They would sing and do the readings and, after the homily, they would join in with comments and prayers that were spontaneous and free. With no sign of embarrassment, they spoke about whatever was in their hearts. Those Masses in the daycare center were simultaneously moments of laughter and solemnity. After Mass we would stay on for a snack and a chat. It was such a contrast to the formal, ritualized celebrations of Mass in so many of the big churches being built in Korea at that time. I used to wonder to myself, where would Jesus have been more at home? Was this not what a localized church should look like?

Despite the progress that the Church has made in opening up to cultural diversity since Vatican II, in recent years I have been saddened and disappointed by the push from the central governing body of the Church to emphasize uniformity rather than diversity as a foundation of Church unity. I hope we can steadily challenge and reverse this excessively controlling trend.

The Church in China seems to me to be going through a process similar to that of Korea 40 years ago. However, I live and work in the hope that here we will not move towards the over institutionalization of the Church. In fact, I see signs of hope, one of which is the willingness of young Chinese to listen to outsiders. They are searching; they ask about God, religion, the purpose of life, justice and values in general. I believe that much can be done to help them, provided we offer a warm and open welcome. While it may be difficult for many older priests to be adaptive and welcoming due to the years of persecution that pressured Church leaders into a closed, protective and suspicious mentality, I see younger priests who do have a wider, outward-looking vision.

I see this re-emerging Chinese Church as having the potential to offer today's youth hope and direction. I feel privileged to be able to contribute. I like the approach that focuses on how we can be more Christian by searching together for more authentic ways to live our faith. Drawing on the insights and religious practices of those who lived in the locality before us is part of the process. In doing so, we grow spiritually. Ultimately this is about how we might walk with and know Jesus Christ.

Link to our tradition:

In the Church there was unity in diversity from the beginning. See Acts 2, 1-11: "When the time for Pentecost was fulfilled, they were all in one place together. And suddenly there came from the sky a noise like a strong driving wind, and it filled the entire house in which they were. Then there appeared to them tongues as of fire, which parted and came to rest on each one of them. And they were all filled with the Holy Spirit and began to speak in different tongues, as the Spirit enabled them to proclaim. Now there were devout Jews from every nation under heaven staying in Jerusalem. At this sound, they gathered in a large crowd, but they were confused because each one heard them speaking in his own language. They were astounded, and in amazement they asked, "Are not all these people who are speaking Galileans? Then how does each of us hear them in his own native language? We are Parthians, Medes, and Elamites, inhabitants of Mesopotamia, Judea and Cappadocia, Pontus and Asia, Phrygia and Pamphylia, Egypt and the districts of Libya near Cyrene, as well as travelers from Rome, both Jews and converts to Judaism, Cretans and Arabs, yet we hear them speaking in our own tongues of the mighty acts of God."

## Becoming More Missionary

### By Columban Fr. Gerry Neylon

My main contribution to our mission in China is facilitating overseas study for priests, Sisters and laity from both the underground and over-ground parts of the Catholic Church. We don't have accurate figures of how many Catholics belong to each sector of the Church, but it is estimated that there might be about ten million in each. The Government generally turns a blind eye to the activities of the underground members of the Church. They are considered illegal by the government and have to operate secretly. There is a lot less conflict and hard feelings between the two sectors of the Church now. I feel that in my present role in China that I am more missionary now than I have ever been in my 37 years as a Columban priest.

I was ordained on Easter Sunday 1973 and took up an appointment to South Korea in August. At that time all the Christian Churches were attracting lots of new members, because the Churches were standing up for those who were being harassed by the Government, in particular the industrial laborers. I was there for four years, two years in language school and two years parish work. We were kept very busy with programs helping catechumens understand and appreciate the Catholic faith, a variety of catechetical programs for Catholics, sacramental ministry and plenty of opportunities to be involved with parishioners. Most of our contact with parishioners was related to the Church. The language was difficult, but we had every opportunity to practice and plenty of people willing to help us.

After four years in Korea I was asked to go to Taiwan and spent seventeen years there, from 1979 to 1996. I found it a totally different scene, where there was little interest in the Church. There were large numbers of Catholics on the books, but not many came to church. Many had come into the Church during the 1950s and 1960s when relief goods were distributed through the parishes. Once the goods stopped most of these so-called "rice Christians" ceased coming to church. On weekends we would have only 70 to 80 worshippers at Mass, so there was no way we could approach the mission as we had been doing in Korea. Another factor that affected Mass attendance was the work pattern of many parishioners. They did not, quite simply, have time to go to church. They often worked two jobs, one during the day and one at night, and had just two consecutive days off each month!

In these circumstances we had to ask ourselves how we might be relevant to the lives of those around us. After much discussion with parishioners and the local people, another Columban priest and I opened centers for mentally impaired children in our parishes. Taiwanese society looks down on these children. They feel that they are useless, and many are locked up at home because they do not want the neighbors to see them. Parents give them no personal training of any kind. Some children are sent to huge state-funded institutions where conditions are horrific, where many are locked up in cages like animals. Parents often forget about them once they are institutionalized. Lay missionaries from the U.S. with expertise in special education came to work with us. They insisted on one teacher per five children and emphasized helping the children to help themselves, so that they might be as independent as possible. The centers are still going strong, and the children's progress and well-being are wonderful to behold.

This work made sense to me, but I was also challenged in other ways. On one occasion, while traveling on a train, a fellow passenger asked me, "Is your wife also American?" I replied, "I'm from Ireland and I don't have a wife." He continued, "You're not married? You know, we Chinese all marry" I said, "I'm a Catholic priest, and Catholic priests don't marry." He was totally taken aback at this. Noting his reaction, I said, "What do you think of this?" He said, "I think you're very selfish." So I said, "Why is that?" He said, "We Chinese all marry, because it's our duty to produce grandchildren for our parents. You're not doing that. You're only thinking of yourself." Obviously the value that I, and Catholics generally, put on celibacy meant nothing to him.

My fellow passenger's comments had a big impact on me and suggested a need to be more in touch with his way of thinking and the values of non-Christians in Taiwan. In Korea I had been immersed in doing obviously priestly work in a busy church, but in Taiwan they were not buying that.

However, my missionary journey in Taiwan came to an end when, in 1996, I received a phone call from the Columban leader asking me to go to China. Ned Kelly, a fluent Chinese speaker, had died in 1994. He had spent the previous ten years researching possible openings for Columbans working in post-Chairman Mao China. The other Columbans who were in China at the time primarily taught

English in Chinese universities as an effective form to witnessing to Jesus Christ in a country where non-Chinese are not allowed to be involved in religious activities.

By 1996 my emphasis had moved from parish work to outreach to mentally impaired children. The idea of moving to China did not sit well with me. I didn't see the need for it. How could teaching English compare with working with children who were shunned and ignored at home, or forgotten in some large institution?

After much soul searching and discussion on my particular role, I came to China with the intention of doing more or less what Ned had been doing. I arrived a month after the British handed over Hong Kong to the Chinese on July 1, 1997. In both Korea and Taiwan I had been free to do as I wanted, finding my way along with other missionaries as best we could. In China, as non-Chinese, we are restricted in many ways. My training as a priest, and my experience of working with special needs children could not be used directly in China. Most of the props of my Irish cultural background, my seminary training and my experience as a missionary in Korea and Taiwan were effectively removed in my new situation.

My new mission forced me to put all my emphasis on witnessing to Jesus Christ by the very way I live my life as a Christian. There is no shortage of opportunity to do that in a country that attaches no importance to religion. My being in China is about forming relationships, interaction with the people here in as deep and intimate way as I can, and letting them see for themselves what a Christian is. My mission obliges me to adopt a low profile. I cannot talk about my Christianity, but I can witness to it as I relate to others. I would like to include a short story to illustrate this point.

On May 12, 2008, there was a massive earthquake in Sichuan Province which killed almost 90,000 people. It happened at 2:28 p.m. in the middle of a school day. Many local schools collapsed, and thousands of children died in the ruins of poorly built school buildings. Because of the one-child policy this meant the end of the line for many couples, which translates into unimaginable desolation for Chinese people.

A woman doctor was working her shift in a local hospital when the earthquake hit. She lived alone with her mother and wondered all afternoon what might have happened to her mother. She was so busy with the dead and dying arriving at the hospital that she could not contact her mother. After work she returned home to find her house destroyed and then frantically searched the area for her mother. To her great joy she found her alive but pinned under a boulder. They talked for a while, and then her mother died suddenly. She was totally distraught and inconsolable. She had no religion of any kind. She was a convinced materialist. For her, her mother was dead and that was the end of her.

A few weeks after that, in the course of my work, I was asked to see this woman. I talked to her but, because I am not allowed to be involved in any form of proselytizing, I spoke to her about my own belief in the afterlife and what it meant to me when my mother died. I was able then to introduce her to the local Chinese priest. She is now taking instruction in the Catholic faith with him.

I am convinced that it is at the level of witness that we can make the most impact. I can facilitate, but I cannot instruct people in the faith. However, I can show others what my faith means to me, and they can decide to take or not to take the next step. In fact, I have come to believe that witness by my lifestyle is the most effective form of evangelization. I take very seriously the advice of St Francis of Assisi: "Preach the Gospel at all times—if necessary use words."

Link to our tradition:

"But Ruth said [to Naomi], 'Do not press me to go back and abandon you! Wherever you go I will go, wherever you lodge I will lodge. Your people shall be my people and your God, my God. Where you die I will die, and there be buried. May the LORD do thus to me, and more, if even death separates me from you!'" (Ruth 1, 16-17)

"When they had gathered together they asked him, 'Lord, are you at this time going to restore the kingdom to Israel?' He answered them, 'It is not for you to know the times or seasons that the Father has established by his own authority.

But you will receive power when the Holy Spirit comes upon you, and you will be my witnesses in Jerusalem, throughout Judea and Samaria, and to the ends of the earth.' When he had said this, as they were looking on, he was lifted up, and a cloud took him from their sight." (Acts 1, 6-9)

## Women of Faith

### By Vida Hequilan

"Let us give something to each person we meet: joy, courage, hope, assurance, or philosophy, wisdom, a vision for the future. Let us always give something."
(Daisaku Ikeda, Buddhist peace activist and writer)

In my four years with the aboriginal ministry in the mountains of central Taiwan, I met two women who made a big impact in my life: Yada and Yaki. While some of us are driven by ambition to strive for bigger and better things, these two women strive simply to survive. Both of them have had a life of constant struggle but have taken on their struggles with courage, determination, and an undying faith in life.

Yada works hard to provide for her family and looks after her cancer-stricken husband. She has three daughters, all of whom are married, and a son who still lives with her in the family home. Even though her husband's cancer is in remission, he is too weak to work, and so Yada takes on the responsibility of sustaining the family. Every day she wakes up early to work the farm; then she works in the parish's after-school program as one of its teachers. I sometimes wonder where she gets her energy to do all these things. I often refer to her as "Super Woman," because she makes everything look easy. She never complains nor blames God of her situation. She has the grace to see the beauty in life despite her difficulties.

One time, she shared with me that she never wanted to marry at an early age because she wanted to study and get a degree. But she eventually gave in to the mounting pressure, not just from her family, but from the tradition of her culture that women should marry to have a secure future. And so she got married at eighteen, and right away struggled to live as a wife, a mother, and as an extra hand on her husband's farm. Also she has had to deal with her husband's drinking problem and the cultural demands placed on her as a woman.

Yaki is just one of the few elderly women in the village who still work in the mountains. Like Yada, she also looks after a sick husband and provides for the two of them. She does everything since her husband had an accident that took his leg. She works in the farm every day and sells produce from their land, such as vegetables and fruit, to local tourists on weekends. Her determination is just unbelievable. She never accepts any financial support from her children or relatives. Every time I see her I never detect any sign of tiredness or sadness; she is the epitome of happiness and courage.

These women have stories of a lifelong struggle, as do most of the women here. In their culture, the demands of their role as daughter, mother, and grandmother dictate that men should always take the front seat. Yet, as I listened to the stories of these two women, I heard strength, determination, and love for life.

Their choices have been limited, but they lived with those few choices and took time to celebrate the joys and successes they experienced along the way. They never gave up on life and their stories gave me the gift of courage and hope—to be thankful for my life, and to be able to wake up each day with the determination to take on life, be it bad or good. I learned a great life lesson from these two wonderful women, and that is to not let your struggles bring you down. Instead, face up to life with determination and faith.

Link to our tradition:

Miriam, a woman of faith, gave birth to Moses. See Exodus 2, 1-10: "Now a man of the house of Levi married a Levite woman, and the woman conceived and bore a son. Seeing what a fine child he was, she hid him for three months. But when she could no longer hide him, she took a papyrus basket, daubed it with bitumen and pitch, and putting the child in it, placed it among the reeds on the bank of the Nile. His sister stationed herself at a distance to find out what would happen to him. Then Pharaoh's daughter came down to bathe at the Nile, while her attendants walked along the bank of the Nile. Noticing the basket among the reeds, she sent her handmaid to fetch it. On opening it, she looked, and there was a baby boy crying! She was moved with pity for him and said, 'It is one of the Hebrews' children.' Then his sister asked Pharaoh's daughter, 'Shall I go and summon a Hebrew woman to nurse the child for you?' Pharaoh's daughter answered her, 'Go.' So the young woman went and called the child's own mother. Pharaoh's daughter said to her, 'Take this child and nurse him for me, and I will pay your wages.' So the woman took the child and nursed him. When the child grew, she brought him to Pharaoh's daughter, and he became her son. She named him Moses; for she said, I drew him out of the water.'"

## Let Your Light Shine

### As told to Peter Woodruff with Colin McLean translating

It all started when I was about seventeen years old and doing the confirmation program. At that time (1983) there was a Eucharistic Congress in Salvador, which provoked lots of discussion about religious topics. Also, I had contact with a youth movement, Youth Apostolate on the Periphery, which at that time was active in most dioceses in Brazil. This movement's approach to the apostolate helped me lay the foundations of a spirituality that continues to mark and shape my life.

**Harsh Reality**

In this disturbed world
In the midst of so much rejection
Many live stripped of everything
Without work, without happiness
And without anything to achieve
What passion does s/he hold in his/her hands?

There are no vacancies in commerce
There are no vacancies in industry
In the interior of the north-east the situation is
serious.

Oh, my God, what anguish!
The despair, the violence,
Hope disappearing little by little.
Decadence growing little by little.

The courageous take up the struggle for survival
But come up against the system,
That merely metes out suffering.
Persecuted in toil and drudgery
Under the claws of power
Bereft of the chance for a full life
Only united can they prevail.

Wake up, my people! Arouse yourselves!
Challenge the oppressors.
New blood is needed
To water Freedom.
Let's uncross our arms,
Enough of doing nothing.
For the sake of new life
We need to join hands.

New blood is needed
To water Freedom
For the sake of new life
We need to join hands.

To prepare for confirmation we met every Saturday in our local parish for two years. After I was confirmed I was invited to coordinate the youth groups in our parish. There were many communities in the parish and my job was to help them work together to help the youth grow in the understanding and establish the practice of reflecting on their lives in the light of Christ's teaching. We wanted to help them discover and deepen the spirituality that grows out of and is nurtured by their own life experience.

When the youth movement ran its fifth music and poetry festival I represented my parish in the poetry section with a poem titled, "Árdua Realidade." Since that time I became seriously involved with the movement. I have always liked to sing and play the guitar and, in later years, participated in the festival with songs that I wrote and won two prizes.

The movement organized youth formation seminars, which in turn motivated others to join the movement's work. We soon formed a branch of the movement within our deanery to work specifically with poor youth. The basic purpose of our work was to help the youth find their way in life in the light of the teaching of Jesus of Nazareth. Our work was reinforced by our participation in the Basic Ecclesial Communities that constituted our parishes.

When the occasion warranted we took our moral conviction to the streets. I remember such a moment in 1988, when, with the support of Columban Fr. Arturo Aguilar, we organized a public protest about the fatal shooting of five young people at a train station. Private security guards accused them of jumping the barrier to avoid paying the fare and then shot them.

We wanted to help the youth develop a critical awareness of all aspects of their lives. We urged them to question and analyze all they were confronted with. We provided them with tools to look critically at the mass media. Housing is always a problem for the poor, so we helped our youth look at that area of their lives on the basis of more information than they normally have. We helped them question some of the accepted ways of seeing things, e.g. beauty according to predominant view in our society. Many were unemployed, and we would help them deepen their understanding of why they found it more difficult to get a job than young people from other sectors of society, which still sees "white" as a hallmark of beauty. We helped them become more aware of their own rights, women's rights, and the rights of the indigenous peoples. We delved into the economy, and the land issue, which dates back to when this area of Brazil was predominantly huge landed estates (fazendas), growing sugar and/or coffee with slave labor. We accompanied them as they worked through personal issues, such as relationships and sexuality.

Of course, this youth movement was more significant for some than for others. While we had big dreams we also knew that we were merely one part of a nationwide social process that was transforming our country as millions of downtrodden men, women and children discovered and affirmed their dignity as sons and daughters of God. In our movement our Christian faith was nourished by prayer and celebration. The annual music and poetry festival was a highpoint of the year for so many of us. What we wrote and sung was an expression of our spirituality, and every year the festival finished with a Eucharist in which all had an active part. We did not just go to Mass but rather we celebrated our faith as a dynamic and faith-driven youth community.

As we know, all good things come to an end at some stage. That happened for us in the periphery youth movement when the priest appointed to oversee the youth work in our diocese changed the orientation so that the youth were encouraged to focus their energies on activities such as, teaching catechism to children, liturgy and the parish choir. Instead of helping Catholic youth look at the world and the challenges of life with the eyes of Christ the youth were channeled into internal Church work.

Many of us in the youth movement were deeply disappointed by this change. We lost support by the weakening of our movement, but we did not lose our Christian faith. We found other ways to grow in our faith and contribute to the life of our Church. Youth Apostolate on the Periphery lost the support of the Archdiocesan leadership and petered out around 1995, but I am still close to friends of those days. Also, many of the movement members remained active in the Basic Ecclesial Communities.

> **Themes for Action and Reflection in the Black Apostolate**
>
> There are five key themes in the work of evangelization and the promotion of human and Christian dignity among people of African descent, which are developed in the Black apostolate:
>
> - Spirituality
> - Inculturation
> - Black Identity
> - Black Identity and Citizenship
> - Interreligious Dialogue

I had my first contact with Columbans in 1986, when I began to work with Columban Fr. Arturo Aguilar (U.S.). I later met Columban associate priest, Adrian Carberry (Ireland), and was still working with the youth in our parish when Columban Fr. Colin McLean arrived as parish priest in 1997. Also, around that time, a black auxiliary bishop, Don Gilio Felicio, was a major force in setting up a training course for the black apostolate in Salvador. Fr. Colin sent me, two other men and a woman to this course, consisting of three live-in weekends. I have been committed to the black apostolate since that time. In 2007, I was invited by the priest in charge of the black apostolate in our diocese to take charge of its diocesan office.

That was the first of three major changes in my life around that time. Getting married was the second in chronological order but, in terms of significance, the most outstanding. My wife, Elania, and I were together for three years before we married in 1999. Elania is supportive and understanding, but at times I have difficulty balancing the demands of the apostolate and family life. She both complains and counsels me; I listen to her and we continue to grow together.

The third major change began to happen when our parish priest, Fr. Colin, sent me to the course for permanent deacons. I went three times a week for three years and was ordained deacon in 2006. Being a deacon is for me an opportunity to be of service. I had learned an approach to being a Christian in the periphery youth movement and the Basic Ecclesial Communities, which is not clerical or institutional. It does not separate the Church from the World but rather helps Christians be in the Church in the World and, in my case, in solidarity with Afro-Brazilians in our search for dignity and full inclusion in our society.

Link to our tradition:

Marcelo Batista dos Santos, a member of a Church community committed to solidarity with the poor, describes the evolution of his Christian faith. Peter's faith also grew strong in love. See John 21, 17-18: "He said to him the third time,

'Simon, son of John, do you love me?' Peter was distressed that he had said to him a third time, 'Do you love me?' and he said to him, 'Lord, you know everything; you know that I love you.' [Jesus] said to him, 'Feed my sheep. Amen, amen, I say to you, when you were younger, you used to dress yourself and go where you wanted; but when you grow old, you will stretch out your hands, and someone else will dress you and lead you where you do not want to go.'"

## Shapes of Solidarity

Columban Fr. Peter Woodruff reporting on an interview with Pat Eagan

I met Columban Fr. Pat Eagan while passing through Santiago, Chile, in May 2011. In my memory of Columbans in Latin America, which only goes back to 1968 when I first arrived in Peru, Fr. Pat has always been in Chile. In fact, he first arrived in Latin America in 1960 and worked in the port chaplaincy in Buenos Aires for three years before moving to Chile. I asked Fr. Pat to tell me how he saw the Columban contribution in Chile since his arrival and the following is my attempt to summaries his reply. In the final paragraph Fr. Pat says a little about how he sees the future of Columban mission in Chile, but it is much more difficult to talk about that than what has already happened.

The Chilean Church was much more visionary than the English speaking local churches from which Columbans were drawn, so we arrived to work with a local church with ideas, questions, ferment and passion for change. Of course, we tuned in as best we could and, with the help of the local vision, began our work among the poor and marginalized.

We were happy to live and work with the ever increasing numbers of poor who, during the latter half of last century, came in their thousands from the countryside to the major cities in search of a better life, a life that offered the possibility of more choice as regards work and the possibility, slim though it may have been for most, of greater prosperity.

Our main contribution was setting up the Church in poor and marginalized areas of Santiago, Iquique and Valparaiso. We would move into an area in its early stages of settlement. We would look for suitable sites to establish community centers and promote the formation of Christian communities. We would do this in coordination with the residents of the area as we were always intent on promoting the laity to their potential of responsibility and leadership.

We would live in simple houses and share our lives with our neighbors. We did not set ourselves apart. Eventually with the people we would build chapels and encourage the development of communities based in the chapels. We also built bigger central churches which were more open to all and helped draw the chapels out of an inward looking isolation. For our buildings we had both local and foreign financial support.

We helped people organize in order to meet basic needs in a communal way. We could not help solve all the personal, family and social problems but those with whom we worked knew we were on their side and were grateful for our solidarity. While we did our best to help set up a local parish church, at the same time we were involved in a variety of ways in supporting our parishioners in their struggles to make a go of life. Many of the social and educational activities were also community building as they helped residents meet and get to know each other, which was important in the new suburbs of the city populated by people from many different towns and villages and without previous experience of each other's customs and history.

In bad times, we helped organize soup kitchens. We introduced the idea of parish centers for the third age, which have now become a standard part of parish life in the archdiocese. Many of us helped tackle the endemic problem of alcoholism, especially among the men. In the early years, before all had a chance to go to school, we helped organize literacy classes. In many of our parishes we ran short courses in basic skills, such as plumbing, carpentry and electricity, something which many men were most grateful for. In fact, I saw some at class on evenings when everyone else in Chile was glued to the television screen watching some important international soccer match in which Chile was playing and, for a Chilean, that really does point to serious commitment.

Parish development required setting up sacramental programs run by local laity. We never brought in better educated people from other parts of town, unless it was to help the locals equip themselves better to do whatever needed to be done. Such programs were part of the archdiocesan pastoral plan with which we always collaborated. We did not see ourselves as being here to do our own thing but rather to work with the local Chilean Church.

We would move into a developing area and work there until we had a viable parish up and running. We would then ask the archdiocese to take direct responsibility for the parish and negotiate a new commitment for ourselves. We have done this in 28 parishes of the Archdiocese of Santiago and also in parishes in Iquique and Valparaiso. In 1963 I began in Santa Luisa, San Antonio, then moved to San Marcos, south Santiago, then to San Gabriel, west Santiago, then to San Luis Rey in Conchalí, north Santiago, then to Santa Cruz parish in Vallenar, a city founded by Ambrosio O'Higgins (Irish born Spanish governor of Chile from 1788 to 1796) and in the same area as the mine in which miners were trapped and rescued in 2010, where I was for eleven years, the longest I have been in any parish, then in Maria Misionera in Santiago, and now in San Matías in Puente Alto, far south of Santiago. Only the last of these parishes is presently run by Columbans.

Other pastoral emphases came into play during the period of the military dictatorship (1973 to 1990). The Pinochet government closed down all forms of popular participation forbad meetings of more than three people and rode roughshod over the human rights of thousands of individuals and families. The Chilean Church took a strong stand in favor of human rights, and Columbans working in Chile wholeheartedly backed our church leadership.

Maybe not all bishops agreed with the emphasis on human rights, but they went along with it. The Church was unified in its stand. Some of our priests had to leave the country, and all of us were deeply affected, especially when special government police raided our center house and shot Maria Reyes, a Columban employee, as they stormed the house. They took Dr. Sheila Cassidy prisoner and tortured her.

When the Pinochet government demanded that the parishes hand over a list of places where our communities met, the names of those attending the meetings and the topics being discussed, the Cardinal Archbishop of Santiago ordered us to refuse this demand. He insisted that acquiescence to such an intrusive government directive would be the end of us. The grassroots movement heeded the Cardinal and the government did not insist. However, we did shift our emphasis from Basic Christian Communities, which met in private houses, to Basic Ecclesial Communities which met in parish chapels.

We also supported the local church's organizations, especially the Vicariate of Solidarity, which was on the front line in the defense of human rights. When the military took over the government in 1973 the Church was very well organized, which stood us in good stead. We were used to working in and with the institution, and Columbans had always supported this approach. Even today two of the Episcopal vicars in the Archdiocese of Santiago are Columbans.

As regards our contribution to the life of the Chilean Church and people, I can say quite clearly what we would like to do but, as in many visionary enterprises, working out the strategies for achieving our goals can become quite complex. We are a missionary society, and we believe that the Church of its nature is called to be missionary, so we want to find ways of effectively inviting the Chilean Church to become more missionary. I see two major factors that hinder this: first, the relative geographic isolation of Chile, bordered on the east by the mass of the Andes Mountains, on the west by the Pacific Ocean and between Chile and Peru to the north barren stretches of desert; second, the fact that the Chilean Church is still far from self-sufficient in priests, so the prime focus continues to be the building up of the local church.

However, we have agreed that despite the difficulties this will be the priority of our mission in Chile. While we strive to work out how we might best go about achieving our goal, we continue to do what we have always done. The composition of our Columban group in Chile has changed a lot in recent years as men and women, priests and laity, from countries such as Korea and Fiji, join our ranks. This puts pressure on us to work cross culturally among ourselves. Despite all the difficulties that slow our progress towards defining and implementing strategies to achieve our goals, I am hopeful.

Link to our tradition:

The Apostle, Paul, did similar missionary work in Corinth, Greece. See Acts 18, 1-11: "After this he [Paul] left Athens and went to Corinth . . . . [he] stayed with them [Aquila and Pontus, fellow tentmakers]and worked . . . Every Sabbath, he entered into discussions in the synagogue, attempting to convince both Jews and Greeks. When Silas and Timothy came down from Macedonia, Paul began to occupy himself totally with preaching the word, testifying to the Jews that the Messiah was Jesus. When they opposed him and reviled him, he shook out his garments and said to them, 'Your blood be on your heads! I am clear of responsibility. From now on I will go to the Gentiles.' . . . many of the Corinthians who heard believed and were baptized. One night in a vision the Lord said to Paul, 'Do not be afraid. Go on speaking, and do not be silent, for I am with you. No one will attack and harm you, for I have many people in this city.' He settled there for a year and a half and taught the word of God among them."

## A Spirit Filled People

### By Columban Fr. John Hegerty

In the spirit of the catechetical renewal recommended by the Latin American Bishops' Conference (CELAM), held in 1968 in Medellin, Colombia, in 1992, the Latin American Conference of Religious (CLAR) presented a Biblical study program to CELAM. They also wanted to make a creative, forward-looking gesture on the occasion of the 500th anniversary of the beginning of both Christian evangelization and the clash between the cultures of Europe and Latin America. CLAR had commissioned two well-known Biblical scholars, Carlos Mesters, a Carmelite from Holland, who has worked and studied in Brazil for over 50 years, and Javier Saravia, a Mexican Jesuit working in his own country, to prepare a program that would facilitate access to the Word of God by the poorly educated faithful of Latin America.

In chapter 8, section 3, paragraph 6 of the Medellin conference conclusions the Bishops state:

. . . present day catechesis must take on in their entirety the sufferings and hopes of people today in order to offer them full liberation, the wealth of an integral salvation in Christ, the Lord. And so, it must be faithful to handing on the biblical message, not merely as regards its intellectual content, but also as regards its living personalized reality in the experience of life of people today.

Real life situations and authentically human desires make up an essential part of the content of catechesis. They must be analyzed carefully within their actual context in the light of the lived experiences of the People of Israel, of Christ, and of the ecclesial community, in which the Spirit of the risen Christ lives and works continuously.

The proposed program was not accepted by any national conference of bishops in Latin America basically because of the methodology used. Its starting point was a reflection on the life situation of the people studying the Bible. This was similar to the method of Liberation Theology, which for many was a divisive experience in their diocese and had already been questioned by the Congregation for the Doctrine of the Faith.

While the CELAM conference in Medellin used a methodology of discernment and investigation which took as its starting point the life situation of the peoples of Latin America, as did the following CELAM conference in Puebla, Mexico, in 1979, the CELAM IV conference in Santo Domingo in 1992 did not adopt that methodology. Supporters of pastoral initiatives that inspired and in turn were inspired by liberation theology were on the back foot at the CELAM meeting in Santo Domingo.

Episcopal appointments in Latin America during the papacy of John Paul II did not take into account candidates closely associated with the development and practice of liberation theology. Also, in 1984 and 1986 two documents from the Congregation for the Faith were read by many as an implicit rejection of the methodology espoused by liberation theology.

On August 6, 1984, the Congregation for the Doctrine of the Faith (headed at that time by Cardinal Joseph Ratzinger, later Pope Benedict XVI) published an INSTRUCTION ON CERTAIN ASPECTS OF THE "THEOLOGY OF LIBERATION," which met with both approval and disapproval of theologians and church leaders depending on the stance of the individual. In the light of the challenges from bishops, theologians and priests, Sisters and laity working among the poor, a more comprehensive and nuanced statement, titled INSTRUCTION ON CHRISTIAN FREEDOM AND LIBERATION, was published by the same Congregation on March 22, 1986. However, many Latin American bishops became wary of any pastoral approach that seemed to have a whiff of liberation theology.

At stake was the validity of bottom up theological reflection as distinct from top down, which is what has predominated in the Church for centuries. For those who propose the former, it is not a matter of "either or," but of "both and." However, many church leaders insist that theological reflection must develop out of the Magisterium of the Church, tradition and the Bible, without necessarily taking into account the historical context, for example, the 1993 "Catechism of the Catholic Church." Many involved in grassroots pastoral work with the poor, especially in programs for forming lay leaders, have continued to insist on the need to contextualize Biblical and theological courses.

Even before CELAM's rejection of the CLAR Bible study program, José Mizzotti, an Italian missionary priest of the De Montfort religious order, had formed a team in Lima to promote the use of the methodology proposed in the CLAR study program. It was originally called "Popular Reading of the Bible," but he with his team renamed the program, "A Pastoral Reading of the Bible." The team had a lot of initial success and received invitations to run workshops in dioceses and parishes all over the country. It was not generally recognized that this was basically the program that had been discarded by CELAM in 1992.

However, it was not long before a whistle blower in a country diocese, by means of an anonymous letter, notified one of the bishops, and the initiative was closed down. The specter of liberation theology was raised to the bishops and also the accusation of fostering the formation of a parallel church.

Between 1995 and 2000, José Mizzotti's team entered into dialogue with the local committee for the Doctrine of the Faith, which is headed by a bishop, to see what was acceptable and what might need to be changed. The bishop in charge postponed any decision and let the matter drag on for about four years as the only plausible basis for totally blocking the program was fear, not content or methodology.

The team took their case to Rome, to the Congregation for the Doctrine of the Faith, requesting an assessment of the Bible study program. In due course the reply came back recommending changing a few words, and with that approved both the content and the methodology.

Subsequently, in 2000, the Peruvian Bishops' Conference, through the President of the Peru Commission for the Doctrine of the Faith, approved the program for pastoral use. The text of our booklets has been revised to the satisfaction of the bishops, and in 2005 our team has been recognized as a not-for-profit religious association of the Catholic Church.

The conclusions of the CELAM conference in 2007, in Aparecida, Brazil, gave further formal church backing to the work of Mizzotti and his team. Near the beginning of this document the assembled Bishops describe the methodology they intend to use at that Episcopal Conference:

19. In continuity with the previous general conferences of Latin American Bishops, this document utilizes the see-judge-act method. This method entails viewing God with the eyes of faith through his revealed word . . . Believing, joyful, and trusting adherence to God, Father, Son, and Holy Spirit, and involvement in the church are preconditions for assuring the effectiveness of this method.

This is precisely the approach that José Mizzotti and his team have advocated for many years.

Link to our tradition:

The above, which describes a project designed to help the poor of Latin America read God's word in the Bible from the perspective of their life experience, recalls the words of the prophet Jeremiah 31, 33-34: "But this is the covenant I will make with the house of Israel after those days—oracle of the LORD. I will place my law within them, and write it upon their hearts; I will be their God, and they shall be my people. They will no longer teach their friends and relatives, 'Know the LORD!' Everyone, from least to greatest, shall know me— oracle of the LORD—, for I will forgive their iniquity and no longer remember their sin."

## A Pastoral Reading of the Bible

### By Lucy Cardenas

Twenty years ago I began to go to weekend workshops to learn about new Bible study methodology. We now call our program "A Pastoral Reading of the Bible," and it is aimed at Christian communities among the poor of Latin America and the Caribbean.

We call it pastoral, because it is designed to help participants take on the responsibilities and challenges of their lives with courage, love and compassion and deep faith in Jesus Christ.

The program runs in a communal setting, which facilitates sharing of problems and insights among participants; in fact, it is a community builder as it generates friendships and an attitude of mutual care. The main beneficiaries are the grassroots church communities of Latin America, and it can function quite well even with those who cannot read or write. However, most participants have the basics of literacy.

Our program is educational in that it helps participants grow into a method of interpretation that helps them find their own way with the Bible, but always reading and reflecting on the text in community. All reflection begins with what participants are living and eventually returns to that, and so helps the readers see with greater clarity their way in life according to the Word of God.

CELAM, Aparecida, (2007) explicitly identified and affirmed our approach to prayerful Bible study:

249. Among the many ways of approaching sacred scripture, there is one privileged way to which we are all invited: Lectio divina or the practice of prayerful reading of sacred scripture. This prayerful reading, when well-practiced, leads to the encounter with Jesus-Master, to the knowledge of the mystery of Jesus-Messiah, to communion with Jesus-Son of God, and to the testimony of Jesus-Lord of the Universe. With its four moments (reading, meditation, prayer, and contemplation), prayerful reading fosters the personal encounter with Jesus Christ in the manner of so many figures in the Gospel: Nicodemus and his longing for eternal life (cf. John 3, 1-21), the Samaritan woman and her yearning for true worship (cf. John 4, 1-42), the man born blind and his desire for inner light (cf. John 9), Zacchaeus and his wish to be different (cf. Luke 19, 1-10), and so forth . . . . They did not [merely] open their heart to something of the Messiah, but to the Messiah himself, route of growth in "maturity according to his fullness" (Ephesians 4, 13), process of discipleship, of communion with brothers and sisters and commitment to society.

For one year around ten people from our parish went to the training workshops each weekend, and one evening during the week we replicated a shorter version of the sessions with communities in the parish. They liked it so much that they kept coming. The methodology encouraged participation so the meetings were not boring. The educational approach differed radically from what participants had known during their time at school. Maybe they were also surprised to find that they were learning a lot in such a simple way. Together we learned to approach both life and the Bible text in a critical way, not to undo the good that we knew and did, but to see how to act even better.

For me it was a place to meet and dialogue with others and, in that encounter I feel that I meet God. I grew stronger in my calling as a lay person. What I learned I would apply in my work as a nurse in the police hospital and the nurses' training school. Perhaps one of the most important things that I learned was to approach others as one person to another. There is a lot of class and racial discrimination in our Peruvian society, and our Bible study program helped me question and act contrary to this discrimination, especially in its more subtle forms. I realized that I did not feel or act either superior or inferior to others, regardless of who I was dealing with.

I believe that I learned to be a faithful link or bridge between life and the Word of God in the Bible—faithful to the person looking for enlightenment and also to the Bible text. Also, all that we had shared in our community over the years stood me in good stead when, along with a group of senior nurses, I was transferred from the nurses' training school where I had been working for 21 years. The government had made major budgetary cuts, and I found myself in limbo for three long months.

Being moved in this way from the job I had dedicated myself to for years really shook me up. It was as if my whole professional career had collapsed from one day to the next. I was not married and did not have a family, so my job in the nursing school had become a very important part of my life. Possibilities of professional advancement in this area were eliminated. After three months of uncertainty, they transferred us to a new unit where we worked on investigation, prevention and control of infections within the hospital. All this happened in 2002 and in fact, not long after that, in 2006, I retired from nursing. My Dad became quite sick at that time, and I helped look after him until he died that same year.

The problems of my life did not make me feel more or less, as my dignity does not hinge on whatever position I may have been occupying, rather it stems from knowing that I am one more daughter of God.

More recently, our Bible study teams (there are now two working in two parishes) have been running workshops for new team members in order to offer pastoral workers and members of parish communities, not only methodology and theoretical knowledge, but an experience of meeting the Lord. In each community, we would like see these meetings for Biblical reflection given ever greater importance. We would like pastoral workers to apply what they learn in their pastoral work so that catechetical meetings, other activities and Sunday celebrations may be experiences of meeting the Lord. All this should strengthen the life of the community and the everyday life of each person.

We meet every Thursday, and it's always a special moment in my week. For me it's all about dreaming, imagining and believing that another kind of world is possible. Now I also do Bible study with my Mum. At 7:00 a.m. each day she is there with her Bible open at the text we are to discuss according to the see-judge-act method that has served me so well for over 20 years.

Link to our tradition:

A pastoral team develops a Bible study method that helps participants grow in community as they reflect on their life experience in the light of the Word of God. The 2007 Latin American and Caribbean Bishops' Conference (CELAM) met in Aparecida, Brazil and supported such endeavors. See No. 248 of its conclusions: ". . . Disciples of Jesus yearn to be nourished with the bread of the Word: they want to have access to proper interpretation of the biblical texts, to use them as mediation of dialogue with Jesus, and that they be the soul of evangelization itself and of proclamation of Jesus to all. Hence, the importance of a 'biblical ministry' understood as a biblical impetus to pastoral ministry, . . . This demands that bishops, priests, deacons, and lay ministers of the Word approach sacred scripture in a way that is not merely intellectual and instrumental, but with a heart 'hungry to hear the Word of the Lord.'" (Amos 8, 11)

## Two Steps Forward and One Step Back

### By Columban Fr. Paul Prendergast

Andeans have organized on the basis of community for centuries if not for millennia. The identity of most was intimately linked to a sense of belonging to a community of anywhere from 40 to 400 families. From time immemorial people's lives have been worked out within the framework of the community, and little seems to have changed in this regard in spite of the social upheavals of Spanish colonial rule.

At the heart of the Andean way of life is an ethic of strict reciprocity. Its demands may at times be quite complex, but all members of an Andean community are aware of their rights and duties as determined by the norms of reciprocity. It governs the way community members relate to each other. It does not exclude the loving care proposed by Christianity, but nor does it integrate that basic Christian moral demand into the reciprocal dynamic that governs the life of a community. If a community member wants to go that one step further that Christian morality urges there would be no objection, but it is certainly not demanded of him/her.

The law of the ancient Hebrews protected the weaker members of the community (Deuteronomy 22, 22-27). This spirit of compassionate concern for the widow, the orphan and the stranger might also be part of the moral vision of many Andean Catholics, but it has not penetrated the whole of society. We clearly still have a long way to go.

Until the 1960s an Andean parish functioned according to a centuries old pattern. The typical parish embraced many communities, maybe 30, 50 or even more, and usually there was a central town where the main parish church was located. Each community had its chapel and patron saint, whose feast day was celebrated each year. The parish priest was expected to visit each community at least once a year but, due to the age of the priest or the harsh terrain of the parish, he may not have always managed to do this.

The Catholics of these communities had a strong devotion to their patron saint, whose power they trusted to protect them from harm. They felt close to the suffering Christ, a relationship that they highlighted especially over the Easter period and at the times of the fiestas in honor of the Holy Cross. They frequently placed crosses on hilltops near their villages.

Each community had a well-organized system of Christian life that probably dated back to the time of the Spanish missionaries. Each community had its religious leader who was responsible for bringing the children together during Lent to learn the basic prayers and hymns, in particular those referring to Christ's suffering and death. All of this was of course in the Quechua language.

A major change began to get underway in the 1960s, stimulated of course by Vatican II and the CELAM meeting in Medellin, Colombia, in 1968. Church leaders began to take a serious interest in catechesis regarding doctrine and moral teaching. Prior to this there had been a deeply ingrained pattern of religious activity, but it was not underpinned by an appreciation of the Church's teaching. It was a religious faith and practice often divorced from an understanding of both doctrine and morality.

Despite Church leaders' efforts to foster a more integral approach to being a Christian I feel that we are far from achieving that goal. I feel that we have attempted to help our people integrate Catholic moral teaching into their lives, but so often we have adopted an approach one or more steps removed from their lives. We have also addressed many social justice issues from the standpoint of Christian moral teaching, but we have failed to hone in on the way community members relate to each other. We have worked the big picture reasonably well, but I sense that we've not been able to get at the heart of the people's way of thinking and acting.

Then there is the question of public debate about issues, mainly related to water and industrial development, which might impinge on the lives of a village, a district, a department, etc. The Andean approach to a public discussion on such matters is quite different from that of westerners. There is certainly nothing straight forward about the debate, and there is definitely little interest in a dispassionate study of the pros and cons of a public proposal, nor would the "common good" be a significant commonly accepted value. This is not to say that in our countries of origin we tackle our social issues more effectively, but rather that we do things differently.

Another major difficulty has been that the people we are trying to reach with our modern catechesis speak and think in non-European categories. However, there has been a huge effort over a long period to help both children and adults know more about the life and teaching of Jesus of Nazareth. Through catechesis and the celebration of the Sacraments we have done our best to introduce our people to a flesh and blood Jesus, to help all see beyond the plaster or wooden image, beyond the idea of a divinity without thoughts or feelings, to a man who grew up in a family, searched for His way in life, loved those with whom He shared life, spoke and lived by the truth and finally died for being who He was. Our people have never been in any doubt about Jesus being the Son of God but, except for His final hours of suffering, His humanity was not sufficiently taken into account.

Still, they are Quechuas of the Andes, and we church leaders are Europeans. Even those Quechuas who accept the invitation to join our ranks as priests or religious tend to leave aside their Quechua ways and adopt a European approach to life. They separate themselves from their cultural roots so have little interest in communicating the truths of our Christian faith to their own people in terms that they will understand. Rather, many would tend to think that their people should strive to move forward into the modern world and leave behind a way of life that has become obsolete.

Despite the shortcomings of all that we have done, I can say with confidence that our people now have a sense of being part of the parish with opportunities to contribute creatively to parish life. The parish is no longer seen as simply the religious institution that gives the priest a living, nor is it just the small group that hovers around the parish priest in the main parish center. The communities of our parishes are alive and active and well able to say who they are with self-belief.

Link to our tradition:

Andean subsistence farmers in the south of Peru strive to move towards a post-Vatican II understanding and practice of their Catholic faith, an experience of discovery not unlike that of some in the early Church. (See Luke 24, 13-35): "And it happened that while they were conversing and debating, Jesus himself drew near and walked with them, but their eyes were prevented from recognizing him . . . . we were hoping that he [Jesus] would be the one to redeem Israel; and besides all this, it is now the third day since this took place. Some women from our group, however, have astounded us: they were at the tomb early in the morning and did not find his body; they came back and reported that they had indeed seen a vision of angels who announced that he was alive . . . . beginning with Moses and all the prophets, he [Jesus] interpreted to them what referred to him in all the scriptures . . . . he went in to stay with them . . . . he took bread, said the blessing, broke it, and gave it to them. With that their eyes were opened and they recognized him, . . ."

## An Evangelizing Faith Community

By Columban Fr. John Hegerty

This now vibrant parish community began to get under way in 1990, just five years after the first residents began to move to a recently urbanized sector of what had been, until the 1969 agrarian reform, a large feudally run farm. In 1993 the housing association of the area donated 900 square meters of land to our parish, and it is on that land that we have slowly built a parish hall, half the walls of the chapel and a few rooms in which we run our parish meetings and programs. We now have a well-organized and active local parish community.

We celebrate Sunday Mass in our hall twice a month, and on other Sundays we have a lay-led liturgy. About 300 parishioners come to our Sunday celebrations. There are four baptismal preparation teams for the parish so our people coordinate with them, and we have a few baptisms in our hall each month. The six month first communion preparation program involves the parents of the children and is run by a team from our local community. Each year we have around 40 to 45 children making their first communion. We also have a team that runs a follow-up program with the children who wish to participate. There are 28 youth in our local confirmation program this year. A couple from each parish community joins the team that runs a centralized marriage preparation course. This course has recently been renewed, and the couples have given us significant positive feedback. They report that they are discussing for the first time matters of major importance for their lives together. Some of the youth participate in one central parish youth group with the youth from each of our twelve communities always making a point of affirming their local community identity. There is a prayer group that meets once a week for an hour's prayer before the Blessed Sacrament, and we have a choir to animate the singing on Sundays and another to sing at weddings, Baptisms and weekday Masses. Each Tuesday a group of ten to twelve community members meets for an hour and half to reflect on and discuss the Bible readings for the following Sunday's liturgy.

To continue doing all this and more we need to continue to develop our local community parish center. We have plans for a chapel, and the foundations and some walls have already been built. We run two or three fundraising activities each year, from which we raise between $500 and $1,000 each time. We ask local residents to donate money or material towards our chapel project. To date we have been able to find the resources to get the building materials for our local community center, but the parish looks for funds to help with the cost of building, especially major sections such as the roof, plans and builders' wages. I have always believed that this parish community project deserves our time, effort and financial support. To verify and support this conviction I asked a few pillars of our community (Jorge, Doris, Martha, Adela and Rosario) what belonging to the local parish community had contributed to their lives and what, in their opinion, did the community contribute to the life of the broader civic community.

Jorge used to be on the fringe of parish life; he went to church occasionally, maybe for a special celebration, such as a funeral, wedding or Baptism. He accepted an invitation to do a retreat, which motivated him to become active in the parish. He said, "That experience changed my home life and helped me be much more communicative." He also told me that, in his opinion, many neighbors are searching for a deeper spiritual meaning in their lives, and the parish community has helped in that. It has provided many with the opportunity to meet other residents, to get to know each and so not feel isolated from neighbors.

Doris told me that she used to be like the prophet Amos—slow to hear the call of God. What her husband, Jorge, had done had a major impact on her, and she began to go to church more frequently. She said, "Now I like going to Mass and have gradually come to understand better what it's all about. I also feel that I have become more tolerant." She feels that the parish community has been able to instill a certain joy into the life of the local civic community. She remarked, "All of us have something to complain about but that does not have to be our main agenda."

Martha felt that the parish community had helped her change her way of being with others, helping her to be less impatient and more able to put herself in the position of others, and so appreciate their point of view or experience of life. The parish community has helped her feel part of a wider community; it has helped her feel at home here. She said, "This parish community helps its members and also the members of the broader community to break out of their isolation."

Adela was not active in the parish when she first came to live here but, thanks to an invitation from Doris, she came along to the first communion program for her daughter, felt welcomed and began to want to participate. She said, "When Columban Fr. John Boles invited me with my husband to be guides for the adults in the first communion program I felt a deep joy." Her husband does not participate and, at one stage, put pressure on her to pull out of parish activities but she put her foot down, so now according to Adela, "He does not participate but he does support me, and I feel so happy to see the joy of others as they become part of our community."

Rosario put it simply, "This community allows me to live my faith. It gives us the chance to reach out to others to speak of a God who loves all of us."

Link to our tradition:

The life of Christ the Savior parish community, one of twelve communities in the parish, "Our Lady of the Missions," San Martin de Porres, Lima, Peru, brings to mind a parable of Jesus. See Luke 13, 20-21: "Again he [Jesus] said, 'To what shall I compare the kingdom of God? It is like yeast that a woman took and mixed [in] with three measures of wheat flour until the whole batch of dough was leavened.'"

## Peruvian Laity on Mission within Peru

By Columban Fr. Bernard Lane

In the mid-1990s the Columbans in Peru were looking for a strategy that might help committed lay people with initiative and leadership skills to think and act beyond their own parish. The invitation to participate in an organization dedicated to sending adults and youth on mission within Peru met with an enthusiastic response. We Columbans were delighted to be able to do a bit more to pass on our missionary emphasis. It was good to see people I knew and with whom I'd worked taking interest in such a mission project.

We believe in and want to do what we can to promote a mature and co-responsible laity in the proclamation of the Gospel in order to help make real the Kingdom of God among us. This vision continues to be nourished and affirmed by people who are still signing up for our mission program. However, our lay missionaries tend to focus solely on building up the Church and ignore the challenge to transform society, which, according to the Church's teaching, is the prerogative of the laity.

Even though we have tried to encourage our laity to work at the link between their Christian faith and the issues facing our society we have had limited success. Maybe this is such a daunting task that most feel that it's not worth even trying to undertake it. In our preparation courses we constantly strive to open participants to the social issues of Peru. Most would see such matters as important but the business of government and politicians, with little opportunity for anyone else to do anything about them.

However, there have been a few exceptions to the rule. Recently, Isabel, one of our long term missionaries, ran as a candidate in local municipal elections. Another, Aliseo, is committed to a development project with youth and women in his local community. Adela worked on a committee to pave a road in her locality.

There are other frustrations such as, missionaries sometimes ceasing to be outgoing. Instead of going around the barrio knocking on doors when they go to a community, they just sit and wait in the chapel or communal hall. Some promise to do something and then don't turn up. Perhaps, the biggest difficulty stems from home and school formation which has geared most people to reproduce what they have been taught, rather than think and act creatively.

Despite the difficulties we plan to continue to invite people to live an experience of Christian commitment that moves beyond a Church focused project. We want the Church to be for the Kingdom of God not just for itself.

This year one of our priorities has been to encourage our lay missionaries to feel that all of us are members of a community in which we care for each other, get to know each other, reflect and pray together, and also celebrate together. We want the community in which the members are seen to love each other to be our prime witness of our faith in Jesus Christ. I can already see this happening in some parishes where our missionaries meet regularly for study and prayer. In other parishes absurd divisions and squabbles can be quite disheartening as there is so much potential good waiting to be unleashed.

Also, this year there has been a shift in how we organize our principal formation program—the annual five week summer course. Formerly it was open only to those committed to going on mission to some other part of Peru, but now it is open to all active pastoral agents in our parishes. Also, we have made a point of looking for qualified Peruvian laity to lecture and run workshops, giving less prominence to priests and religious. Pilar helped us with social analysis, Milka with gender issues, Clarisa with psychology, and Walter with planning and organization.

We no longer have missionaries available to go to places for three or four months, so we have been consulting the receiving parish or diocese to see how we might help out with formation workshops that run for a few days. Our numbers have decreased in recent years, but we still have 50 active missionaries, drawn from eight parishes, three of which are still Columban-run and the rest used to be run by Columbans. About 75% of our missionaries are women.

When asked by Peter Hughes, a fellow Columban from Ireland who first came to Peru in 1966, how this experience of coordinating and accompanying the Columban lay missionary program within Peru, had enriched me, two things came to mind.

First, I feel certain that at this stage of my life my growth as a person requires the opportunity to be able to work closely with an adult community outside the parish context and this is what my present job explicitly invites me to do. In the parish situation I ended up feeling as though I was just doing jobs as if I were simply a functionary around the place. I would so easily respond to the numerous requests for this and that in the parish and end up without quality time for any particular group of people. In my present job I have ample opportunity for person to person relating and genuinely feel that I do belong to a community.

Second, I feel that this program responds to what we define as Columban mission, because we are preparing and facilitating laity who want to go on mission, and this is my fundamental commitment and interest—to help others be pilgrims for Christ.

Link to our tradition:

The above Columban pastoral project offers lay men and women the opportunity to go beyond the familiar setting of their lives to be part-time missionaries in their own country. Such an opportunity offers them a special opportunity to do as Christ urged His disciples in Matthew 5, 14-16: "You are the light of the world. A city set on a mountain cannot be hidden. Nor do they light a lamp and then put it under a bushel basket; it is set on a lampstand, where it gives light to all in the house. Just so, your light must shine before others, that they may see your good deeds and glorify your heavenly Father."

## Rural Missionary Catechist

By Benigna Alvarez Zavaleta

Since I have been in Combapata, my main aim has been to form Christian communities, which meet regularly. It would be impossible for me to attend to all the communities alone. I have been very fortunate to have a group of local lay missionaries working with me. Benigna is an outstanding example of the parishioners who are helping me and I am extremely grateful to her and the rest of the missionary team. Columban Fr. Don Hornsey

I have lived all my life in Amahuaylla, a hamlet with just ten families, four kilometers up the valley from Combapata. My father died some time ago, and I live with my mother and niece. We have a small farm of a little less than one hectare where we grow broad beans and potatoes for our own consumption and maize and vegetables to sell in the market. We also have chickens and ducks, six sheep and four bulls. We hire a man to help with the heavy work and also the harvest.

Since I was a small girl I have been coming to the parish to participate in whatever was going on. I come to town each day on the minibus that brings the school children in to school.

In the mornings on Monday, Wednesday and Friday I work in the department for catechesis in Sicuani where we prepare material for catechists and organize courses. All our material is bilingual, and the formation courses are scheduled for nine, live-in, five day sessions each year in the Combapata parish center and an annual retreat.

In the afternoons, plus Sunday, I work as the Combapata parish secretary. However, I do my grassroots pastoral work in the evenings from Monday to Friday.

Seven years ago, soon after Fr. Donald arrived in our parish, I began to work as a missionary to our rural communities. It takes me up to an hour to walk to most communities where I meet with men, women and children. I help the children to prepare for baptism and first communion, and the youth for confirmation. I work with the adults to help develop a sense of being a Christian community. At our meetings we discuss the Bible text of the day or a theme that Fr. Donald has asked us to study together. In the countryside everyone's mother tongue is Quechua so all our religious programs are in that language.

To date I have been able to foster the development of ten Christian communities in local rural communities. I help them get established and find a member of the community who is willing and able to continue as leader, and then move on to the next place. Over the past seven years I have helped ten communities become established with their own leaders. I hope to be able to do something similar for three more rural communities. In this pastoral outreach I see myself as a rural missionary catechist. I try to do as St. Paul did in the early days of Christianity—travel from place to place to announce the Good News of Jesus Christ and establish a community of believers who will in turn continue to announce the same message by deed and word.

At the moment I am going to five communities, which keeps me busy on the evenings from Monday to Friday. Our meeting lasts for one hour. During the months when there is little to do in the fields we might have from 20 to 25 adults participating a community meeting, but the numbers go down to around fifteen during busy periods, such as sowing and harvesting. Our parish work has to take into account the rhythm of work in the fields.

I am so pleased to be able to do this missionary work. There have always been small rural communities, and even though each may have had its own chapel they did not have a vibrant Christian community that could read and discuss Bible texts and apply them to their daily lives. I know for sure that the residents of our rural communities appreciate what I do because they continuously search me out to do this and that.

I feel most grateful that our Bishops meeting in Aparecida, Brazil, in 2007 for the fifth meeting of the Conference of Latin American Bishops, explicitly supported our missionary outreach.

Link to our tradition:

CELAM, Aparecida, 2007, No. 178: "In the ecclesial experience of some churches of Latin America and the Caribbean, basic (base) ecclesial communities have been schools that have helped form Christians committed to their faith, disciples and missionaries of the Lord, as is attested by the generous commitment of so many of their members, even to the point of shedding their blood. They return to the experience of the early communities as described in the Acts of the Apostles." See Acts 2, 42-47: "They devoted themselves to the teaching of the apostles and to the communal life, to the breaking of the bread and to the prayers. Awe came upon everyone, and many wonders and signs were done through the apostles. All who believed were together and had all things in common; they would sell their property and possessions and divide them among all according to each one's need. Every day they devoted themselves to meeting together in the temple area and to breaking bread in their homes. They ate their meals with exultation and sincerity of heart, praising God and enjoying favor with all the people. And every day the Lord added to their number those who were being saved."

## Christian Communities Growing towards Maturity

By Columban Fr. Liam O'Callaghan

Helping a Network of Parish Communities Develop into an Effective Instrument for Mission

The Diocese of Lahore was established in 1886, with the Capuchin religious order assuming responsibility for its early development. From early days the Capuchins sought to establish the basis for a strong local church. They recruited and prepared young men for the diocesan clergy. They trained lay leaders who are known as catechists, who have traditionally been responsible for grassroots pastoral work in the hundreds of villages in what has been up until recent times a predominantly rural landscape. The local church was well placed to respond to the massive influx of mainly lower caste Pakistanis into various non-Muslim religious groups, including the Catholic Church.

Ours is a large urban and rural parish, created in 2007, on the southern side of the outer rim of the metropolitan area of Lahore (estimated population of 8.6 million). We have about 2,500 Catholic families in the parish. As Catholics make up roughly 1.5% of the population of Pakistan, our parishioners are quite scattered over a large area.

To help our parishioners acquire a sense of belonging to a local community we have built eight chapels adding to the ten that already existed. Some of our chapels function as multi-purpose facilities—meetings, Sunday school, literacy classes. These are centers around which the Catholics of the area celebrate and grow in a sense of belonging. I am the only resident priest, and a local Dominican also helps out on weekends. On average we have Mass in five places each Sunday, and in the other chapels we have lay-led liturgies of the word with communion.

Paid, fulltime, diocesan catechists and paid, part time parish employed catechists are the backbone of our parish pastoral team. We have four diocesan and six parish catechists. One parish catechist runs the office, and the other nine have an area each of the parish, in which they have responsibility for the pastoral development of 250 to 300 families living in the vicinity of one, two or three chapels. All our catechists are married and live with their families in an area of the parish. They are responsible for pastoral care, catechetical and Biblical formation and the celebration of baptisms, marriages and funerals. For over 50 years catechists have been entrusted by the bishops of Pakistan with the responsibility to administer these Sacraments and lead liturgies.

The diocesan catechists do a three year formation course and then are officially appointed by the diocese to each parish. They can officially do what deacons do elsewhere, but they are not part of the clerical world, nor are they permanent in their diocesan role. In fact, most retire to some other job after about 30 years. The parish actually pays the wages of all the catechists but, in the case of the diocesan catechists, the diocese looks after housing, insurance and medical cover.

Since many families, especially those who have come into the parish from country areas, have not had the chance to learn about their faith or belong to a Christian community we are taking a number of steps to help them grow in understanding and experience of our Christian faith in action.

I feel that this parish is genuine mission territory as most of our parishioners have been terribly neglected pastorally. New residents are moving into the area all the time, and many Catholics have had little contact with the Church. Most respond positively to our outreach and welcome. In one new area last month we had around 50 baptisms, and this month it will be the same.

Lay formation is high on our agenda of priorities. Mushtaq Asad, a lay theologian on our parish staff since 2008, works tirelessly giving Bible courses in the parish center and in the chapels. He is busy with Bible study groups most nights. He also facilitates a monthly session with our parish catechists as part of their ongoing formation.

Due to the lack of pastoral care many have a weak sense of being Christian. We work with them through our team of catechists who do visitation and organize religious instruction. We have parish schools in five areas of the parish, so we find we can also work with the parents through the school. Still, there is a majority that does not go to school.

In recent years, we have run a mission exchange program with the Badin parish in the south of the country. We send six parishioners down to Badin, and they send six of theirs to us for a period of time. Thanks to the ethnic and linguistic difference[27] we have benefited from the exchange. Our people have learned from families and communities with whom they stayed in the south. Their hosts speak another language and have different customs but also profess the same Catholic faith. This experience has given so many of our people a deeper understanding of what cross cultural mission is about.

This exchange experience has helped motivate our catechists and other pastoral agents to be outgoing and missionary within our own parish. We need this broad missionary commitment if we are to build up our local church. With renewed understanding of our faith, we will have more confidence and so be more willing to enter into dialogue with others.

Members of the various parish communities also gather a few times a year to share among themselves, maybe to celebrate together or perform for each other. Recently we gathered the thirteen choirs of the parish to sing Christmas songs. Such meetings help people from the various communities get to know each other and cement a sense of belonging to the parish community.

I for one feel a deep joy in being part of this emerging Catholic parish community as I witness the active and committed involvement of so many parishioners who are doing their best for the community and taking advantage of opportunities to reach out to others. They have become more aware of their responsibility in mission.

Link to our tradition:

The Apostolic Exhortation, Evangelii Nuntiandi, 1975, No. 75, sums up the spirit of a parish's development in Lahore, Pakistan: "Evangelization will never be possible without the action of the Holy Spirit. The Spirit descends on Jesus of Nazareth at the moment of His baptism when the voice of the Father—'This is my beloved Son with whom I am well pleased' (Matthew 3, 17) . . . Jesus is 'led by the Spirit' to experience in the desert the decisive combat and the supreme test before beginning this mission (Matthew 4, 1). It is 'in the power of the Spirit' (Luke 4, 14) that He returns to Galilee and begins His preaching at Nazareth, applying to Himself the passage of Isaiah: 'The Spirit of the Lord is upon me.' And He proclaims: 'Today this Scripture has been fulfilled.' (Luke 4, 18) To the disciples whom He was about to send forth He says, breathing on them, 'Receive the Holy Spirit.'" (John 10, 22)

---

[27]    The people here are Punjabi and speak Punjabi, while in the south they are Sindhis, Parkari Kholis, Kutchi Kholis and Bheels, all of whom speak their own language; the common and official national language is Urdu.

# Christmas Gift

By Emmanuel Neno

It was December 21, 2007, when Joseph and Mary were visiting one of their relatives who had been hospitalized. Following their visit, as they were leaving the hospital, two women were standing at the main exit. One of them called out for Mary and asked her to come into a corner to talk in private. She hesitated but followed the women to an isolated corner. The air was still filled with doubt about what the women wanted to talk about. They opened a basket to reveal a newborn baby girl whom they wanted to pass on to some couple with no kids. They asked Mary if she knew any family who would be willing to adopt the baby.

Mary was confused about the reason why they wanted to give the baby away and asked, "Where are her parents?" They said, "My dear sister, what are you going to get out of knowing her parents? Just take a moment to think that if she had her parents, would we be hanging around here in public with her?" That did not clear things up for Mary. The women continued, "We want to give this baby away to some family that can look after her. If no one takes her then we would just have to dump her somewhere." Mary soon worked her thoughts into the bottom of all this. She asked the women to wait while she went and spoke to her husband.

Upon discussing things with Joseph, they both started pondering how to deal with the situation at hand. Joseph recalled that a young couple that he knew was having difficulty conceiving. Hoping that they might want to adopt the baby, he gave them a call and told them the good news. But he was soon disappointed with their reply that they didn't want to raise someone else's baby. He kept trying other people off his phonebook, but no one agreed to the idea of adopting a baby that was not from their own blood. Joseph and Mary were deeply puzzled about what to do. They wondered whether they should walk past this situation like the priest and the Levite or be the good Samaritan and help the women out. The situation was testing Joseph and Mary's faith. While the clock kept ticking, they were lost deep in thought about what they could do. The hospital had a canal running by its side; they were afraid that the women might put the baby in the canal.

Joseph and Mary decided that they would take the baby home, and as soon as they could find someone to adopt her, they would pass her on. It was bitterly cold outside and there was nothing to wrap the baby in. Joseph went to the market to buy a blanket, but due to Muslim Eid, the shops were closed. He came back empty handed. He asked his wife to take off her long scarf and wrap it around the baby. And so, they took her home.

Three days went past, and the baby was still with Joseph and Mary. Visitors to their home would ask questions about her and offered unsolicited suggestions about the baby's future. The newborn was lying in Mary's lap looking up at her. It seemed as if she was carefully listening to the conversation about her future.

Joseph and Mary looked down at the baby's face that showed her innocence and anxiousness. They felt as if her eyes were questioning them, asking "Does this house have no place for me?" Since it was Christmas time, they decided that they would take the baby as a Christmas gift from God and keep her. If anyone were to ask about her, Joseph and Mary decided that they would tell them that the baby was their own and part of the family.

Yet, people still expressed their concerns about the child. They told Joseph and Mary that she was too young, and when she grows up, her education and marriage will be a heavy burden. Joseph and Mary put their foot down and insisted upon their decision. They said, "Education and marriage will be a responsibility later. For now, the child does not have those needs. Our responsibility at the moment is to look after her and give her the love she needs. The rest we leave to God's providence."

Emmanuel Neno, Executive Secretary, CBCC, Catholic Bishops Commission for Catechetics

The above is a true story and the true identity of Mary and Joseph are Emmanuel and his wife.

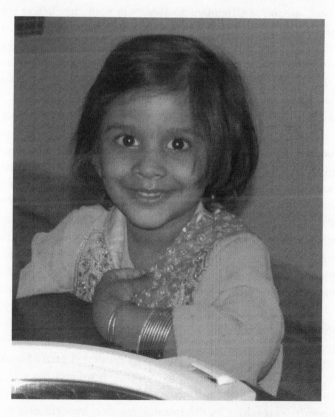

Link to our tradition:

The story of adopting a recently born baby who might have been left to die brings to mind the teaching of Jesus: "When did we see you a stranger and welcome you, or naked and clothe you? When did we see you ill or in prison, and visit you?' And the king will say to them in reply, 'Amen, I say to you, whatever you did for one of these least brothers of mine, you did for me.'" (Matthew 25, 38-40)

# On Being Good News

### By Mushtaq Asad

Columban missionary, Fr. Tanvir O'Hanlon, invited me to work with the Columbans for the promotion of mission in our local church. He said to me, "We have this gift of mission and we want to give it to the people of Pakistan." That was in 2007 when I had recently completed a four year contract in a pastoral institute dedicated to the formation of religion teachers. However, the story of my faith journey began about 30 years ago when I was in my early twenties.

For two years I trained to be a catechist and then the De La Salle Brothers decided to send me to the Urbaniana University in Rome for further studies. After two years study I graduated with a licentiate in missiology. One of my favorite authors at the time was Cardinal Carlo Maria Martini, and I had the good fortune to spend a three month summer break in his Milan diocesan lay missionary center for Africa. I took part in the program for the lay missionaries and was deeply impressed on seeing whole families preparing to go on mission.

Cardinal Martini visited occasionally, and even though he did not say much his presence was the message that stayed with me. I liked the way he commented on the Bible; it was as if he did not merely have the mind of the Church but the Church was in him. He would say, "You are not merely in the Church but the Church is in you." His presence and what I experienced at that center for mission became the main source of my inspiration for subsequent work with laity.

On my return from Rome I took up a teaching post at the national catechists' training center in Faisalabad. The center was run by the De La Salle Brothers for all the dioceses of Pakistan. My life there was one of books, classes, correcting assignments and all that goes with a teaching job in an academic institution. I was happy in my work and in my home life, but then in 1996, ten years after I had begun teaching, tragedy struck. My wife, who was only 28 years of age, died. We had three children, the eldest a boy (8 years), then a girl (6 years) and a boy (4 years).

I stopped teaching and did nothing for six months. I grieved and wondered how this fit into God's plan for me. I felt so broken up and did not understand what God wanted of me. I did not know where my life was headed and I could not simply return to teaching in the institute for catechists. Then a priest friend,

Fr. Emmanuel Asi, opened a door for me, and I walked through it into a new life. He invited me to coordinate a newly established theological institute for laity— MAKTABA-E-ANAVEEM (School of Thought of the Poor). The name is in Urdu, our common language in Pakistan. The root of the first word is Arabic and of the second it is Hebrew.

The new institute's work was not done primarily in the classroom. My job put me in direct contact with lay men, women and children in the grassroots of our local church. We promoted the formation of theological groups in every city of the country, forming the groups with the help of parish priests and catechists. I realized that this work with laity was God's will for me. There was so much opportunity for further study for clergy and religious, but lay men and women were not valued for the work of doing theology. In fact, some priests opposed our work and said that theology was not a suitable topic for the laity, but other priests supported us.

My brokenness prepared me to go with people, to be with them in a common search for our way in life. I reflected anew, and my reflection was fresh. As I got into the job I came to appreciate the fertility of my pain.

Our priority was fostering the life of Christian communities, forming laity for mission, developing a network among the theology groups we formed. I was doing all this under the directorship of Fr. Asi, but when he moved on and another person took over, he destroyed what we were doing. The church leadership became concerned, and our nascent movement of lay theology became dormant. However, there is still a spark there, but it needs someone to breathe air on it. It seems to me the church leaders want the institution of the Church to be a priority in itself. In contrast, we focused on the everyday lives of ordinary lay people. What does the Word of God have to say to what we are living? What is God calling us to in our daily lives? How might we build a more harmonious, inclusive and just society?

We worked to give birth to a local contextual theology. Our basic inspiration was the opening lines of Vatican II's great document, "Pastoral Constitution on the Church in the Modern World" (*Gaudium et Spes*), Promulgated by Pope Paul VI on December 7, 1965: "The joys and the hopes, the griefs and the anxieties of the men of this age, especially those who are poor or in any way afflicted, these are the joys and hopes, the griefs and anxieties of the followers of Christ." I believe that the mystery of mission is hidden in the words, "the joys and the hopes, the griefs and the anxieties of the men [and women] of this age, especially those who are poor or in any way afflicted."

I was totally changed by the task I had taken on. I was no longer preparing and teaching class but rather reflecting and sharing my faith with other lay men and women. I learned to express myself in the language of everyday life, to listen carefully to the reflections of others and I soon discovered the marvelous mystical depth in so many of the people with whom I was working to build up our network of contextual theology. In fact, I began to realize my potential as I moved more and more into dialogue rather than being the one who knew and explained things to others. We had moved beyond catechetics, the task of communicating the essentials of our Christian faith, to theologizing, the task of reflecting creatively on the implications of the Word of God for our lives and for our planet earth on and with which we give shape to our lives.

Many lay members of the network were diocesan catechists who rely on the diocesan salary to support their families. Consequently the network we created could not prosper without the support of church leaders. When the catechists have a national meeting I still sometimes receive an invitation to speak, and I like to go as I know so many of them; they were my students and later, collaborators in creating something new among the laity in our local church. Some may have seen my going from one institution to another as failure but I feel that I have lived my calling in a missionary way. I never became installed anywhere. I resigned from Maktaba-e—Anaveem and moved to a pastoral institute run by the Dominican Fathers to work on the formation of religious teachers, so I was again busy with the formation of the laity.

And so I come to the fourth stage of my missionary adventure, I am now with the Columban missionaries. I had come to understand that we do not necessarily see the fruits of our mission, but rather our calling is to die as a seed of mission. We can easily become over invested with tangible and verifiable evidence of success. With this in mind, I began to collaborate with Fr. Tanvir in a mission exchange program, in which one parish community in Lahore sent missionaries to another community in Sindh, and the parish in Sindh reciprocated. We had sown the seed of this exchange in study groups that we run every evening in various parish centers. In our culture we are considered "People of the Book," so we readily discern the will or call of God in our reflection on Bible texts. Once we have chosen those we wish to send, we give them an intensive preparation before they go on their two to three week missionary journey.

On arrival at their destination our missionaries are welcomed into the homes of the families with whom they will stay. Over the course of their time on mission they share their faith story with their hosts, be it with the family where they are staying or with a parish community. For all missionaries this is a cross cultural experience even though all participating in the program are Pakistanis. On returning to home base our missionaries share with their friends how the experience has changed them. Sometime later missionaries from a Sindh parish community came to Lahore to enjoy our hospitality and share their faith stories with us. In both cases, on the day of departure the missionary group is given a public send-off at the end of Mass in the presence of the whole community so they have a sense of being sent by the community, not just by the priest.

It is a great experience for both sides when grassroots parishioners can recognize and say, "We are missionary." They had thought that only the foreigner is missionary. As we locals own that same calling, we change our awareness of who we are as Christians.

Link to our tradition:

A Pakistani layman dedicates his life to helping other Pakistani lay men, women and families take on their rightful missionary vocation, as affirmed in the Vatican II document of Christian Mission, *Ad Gentes*, No. 21: "The church has not been really founded, and is not yet fully alive, nor is it a perfect sign of Christ among men and women, unless there is a laity worthy of the name working along with the hierarchy. For the Gospel cannot be deeply grounded in the abilities, life and work of any people without the active presence of laymen and women. Therefore, even at the very founding of a Church, great attention is to be paid to establishing a mature, Christian laity."

## Living My Faith Quietly

### By Jia Xiuqin

I graduated from engineering school in 1966, the year the Cultural Revolution began. That was when the government began to close down schools, universities and come down even heavier than previously on religious practice of whatever kind all over China. I had been brought up a Catholic and as a child went to church regularly and said my prayers from our prayer book. I had registered as a Catholic at my high school, but in my graduation papers that item did not appear, an omission which permitted me to get into engineering school. After graduation I was able to get a good job. I was lucky to finish just before the engineering school was closed.

I remained a Catholic in my heart but did not have a chance to go to church for years. I did not say my prayers as I did not have my prayer book. The Cultural Revolution cut me off totally from the practice of my Catholic faith. However, I was lucky in that I did not suffer personally, nor did my family. There was a gap in my life, and I could not share my faith. For those years, religion was a very private matter between God and me.

The man I married, Li Zhendong, is also an engineer but he is not a Catholic, nor did he find out that I was a Catholic for 20 years after we were married. It was never a matter of conversation. It never occurred to me to talk to him about my religious faith. In those times no one talked about their religious beliefs, because neighbors were encouraged to report on those who showed signs of such retrograde, unpatriotic tendencies. However, I know he supports me in my religious commitment, and he helps me improve the text of articles I write for the main Catholic newspaper in China. He has a great mastery of our language, something which I think our daughter has inherited from him.

In those difficult years from the mid-1950s onwards all the priests and Sisters scattered or were jailed, and the churches were closed and taken over for other activities. The organized churches of whatever kind were effectively wiped out. The only sign of religious practice in those times was a family praying quietly at home at night or a grandmother almost in a whisper teaching her grandchildren their prayers.

My daughter, Li Baochun, was 15 years of age when she found out that I was a Catholic. At no level of our family life was there any talk about religious faith. She grew up in an environment that at every level emphasized that there is no God, at school explicitly so and at home by not mentioning the matter. She subsequently became a Catholic in her late twenties. In our family tradition, she also became an engineer.

My husband and I are now retired, but we know that people in the workplace generally see us believers as a little odd. Our daughter continues to verify this ongoing prejudice against religious belief among most of our people. However, there are signs of questioning the totally materialistic approach that has come to imbue our society. Recently our daughter worked on the construction of a building for an art museum, and she was chatting with a fellow engineer who commented, as he looked around at the art work, that maybe we do need something that stirs our spiritual nature, especially when we get to 50 years of age. She agreed with him, and he asked her whether she had a faith; to which she replied that she was a Catholic and later gave him some literature on the Catholic faith, without pressing him to go to the church.

While it is true that there has been much resistance to and persecution of my Catholic faith, I am proud to say that there are now four generations of women in my family who are Catholic and still alive. My 90 year old mother is the first and lives about 700 kilometers away near Beijing. My ten year old granddaughter Qiqi who lives with us here in Wuhan is the fourth generation. In view of the history we have lived through, this living faith is precious to us.

Link to our tradition:

The following promise of Jesus seems to be verified in the experience of Jia Xiuqin and her family—John 7, 37-39: "On the last and greatest day of the feast, Jesus stood up and exclaimed, 'Let anyone who thirsts come to me and drink. Whoever believes in me, as scripture says: Rivers of living water will flow from within him/her.' He said this in reference to the Spirit that those who came to believe in him were to receive. There was, of course, no Spirit yet, because Jesus had not yet been glorified."

# Rebirth

## By Columban Fr. Dan Troy

I am grateful for the opportunity to have met Bishop Peter Zhang, the first Chinese bishop of Hanyang, on a number of occasions in the few years before he died in 2005 at the age of 91. He succeeded Bishop Edward Galvin, co-founder of the Columbans and a native of my own County Cork in Ireland. As one of many victims of religious persecution by the Chinese government, Peter Zhang spent 24 years as a priest in prison. He was a strong and faith-filled leader until his death. It has taken some time for a new leadership to begin to emerge, but I now sense new life in what was the first mission of The Missionary Society of St. Columban.

Fr. Chen Tian Hui was in his first year of theological studies in 1956 when the local seminary was closed. He found a job as a bus driver until 1993, when Bishop Peter Zhang invited him to be ordained a priest for the diocese. Even though he is now 83 years of age, since the bishop died he continues in the role of Apostolic Administrator. There is little hope that a new bishop will be appointed to Hanyang Diocese in the near future due to its weakened position.

In the meantime, Fr. Joseph Li Chang Jie, from Lu Lin Hu, a local town, has taken on the administrative and planning work. Due to lack of freedom at the time, Joseph was ordained in 2001 in an out-of-the-way church with twelve or so present in a very short night-time ceremony. But, so much has changed in just ten years; this year Fr. Zhang Wei, who recently returned from three years of theology studies in Rome, was ordained with great public fanfare at Huang Lin church, followed by a sit-down meal with 850 guests in a local restaurant.

Prior to 1949 there were about 100 churches and chapels in the Hanyang diocese, but after 1953 there were no public religious activities in any church. Most were demolished or transferred to other use during the Cultural Revolution. Recently I saw one church in the countryside being used as a chicken coop; our cathedral in the city was converted to a factory in the 1960s for making electrical fittings. The Church is still in the process of recovering property confiscated in that period. Fr. Joseph tells me that during the Cultural Revolution people were forbidden to pray, but in the early 1980s he saw his parents praying in a dark room with some neighbors. Clearly persecution and government decrees did not prevent all practices of our faith. Fr. Joseph tells me that he was nine years of age when he first attended Mass in 1985 and that over the past 20 years they have enjoyed ever increasing freedom to practice their faith publicly.

Fr. Joseph speaks energetically about the diocese's five to ten year plan. He recognizes the limited opportunities for the Church in the rural area, which was the heartland of church life in Hanyang diocese prior to 1949. There is still work to be done in the rural area, primarily with the very young and the elderly. In many country churches the Sisters run a summer course for children from nine to sixteen years of age where, among others things, they teach the children some of the basics of the practice of our faith. Simplicity of life is close to hand even when running such summer courses. There are usually problems with power cuts, probably due to overload resulting from the extensive use of air conditioners, but they get by with candles. When the water is cut off because there is no electricity for the pump, things become more difficult.

However, priests and Sisters agree that they need to give priority to pastoral work and missionary outreach in the urban centers. In the words of Fr. Joseph, "The majority of the youth have gone to the city so we must follow them there." That may be easier said than done. In the city the Church has limited access to land so the first step is to negotiate with the government to acquire a place to build parish centers. This is not a simple matter in any part of China but in some places it is more difficult than in others. In Hanyang diocese it continues to be rather difficult. Recently, in one town, after a public demonstration by Catholics protesting the government's inaction on the matter, land was assigned to the Church. The basis of the land grant is a state commitment to compensate for property confiscated since 1949.

The twelve Sisters who belong to two communities in the diocese are committed to the project of Church revival, but they also need to ensure an adequate income. Sr. Li Shuang Qun told me that they want to run a home for the elderly. There is a need, and there are facilities that could be modified for the purpose but it seems that other interests have so far stood in their way. The Sisters would like to make a living from running the home and at the same time dedicate themselves to the care of the elderly as an apostolate.

The diocese has five priests, twelve Sisters and five seminarians. They want to put more energy into formation of Church personnel, including laity, but locally there is little opportunity. A few laity are currently preparing for the mission, one in a two year course in Beijing, another in a six month course in Handan. Fr. Joseph wants to specialize in personal faith development. He also wants priests and Sisters to help train catechists at a local level, but the problem of adequate facilities has yet to be solved. He has been behind the organization of a local one year course for catechists in which 20 are participating, but the facilities are poor, and it costs U.S. $15,000 a year to cover the cost of teachers' wages. A former seminarian from Hanyang directs the program. The active priests and Sisters are relatively young and want to attract youth to the Church but other than personal contact they have no organized strategy for this. They desperately need urban centers from which they can work and to which they can invite youth. For a Church that has been through so many difficulties in the past 60 years, it is also likely that they will now find a way forward in faith through these more recent challenges.

## Steady Comeback

An interview with Hanyang Sisters Shen Ai Yun and Zhang Jinping, the former now the community leader and the latter the leader for the previous six year term.

In the late 1940s, as the People's Liberation Army (PLA) advanced towards Wuhan, located on the Yangtze River, 700 kilometers inland from Shanghai, Columban Bishop Edward Galvin met with the Sisters of a community he had founded. There were tears all round as he released them from their vows and asked them to return to their families. Thirty years later, after China's Cultural Revolution was over, some decided to regroup. In November 2010, two were still alive, Sr. Li Fen Fang, aged 92 years and Sr. Zou Wen Bin, 97 years of age. Sometime later the Sisters began to invite young women to join them. The following describes some of their dreams and plans for the future.

What would you like to be doing in 15 years and how do you plan to go about realizing your plans?

First, I dream of a bigger community; we need to grow in order to do what needs to be done here in Hanyang. We want to do mission work in the Hanyang Diocese. We would like to help improve the spirituality of Catholics and attract others to the Church. We would help Catholics deepen their spirituality through courses about our faith and the Bible, and by inviting them to come to church more regularly. Then, in order to interest others in our faith we would begin by visiting them, especially in their time of need. Showing compassion and friendship is very important in Chinese culture regardless of religious belief. We would also encourage Catholics to invite their friends to church. Some Catholics might ask us go to homes or the work place of friends to talk about our faith. Many people in China are searching for a deeper meaning in their lives; this is so especially among the youth.

In order to tackle these tasks we would need preparation and there are courses in theology and Bible for Sisters in three cities in China—Taiyuan, Beijing and Shijiazhuang. Some of our Sisters have already done the two year course in Taiyuan. A three year course will soon be available in Beijing, for which the entry standard will be quite high.

There is very little missionary work being done in the diocese of Hanyang; we lack organization. We could start a training center here in Hanyang for Catholics so that priests, Sisters and laity might work together to help renew the faith of our people and, at the same time, reach out to others with the Good News of the Gospel.

Pope Benedict XVI, in his encyclical *Deus Caritas Est*, tells us that our faith in Jesus Christ urges us to respond in three ways: first, to preach the message of Jesus; second, to live a religious life, by the practice of the prayer and the celebration of the Sacraments; third, serve those who are in need. Being religious Sisters we should care about those whom society does not care about (and their number is increasing).

Maybe we should not say that society does not care at all, but what we can say is that it does not care enough. For example, younger family members may give money to help the elderly of their family, but then do not live with them, accompany them in their illness or loneliness. There is so often a lack of personal care rather than a lack of money.

To help do even more of this outreach work we have formed a lay group called "Love Heart Small Group," which has seventeen members. We know we cannot solve other people's problems, but they like us to visit them in their homes. We find this is so with both Catholics and non-Catholics. We have also seen that this kind of outreach opens up a way that connects our hearts with the hearts of many local people.

Link to our tradition:

The above two stories describe how initiative, patience and new church leadership in Hanyang diocese are giving shape to a vision for our times, a vision nurtured by a hope dating from the early days of the Church. See Revelations 21, 1-6: "Then I saw a new heaven and a new earth. The former heaven and the former earth had passed away, and the sea was no more. I also saw the holy city, a new Jerusalem, coming down out of heaven from God, prepared as a bride adorned for her husband. I heard a loud voice from the throne saying, 'Behold, God's dwelling is with the human race. He will dwell with them and they will be his people and God himself will always be with them [as their God]. He will wipe every tear from their eyes, and there shall be no more death or mourning, wailing or pain, [for] the old order has passed away.' The one who sat on the throne said, 'Behold, I make all things new.' Then he said, 'Write these words down, for they are trustworthy and true.' He said to me, 'They are accomplished. I [am] the Alpha and the Omega, the beginning and the end. To the thirsty I will give a gift from the spring of life-giving water.'"

## The Journey of Our Local Church in Myanmar

### By Fr. Marino Nanjha

I am a priest of the diocese of Loikaw in eastern Myanmar (formerly Burma), a country with a population of 60 million, and ruled by a harsh military government since 1962. We do not have much industry; the people look to the soil for a living. Our natural resources of gas and oil are exploited by foreign countries, principally China. I have been working as a missionary with the Columban Fathers in Peru for the past six years. I have been asked to write on the how and why of my vocation, and I have tried to do so in a historical context. I hope you enjoy it.

## Historical Background

There is evidence of the presence of Christianity in Myanmar as early as 1287. Archaeologists have found frescos containing crosses, and Latin and Greek words in some places in Pagan, once a flourishing kingdom in central Myanmar.

After the discovery of the sea route to India by Vasco da Gama in 1497, Portuguese missionaries set out for the Far East as chaplains to Portuguese soldiers, sailors and settlers. Portuguese traders, after founding Goa as the Sea port to the East arrived in our country in 1510, befriending the King of Pegu. The great Portuguese missionary, Francis Xavier, wrote to his fellow Jesuits in Europe and stated that the kind of missionary sent out should be capable of going unaccompanied or accompanied wherever needed, be it to the Moluccas, China, Japan, or to the Kingdom of Pegu.

In 1622-Pope Gregory XV set up the Sacred Congregation for the Propagation of the Faith to take care of Christian missions independently of secular powers such as Spain and Portugal who had many ulterior motives. The Paris Foreign Mission Society, which was purely a missionary society, was approved in 1659. The first MEP (The Parish Foreign Mission Society) came to Burma from Siam, helped by the Burmese Ambassador in Siam. They reached Pegu and set up a hospital that had enormous success. But the King of Ava, fearing their influence over the people, condemned them to death.

In 1743 the first group of four Barnabites, the popular name of the Italian religious order canonically known by the title, Regular Clerics of St. Paul, arrived in Burma from Rome. They were accompanied by an experienced surgeon. Within a few years all were dead, victims of local political conflicts or natural disaster. In 1754 a second group of Barnabites were sent. They set out from Paris in two different ships which never arrived at their destination. The first sank in the Atlantic and the other in the Gulf of Martaban. In 1760 a third group of three Barnabites were sent out, but only two survived the sea journey to arrive in Rangoon in 1761. During the following years more Barnabites were sent to Myanmar and enjoyed some periods of acceptance by the Myanmar authorities.

The number of Barnabite missionaries dwindled, and the Oblates of the Blessed Virgin Mary initiated their work in Burma (1830-1860). By 1837 many Oblates had arrived and, like the missionaries before them, worked among the Burmese in the lowland plains.

When the British-Burmese war began in 1852, the situation became very difficult for the Oblates so Bishop Balma, the man in charge at that time, sought help from the Paris Foreign Mission Society. Bishop Paul Bigandet was appointed Vicar Apostolic of Southern Burma in 1870, and at the time of his death in 1894, there were 35,000 Catholics in Burma.

Thanks to the undaunted courage and effort of so many zealous foreign missionaries the Catholic Church in Burma put down strong roots and established herself firmly in the various parts of the country. The dioceses of Rangoon (lower part of Myanmar), Mandalay (upper region), and Toungoo (eastern part) were well established by the end of the 19th century. During the latter part of the 19th century the missionaries, especially the PIME (*Pontificum Institutum pro Missionibus Exteris*) missionaries from Italy, began to move up into the hills to work with the non-Burmese tribal peoples living there. This initiative came especially from the Toungoo diocese in the east.

During the Second World War (1939-1945) the Japanese armed forces wrought havoc in Burma. Churches were bombed, foreign priests were deported, people were forced to flee to distant places and in several places priests, Sisters and lay people were ruthlessly murdered. In 1945, when the war was over, the Catholic Church had a difficult time re-constructing churches, schools and parishes.

In 1936, the first group of Columban missionaries arrived in Banmaw to take charge of the area, and in 1939 the Kachin State became a separate Prefecture Apostolic with Banmaw as its center. In 1961, it was erected into the diocese of Myitkyina. The Catholic faith spread rapidly during the time of Columban missionaries as more mission centers and schools were established. But, in 1966 the government ordered missionaries to go home. Schools, hospitals and dispensaries were nationalized. However, some foreign missionaries were able to remain with special permission from the government.

The church continued growing slowly, and the number of native priests and religious increased. On April 3, 1976, Bishop John Howe ordained Fr. Paul Grawng as the first Kachin Bishop. On April 24, 1977, Bishop John Howe handed over the diocese to Bishop Paul Grawng and the indigenous clergy. The Columbans withdrew by July 1979.

The former mission of the Columbans is now three dioceses, Myitkyina, Banmaw and Lashio. People, priests, Sisters and the bishops of these dioceses came together in Banmaw to celebrate the 75th anniversary of the arrival of the Columbans in March 2011. The archbishop of Mandalay, Paul Grawng was there. He was the first priest of the Kachin people, ordained in 1965.

Fifty years after the establishment of the hierarchy of Myanmar, there are fourteen dioceses (three Archdioceses and eleven Dioceses), and currently fifteen Bishops, 677 priests, 333 men religious, and 1,958 women religious working in the vineyard of the Lord.

## The Present Day

The Catholic Church in Myanmar is gradually gaining momentum in its work of Evangelization. It is one of the few countries in Southeast Asia where most of the priests and religious are indigenous. The Church's activities are pastoral and social with little emphasis on education or health care as the state insists on total control of those areas.

Myanmar priests, nuns, and laity are contributing to the mission of the Church in all continents of our planet. Myanmar missionaries are found in countries such as Fiji, Japan, Philippines, United States, Italy, Papua New Guinea, France, Tanzania, Peru, Australia, Thailand and more.

When I began to work in San Pedro y San Pablo parish I felt quite powerless. I spoke just a little Spanish; I did not know the people, and I was unfamiliar with local customs. I decided to catch buses that took me to different parts of this huge city; I wanted to get to know Lima. Along the way I observed the struggle of so many people to get to and from work and how the bus drivers and conductors treated their passengers. I also went to places in the parish where people gather to get to know others and to make myself known to them. I visited the markets, the schools and the soup kitchens (29 in our parish). And so, I gradually began to build up relationships and feel confidence in myself to do something.

Language was a challenge as I needed to become proficient in two languages simultaneously. Most of the Columbans are English speakers and generally spoke English among themselves, so I felt that I needed to build on the basic grasp of English that I already had. Becoming more fluent in Spanish was easier as I had the chance to speak and hear Spanish all the time in my pastoral work. I would always make an effort to speak with others; if I passed by a shop I asked the sellers the names of things on display, and they helped me. I found men, women and children to be generous with their time and very kind; they became my Spanish language teachers.

I felt happier in myself going out to meet people rather than just hanging around in the parish house. However, I did make some problems for myself by eating food from street vendor stalls. My parish priest, Columban Fr. John O'Connell, who first came to Peru 53 years ago, insisted that I didn't eat in such places; he told me, "Marino, your stomach is not used to what Peruvians are used to, so please be careful."

During my six years in this parish I did not build any chapels or support any other construction project, but other priests had already done that. I focused on building up relationships with the people and am so happy to have chosen that focus during my brief time here, but saying goodbye can be sad.

I found the faith life of Peruvians to be quite different from ours in Myanmar. Here they believe in God very present in their lives. One time I went to the celebration of the feast in honor of St. John the Baptist and saw how the devotees danced before the image of the saint in homage to God. They seem to include all that they are living in their relationship with God. All I could do was to affirm the beauty of what they do.

On the other hand, our religious practice in Myanmar is more along the lines of Romanic ritual. Our Catholic faith has not been integrated with ancient religious rites of our people. We have not put our own stamp on the practice of the Christian faith as have the Peruvians with whom I worked. Also, in Myanmar our church life is quite clerical with little lay participation at any level of leadership. The laity, at least as regards religious practice, are simply expected to do as directed by the clergy and religious.

I am now looking forward to returning to my own people and taking on the mission that my bishop may entrust to me. I am very much grateful to the Good Lord who disposes me in this mission and to all the Columban missionaries who have been unconditionally supporting me with magnanimous hearts. I am happy to have been an overseas missionary. I am proud of my family who is always present with me through prayers and moral support. I am proud of my country and my people who once were evangelized and now can contribute some of its own men and women to be missionaries. I consider it as great blessings for Myanmar to have been a country evangelized and now has become a country which evangelizes. We, as missionaries in the foreign land, are the fruit of the mission works realized by those former missionaries who had shed their blood generously on our soil. Indeed I have nothing to be proud of myself but of them and their zeal, dedication, sacrifice and love for us. And I am confident that there are more overseas missionaries to come from Myanmar soil.

Fr. Robert Kuhn (Phekhon Diocese), who recently returned to Myanmar, and I (Loikaw Diocese) are the first missionaries to South America. I am from the Kayah State and belong to the Kayan Kangan tribe. We are one of seven tribes in the state, each with our own language, so our common language is Burmese, the language of the tribe that occupies the low plains of Myanmar and presently rules our country. We come from the part of Myanmar evangelized by the PIME Italian missionaries. We have been blessed by the foreign missionaries, and we feel indebted. To respond to the call of mission our Myanmar bishops constantly invite all Catholics to become missionaries, either locally or in foreign lands.

We are proud to have been missionaries in this continent, and we thank the Missionary Society of St. Columban, which has given us this historical opportunity to be short-term, overseas missionaries. With this experience, I am sure we have a deeper understanding of Christian mission, which will help us immensely in our work as Christian missionaries wherever we go.

Link to our tradition:

The gradual progress from being evangelized to being evangelizers is also the story of the inculturation of the Gospel in a local church. The local church is ready to go out to others when it has put its own cultural stamp on the Christian

Gospel. The Church has been open to this process from the time of the first generation of Christians. See Acts 15, 1-2, 22-29: "Some who had come down from Judea were instructing the brothers, 'Unless you are circumcised according to the Mosaic practice, you cannot be saved.' Because there arose no little dissension and debate by Paul and Barnabas with them, it was decided that Paul, Barnabas, and some of the others should go up to Jerusalem to the apostles and presbyters about this question." Acts 15, 22-29: "Then the apostles and presbyters, in agreement with the whole church, decided to choose representatives and to send them to Antioch with Paul and Barnabas . . . . This is the letter delivered by them: '. . . Since we have heard that some of our number [who went out] without any mandate from us have upset you with their teachings and disturbed your peace of mind, we have with one accord decided to choose representatives and to send them to you along with our beloved Barnabas and Paul, who have dedicated their lives to the name of our Lord Jesus Christ . . . . It is the decision of the Holy Spirit and of us not to place on you any burden beyond these necessities, namely, to abstain from meat sacrificed to idols, from blood, from meats of strangled animals, and from unlawful marriage. If you keep free of these, you will be doing what is right. Farewell.'"

## Wedded to the Church of the Pacific

### By Columban Fr. Donal McIlraith

On completing my doctoral studies in sacred scripture in Rome in 1989 our Superior General, Fr. Bernard Cleary, asked me to teach scripture for one year in the Pacific Regional Seminary in Suva, Fiji. That one year has become 25 years, and I have been teaching six to nine courses each year since I arrived.

Fiji was not my first mission; I was first appointed to Japan. Then I was asked to do post graduate studies in sacred scripture. An Argentinian Biblical scholar, Ugo Vanni SJ, had recommended me to do my doctoral studies with him in the Apocalypse. I completed my formal academic studies with a thesis on the marriage imagery in the Apocalypse, a topic that, over the years, I have been developing not only with my students in the seminary but also with lay leaders in the Church.

I am at heart a pastoral priest and, despite the way things have worked out for me, I know that I did not join the Columbans to be an academic. Every Christmas, Easter and August 15, I have tried to get to the Kandvu islands where I minister to the island communities. They have not had a resident priest for 40 years, so their catechists are the backbone of church life. Even though most of the youth tend to look for a future in Suva or another urban area, the village residents farm their land, fish and take on a full family and communal life. Over there I stay in Nasalia village, and community members take me by boat to the communities on other islands.

There was a moment ten years ago when it became very clear to me that it was not a matter of choosing between being pastoral or academic, but rather of feeling that I was committed to the emerging Church in Fiji and, more broadly, the Church in the Pacific from Guam to Tahiti, which is organized under the umbrella of CEPAC (Episcopal Conference of the Pacific), the post Vatican II Bishop's Conference that founded and runs our regional seminary which currently has 150 seminarians.

Cyclone Amy hit northern Fiji damaging or destroying all that was caught in its path. I went with a lorry (truck) load of food up to Taaremon's (a Columban student at that time, who was ordained recently) island. Taaremon and his brother in law met me with a boat to take me and the food to Rabi, their island. We had problems with the engine and the boat drifted for two days, during which I was quite frightened but, at the same time, felt that experience wedded me to the Pacific.

I was frightened but calm as the two lads seemed unconcerned. They, it later emerged, felt safe because they were traveling with a priest. Also at a very distracted evening prayer the night before our engine fell off, the final verse of Psalm 121 had jumped out at me: The Lord will bless your going and your coming now and forever. It may have not meant much to me before the engine failure but it took on powerful meaning during the time of our drifting.

I have taught the majority of the local priests working in the CEPAC region; I have also taught a number of the bishops. Visiting other Pacific islands I feel very much at home; I am welcomed by friends. Soon we will no longer be needed to staff the seminary. Most parishes are already staffed by Pacific island priests. However, before I hang up my boots I feel there is something more that we Columbans might do.

Our Church is essentially missionary, so I would like us to do more to help the local Church, through their priests, become more missionary. We Columbans already support a sending and receiving program for lay missionaries, and in other countries we have a program to help local priests spend a few years in a situation of cross cultural mission. For over 40 years, many diocesan priests have worked with us in our places of mission, especially in Peru and Chile. I feel that now is the time to promote this missionary endeavour among the diocesan priests of the CEPAC region.

Since the seminary's foundation Columbans have been a constant presence on the staff. Columban Fr. Dermot Hurley was a spiritual director at the very beginning; Columban Fr. J.J. Ryan taught systematic theology for many years; Columban Fr. Kieran Maloney also taught here; Columban Fr. Gerry McNicholas taught history for a time; Columban Fr. John Morrissey taught moral theology; Columban Fr. Dick O' Sullivan, who arrived in Fiji in 1959, continues to teach systematic theology; Columban Fr. Pat Colgan taught scripture for a number of years; Columban Fr. Iowane Gukibau, a Fijian Columban with missionary experience in Brazil and Peru, has begun teaching missiology and history this year.

And so, I would like to continue to assist the CEPAC region become ever more missionary, and I hope to encourage the Columbans to promote our program of priest associates among the diocesan priests of this region. Having Columban missionaries from here (both priests and lay missionaries) working in places as far apart as Peru and Pakistan, means that we are already a small but vital part of this missionary Church.

Link to our tradition:
Vatican II in *Ad Gentes,* on the missionary nature of the Church, stated:

The pilgrim Church is missionary by her very nature, since it is from the mission of the Son and the mission of the Holy Spirit that she draws her origin, in accordance with the decree of God the Father. # 2

The Council also went on to make it clear that the disciples of Jesus had a responsibility to ensure that the Church is indeed missionary:

Now, the Lord Jesus, before freely giving His life for the world, did so arrange the Apostles' ministry and promise to send the Holy Spirit that both they and the Spirit might be associated in effecting the work of salvation always and everywhere. # 4

# CHAPTER 6

## The Ministry of reconciliation

This has been proposed as a paradigm for mission for a number of reasons. Major historical shifts, such as the fall of communism in the Soviet Union and the China's move to state supervised capitalism, have resulted in opportunity for some, confusion and misery for others. Massive social disruption, armed civil conflict and genocide mark the political process in some parts of our world. Indigenous peoples in the Americas, Oceania and parts of Asia continue to struggle to claim their heritage in the face of a continuing onslaught by the descendants of European invaders. At the global level, the ever increasing gap between rich and poor promises to continue to be a fertile seedbed of resentment, hatred and violence.[28]

Human beings have always struggled to find ways to live in harmony at all levels—family, clan, tribe, neighborhood, city, nation state, regionally and globally. Over the course of history power has been exercised in a variety of ways to maintain a certain order or stability and also to increase the power of individuals, groups or nations. Force, the most drastic expression of which is war[29], has frequently been the main means of ordering human affairs. However, diplomacy and negotiation have also played a significant role in the evolution of society at all levels. Clearly force of any kind does not cure hatred or resentment in those who may consider themselves the victims of abuse or oppression, even though it may achieve periods of superficial tranquility which, under some regimes, have lasted centuries.

---

[28]  Robert Schreiter is a well-known proponent of reconciliation as a paradigm for mission in the 21st century—cf. *Robert. J. Schreiter*, RECONCILIATIAON AND HEALINAG AS A PARADIGM FOR MISSION, *International Review of Mission, Volume 94, Issue 372*, pages 74-83, January 2005

[29]  Genocide is clearly more vicious than war but its purpose is not superiority over but the elimination of another people.

However, such a strong reliance on force to maintain order on our planet seems ever less likely to succeed. The rapid rate of globalization is creating ever greater interdependence between nations, which in turn obliges all to enter into a global conversation, the main forum for which in our times is the United Nations organization. The development of weapons of mass destruction and ever more lethally efficient conventional weapons pressures the whole of humanity to look for ways other than warfare to settle disputes. So, obviously, the more that can be done to heal the wounds of our world, to address the issues that have traditionally provoked lethal violence, to foster harmonious communication between peoples who are ethnically, linguistically and religiously different, the more we guarantee the survival of our race and our planet.

Jesus of Nazareth put forgiveness at the heart of his message. Revenge not exceeding the injury done or evening the score had been the only recognized way of honorably dealing with offense, hurt or injustice. Even among the Jews, God's chosen people, the rule of thumb for conflict resolution was: ". . . life for life, eye for eye, tooth for tooth, hand for hand, foot for foot, burn for burn, wound for wound, stripe for stripe." (Exodus 21, 24-25) Jesus, also a Jew, challenged this and proposed an alternative, which essentially reversed the previous approach: "You have heard that it was said, 'You shall love your neighbor and hate your enemy.' But I say to you, love your enemies, and pray for those who persecute you, that you may be children of your heavenly Father, for he makes his sun rise on the bad and the good, and causes rain to fall on the just and the unjust . . . . So be perfect, just as your heavenly Father is perfect." (cf. Matthew 5, 38-48) Forgiveness, not revenge, is the way to be children of our heavenly Father and to "be perfect as He is perfect." Such an approach to human relationships may be at the heart of Jesus' teaching but we, His followers, have always struggled to make it the basis of our approach to human conflict. The English missionary, E. Stanley Jones, reported Mahatma Gandhi as saying, "I don't reject Christ. I love Christ. It's just that so many of you Christians are so unlike Christ."

In terms of our relationship with God our challenge is to repent; we can count on God's forgiveness. In terms of relationships among humans we must take responsibility for both repenting and forgiving, both of which are often extremely difficult. Often, when we do harm we so easily find ways of justifying our act. We become self-righteous and blind to our fault for the resulting evil. How can we come to repentance if we cannot even recognize that we have acted wrongly? It may be even more difficult for the person or persons who have suffered at the hands of another or others. It is nigh on impossible for those outside a particular situation of conflict and hurt to imagine the feelings of hurt, resentment, anger and hate that might be driving the victim or victims towards some form of revenge or retaliation.

Then there are the massive social evils that must be faced in a spirit of forgiveness and reconciliation because the ultimate goal is healing and so renewed life. The following is by no means an exhaustive list but some major present day challenges are:

The many local and civil conflicts that have come to the fore in various parts of the world since 1989—wars in the Balkans, genocide in Ruanda, polarization of politics in U.S., dispossessed indigenous peoples reclaiming their heritage, conflicts related to the so-called "Arab Spring" in the countries of the Middle East and North Africa, etc.;

The constantly increasing gap between the world's rich and poor provoked by the neo-liberal economic policies that have been put in place around the world during the past 40 years;

The devastation of the lives of individuals and of societies by the spread of HIV/AIDS, especially in poorer parts of the world.

The rest of this chapter is made up of mission stories illustrating the above paragraphs. After each story or, in some cases groups of stories, there is a link to our religious tradition, which, for the most part, is taken from the Bible but, also from teachings of the Popes, General Councils and Episcopal Conferences.

## Beginning of a New Life—March 16, 1992

### By Columban Fr. Sean Conneely

I took my last drink with my close friends in Mexico City. I was on a trip from Korea to a rehabilitation center in U.S. via Chile, Peru and Mexico. I had intended to have my last drink at a St. Patrick's Day party in Los Angeles, but on arrival there I decided that enough was enough and had a most enjoyable party with my Columban brothers and sisters without taking a drink.

I last met fellow Columban, Fr. Peter Woodruff, just over twenty years ago in Peru and today he asked me where I was at now and then added the rider: how did I get to that place? I'm known to be a great talker, great in the sense that I'm disinclined to stop once I've started. I now help others deal with deep, personal problems, which are having major negative repercussions on relationships that matter to them.

I work with teams of married couples who run weekends for couples who are trying to put their marriages back together. The program we use, Retrovaille (rediscovery), was developed in Canada. We try to help each person who comes to these weekends to look deep into themselves and then bring what they have discovered and owned to the conversation with their spouse.

I work with addicts of various kinds in 12 Step Programs for alcoholics, drug addicts, food addicts, sex addicts, etc. I know the 12 Step Program intimately as I have been through it myself. I do group and one on one sessions. These programs can help participants recover power over aspects of their lives that have run rampant. They can empower addicts to retake their lives.

I also offer spiritual accompaniment to people, mostly religious Sisters, who seek such support for their life journey. The issues are very personal as those I accompany grapple with inner turmoil in regard to their own calling and in terms of how to relate with the members of their community.

Growing up in the 1960s, I became aware of social issues as being an integral part of the Gospel and Church`s teaching, and I try to play my part in the movement. I`m not able to be part of the activity on the streets as I would like anymore, but in sermons and Bible teaching I try to make it central always and support those involved actively as much as I can. I hope it will be always close to my heart.

I attempt to walk with all on their journey from pain to serenity. I do this with confidence because for more than twenty years I have been on this journey. I strive also to do this with God. When I was young, healthy and athletic I over-trusted in my own prowess and strength. I have since learned to focus on the work of the Spirit of God in my life and that of others. I now feel that the stronger my relationship with God the better equipped I am to accompany others as they search for inner healing and honest relationships.

I will say a little about key people and events in my life and maybe that will explain, in part at least, how I have come to where I am. There is also a short passage in the Bible (borrowed by The Seekers for one of their songs) that offers an explanation for the variety in our lives:

> There is an appointed time for everything, and a time for every affair under the heavens.
> A time to give birth, and a time to die; a time to plant, and a time to uproot the plant.
> A time to kill, and a time to heal; a time to tear down, and a time to build.
> A time to weep, and a time to laugh; a time to mourn, and a time to dance.
> A time to scatter stones, and a time to gather them; a time to embrace, and a time to be far from embraces.
> A time to seek, and a time to lose; a time to keep, and a time to cast away. A time to rend, and a time to sew; a time to be silent, and a time to speak.
> A time to love, and a time to hate; a time of war, and a time of peace. (Ecclesiastes 3, 1-8)

I grew up in a poor part of the west of Ireland. My mother insisted on all things Irish. We spoke the Irish language at home. We recalled the days when the Irish were free from the yoke of the English. My mother and my primary school principal, Tadhg O'Shea, never tired of reminding us of great Irish saints, many of whom were missionaries. St. Columban was high on the list. I grew up with a passion for social justice. My other passion was sport and all that comes with that, especially the friendships forged in the playing and partying together, friendships that have endured to this day.

When I went to boarding school at St. Jarlath's, Tuam, at the age of thirteen, I was made to feel ashamed of the way I spoke English and that left deep wounds that took much time to heal. And yet it was there at St. Jarlath's that I was further inspired by the modern Irish missionary movement as a co-founder of St. Columban's Missionary Society, John Blowick, had studied there.

I entered the seminary in September 1962 and Vatican II began in October of the same year. During the 1960s the civil rights movement with Martin Luther King at the helm was inspiring people around the world. In the late 1960s the civil rights movement in Ireland began to question and challenge us. Students and civic activists were naming problems as they saw them. Many of my generation felt part of this movement of hope. We also felt encouraged by the conclusions of Vatican II. Things were happening in society and in our Church that urged us on to radical commitment in the cause of a more human world. In that spirit I set out on my first missionary journey to Korea.

As I look back on all that has brought me to the present moment, I feel that I have been carried by the current and I have navigated my own passage in what has been the story of our world over the past 70 years. I feel that in so far as I am close to God I have a better chance of being my own navigator.

Link to our tradition:

William Cowper wrote in his poem, The Task: "Variety's the spice of life, that gives it all its flavor." The following Bible text, Ecclesiastes 3, 1-8, may have inspired the saying, as it did The Seekers' song, 'Turn, Turn, Turn': "There is an appointed time for everything, and a time for every affair under the heavens; a time to give birth, and a time to die; a time to plant, and a time to uproot the plant; a time to kill, and a time to heal; a time to tear down, and a time to build; a time to weep, and a time to laugh; a time to mourn, and a time to dance; a time to scatter stones, and a time to gather them; a time to embrace, and a time to be far from embrace; a time to seek, and a time to lose; a time to keep, and a time to cast away; a time to rend, and a time to sew; a time to be silent, and a time to speak; a time to love, and a time to hate; a time of war, and a time of peace."

# A Scout Troop Drawn from Sons and Daughters of Malate Street Families

By Columban Fr. John Leydon (Parish Priest of Malate Parish)

I belong to a Malate parish, Our Lady of Remedies, in Manila. The majority of our parishioners are urban poor. In a scene like this you soon realize that there are many degrees of poverty and that the bottom rung is those who are homeless.

There are no street children here as such; we have street families. These are usually families who have fallen through the net, and there is usually a degree of dysfunction due to drugs or some other factor. However, I personally have no idea how these families survive on the street. I feel that I'd last no time at all in a situation like theirs. I am in total admiration of them.

We have a program for the settled areas, which are poor. We also have a program for the street families. The street families have a degree of stability, but you can imagine what it might be like not having a house, living on the street.

A lot of the kids from the street families drop out of school, so we have a class room program for them to help them get back into school. It's a daily program from Monday to Friday; there's a feeding program for them as well, so at least they'll get one decent meal a day.

A few years ago the scouts approached to see if we would be interested in setting up a troop for the children of the street families. It seemed like a good idea to us, especially Fr. Enrique Escobar (a diocesan priest from Peru who worked with the Columbans in Manila for six years), who was very close to the poor and had a scout background himself. We were also very impressed with the scout's person in charge, Sophie, a dynamic woman with intense commitment to the children who have joined our local troop.

Twenty four children joined the first year, seven of whom were totally wild and unmanageable and were intent on wrecking the program, so were asked to leave. At that initial stage they might have killed the project before it got off the ground.

At first it was so difficult to get the children to come to the meetings, and the teachers involved had to go and almost drag the children to the regular meetings of the troop. But, after a while the youngsters began to turn up on time waiting for it to happen. It responded to some needs they had, maybe something along the lines of structure, mentoring and opportunity for growth.

The following year the seven who had been put out during the early days of the troop's formation were outside with their noses to the window clamoring to join again. When the troop consolidated they were able to take them in again. There was now no possibility of them wrecking anything, and they had also seen the benefits for their companions and wanted to share in that as well. They knew that joining demanded they pay a price, but they were persuaded that it would be worth it.

Sophie and her husband are full time workers with the scouting movement; they are most impressive people. They have two children, and I noticed that when they took the scouts off on a camp they took their children along too. Normally middle-class parents, who are involved with the poor, and especially with street children, would be very protective of their own children and would keep them apart from the poorer children with whom they are working. Sophie's children simply joined in the scouting business with the rest of the troop. The children of the street families also mix with the other children of the parish, but there is a gap, even though all of them are poor.

The children in the Malate parish troop are part of a scouting movement program called, Ticket to Life Scouts (TTL), which is a project for Children in Especially Difficult Circumstances (CEDEC) aged six to sixteen years. The program is designed to help the children develop a plan for their lives by schooling them in responsibility and, in general, fostering their personal development through the scouting movement. More than 5,000 children within the Asia-Pacific Region belong to TTL in eight pilot countries—Bangladesh, Nepal, Pakistan, India, Indonesia, Mongolia, Sri Lanka and the Philippines.

Our scout troop went to a Jamboree in December 2009 where 13,000 scouts from the Asia Pacific Region gathered for their 26th Jamboree. It was a great experience for them to be able to mix with boys and girls from many countries, especially street children from other countries, and feel that they belonged.

Sophie is totally committed to scouting, is very vivacious, but what comes across is her love for the kids; it's palpable, so to speak. She knows each child intimately. She has to deal with their families and at times has trouble convincing them of the worth of the scouting program for them and their children. The family depend on the children for income, so they are always asking (themselves at least) how the scouting movement might enhance family income—begging or watching cars or some other small chore for which they might earn a tip.

On one occasion recently I attended a feedback session with the parents, many of whom were over the moon about the way their children had matured in a way that they thought would never happen. I found what many parents had to say to be so inspiring; they helped me see that this program is having an impact on their lives; it goes beyond just meeting a basic need without any human development. This program has a promise of real change; you see it reaching children who are both quite vulnerable and also open to learning. What the troop is doing with them is, in some way, helping them to push and dream beyond the directionless and poverty stricken routine of street life.

# Finding Hope through Scouting

## By Sophie Castillo

(Sophie Castillo works fulltime for Boy Scouts of the Philippines. She is the youth program assistant and the coordinator of the TTL program in Manila and Davao. She works with the troop in Malate on a voluntary basis.)

Ticket to Life (TTL) is about taking scouting to street children to help them have a better life; scouting will be their ticket to life. TTL began in Nairobi, Kenya, in 2004. For our program in the Philippines we secured funding for five years from the World Scouting Movement in 2007.

The administration of the city of Davao provides support for the TTL troop in Davao. They have a benefactor high up in the administration who was once a scout.

Through Fr. John Leydon, the parish priest of the Columban-run parish of Malate, Our Lady of Remedies, we have the use of a place to meet, and the parish covers the cost of transport when we go somewhere with the children. The parish also helps with the cost of schooling of some of our young scouts.

Derek Bonifacio is the Malate troop leader, which he does as a volunteer. He is also a fulltime employee of the Boy Scouts of the Philippines. He works as artist, photographer and personnel assistant.

"The children want a meeting every Saturday afternoon so, even if Derek cannot attend, my husband or I or other adult collaborators always step in as substitutes. In the beginning we had to ask the parish social worker to visit the children and urge them to come to the meeting. Now the children are waiting for us to open the door. Scouting has become an important aspect of their life routine. For the first three months only ten or so would come along to the weekly meeting but, when they realized what it was all about, we had 30 or so coming each week."

I urge the children to think and dream beyond their present situation: "Don't limit your dreams. You don't want to stay living in the street. Work for and follow your dream."

I insist that even though the children live in very difficult circumstances they are close to their families. Even though at times their parents are not good to them, they love their parents. They want to continue to live with them on the street. The street is the home they know.

It is true that we have to deal with many problems, but our problems are not with the children but with the parents who, at times, do not allow or encourage their children to attend the Saturday afternoon meeting. They are concerned that we are taking them away from work and so depriving the family of much needed income.

We usually have two or three adults at the troop meeting and actively involved with the children. We don't simply leave everything to Derek, our troop leader. We have seen that it is important that we adults win the trust of the street children, who often find little support from their parents.

Jerwin is fourteen years of age and lives with his family on the street. He is the eldest of six children. He works at night driving a pedi cab, earning between 80 and 100 pesos a night (40 pesos = $0.92). He pays his own school expenses.

Jerwin is from the first group in May 2008. He attended the orientation, and one day when he arrived late we observed he was using drugs (sniffing glue). He did not come again for a year. His sister was attending, and he would come and watch from behind the fence.

In May 2009 he joined the second group, attended twice and then stopped coming. When he came to the parish feeding program the teacher told him that I was looking for him. That made him so happy, and he has been attending the meetings ever since. I told him that I was really happy to see him again and, on his own initiative, he returned to school.

Jerwin is no longer using drugs and, even though he is only in grade three, he has decided that he wants to be a lawyer. However, his mother, who is on drugs, tells him to work and not be bothering with school or scouts. His sister has stopped coming to the scout meeting, and I see her selling flowers on the street.

Marlene is fourteen years old and joined the first group in May 2008. She has always gone to school and is now in first year of high school. She lives on the street with her family, has two older brothers and two sisters. She helps her mother who is a street vendor, selling cigarettes, soft drinks, snacks, sweets and so on.

Her father and two brothers hit her mother and sisters when they are drunk. They ask her for money to buy drink, and when she refuses they beat her.

Marlene used to be very shy but has developed leadership skills and is quite responsible. She wants to be a teacher, and her mother is most supportive.

## "We are the miracle girls!"

### By Columban Fr. Seán Coyle

"You won't laugh at me, will you?" asked 11-year-old Lourdes (not her real name), just before she got up to sing at a program in Holy Family Home, Cabug, Bacolod City, Philippines. It was the feast of the Holy Family, December 2002, and I had been invited by Sr. Letty Sarrain, a Panamanian Capuchin Tertiary Sister of the Holy Family, to celebrate Mass.

Not only did I not laugh when Lourdes sang, I was astonished at the purity and clarity of her soprano voice which made me think of mediaeval cathedrals. I was deeply touched too by the utter trust of her question, even though she had never met me before. I learned later that she had had a particularly bad experience with an older male member of her family.

Knowing what had come to light in the Church in a number of countries, including my native Ireland, I was a little hesitant to get involved with the girls. There are between 40 and 50, some as young as four, some in their early 20s, at any given time. Most live in Holy Family Home, just outside the city proper, within sight of Mount Kanlaon, an active volcano. Most of the girls taking third-level education live in another house near the city center, under the supervision of a house-mother.

Nearly all the girls have been referred to the Sisters by social workers in the cities and towns of Negros Occidental. Most have had experiences similar to that of Lourdes though some come simply from a background of poverty.

At first I used to visit once or twice a month, usually on a Sunday afternoon, sometimes bringing "goodies" from a doughnut store. Then I found myself celebrating Mass fairly regularly until finally I did so almost every Sunday and on special occasions. I often hear confessions, and some of the girls will remind me to do this.

A breakthrough in my relationship with the girls was in March 2003 when Sr. Alma Alovera, until recently in charge of the Home, was with a group of the girls who had made the honors list in the local public elementary and high schools. One of the older girls with a big smile on her face said to me, "What about a 'blow-out,' Father?" I didn't respond as I didn't know how to. I later consulted Sr. Alma, and she told me to go ahead. I insisted that she come with us when we went one afternoon to McDonalds.

By the following year, when I had come to know the Sisters and the girls much better, I decided to bring the graduates and the honor students to a popular family restaurant for a meal. It didn't bankrupt me, and I got great delight in seeing the girls being served by waiters. I've made this a yearly practice, going to different restaurants, one with an "all you can eat" promo. We usually end the evening with ice-cream.

I hardly ever ask a girl about her situation. They get professional care for that. Sometimes one of them tells me that she has a court hearing coming up and asks me to pray for her. I get angry when I learn that a hearing has been postponed, as so often happens, because one or other lawyer or the judge hasn't turned up. I see this as a continuation of the abuse.

The girls know that I'm aware of their background as I often refer to it in my homilies, Even more often, I let them know how I see them welcoming a new girl and helping her through her initial difficulties. Each year too we combine the celebration of the feasts of St. Agnes, January 21, and Blessed Laura Vicuña, January 22. Blessed Laura was born in Chile in 1891 and died in Argentina a few months short of her 13th birthday, having offered her life for the conversion of her widowed mother who was living with a man who tried a number of times to abuse Laura. St. Agnes of Rome was born and died exactly 1,600 years before Blessed Laura and is the patron of rape victims. We also celebrate the feast of St. Maria Goretti on July 6.

The girls in Holy Family Home have brought great joy into my life. I'm aware too that for some, when they eventually leave Holy Family Home, it's not a question of "And she lived happily ever after." But I see so many who have been healed, who have learned to forgive, who have lived in a loving environment, who have been enabled to go to school when otherwise they would never have the chance.

On the first Saturday of each month the Sisters have a two-hour vigil before the Blessed Sacrament for vocations to their congregation. The girls are invited to join this and most attend, though the younger ones usually leave early before they fall asleep. The prayers of both the girls and the Sisters are being heard, because there is a steady stream of young women become aspirants each June. And when Columban Fr. Michael Sinnott was kidnapped in 2009, I asked the girls to pray especially for him. They prayed their hearts out and jumped with joy when they heard of his release. One of them came over to me and said, "We are the miracle girls!"

A few weeks before the elections held last May in the Philippines I said to Lucy (not her real name), a 19-year-old who will graduate from elementary school in March and who comes from a background of utter poverty, "Vote for me! For what? Para presidente, para gobernador, para mayor, para sa tanan! For president, for governor, for mayor, for everything!" Lucy replied, "Para pari! For priest!"

Though we were only bantering I was delighted that Lucy had gone to the heart of the matter. "The miracle girls" have brought great joy into my life, the kind of joy I imagine a father or grandfather has. They enjoy going to a restaurant, enjoy the ice-cream, but above all they love me as a priest.

Link to our tradition:

The above three stories tell of projects of inner healing, which depends significantly on the experience of being accepted. See John 8, 3-11: ". . . the scribes and the Pharisees brought a woman who had been caught in adultery and made her stand in the middle. They said to him [Jesus], 'Teacher, this woman was caught in the very act of committing adultery. Now in the law, Moses commanded us to stone such women. So what do you say?' They said this to test him, so that they could have some charge to bring against him. Jesus bent down and began to write on the ground with his finger. But when they continued asking him, he straightened up and said to them, 'Let the one among you who is without sin be the first to throw a stone at her.' Again he bent down and wrote on the ground. And in response, they went away one by one, beginning with the elders. So he was left alone with the woman before him. Then Jesus straightened up and said to her, 'Woman, where are they? Has no one condemned you?' She replied, 'No one, sir.' Then Jesus said, 'Neither do I condemn you. Go, [and] from now on do not sin anymore.'"

# Breakfast in Nancheng

By Columban Fr. Peter Woodruff

On November 23, 2010, the feast of St. Columban, Columban Fr. Gerry Neylon and I had breakfast at 7:00 a.m. with Fr. Tommy You Guojie, a priest of Nancheng Diocese. Nancheng is the county capital, and Nanchang is the capital of Jiangxi province, China. Fr. Tommy remembers Columbans from his youth in his home village, Yujia, where he came to know Columban Fr. Peter Toal. Fr. Tommy is now 81 years old. He went to the minor seminary in Nancheng from 1945 to 1949, where Fr. Ted McElroy was rector. Of course, he also knew and appreciated very much Columban Bishop Pat Cleary, who first arrived in China in 1931 and was consecrated bishop of Nancheng Diocese in 1939. Fr. Tommy had studied two years of theology in the Shanghai seminary when he was imprisoned in line with China's communist government's crackdown on public religious practice. However he was released from prison in January 1957 and was ordained priest in April of the same year. In December 1958 he was imprisoned once again and remained in prison or a labor camp for the next 30 years.

Released in 1988, he was free to resume evangelization in his home diocese, but in 1989 he was asked to take a three year appointment as spiritual director in the Shanghai seminary. He had a friendly approach to the students who grew to appreciate his style and the spiritual message he had to offer. The Communist Party cadres who watch over what goes on in the seminary decided he was becoming too close to the students and therefore more influential than they wanted, so after just one year he was obliged to return to his own diocese. He was then appointed parish priest of Nancheng, where he worked until his retirement in 2009.

I had the chance to ask Fr. Tommy how he saw the future of the Church in China. He said immediately that he thought the Church would be much better than now. He put it this way, "There has been progress in recent years in many parts of the country; now the Chinese government consults Rome before appointing bishops, whereas before this the Holy See had no say in the matter. Recently, the Pope approved the government appointment of our own local Bishop of Nanchang, Li Shuguang, who was consecrated on October 31, 2010.

Bishop Li Shuguang was once pulled up by the police while driving his car and, after a phone call to the Governor of the Province, the policeman let him go, which might indicate that he is basically the government's man. However, I am confident that this bishop will not become anybody's puppet. He is his own man.

I also see great hope if diplomatic relations between the Holy See and the Chinese Government are established. This would make a huge difference for the underground members of the Church as they would then be recognized by the

Government. In fact, the relations between the underground and over-ground parts of the Church have improved, except in a few specific places."

In reply to my question about significant moments in his life as a parish priest, Fr. Tommy replied:

"My greatest consolation, especially during many years in prison, was being able to say the rosary and sing the Salve Regina (Hail Holy Queen) and the Dies Irae. Of course, I still know both by heart in Latin (He then sang them for us in the original Latin).

My greatest joy as a priest after coming back to work in the parish was being able to visit the Catholics and to minister to them. It felt great to have no restrictions placed on me; I was left free to get close to my people.

In the year 2000 I distributed leaflets promoting the cause of the canonization of 120 Chinese martyrs, and the authorities ordered me to take back the leaflets I had handed out. I refused, so they put me under house arrest under the supervision of a college student. I chatted with him, befriended him and persuaded him to read parts of the Bible, so I had little problem with my 22 days of confinement."

Fr. Tommy celebrated his 50th anniversary of ordination in Nancheng in 2007, and the locals made a big thing of it. However, fifteen local diocesan priests were ordered by government officials not to attend the celebration, but they disobeyed the order and went.

One of Fr. Tommy's sisters, Teresita, who died in 2006, was a Columban Sister, so it seemed right that we remember her and St. Columban at that early breakfast in his family's house before beginning the seven hour bus, train and taxi journey back to Wuhan, a journey that I was able to undertake thanks to Fr. Gerry's fluency in Mandarin and his familiarity with the local public transport system.

Link to our tradition:

Ephesians 6, 10-17 offers advice that Fr. Tommy seems to have followed: "Finally, draw your strength from the Lord and from his mighty power. Put on the armor of God so that you may be able to stand firm against the tactics of the devil. For our struggle is not with flesh and blood but with the principalities, with the powers, with the world rulers of this present darkness, with the evil spirits in the heavens. Therefore, put on the armor of God, that you may be able to resist on the evil day and, having done everything, to hold your ground. So stand fast with your loins girded in truth, clothed with righteousness as a breastplate, and your feet shod in readiness for the gospel of peace. In all circumstances, hold faith as a shield, to quench all [the] flaming arrows of the evil one. And take the helmet of salvation and the sword of the Spirit, which is the word of God." Then, Galatians 5, 22-23 sums up: ". . . the fruit of the Spirit is love, joy, peace, patience, kindness, generosity, faithfulness, gentleness, self-control."

## Reclaiming Space

By Columban Fr. Peter Woodruff

My host in Salvador in north east Brazil was Columban Fr. Colin McLean who grew up in Bentleigh and Brighton, Melbourne, Australia. He has spent the past 26 years in poor barrios and Catholic parishes of Salvador, where he has done his best to work in solidarity with Afro-Brazilians who continue to be discriminated against in many not so subtle ways.

One night, Fr. Colin with a few local friends took me to the historic center of the city. We sat at a table in the main square, listened to music and drank beer. The square used to fill every Tuesday night. It was an Afro-Brazilian cultural event to which anyone was welcome and the fun went on until the early hours of the morning.

The present mayor of the city decided to implement reforms, supposedly to make it safe for tourists and clean up the vice. He has effectively destroyed a joyous, maybe even wild, Afro-Brazilian gathering in which these people claimed this as their space in a non-exclusive way. They had learned to celebrate precisely in the places where their ancestors were bought, sold and whipped.

That night, despite the musical contribution of a local band we were soon bored and decided to walk around the streets near the main square to see if anything was happening elsewhere, and for a while that was even more boring. We went into a beer hall where there was another band playing and a few young people dancing, but one could hardly say that the place was alive, so once again we went walking.

We heard the noise of drums long before we saw the drummers. There were about twelve young men walking six abreast up a narrow cobbled street, each with a drum of some kind. The beat of the drums was deafening. I have never heard such musical volume that was not in any way amplified. They played with such verve and energy. I was not sure who was leading the band, but they played as a unit and obviously reveled in what they were doing.

A few young people, mostly tourists, followed them vainly attempting to imitate the vigor of the dance that was led by a young Afro-Brazilian dressed in half-mast white trousers and naked from the waist up. His skin glistened with sweat in cool humidity of the night. Most of us stood on the footpath as they slowly moved past.

Fr. Colin and Tonhaõ, one of the drummers, sighted and recognized each other. The young lad's face lit up, and he seemed to beat his drum with even more enthusiasm. I stood and watched, totally rapt by the sight and the music; it was deafening and magnificent. Once again these young men seemed to be gradually reclaiming a space that had been taken from them through the dictatorial decree of a city mayor, a man for whom Colin's Afro Brazilian friends might pray, "Forgive him, Father, for he knows not what he does."

Link to our tradition:

Jesus reclaimed God's space. See Mark 11, 15-17: "They came to Jerusalem, and on entering the temple area he began to drive out those selling and buying there. He overturned the tables of the money changers and the seats of those who were selling doves. He did not permit anyone to carry anything through the temple area. Then he taught them saying, 'Is it not written: My house shall be called a house of prayer for all peoples? But you have made it a den of thieves.'"

## A Valiant Community

The residents in a poor suburb of Santiago de Chile, together with their pastor,
face up to social ills that threaten their personal and family lives
By Columban Fr. Peter Woodruff (with Columban Father Mike Hoban from the
U.S. and Fr. Gerardo Ouisse from France)

Columban Fr. Mike Hoban is presently the Episcopal vicar of an area to the south of the city, which includes 38 parishes. Columbans have been working in the southern Zone since 1964 and still staff three parishes in the vicariate: San

Columbano, Santo Tomás Apóstol and Jesús de Nazaret. They also staff San Matías parish, which is even further south in Maipo Vicariate. This is one of the largest parishes in the archdiocese with 80,000 residents and is staffed by Irish, Fijian and Korean Columbans. Fr. Mike was also Episcopal vicar in the Maipo vicariate for a time.

The archdiocese is divided into seven vicariates with a priest appointed as Episcopal vicar in each. He visits the parishes to support the work of the parish team and encourage them in their efforts to implement the archdiocesan pastoral plan that is reviewed and updated regularly in a process of consultation with the pastoral agents of the archdiocese, which includes priests, religious and laity. He also goes from parish to parish to do confirmations. The Episcopal vicar is an experienced parish priest who helps keep the lines of communication open between the Archbishop and the grassroots church communities of the city.

Fr. Mike first arrived in Chile in 1972, just one year before the military coup against President Salvador Allende that set Chile on a path of military dictatorship until 1989. He has worked in a number of parishes in poor areas of Santiago, Chile. He has also been responsible for a number of non-parish apostolates.

I had not seen Fr. Mike for at least fifteen years but found him as active and informative as he ever was. I told him I was looking for mission stories for the Columban mission magazines that are published in the English-speaking countries where the Columbans have found support since the early years of our missionary enterprise. He took me to meet the parish priest of one of the toughest parishes in his vicariate.

Fr. Gerardo Ouisse, from Nantes, France has worked in Chile for 25 years and is now in his early seventies. He was also a worker priest in France for sixteen years. He arrived at San Cayetano de la Legua parish nine years ago. La Legua is located four kilometers south of the city center and belongs to the municipal district, San Joiquin. Gerardo had to face a double challenge: take over the direction of a parish that had been run for years by the well-known charismatic priest, Mariano Puga, and work pastorally in a situation mired by endemic and entrenched social problems related to poverty and a criminal culture.

He said to me, "I had to be careful to respect what I found going on in the parish. Yet, I had to relive the dialogue between God and Moses:"

Moses said to God, "Who am I that I should go to Pharaoh and lead the Israelites out of Egypt?" He answered, "I will be with you; and this shall be your proof that it is I who have sent you: when you bring my people out of Egypt, you will worship God on this very mountain." "But," said Moses to God, "when I go to the Israelites and say to them, 'The God of your fathers has sent me to you,' if they ask me, 'What is his name?' what am I to tell them?" God replied, "I am who am." Then he added, "This is what you shall tell the Israelites: I AM sent me to you." (Exodus 3, 11-14)

Fr. Gerardo related some of his first impressions: "I was struck by the number of youth gathered at street corners; they dawdled from corner to corner without any apparent purpose; they seemed bored and maybe drugged. There were many children of school age hanging around on the streets. I heard stories of drugs destroying families and provoking armed street violence."

But to counter this he said of the local parish community, "I also met a very strong Christian community formed in our faith over a period of 60 years. Local church identity was strong—*Somos del Señor, somos de La Legua* (we are the Lord's, we are from La Legua). I realized that I had arrived in the midst of a people who were accustomed to fighting for every little bit of communal progress. From this parish 60 people were killed by the repressive forces of the Pinochet dictatorship. Many were tortured, disappeared or shot."

In recent times La Legua has been plagued by daily shootouts in the street, often at around 4:00 p.m. when the children were coming home from school. Many would call home on their phones to find out whether it was safe to go home. Fr. Gerardo told me:

"The Christian community together with local civic leaders organized a march for peace in the area but along the route some marchers insulted the police so we had to find another approach to the problem. In fact, as a consequence of what happened on that march, fifteen days later 200 police did a search and destroy operation in La Legua, took away seventeen people who were subsequently jailed for drug trafficking, an act for which the criminal element in the community blamed us. That happened five years ago and now their children, who were simply abandoned on the street and did not go to school, are in the street gangs peddling drugs."

"Through the Latin American Bishops Conference headquarters in Colombia we contacted people who'd had an experience of facilitating a reconciliation process between ex members of the Colombian guerrilla movement (FARC) and ex members of Colombian para military forces, who were living in the same suburb. They came to Santiago and helped us do something similar here and then we were able to organize more marches for peace. Most probably another factor that has helped the reconciliation process among us is that I am quite active pastorally in the prison which for now is home to thousands of prisoners, 600 of whom are from La Legua; I do my best for them and they respect that."

"However, the community was well aware that we needed to do more than march for peace and facilitate reconciliation. We wanted to look into ways of getting at some of the roots of the social problems of our parish. I believe that I am pastor of all who live in La Legua, not just those who are actively part of our parish."

"At our 2010 parish planning meeting we decided that we just had to do something about the constant deaths from shootings and knife attacks. We prepared a letter for the government but no one was prepared to sign it for fear of reprisal from criminal elements in our community, so I signed it and am now under round-the-clock police protection."

"In the letter our Christian community stated that, 'We live each day in a climate of intolerable violence . . . . Drug traffickers control the streets and walk around freely with guns in their hands. Parents usually call home from work to find out whether or not it is safe to return home or should they wait until the current shootout is over. Collective fear is destroying the fabric of social and community organizations that have been developed by decades of struggle and sacrifice . . . . Many of us in our daily lives live as prisoners of a dictatorship established by drug traffickers . . . . We expect the dignity of any Chilean as regards access to education, health, housing, honest work, but in this letter we are asking for something even more basic: that weapons are removed from our suburbs . . . . We will not be resigned to continue living in this way because La Legua is a place of struggle and dignity. Because of our faith in Jesus Christ we will not vacillate in the defense of the life that has been entrusted to us . . . .'"

While this letter was sent to the government it also circulated to all parts of the country because many suburbs experience similar social problems that were not being faced up to by the authorities. Government authorities came to verify what was stated in the letter and subsequently entered into dialogue with our community to see how to tackle the problems. Some wanted to embark on repressive police action but were persuaded by the community that this would not work as La Legua and many other poor barrios have an historic memory of resistance to and struggle against the repressive tactics frequently used by the Pinochet dictatorship.

Gerardo smiles as he tells me, "We are in the process of working things out. Something is happening. We don't feel hopelessly bogged down in a situation that is slowly destroying us. It will be a long road but we want to walk it together and will do all in our power to encourage the government to work with us."

## A Program that Works

People with HIV/AIDS being empowered to manage their lives positively
By Columban Fr. Cathal Gallagher

In 1997 I was parish priest in Villa Maria, one of the poorest suburbs of Lima, Peru, when I received a phone call to go to the local barrio clinic run by Sr. Mildred McNamara, a Sister of Mercy from Ireland who first arrived in Peru in 1969. Two brothers had died of AIDS in the same week and a third brother was in the throes of an emotional fit as he believed that he would be next to die.

At that stage I knew nothing about AIDS so began to ask around and found out that many were dying from it but none of my Columban friends were talking about it. Even the families of the victims would refer to their relatives' illness as tuberculosis or leukemia. It was as if we Columbans were colluding in the generalized denial in the population. My fellow priests would sympathize with the families of the deceased, do whatever religious ceremony was appropriate and leave it at that.

I called together a group that I thought might help find a way to respond to a steadily worsening situation. I met with a psychologist, a teacher and a lawyer, but we did not know enough to go beyond the basic recommendations of prevention. In 2002, for personal reasons, I left Peru and went to London where a friend, who was working with people suffering from HIV/AIDS, urged me to apply for the position of Coordinator of a Multidisciplinary HIV/AIDS Team that was based in a hospital in north east London. I did and landed the job.

There I learned about the Stanford University program for self-management of chronic conditions, which was implemented by the National Health Service under the title of "The Expert Patient." I eventually got the top qualification for running the program; at the time, there were only three people in the United Kingdom trained to that level for work with HIV/AIDS sufferers. After three years I decided to bring the program to Latin America, so returned to Lima in 2005.

The program's purpose is to educate people living with HIV/AIDS in the self-management of their chronic condition. Through the program we set out to empower people so that they might discover within themselves the tools and ability to manage their lifestyle while living with HIV/AIDS. We constantly talk about response-ability, i.e. the ability to respond to a new situation in their lives. We further train suitable participants as future trainers in the program and as promoters of prevention in high risk populations in the metropolitan area of Lima.

The basic program consists of seven, consecutive, weekly, two and a half hour sessions, to which we have added an eighth session one month after completing the seven sessions. This is to get feedback about how participants are implementing the program in their lives. Over 1,000 people have been through this program over the past five years, 70 of whom have been trained as trainers of the program, and 20 of whom are soon to be accredited by Stanford University as master trainers of the program. Thirty of the seventy continuously run programs in more than twenty locations, scattered for the most part around the poverty belt of the city.

From my experience to date I can see that a major issue for many is the lack of a good father figure. Correcting that will require major changes in Peruvian society, especially as regards the authoritarian, patriarchal mindset of many men and also the strong tendency in many to avoid responsibility for their children, in particular those born of a woman other than their wife.

In our center we coordinate our work and also offer ongoing education for the trainers on topics such as, human dignity, human rights, self-esteem and leadership. This is over and above what is stipulated in the Stanford University

Program. We also run a support group in the center, which is open to all who have been through the basic program. This allows us to help many combat depression, shame, social stigma and discrimination. In our center we also do advocacy work in cases where the government fails to provide certain medicines that are guaranteed by law and when a person is illegally dismissed from their job because of a positive HIV/AIDS diagnosis.

I see men and women who live with HIV/AIDS as the present day lepers. Our job is to help them move from exclusion to inclusion, as did Jesus of Nazareth when he acted to help the lepers of his day belong once again to society. I see HIV/AIDS as largely an illness caused by poverty, poor education and inadequate health facilities. I would like all to feel welcome at the table of the banquet of the Kingdom of God.

Changes that workshop instructors have seen in people through their participation in "Si, Da Vida"[30] Workshops:

As an HIV-positive homosexual, I thought the program would give me the chance to help my fellow homosexuals. The program is effective and has a broad scope. As an instructor, I have been able to help HIV-positive heterosexual women look after their health. I have also been able to help women who support HIV-positive husbands and grandchildren by keeping them informed and helping them manage the health of their relatives. Gichin Gamarra Yzquierdo.

Carlos Vicente Arias Murillo is married and is a patient at a local hospital. I met him in February 2011 while looking for people to participate in our workshops, "Si, Da Vida." Carlos had been diagnosed with an eye infection and AIDS, along with depression. I persuaded him to join in the seven week workshop on the self-management of his illness. I was so pleased that he came with his wife, Elvira, who also had AIDS. With just two sessions to complete the workshop Carlos was admitted to hospital to treat the eye infection and was released after one month. One day we met by chance in the hospital, and I was so surprised to see him looking like another person. He had overcome much of his depression and thanked me for getting him involved in the workshop. I congratulated him on making the effort to push on and also attend the workshop sessions, and so not fall into the trap of the vicious circle of the addict. I was pleased to have been able to help him find a way to manage his own illness and hope to continue to do similar work with others. Karling Jack Ramon Vela

I was helping run a workshop on self-management of one's own health in Villa el Salvador (a poor area on the southern edge of Lima) when I met Enzo; he did not talk much and kept to himself. He took drugs to help himself cope. During the seven week workshop he learned to share, participate and ask questions. He grew in self-confidence and began to do things that he had stopped doing due to

---

[30]   Yes, it is life giving—the Spanish is a play on the word for AIDS, which is SIDA

lack of self-confidence and motivation. He joined in group dancing; he worked; he stopped taking drugs and looked for professional help. He was clearly happier, which showed in his face and in his attitude to life.

I had another experience in another hospital when helping a mother with her small children. She always arrived late but still she came. Her husband gave her a hard time both physically and psychologically. The program helped her improve communication with her husband, in the sense of being more assertive with him and so reclaiming her dignity as a woman and a person, something that all of us have. This also helped her grow in confidence. She took her husband to the following workshop in Villa el Salvador so that he might also live the experience. She had managed to convince him to go with her as it was good for both of them. Rafael Cruz (instructor)

My name is Hugo Cesar Lopez Rocha, and I am an instructor of "Yes, it gives life" in the workshop on managing our health. In 2011 I met a participant, called Jose Luis, and as I was talking with him I realized that he had a problem with his sight that was similar to my own. He shared various experiences related to the cytomegalovirus attack on his eyes. He told me that he could not go out because he had trouble seeing, he tripped over in the street, could not cross the road, and fell in potholes and puddles. What I liked was that one of his first decisions was to attend the seven week workshop, which he did faithfully. It was a real lesson for me and I thank the program for it. Hugo Lopez

On one occasion I was running a workshop in a hospital when I met Flor, mother of three children, who had recently been diagnosed with HIV/AIDS, with which she had been infected by her partner. She was timid, knew little about HIV/AIDS, was very poor and told us that all she had with her was two or three soles for her bus fare—this because of the sexist attitude of her husband and not having a job herself as she had to look after their home. But, she really wanted to learn.

We were in the fifth week of the workshop and we began asking the participants if there was something they wanted to share. Flor timidly raised her hand, started to cry and talked about her problems at home, the abusive treatment by her husband and the difficult economic situation. She was on the point of taking her own life by eating rat poison. I asked her what she thought and did at that moment. She replied that she remembered that the previous week we had talked about when we have negative thoughts we should exchange them for positive thoughts. So, she remembered that her daughter would soon be turning fifteen years of age (a major birthday for girls in Peru) and that she also had two more children for whom to continue with her life.

From that moment Flor changed, participated more and became part of the group. I realized that she needed to be listened to. She began to smile and enjoy herself in so far as she could. Ronny Rios

Noah is 25 years of age, has a partner and a baby. I met him in a workshop in a hospital in the north of Lima. Both his partner and his baby are HIV negative.

However, on being diagnosed HIV positive Noah changed, isolated himself, became antisocial, had problems with his partner, even left her for a time and went off to the jungle (the other side of the Andes Mountains) for two years. I met him when he returned and invited him to a workshop. He trusted me and came along. He wanted help so as not to lose his wife. The first thing he learned to do in the program was to work out how he might please his wife. He became more attentive to her wishes and did not insist on his own opinion. He then saw how the atmosphere of his home began to change and also realized that he had been living in a vicious circle, undermining himself. At the close of the workshop he stood and asked for leave to speak; he began by thanking the program for the opportunity to change his life. He said that now he is different; he plays with his friends and, what's more, he now smiles, which he had forgotten how to do. In the future he insisted that he would participate in any workshop to which he was invited. Maria Luz

## Against the Odds

The struggle of a man stricken by polio to make something of his life in one of the
poorest barrios of Lima, Peru
By Walter Berto Flores

Our house was undermined by the river Rimac over a number of years, but we did not abandon it until 1970, 30 years after it was built. The heavy rains came in January and February, and the water cascaded down the valley of our river from an altitude of over 5,000 meters. It was a crashing, surging torrent by the time it reached our barrio, very close to the center of Lima. Year after year the river dug deeper into the coastal plain through which it rushed on the way to its delta near the port of Callao. In years when the rains were particularly heavy the river gouged out the banks twenty meters or so below our house. A little more of the lip on which our house was perched would crumble, followed by bits of our patio and outer rooms. Year by year we retreated into the rooms furthest away from the edge until one day we were forced to evacuate the house shortly before it all fell into the river. That left us without any home or money.

I was the third of five children and the only male. My parents had come from different parts of the Andes Mountains to look for a better future. They met in Lima, married, established that home and struggled all their lives to make a living for themselves and their children. I got polio at the age of one year, just when I was beginning to learn to walk. I was paralyzed from the neck down, but thanks to six years of therapy in the St. John of God Hospital I recovered the use of all my body with the exception of my right leg.

After losing our house beside the river we went to live in the place where my father was a watchman. My father's boss at that time allowed Dad to move the whole family to a small house that had been built for the watchman, and we stayed there for 25 years. When eventually the factory owner told us to leave we had to find places to live and, as my father had not anticipated this, all of us ended up renting in various places nearby and I went to live with a sister.

I did well enough at school to get into the Agrarian University where I studied economics part time between 1981 and 1986. The Rector at that time was Alberto Fujimori, who was also one of my professors. I got around with one crutch, went to university on a minibus and then rode a bicycle around the campus. I used to fall off quite a bit so now, especially in public places, I get around in a wheelchair, and I find people tend to be more respectful and helpful. Also, I could not go into shops with my bicycle, nor could I leave the bicycle outside for fear of it being stolen. However, when I go to familiar places near where I live I continue to use my crutch and bicycle. For financial reasons, I was unable to complete my studies at that time.

After leaving university I earned a living for five years selling groceries as a street vendor. This project collapsed overnight when, in 1991, the newly elected president, Alberto Fujimori, introduced drastic economic measures that literally decimated the value of my capital. One night I had 1,000 soles and the following morning that 1,000 was worth 100 soles. Like thousands of small businesses, I was wiped out as I could not buy the groceries for my small business. Times were hard for many. I was living with one of my sisters and could not get a job.

My sisters could not give me a room as they too were struggling to make ends meet. I just had a space on the floor to sleep. I also got to know hunger as, for a time, I had no work; 1999 to 2006 were the toughest years for me. The only income I had was from giving private classes in mathematics to primary school children. However, I did have something that money could not buy to help me face any amount of hardship. In moments when I was depressed, when despair threatened to take over my life, when all seemed lost and all doors were closed to me, I never lost my faith in God. I firmly believed that my chance would come but had no idea when or how; still, I wanted to be ready for the moment. I never gave up totally. I saw others committing suicide. I cried from despair, but I never resigned myself to the situation that I was in, because I always remembered a lesson in facing tough situations that my father gave when I was a child.

One day, when we were still living in our house above the river, he gave me a task and told me that he expected to see it completed by the time he returned from work. He left me with a pick and shovel and told me to dig a hole, one meter wide and two meters long. I thought he was being hard and punishing me for something I had done. I dug the hole but was angry with my Dad. On returning from work he saw that I was angry and upset, then he hugged me and said, "In your life you will have many problems, many things to do that for others are easy but for you they will be difficult but, come what may, you will have to do them. It will cost you more but you will have no choice but to make the extra effort."

Then, the big chance came when I arrived at ASPHAD in 2006, where I discovered a place that helped me feel wanted, where I could use my talents and also began to know my second family. Although it was an association founded to help people with serious learning difficulties, it does allow people with physical disabilities to join in provided they are willing to help along the ones with learning difficulties. That suited me fine, because now I am involved with dozens of others who have some kind of disability. Because of all I have endured, I can appreciate what they have gone through and continue to suffer. I can empathize with them and see great scope within the association to collaborate with all these special people and their families in making life so much better and enjoyable for all concerned. Fr. Chris and Sr. Millie have given me lots of support.

ASPHAD has its own Center with good workshops for cooking and baking, sewing by hand and machine, producing handicrafts, computing and internet, traditional dancing, with a psychologist and physiotherapist to organize stimulating exercises and games. Thanks to my interest in economics, I'm currently the treasurer for the association, and because I am keen enough to come every day to look after the breeding of *cuyes* (guineas pigs) up on the flat roof, I am appointed to keep an eye also on the daily running of afternoon classes and workshops from Monday to Friday. I enjoy helping special people with computer programs designed for them. For its part, ASPHAD gives me a small living allowance and covers the university fees.

I am now 53 years of age, have never married and have no children. I live just three blocks from ASPHAD in a rented house with one of my sisters, with whom I share the rent. Two years ago I took the opportunity to complete my university studies online and in July 2011 I hope to receive my Bachelor of Economics degree. This will help me continue working for and building up ASPHAD towards economic self-sufficiency. That is part of my job as treasurer and a challenge to show how our people with disabilities are capable of contributing a great deal to family and community life.

Link to our tradition:

The above three stories tell of both personal and communal healing, which can be a slow process that requires commitment from both those suffering and those collaborating with them. Such is the case related in John 5, 2-9: "Now there is in Jerusalem at the Sheep [Gate] a pool called in Hebrew Bethesda, with five porticoes. In these lay a large number of ill, blind, lame, and crippled. One man was there who had been ill for thirty-eight years. When Jesus saw him lying there and knew that he had been ill for a long time, he said to him, 'Do you want to be well?' The sick man answered him, 'Sir, I have no one to put me into the pool when the water is stirred up; while I am on my way, someone else gets down there before me.' Jesus said to him, 'Rise, take up your mat, and walk.' Immediately the man became well, took up his mat, and walked."

# Drug Addiction, Family and God

By Ronald Tasayco

I was around fifteen or sixteen years old and studying in high school when I began to smoke marihuana. I was in it for the fun with a few friends and within three years I realized that I was addicted. Some years prior to that my younger sister had fallen and landed on her head resulting in a serious injury that required constant treatment for years. She was eventually diagnosed with a condition, schizophrenia, which will permanently put pressure on our family's resources.

My Mum and Dad had to work around the clock to help cover costs so I did not see much of them. My Dad was a policeman, but an honest man, so he did not earn much and needed to get a second and third job to help cover the costs of living and medical treatment. His police medical insurance did not cover the expensive medicines and, at times, not even the less expensive common medicines. With my parents so caught up in trying to cover costs I was more or less free to go my own way, but clearly I got lost.

To pay for my addiction I began to steal things from home and from others. I had begun university studies but soon dropped out and just hung about with my friends who were also into drugs. I did not study, had no job and had given up on life, including on my family.

Eventually, on seeing the suffering that I was putting my parents through, I began to take stock of what I was doing. I was only 22 years old, and my only constant activity had become smoking marihuana. I saw my Mum crying; she pleaded with me to stop. She had to hide anything of value in the house. I wanted to drop the marihuana habit but could not do it alone. I desperately needed help and knew my parents were there for me. If it were not for patient and determined insistence that I reform my life I doubt I'd ever have beaten the drug habit.

Because of the marihuana I stopped participating in the parish youth group where I was a catechist in the first communion program. But then, one day somehow my parents really got through to me and Padre Leo (Columban Fr. Leo Donnelly) also came to the party. They took me to a nearby hospital for therapy and Padre Leo helped cover the cost, but I don't think that helped me much. Still, my Dad thinks that maybe it did help me more than I think.

He became really concerned when one day last year I stole his police revolver to go out and rob some place with my friends. He was so stressed and worried that he suffered partial paralysis of the face. If I had done any harm or been caught with the weapon he would have been punished severely by the police for being irresponsible with his pistol. Dad got a real fright and that also frightened me; I realized the gravity of the problem I might have caused.

Then, around that time some women from our small parish community came to the house to invite my Dad to a retreat and he persuaded them to invite me. Of course, he told them about the problem I was trying to deal with. That invitation came at just the right moment for me. They agreed to come to the house to collect me on a Friday evening at 6:30, and I was packed and ready at 5:00 p.m.

During the weekend retreat things changed for me in a major way. I met others who had been through a similar struggle. I saw what their faith in God had led them to. I saw how happy they were with their renewed lives. Their families were happy too. I began to read the Bible and to pray the rosary. I'd already broken with the drug habit thanks to the support of my parents and Padre Leo, but I needed something more to keep going with my life, to be hopeful and happy about myself. I found that through the community that ran these weekend retreats. I had returned to my family and the retreat helped me return to God.

Things began to change for me. I got a job. In consultation with my parents I moved out of our home in order to put some distance between me and my marihuana smoking friends. I made friends at work and lived by myself near to my place of work. I feel so grateful to God for all that I have been able to change in my life. Prayer and faith have given me so much inner strength to face up to this terrible addiction that I'd allowed bury me alive when I should have been pushing ahead with my life.

My Dad tells me how I used to cry and promise him that I'd change but, at the same time, he was finding little packets of marihuana in my room. My Mum was tough with me but my father chose to be patient and kind; without planning, it was like a good cop, bad cop act. I tended to confide in and depend on my Dad. Things got so bad at one stage that I left home, but I kept going back. My Mum would buy me clothes because all I had was old and unwashed, but then I ended up selling what she had bought me. My Mum did not ask me what I did while away from our home but friends and neighbors commented to her; I know it all hurt her so much.

My Dad was often away from home because of his work. When I was small we lived in Chincha, three hours by bus to the south of Lima, but my Dad was working as a policeman in Lima. When we moved to Lima, we lived in rented houses for a while but, because Dad was away so much doing extra jobs to cover living and medical costs, we did not have a close family life. I know that he later felt that maybe, because he was not there as much as he would have liked to be, I had not had the stability necessary to help me steer a straight and narrow course. However, I don't want to blame Dad for anything; I feel he did the best he could.

After 20 years in the police Dad retired and with his severance pay bought the block of land where we now live. Here we've had more of a family life and I've come to know my Dad. In fact, we have become very close through sharing the trauma associated with my drug addiction problem. He bought me a Bible and a picture of Our Lady, both of which I will always treasure. Dad has become a real friend to me. He is an honest man and also a man of God; he always goes to his Bible study meeting in the parish.

I am now 27 years old and have a reasonably good job selling financial products in a credit union. I feel so grateful to Dad and Mum for hanging in there with me and for Padre Leo who in supporting my parents, helped make my recovery possible.

Link to our tradition:

Ronald's story brings to mind Jesus' parable of the lost sheep. See Luke 15, 4-7: "What man among you having a hundred sheep and losing one of them would not leave the ninety-nine in the desert and go after the lost one until he finds it? And when he does find it, he sets it on his shoulders with great joy and, upon his arrival home, he calls together his friends and neighbors and says to them, 'Rejoice with me because I have found my lost sheep.' I tell you, in just the same way there will be more joy in heaven over one sinner who repents than over ninety-nine righteous people who have no need of repentance."

# Growing

### By Rosa Blanco

It was 1987. I had three children, Patricia (born 1974), Enrique (born 1979) and José (born 1986). I had separated from my husband and had been living with my parents, who were very good to me. However, my mother kept interfering with my children as if she were responsible for bringing them up. I really had no choice but to move out. I joined an invasion and built a temporary house. I made a little money by taking in washing, but there were days when I wondered whether there would be anything to eat the following day.

At that time I first met Fr. Martin Collum. Our barrio leader had invited him to one of our regular meetings, at which we needed to resolve an issue among ourselves. A number of us were in disagreement with our elected leader over a certain internal matter. He hoped to calm the waters with the mediating presence of Fr. Martin. I spoke up and suggested to Fr. Martin that he go home and leave us to work out our own problems. I can still picture him sitting on a rock with his head in his hands looking at the ground. He had thought he was coming to help but did not realize that he was being used by our leader.

Not long after that, in 1991, the newly elected president of Peru, Alberto Fujimori, introduced drastic economic measures that overnight moved thousands of families from a state of poverty to one of misery. All over Peru we organized communal kitchens. I became the president of our local kitchen. To help us gain access to emergency food relief Fr. Martin invited the leaders of 75 such organizations, within the jurisdiction of our parish, to a meeting. Fr. Martin and I became firm friends, and he also became godfather of one of my children.

From the leaders of the 75 kitchens we elected a commission of fifteen people, and I was one of those elected. I began to work closely with Fr. Martin in the coordination of the work of the communal kitchens. We had a monthly meeting in the parish, and we also had to check to make sure that each communal kitchen was getting the food aid to which they were entitled. Also, we ensured that the most desperate cases were taken into account.

On one occasion Fr. Martin asked me to go to a meeting of an NGO that was helping us with the practical application of a new law that allows mothers to inscribe their children in the register of births with the father's surname even if he is not present. She was required to go with two witnesses who would sign to support her claim. I was not sure what I was going to do at such a meeting, and I turned up in my scruffy clothes and broken shoes. The rest of those attending seemed to be well dressed professional people. I was so nervous; I did not know what I was going to say. I waited until everyone else had spoken.

All I could think of was the case of the woman I had accompanied to the municipal office to register her young boy. The functionary was being awkward and even told her she would have to get a blood test as he needed proof the child was hers. That really made me angry; this poor woman was having enough trouble just facing up to the daily grind of her life and here was this cheeky office worker insulting her by implying that her child probably was not even hers. I got mad and went for him. Whatever I said he did not make any more trouble for the woman. When I finished speaking about this at the meeting everyone applauded; I was so surprised. That was the first time I spoke in public.

Some years later, that same small boy, now a man, greeted me in the street, but I did not know who he was. He remembered that I had spoken up for him and his mother.

In 1994, when Fr. Martin was leaving the parish, he introduced me to Fr. Ned with whom I continued to work. When he was leaving the parish he did his best to ensure that I not be left without a job, and he recommended me to the Diocesan Social Outreach program. That was when my life changed, as I had a small income to help pay for my children's education, food and clothing. I was also able to gradually improve my house.

I began to feel freer as I realized that I was no longer wondering whether my children and I would have something to eat the following day. I had the opportunity to begin to look at myself. In the course of the work in social outreach program I found that I was able to be myself; I met many dedicated people. All this helped me value who I am, my own way of being.

I began to learn reflexology the same year I joined the social outreach team. That also helped me move on. I have done training courses and found I was a good therapist so have continued to work in the field. I have enough work and know that patients have learned to value my work. All this affirmation has helped me move on, so now, at 62 years old, I continue to feel quite enthusiastic about my life.

Years ago, when things were really hard for me, I could have taken on a way of life that I would later regret, but I did not go down that track despite the insecurity and poverty of my life at that time. My own determination and my faith in God helped me overcome the difficulties I had to navigate.

Link to our tradition:

Rosa has raised her three children without the support of their father in a Lima shanty town. She has found ways to choose life, a profoundly healing option. See Deuteronomy 30, 19-20: "I call heaven and earth today to witness against you: I have set before you life and death, the blessing and the curse. Choose life, then, that you and your descendants may live, by loving the LORD, your God, obeying his voice, and holding fast to him. For that will mean life for you, a long life for you to live on the land which the LORD swore to your ancestors, to Abraham, Isaac, and Jacob, to give to them."

# A Space for Children

By Nora Cepeda[31]

> To ride on a wooden horse
> is one of their rights.
> Also to open a book
> like the leaves of a cabbage.[32]

Fr. Tony Coney, a Columban missionary priest from Belfast, Ireland, took the initiative to establish and develop this project that opened in 1997. Children come to "La Casa del Niño y de la Niña, Santa Bernadita"[33] to play together, to recreate, and to discover friendship in a welcoming and safe environment. Each day an average of 350 children and adolescents come to the house in two shifts, morning and afternoon, where they are looked after by young workers. In many cases both parents of the children need to go to work so many children are left to their own devices for part of the day as they go to school either in the morning or the afternoon.

A basic principle that shapes the work of those who work in the house is forming the children and adolescents in freedom, and so they can choose what they want to do according to their interest and need.

Initially our experience taught us that teaching and learning to live in freedom requires agreeing on and living according to rules of sharing. It's not about starting something and then giving it up, of doing whatever may occur to us without taking others into account, and so we coupled responsibility to the practice of freedom.

The main strategy for achieving this was to invite the children and adolescents to agree upon rules of sharing in the workshops, games and library, and then review. Another strategy has been to call meetings so that they can give their opinion and join in looking for the solution to problems that affect everyone. For

---

[31]  When Columban Fr. Tony Coney established La Casa del Niño he also created a NGO and invited a number of people with expertise in the education of children to form an institutional directory. Nora worked in primary schools in Peru for 25 years and has specialized in remedial education.

[32]  (Comentary by Arturo Corcuera, Peruvian poet, on Article 11 of The Rights of the Child, http://www.unicef.org/crc/files/Rights_overview.pdf)

[33]  The house is located on top of "Cerro del Choclo" (Corn Hill), also known as "3 de Mayo" since poor farm laborers began to make their home on the hill in the late 1970s. The land around the hill has been farmed for at least 3,000 years but is now covered with houses. Children can see the cream painted house from afar.

example, to avoid scribbling on the walls they decided to designate one wall where they might freely write or draw.

So how do the children and adolescents see things?

"I like the games and I have a lot of fun." (Xiomara, 4 years old)

"My mother used to come here and now I like to come. I like to paint, do jig-saw puzzles and play." (Anderson, 5 years old)

"I like to play mini-soccer; I like the trampoline, playing hide and seek, skipping, having fun, painting and sewing." (Ruby 10 years old)

For the smallest children La Casa del Niño is a safe and easily accessible place to play and recreate. In the house they meet a variety of friends and workers who welcome them, look after them and accompany them with kindness.

Aracelly is 16 years old, expects to complete secondary school this year and has been coming to La Casa del Niño since she was 6 years of age. She says:

"Here, everything that we carry within ourselves explodes and that is reflected in our lives. It's like when a book is closed you don't see anything, but when you open it everything comes out, you can see what is in it."

In the workshops the children and adolescents have the chance to discover and develop their personal talent for drawing, painting, playing a musical instrument, playing sport, participating in theatre or doing handcraft. Such experiences give them security and social recognition; they are the basis of self-esteem; they help them relate better with other children and significant adults such as parents and teachers.

"We learn to offer friendship, to respect friends and if someone needs something we support them." (Anapia, 9 years old, has been coming to La Casa del Niño since she was 4 years old)

The playing spaces, the library and the workshops are designed to help the children and adolescents interact with each other. When they converse, work in teams, share communal space, share toys and tools, they have to come to agreements, organize themselves, resolve conflicts, ask help when they need it, recognize their mistakes and begin again. In this way they develop their own self and their sense of responsibility.

"They support us in the tasks, in what we do not know or understand. They teach us something new." (Analia, 9 years old, has been coming since she was 4 years old)

The library and school homework help are very important to the children and adolescents as in their homes they are unlikely to find help from either books or family members. The workers in La Casa del Niño who accompany the children confirm that the support that they offer does bear fruit because the children's school marks improve. This is a good result but even more important is that their self-esteem and hope for the future improve. There is also a comfortable place with cushions where they can relax, read and discover the value of reading for its own sake, without it being associated with homework.

However, making good use of information will spontaneously as the tendency is to copy what is in the book. The accompanying workers need to motivate them to search, question, think critically and discover creative responses to the many and varied situations of life.

The computer room is one of the most popular in La Casa del Niño. There are educational programs, games and someone to orient the children.

"Just as La Casa del Niño helped me be a better person, now I work as a volunteer supporting a group of seniors . . . Just as they helped me so I help others; I learned that here." (Peggy, 20 years old, presently nearing the end of her training as a nurse)

The children also learn the value of solidarity. Perhaps, for most of the children, La Casa del Niño has not helped them move out of poverty, but it has helped them change how they see themselves, their family and their barrio. This is what Peggy said:

"I am not ashamed to say where I live. Here my self-esteem was shaped; I learned that a person's value is not in what they have but rather in their commitment to be better."

This project has functioned now for nearly 15 years thanks to the generosity of many people in Ireland, U.S.A. and Australia. We see it as a contribution to creating a more just and fraternal society. We believe that similar projects should be promoted by the municipalities of our city so that all children might have safe and welcoming places to discover their talents and enjoy their childhood. This would contribute to laying the foundation of a healthy future for our people.

Link to our tradition:

Helping children enjoy their infancy recalls the admonition of Jesus to his disciples when they attempted to turn away the children. See Matthew 19, 13-14: "Then children were brought to him that he might lay his hands on them and pray. The disciples rebuked them, but Jesus said, 'Let the children come to me, and do not prevent them; for the kingdom of heaven belongs to such as these.'"

# CONCLUSION

Only in recent times, especially since Vatican II, have missionaries in general become more aware of the implications of a dialogical approach to mission. The following paragraph from Vatican II's document on missionary activity homes in on qualities and attitudes necessary in today's missionaries:

In order that they may be able to bear more fruitful witness to Christ, let them be joined to those peoples by esteem and love; let them acknowledge themselves to be members of the group of people among whom they live; let them share in cultural and social life by the various undertakings and enterprises of human living; let them be familiar with their national and religious traditions; let them gladly and reverently lay bare the seeds of the Word which lie hidden among their fellows. (Vatican II, *Ad Gentes*, 1965, No. 11)

Missionaries, who achieve what is advised above, even though in part, probably go beyond their wildest dreams. Bernard Lonergan wrote of five things that need to be done to become authentically human: "be attentive; be intelligent; be reasonable; be responsible and, if necessary, change."[34] We missionaries can so easily fall into the trap of having eyes but not seeing, having ears but not hearing. As strangers among another people we might miss what is being said, be it verbal or non-verbal, and this even though we may speak their language fluently. Perhaps a key factor that allows those, to whom we have been sent, to forgive our inadequacies in this regard, is their perception of us as respecting them as persons, as sons and daughters of God.

Jesus invited us into the very life of God as adopted sons and daughters. So, as God's children we journey with God during our time on earth. After Jesus died and rose from the dead He spent some time with His followers. He promised them ongoing support after His departure. The Father with the Son then sent the Holy Spirit to strengthen, enlighten and accompany the small community of men and women who had faith in the risen Lord. We, as spiritual heirs of that first Christian community, live in the hope of continuing in God's love during our time on earth and beyond. On accepting the invitation to walk with God we also take on the responsibility to welcome others to journey towards God in Christ.

---

[34]    cf. Endnote 9, Chapter 7, Prophetic Dialogue, Bevans, S. & Schroeder, R., Orbis, 2011.

Hopefully, the stories gathered in this volume have helped you, the reader, recall and marvel at God's love for you. As you ponder the experiences of a few men and women of God listening to their people, feeling their pain in the face of diverse hardships, collaborating in their projects, encouraging and standing with them, learning from their courage, faith and wisdom, helping them overcome divisions in family and community life, being moved by their love, explaining Jesus' message to them, being enriched by what they have to say about God and life, putting them in touch with Jesus through the bible, prayer and the sacraments, helping them come to appreciate themselves as sons and daughters of God, you might reflect on and give thanks for your own experiences of doing something similar among those who make up the web of friendship and solidarity in your own life.

Printed in Great Britain
by Amazon.co.uk, Ltd.,
Marston Gate.